HISTORY OF

# BIRMINGHAM

*VOLUME II*

BOROUGH AND CITY

1865–1938

# HISTORY

## OF

# *BIRMINGHAM*

———

### *VOLUME II*

BOROUGH AND CITY 1865-1938

BY

## ASA BRIGGS, M.A., B.Sc.

*Fellow of Worcester College Oxford*
*Reader in Recent Social and Economic History*
*in the University of Oxford*

*Published for the Birmingham City Council by*

GEOFFREY CUMBERLEGE

*OXFORD UNIVERSITY PRESS*

LONDON   NEW YORK   TORONTO

1952

*Oxford University Press, Amen House, London E.C.4*

GLASGOW NEW YORK TORONTO MELBOURNE WELLINGTON
BOMBAY CALCUTTA MADRAS CAPE TOWN

*Geoffrey Cumberlege, Publisher to the University*

PRINTED IN GREAT BRITAIN
AT THE UNIVERSITY PRESS, OXFORD
BY CHARLES BATEY, PRINTER TO THE UNIVERSITY

# PREFACE

IN preparing this book, the second volume of the *History of Birmingham*, I have been fortunate in securing the help and encouragement of many people both in Birmingham and in Oxford. I should like to express my sincere appreciation of the initiative of the members of the Sub-Committee in charge of the project and of the administrative assistance of Mr. E. A. Moseley of the Town Clerk's Department. I am heavily indebted to the City Librarian and above all to Miss D. M. Norris of the Reference Library, with whom I have worked in close co-operation throughout. The Public Relations Officer of the City provided me with useful material, and I have gleaned a great deal from personal contact with representatives of business firms, trade associations, the Chamber of Commerce, political parties, and clubs and societies.

It is impossible to thank by name all the people who have helped me with particular points. Alderman Sir Wilfrid Martineau, Mr. W. B. Kenrick, Mr. H. M Cashmore, Mr. W. A. Cadbury, Mr. D. N. Chester, Mr. Philip Styles, and Mr. D. N. Griffiths have been of great assistance in working through the proofs. Before that stage was reached Professor Gill, Mr. P. M. Williams, Mr. David Henderson, Mr. A. Fox, Mr. D. Foster, and Mr. Cyril Hubbard all added to the information at my disposal. Finally, Miss Alexander, my secretary, has been of invaluable assistance in enabling me to finish the book within a reasonable space of time.

None of my friends and helpers shares any responsibility for the final shape of this book. The history of a city can be told in many ways. I have tried to break down the artificial barriers which separate economic and political history and to describe the evolution of a community. At the end of a long venture I feel that there are still many subjects and problems which need further exploration. Birmingham needs not only a general history but a series of specialized monographs. Often where I most needed the monographs none had been written. Until they are available some phases in local history will remain shadowy and obscure. In the same way English historians urgently need a series of monographs on towns and cities, if they are to interpret intelligently the nineteenth and twentieth centuries. This *History of Birmingham* is offered as a contribution to what I hope will soon become a prominent field of English historiography.

ASA BRIGGS

WORCESTER COLLEGE, OXFORD

*May* 1951

# CONTENTS

# LIST OF PLATES

# FIGURES IN TEXT

# FOOTNOTES

Footnote references have been given wherever a point is of importance and the reader might wish to follow up information. References to Council Minutes are not usually given. The following abbreviations of names of local newspapers have been used throughout:

| | |
|---|---|
| *B.G.* | Birmingham Gazette |
| *B.M.* | Birmingham Mail |
| *B.P.* | Birmingham Post |
| *B.W.P.* | Birmingham Weekly Post |
| *E.D.* | Evening Despatch |

# I
## THE FRAMEWORK OF A COMMUNITY

'IT has long been the complaint', wrote William Hutton in his famous *History of Birmingham*, 'that Local History is much wanted. . . . Many an author has become a cripple by historically travelling *all England*, who might have made a tolerable figure had he staid at home.' The history of nineteenth-century Birmingham, particularly the Birmingham of Chamberlain, is so closely bound up with the history of England as a whole, that a local history of the city is an essential chapter in the history of the nation. Birmingham was important not only in its own right, but because Birmingham men and ideas provided a substantial contribution to English life and thought.

The balance between detailed discussion of local affairs and analysis of important trends in national history is easier to strike in the case of Birmingham than in the case of many other cities. As Oliver Wendell Holmes wrote, 'the axis of the earth sticks out visibly through the centre of each and every town and city', but the local axis in Birmingham is of general interest. This is partly so because Birmingham history illustrates, often in peculiarly striking fashion, some of the main features of city growth in the late nineteenth and early twentieth centuries. More important, Birmingham has offered a special contribution to English history. When all possible generalizations have been made about the growth of suburbia, the development of mass politics, and the planning of large-scale municipal administration, the history of Birmingham remains distinctive and unique, and cannot be contained in any set of categories.

There were three special features of mid-nineteenth-century Birmingham which exercised an important influence on its subsequent history. The first was the strength of nonconformity, the second, the dominance of industry and the wide range of local trades and occupations, the third the close relations, both economic and social, between masters and men. It is only against this local background that Birmingham politics and the revolution in municipal government become explicable.

For 200 years Birmingham had been a shelter of Dissent: in Victorian England it became a stronghold. The leaders of local dissent worked with all their accumulated energies to build up a city which would be worthy of their faith and calling. In Victorian Birmingham they did much to mould the economic, social, and political life of the town. In particular, Unitarians and Quakers occupied important positions in business and in politics. Unitarian mayors held office almost continuously between 1840 and 1880: Unitarian families, like the Chamberlains, Kenricks, Martineaus, and Nettlefolds, provided a compact and tireless leadership in all branches of local life. As if to symbolize their recognized strength, in 1862 they opened the Church of the Messiah, an impressive Gothic building, to take the place of the more humble New Meeting House, in which Dr. Priestley had ministered. These Unitarian families were as important to the Birmingham of the nineteenth century as were the village squires and parsons to the older rural England, which was already in course of disintegration. They were families, as much as individuals, conscious of their birthright, and well established in local life. In national life, however, they were still on the offensive, seeking to redress old grievances, still angry at the sight of social privilege and the insolence of class. In consequence they did not restrict their activities to the local world they knew so well, but plunged themselves into national agitations, in which, as a result, Birmingham secured a position of paramountcy. The National Education League, founded in 1869, was a product of their labours. Of its original capital, Chamberlain and his father gave £1,000 each, and the Kenricks and Nettlefolds over £3,000 more. The League, which had begun as an effort to remove a local evil, made nonconformity a militant political force over the country as a whole, and Birmingham, the centre of the agitation, boasted that it remained true to 'the great principles which have made this town what it is—a stronghold of religious liberty and a fortress against clerical assumption and bigotry throughout the country'.

It was the Education League which launched Joseph Chamberlain in national politics, and it was Chamberlain's ambition and political acumen which extended the movement beyond its 'theological' confines into new fields of social advance. For many years the Unitarians, the Baptists, and the Congregationalists made up his most militant followers. Alongside Chamberlain, John Bright, the Quaker Member for the city, was the acknowledged champion of Liberal nonconformity. Behind him in the

PLATE I

Carr's Lane Chapel

PLATE II

The Church of the Saviour

city were Quaker families, like those of Lloyd, Cadbury, Baker, and Sturge, often playing a leading part in social movements, like the Adult School movement, frequently quite unostentatiously behind the scenes.

It was the clarion call of nonconformist ministers, particularly R. W. Dale at Carr's Lane, the Baptist Charles Vince, and George Dawson, writer, preacher, and 'the first of English talkers', which goaded citizens to social action. Local initiative was never divorced from Christian worship. Speaking of Alderman White, a Quaker who was responsible along with Chamberlain for the making of the great Improvement Scheme, Dale said that he believed his friend 'was trying to get the will of God done on earth as it is done in heaven just as much when he was fighting St. Mary's Ward, just as much when he was speaking in the Town Council, as when he was teaching his Bible Class on the Sunday morning'.[1] This was the effective doctrine behind the development of Birmingham's civic gospel.

The paramount influence of nonconformity often overshadowed the activities of the Church of England, which went on steadily with its work of church building. Indeed between 1851 and 1893 the number of churches within the parishes of Birmingham, Edgbaston, and Aston was more than doubled. The Church Extension Society was set up in January 1865 'to relieve the spiritual destitution of the most crowded parts of the town'.

Religious differences sometimes overshadowed home evangelization. Although Dr. Miller, as Rector of St. Martin's for the twenty-five years before 1866, was a Liberal of Evangelical views, and the Evangelical Alliance dominated Anglicanism in the town, there were frequent clashes between militant nonconformists and churchmen. Religion was a dividing line in the middle years of the century, stimulating intense discussion, and at times, as in the case of the Ritualist riots in 1866, minor skirmishing and violence. By the end of the century increased tolerance had replaced deep-seated animosity, but a price had to be paid. The hold of religion on broad sections of the community was often slackened. It was against this background that Gore came to Birmingham from Worcester as first Bishop in 1905, bringing with him his magnificent gifts of saintly living, powerful preaching, memorable theology, and zeal for social reform. In the six years before he moved to Oxford he left a deep mark

[1] A. W. W. Dale, *The Life of R. W. Dale of Birmingham* (1899), p. 401.

on the city. 'The Church has come to occupy a much more advantageous position than she ever did', wrote a local journalist in 1907. 'The all pervading business spirit of the place—never more dominant than today—animates the clergy, as it does all who come within its influence, and there is no more practical, energetic, business-like man than the Bishop himself.'[1]

The influence of religion and its impact on both individual and social life can be traced in many ways. Edward Burne-Jones, for instance, was writing detailed letters about Calvinist Methodism and the difference between Socinians and Unitarians at the age of fifteen,[2] while Dale was promoting his gospel of civic action, and Newman was meditating on the subtleties of religious explanation. Newman's *Dream of Gerontius* was one of the new books of the day in 1865. Dale and Newman were complete opposites. 'Men of a certain order like Dr. Newman', wrote Callaway, one of Dale's friends, 'perhaps, in retirement see angels; others, like Luther, when withdrawn from turmoil and strife, see devils; and you, I believe, are of this order.'[3] Birmingham found room for both orders of men, and, in an age when religious values have been challenged both by indifference and by direct hostility, it has found room for dynamic and controversial twentieth-century religious leaders as well.

Although the twentieth century has often stressed secular forms of social action, both at work and at play, in the communal life of Birmingham Christianity has always acted as a leaven. In the development of the youth movement, for instance, which provided a bridge between the late nineteenth and the twentieth centuries, the desire to inculcate a practical religious sense was one of the most important incentives. In sport too, with its striking modern mass appeal, a well-known football club like Aston Villa had its origins in the Aston Villa Men's Bible Class, connected with the Methodist Church which gave the club its name.

The vitality of religion in Birmingham explains much in the local story, but leaves a lot unsaid. Birmingham was a city created by industry, and industry was so much a part of its tradition that Hutton claimed that the scythe-blades attached to the wheels of Boadicea's chariot had been made in the city.

---

[1] *B.M.*, 16 February 1907.
[2] See Burne-Jones, *Memorials of Edward Burne-Jones*, vol. i (1904), pp. 22–26.
[3] A. W. W. Dale, op. cit., p. 301.

The economic and social structure of the city depended upon its industrial base. 'Sir,' said Johnson to Boswell, 'we [i.e. Lichfield] are a city of philosophers. We work with our heads, and make the boobies of Birmingham work for us with their hands.'[1]

The hands worked diligently and with inherited skill and craftsmanship at a wide range of tasks. Birmingham was and is a city of many trades. 'The trades of this town are numerous', Baker told the British Medical Association in 1872, 'and the sub-divisions of labour are unusually great; hence the fluctuations of commerce rarely fall heavily upon the entire class of artisans, and famine is of very rare occurrence.'[2] The tradition of skill, the variety of trades, and the adaptability of the finishing industries were to prove as beneficial to the city in the dark days of the Great Depression after 1929 as they had done in the nineteenth century. Birmingham remained fortunate in comparison with other industrial areas. Not wholly dependent on heavy industries, it did not share the long and deep depression suffered in many places elsewhere, and there was a sharp rise in local business activity in the 1930's.

The city attracted new industries, and the growth of engineering and motor manufacturing transformed its industrial structure in a comparatively short space of time, but the variety of trades persisted. When the members of the British Association visited Birmingham in 1865, they were told how dependent they were on the many Birmingham trades.

'At home or abroad, sleeping or waking, walking or riding, in a carriage or upon a railway or steamboat, we cannot elude the reminiscences of Birmingham. Her handiwork is around us in our dwellings: doors and windows, stoves and cupboards, staircase and closet, garret and cellar, the bed we lie on, the very clothes we wear—all testify to her busy craftsmanship. It is well for us that, though she is able to throw a couple of thousand tons of iron up into the air to form a flying roof or to command a palace of crystal to "spring from the grass to meet the sun", she does not disdain to make us serviceable pens for a shilling, or to sell our wives and daughters fifty pins for a penny.'[3]

Seventy years later the manufactures of Birmingham in their endless variety continued to impress and to serve visitors from all parts of the world. Tastes had changed as much as techniques,

---

[1] J. Boswell, *Life of Samuel Johnson* (1791), vol. ii, p. 35.
[2] *B.G.*, 11 April 1872.    [3] *Leisure Hour*, September 1865.

but in 1938 there were still over 1,500 trades represented in Birmingham, and over 10,000 factories, employing on an average less than twenty people each.

The variety of trades and their character meant that considerable reliance was always placed on the skilled artisan. 'At Birmingham, trade depends so much more upon individual skill rather than on great combinations of capital', declared the Report of the Select Committee on the Health of Towns in 1840. Despite the growth of larger units and of new forms of mechanization, the statement remained true. There was a multitude of home workers and of small workshops, and in consequence there was frequently no hard and fast line between employers and employed. This was the third important feature of local society. Business men and working men were not divided by tall walls of social privilege. With few exceptions, down to 1914 the business world of the city still resembled the Warwickshire landscape, a rolling country with no projecting peaks. The small masters were more often than not recruited from among the workmen, the transition being usually by way of sub-contracting and home-work. There was a mesh of complicated social and economic relationships. Outside forces like trade unionism remained weak, and there existed a natural basis for industrial alliances between employers and workmen and for class co-operation in matters of common interest.

The 'small man' system, which accounted for so much in creating the distinctive features of Birmingham's social and political life, had serious disadvantages as well. Lack of capital and of broadly based experience often produced home workshops and converted dwelling-houses of the most cramped and unhealthy kind, as well as a conservatism in methods which led to depression in times of increased competition. The system also opened the way for sweating and unjust treatment by sub-contractors, and made the task of improving wages and housing and of organizing industrial training a very difficult one. Many of the economic and social problems of the twentieth century had their origins in a system which had helped to provide economic vitality and social peace in the middle years of the nineteenth century.

These three features of Birmingham's social structure set the framework of political action. The Victorian business men, who worked on close terms of daily contact with their workers, often lived only one mile away from the centre of the town. They interested themselves both in the gospel of civic action and in the cause of radical reform. At the height of the Reform Bill agitation of 1867 Bright wrote that 'in Birmingham, I believe, the "middle class" is ready to work heartily with the "working class", and I hope a thorough union may take place'.[1] The 'thorough union' made possible the cleaning up of the city and the triumphant vindication of Chamberlain's prophecy, when he became Mayor in 1873, that 'in twelve months by God's help the town shall not know itself'.

Party discipline was used as an instrument of municipal progress. Without the active energies of the Liberal Association, set up in 1865, Chamberlain's programme of civic reform could not have been carried out. What came to be called the 'caucus' marked the transfer of politics from the private province of a few to the general domain of public opinion, and although it was often argued at the time that the new public opinion was being shaped and twisted by powerful secret forces, the initial steps in the growth of large-scale political organization signified a liberation rather than an enslavement. In any case, the caucus, although it seemed to tower like a colossus, was essentially a local organization, far more direct in its appeal to its members than a national political organization of today.

During the age of Chamberlain, Birmingham was a compact society, both territorially and socially. With the process of city expansion, reflected in the increased size of all forms of economic and social organization, much was changed. As the population grew, large factories were set up and the suburbs were pushed farther and farther away from the centre of the town. The relatively small and intimate world of the middle years of the century was broken up. The twentieth century created a bigger city, which needed experts to run it smoothly as well as men of goodwill to stir it to crusades. In place of the nineteenth-century gospel of social progress there has often been substituted a twentieth-century theory of planning, and for local improvement an extension of regional control.

Half-way between these two worlds, Birmingham launched another movement in which it occupied the most prominent place. Tariff reform took the place of civic radicalism as a battle-cry, and although the new agitation was grounded in the

[1] J. A. Langford, *Modern Birmingham and its Institutions*, vol. ii (1867), p. 356.

local structure of business interests, it had national and international repercussions. 'One might almost dramatize the past
history of British commercial policy', Professor Hancock has
written, 'as a struggle between free-trade Manchester and protectionist Birmingham—or better still as a three-cornered struggle, with the old individualist-cosmopolitan City of London
joining forces with Manchester to keep Birmingham in check.'[1]
Although the final triumph of Birmingham did not come until
1932, as G. M. Young has said,

in many ways the change from Early to Late Victorian England is
symbolized in the names of two great cities: Manchester solid, uniform,
pacific, the native home of the economic creed on which aristocratic
England had always looked, and educated England at large was coming
to look, with some aversion and some contempt: Birmingham experimental, adventurous, diverse, where old Radicalism might in one
decade flower into a lavish Socialism, in another into a pugnacious
Imperialism.[2]

The themes of Birmingham history and of Birmingham's
place in English history lend themselves to an analytical treatment, but in presenting a series of analyses, it is important not
to overlook that there was a story as well. The name *Birmingham*
covers all sorts of different communities—the industrial village
of medieval times, the great market town of the seventeenth and
eighteenth centuries, the vigorous, sometimes turbulent, city of
Attwood and Chamberlain, and the centre of a twentieth-century
'conurbation'. The name *Birmingham* is itself a symbol of continuity, but behind the name the city itself has changed, swallowing up not only great tracts of undeveloped land, but also
hamlets, villages, and townships. The great community of the
twentieth century is qualitatively as well as quantitatively
different even from the relatively recent Birmingham of the
golden age of the social gospel during the mayoralty of Joseph
Chamberlain from 1873 to 1876. As the landscape has changed,
sometimes gradually, sometimes with revolutionary speed, perspectives and attitudes have changed with it.

Something of the change is explicable merely in terms of the
rise in population and area. When Hutton wrote his history the
town to which he was so proud to belong was still a small town

[1] W. K. Hancock, *Survey of British Commonwealth Affairs*, vol. ii (1940), p. 92.
[2] G. M. Young, *Victorian England, Portrait of an Age* (1936), p. 124.

PLATE III

Charles Gore: First Bishop of Birmingham

PLATE IV

The Oratory

by modern standards, set in the heart of an unspoilt country-side. Since he wrote the administrative area of Birmingham has grown from a civil parish of 2,660 acres into a county borough of 51,147 acres, and the population of its present area has increased from 70,000 at the first census of 1801 to over a million at the census of 1931. The pressure of an expanding population and an overspilling city has always provided in itself a challenge to local government. *Aris's Gazette* complained in 1751 that 'all the parish offices in the town of Birmingham are become very troublesome, from the largeness of the place'. The same comment might have been made in the middle of the 1930's, when, with the growth of the large municipal housing estates, and the building up of a vast industrial conurbation, an ever-widening range of local government problems faced the Council.

To trace the history of this changing community is itself a challenge. Hutton lamented the fact that Birmingham, 'one of the most singular places in the universe', 'never manufactured an history of herself who manufactured almost everything else'. He set out to meet the need in 1781 by writing a vivid story, quickened by pithy writing and illustrated by seventeen copper-plates 'some of which will be well worth two shillings and six pence each'.[1] Since 1781 the technique of manufacturing a history has changed just as much as the technique of manu-facturing anything else. Hutton's lively imagination, Langford's careful antiquarianism, and Dent's panoramic sketching need to be supplemented. The twentieth-century historian must carry many different instruments in his tool-bag, sometimes the tools of the geographer, the economist, and the sociologist, but he can never overestimate his debt to the skill and craftsman-ship of his predecessors. Some of them, like Timmins and Allen, have written indispensable local economic studies. Others, like Bunce, Vince, and Jones, have sketched the making of local government.

This history sets out to continue Professor Gill's account of the growth of a great community. It begins in the middle of the 1860's, with the start of Birmingham's municipal renaissance. Charles Dickens was reading his *Christmas Carol* to a packed audience in the Town Hall and John Bright was recalling the unfinished campaigns of 1832. The great triumphs of English Liberalism had still not yet been won; the gas-lit city had still

[1] *Aris's Gazette*, 29 October 1781.

not yet been freed from the obvious abuses which held back its progress. But time was hurrying forward, and the pace of change was accelerating even before new leaders arose to direct it. Before the Reform Bill had been passed, before Chamberlain had been returned to the Council, the face of the city itself was rapidly being transformed.

# II

## THE FACE OF THE CITY

'So rapidly are the landmarks of the town of Birmingham being changed', wrote the *Birmingham Post* in 1867, 'that we may shortly be in a position to appreciate the story told of the Parisian, who on returning at night to his lodgings, found that the house—and with it the whole street where he lived— had been demolished since the morning, and the lines of a new palatial block of buildings traced out amid the ruins.'[1]

In the middle years of the nineteenth century the central areas of many large English towns were completely transformed, and the development of Birmingham was not exceptional. The increased demand for business premises, particularly shops, the rise in land values, and the frequently serious congestion of traffic, forced on topographical revolutions. 'In Birmingham', wrote Bunce in 1885, 'the physical conditions of the place have undergone changes which the most powerful memory, based on the most prolonged term of residence, can scarcely enable one to realize.'[2]

It was during the 60's and 70's that the centre of Birmingham began to take on something like its present shape. Down to that time there were few large shops with imposing façades; and small dwelling-houses and tiny factories were often huddled together in what have since become crowded thoroughfares. Many doctors and lawyers continued to live in the centre of the town, and Newhall Street, fashionable Bennett's Hill, the Crescent, the Old Square, and the streets enclosing St. Philip's churchyard had not yet been deserted by tenants of this kind. Thriving tradespeople lived above their shops, quietly and modestly, and it was a rare sight to see a carriage and pair in the streets.

The first agent of change was the railway system. While the North-Western and Midland Lines altered the neighbourhood of New Street and Suffolk Street, the Great Western transformed the area around Monmouth Street, Livery Street, and Snow

[1] *B.P.*, 12 June 1867.
[2] J. T. Bunce, *History of the Corporation of Birmingham*, vol. ii (1885), p. xxiii.

Hill. In both cases insanitary areas were cleared, old streets swept away and new ones opened. The improvements were on a big enough scale for Professor Gill to describe them as 'the first great work of slum-clearance to be done in Birmingham'.[1]

## THE REGIONAL PATTERN OF BIRMINGHAM IN 1859

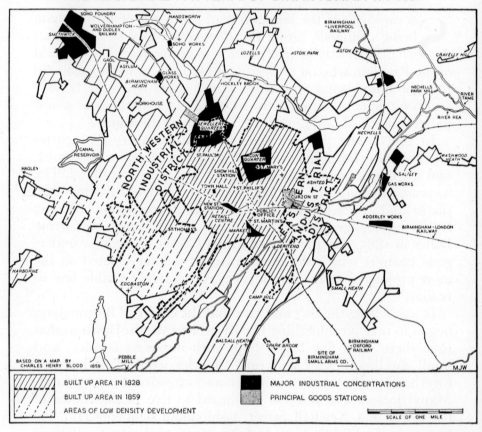

FIG. 1.

The work of pulling down and building afresh was further stimulated by the action of great landowners, a striking example of their action being afforded by the changes in Colmore Row, Edmund Street, Newhall Street and the surrounding neighbourhood, consequent on the falling in of the Colmore Leases from 1866 onwards. Ann Street and Colmore Row were completely remodelled and new rows of imposing buildings erected. On the other side of New Street the undesirable area of the 'Inkleys',

[1] C. Gill, *History of Birmingham*, vol. i (1952), p. 339.

PLATE V

The Old Wharf

PLATE VI

Old Edmund Street

belonging to Colonel Vyse, was bared of all its old half-ruined tenements. There were other changes all over the town in the 1860's and early 70's. The angle of Worcester Street at the bottom of New Street was rounded to ease the growing volume of traffic and a row of large new shops was built. Crooked Lane, where John Cadbury had begun his business in 1831, and Union Street were almost entirely rebuilt. In the Bull Ring some of the old buildings opposite the Market Hall, which had long been used for waxwork exhibitions and sideshows, were pulled down.

The fact that the land was leased to private individuals, firms, or syndicates, and was not developed by the landlords themselves, prevented all this new building from following one common principle of planned construction. The spur to destruction and to building was private commercial enterprise. There were some local figures, like Isaac Horton, who acquired considerable properties during the period of rapid turnover. He leased or owned blocks of buildings in New Street, High Street, Bull Street, Dale End, Worcester Street, Union Street, and Cherry Street. In other cases syndicates, frequently of 'influential local gentlemen', took over enterprises, like the building of the Great Western Arcade, which were too big for private individuals. It was such a syndicate which acquired the Hen and Chickens Inn, one of the best-known and most comfortable coaching inns in the country, 'a place where one could ruminate in comfort, free from the scream of the railway whistle, and the intrusion of the bagman'.[1] It was replaced by offices and shops.

The rush to acquire shop accommodation during the boom years before 1873 forced up the price of land throughout the centre of the city. The shops themselves were on a far more lavish scale than had ever been known in Birmingham before. Hitherto Bull Street had been the main shopping thoroughfare, and old-fashioned local firms clung to old methods of display and salesmanship. Some of them had small bow windows and little panes of glass, which recalled an earlier century. From the 70's onwards there was a vivid transformation. Premises became more ornate, and were designed to attract people not only from Birmingham but from the whole region for miles around. One shop employed nearly 500 people, and sold such a wide range of articles that 'it will indeed be odd if the most capricious and

[1] *The Dart*, 23 June 1882.

exacting of customers cannot find in this vast and motley store the merchandise they require'.[1] Shops like this appealed deliberately to the crowds and not to small circles of accepted customers. Newspapers and advertisements publicized, often garishly, all sorts of new features—elaborate passenger lifts; mahogany counters—mahogany was the favourite wood; glazed glass roofs, and even chandeliers with opal globes. There was a general desire among shopkeepers to secure more space and more light:

> There's J . . . son's, all gas, and so dazzling with brass,
> We might argue without hesitation,
> That the strongest of margarine surely might pass
> For the best butter under creation.[2]

An enormous display of plate glass—with occasional stained glass—was a feature of the exteriors, while inside there were counting-houses comparable with the main offices of the largest town banks.

One of the popular features of the new shopping area was arcades. 'Birmingham seems to be getting quite an Arcadian town', wrote the *Birmingham Mail* in 1882, 'not perhaps in the sense of primitive innocence and pastoral simplicity, but the number and magnificence of its arcades.' The idea of 'shops under glass' appealed to the business instincts of a growing community, and opened a new chapter in the social life of the town. 'Windows stocked with fancy goods, ladies' work, knick-knacks, bijouterie, rare pottery, curios, and *objets d'art* seem well bestowed in a thoroughfare whose construction invites a pleasant dawdle for those who do not use it as a short cut from one street to another.'[3]

There were arcades of all types—the Great Western, sometimes compared with the Burlington Arcade in London; the Imperial with its turret clock, based on a model in Leeds; the Colonnade with its view over the roof of New Street Station; the Central Arcade with 'its gloom and desertion'. 'Features like this give the town a distinctive character', a local journalist wrote in 1889, 'and certainly no other town I have seen in England or the continent can compare with our own in this particular.'[4]

The process of building inevitably meant a great deal of

---

[1] *B.G.*, 22 September 1885.
[2] *The Dart*, 13 December 1889.
[3] *B.M.*, 8 March 1882.
[4] Ibid., 19 April 1889.

demolition of old houses and workshop property, most of it unhealthy and squalid, some of it of considerable architectural interest. The erection of John Bright Street, for instance, necessitated destroying 68 houses and a number of workshops, while new building in progress in 1882 entailed destroying 620 houses, 2 chapels, 2 hotels, and many warehouses and factories. One of the most unfortunate pieces of destruction was the pulling down of Christ Church in 1897, the clearing of the site of 2,475 square yards, and the leasing of the land, the property of the Colmore Trustees, for 150 years to a local syndicate. For every man who thought that Christ Church was 'an excrescence, which still disfigures the very finest site in the whole town',[1] there was at least one other who agreed with the *Builder* that the building should never have been touched.

Another casualty in the process of demolition was the small house with a garden, which had once been such a marked feature of the town. In 1886 a writer could claim that there were 'houses almost in the very centre of the borough where the occupiers possess the advantage of large and fruitful gardens', while in 1911 Walter Barrow recalled playing as a child in his father's garden in Bull Street, where a poplar tree was green in the spring-time, and there was a summer-house at one end.[2] It was to this spacious garden that the shopkeeper in Bull Street could adjourn, if he felt so inclined, to 'smoke a pipe' or chat with a friend within the cool shade of a summer-arbour and be within immediate call for business if required.

These developments in the central districts gradually reduced the gross population densities in the middle wards of the town. In Market Hall Ward and St. Mary's Ward a decline in density set in during the 50's, attributable to the acquisition of land for railways and warehouses. Between 1861 and 1871 the number of houses in St. Peter's Ward decreased from 6,637 to 6,318, in St. Philip's Ward from 1,771 to 1,437, in St. Paul's Ward from 1,869 to 1,486, and in St. Mary's Ward from 3,359 to 3,087. The number of unoccupied houses in these four wards rose from 730 in 1861 to 1,153 in 1871, while the population fell from 51,147 to 42,349. Despite these changes, in 1871 it was still districts within a mile radius of the Bull Ring which showed highest

[1] E. Edwards, *Personal Recollections of Birmingham and Birmingham Men* (1877), p. 5.
[2] W. Barrow, 'The Town and Its Industries', in *Birmingham Institutions* (1911) p. 51.

population densities. St. George's Ward actually increased its house accommodation by 10 per cent. between 1861 and 1871 (from 9,021 to 10,016), and its population density was as great as 196 persons per acre. Twenty years later the decline in density was established in all the central wards. Shops, warehouses, and public buildings had driven out the small houses and workshop-houses of the early years of the century. Birmingham was expanding to become a city of suburbs, while the central area of buildings was beginning to serve the needs of a region. The trend was clear quite early. ' "England, capital London", may have been the geographical lesson taught him at school', wrote a magazine as early as 1879, 'but "Midland Counties, capital Birmingham", has replaced it in his mind for all practical purposes.'[1] At the beginning of the twentieth century Birmingham was once called 'the least self-centred of cities', and of the shopping centre of the town it was said that 'it seethes with people, who have come in from fifteen miles around wearing the looks of release, which a day in town gives'.

The shops were a great attraction, but the shopping area itself was small, probably the smallest in any large English city. Within a few hundred yards of busy thoroughfares there were dark alleys and small workshops, and roads that pointed into the Black Country, and out to Bristol. No other city lost itself so soon. 'I have stood where Aston Street invites to Aston, and Lancaster Street to I know not where', wrote an enthusiastic visitor, 'and have invariably concluded that I would explore on another occasion those vast regions of the children of Tubal Cain.' The centre of Birmingham was like that: there was always the feeling of vast unknown regions beyond.

## II

Even before the advent of Joseph Chamberlain, some attempt was made to encourage the town itself to take an active part in the rebuilding of the central area. In the 1860's improvements were made in St. Philip's churchyard, which had come to be used as a general rubbish-heap, even grave-stones being used as convenient show-places on which to fix printed bills and notices. Tombs were repaired, tottering gravestones laid flat, and fresh turf planted throughout the whole churchyard.

In June 1867 more ambitious proposals were suggested at a

[1] B.M., 1 January 1879, quoting Mayfair.

public meeting, at which a speaker proposed that the town should build 'an ornamental square' on the side of New Street from Stephenson Place to Lower Temple Street. An amendment was carried stating that 'considering the extent of the borough debt and the improvement urgently required in other parts of the town', the Corporation should not provide the necessary funds, although the proposer of the amendment admitted that he might have thought differently had he lived in New Street. The Mayor in the chair said that the scheme should be sponsored, if it really was desired, by private subscription, and he went on to add that he thought that the promoters had been guilty of a want of discretion in bringing the matter before the public at all.

Affairs changed with the rejuvenation of the Council during the golden age of Chamberlain. In the first place, new life was given to an old question, and steps were taken to speed up long-contemplated alterations near the Town Hall. The Improvement Act of 1851 included in the transfer of jurisdiction from the Street Commissioners to the Corporation an agreement for the purchase of land for the redevelopment of the approaches to the Town Hall. At that time the Hall was blocked up on one side by houses built close up to the building, while on the Congreve Street side there was no footpath next to the Town Hall at all. The buildings in Ann Street, now Colmore Row, where the Council House stands, were poor and mean, and Edmund Street was a narrow and awkward thoroughfare, bounded by small houses and workshops. The site of Mason College—later the University building—was covered with a network of dingy and dirty passage-ways and courts. The space now occupied by the Chamberlain Memorial was a piece of waste ground, used as a rough recreation ground by children in the neighbourhood, and occasionally for open-air meetings. 'So poor and neglected was the whole of this central district, that Birmingham people, jealous of the credit of their town, were ashamed to show it to visitors as the heart of Birmingham.'[1]

By the end of the century this squalid district was transformed to become the centre of civic administration. In 1853 the site of the present Council House was brought by the town, with the intention of using it for new Corporation offices, and concentrating in one place the administrative departments of the borough. There were so many delays and misunderstandings in the

---

[1] J. T. Bunce, *History of the Corporation of Birmingham*, vol. ii (1885), p. xxvi.

next few years that the site remained undeveloped, and although the land had been bought on very favourable terms—11,450 square yards for only £33,000—some people were beginning to regard it as a burden rather than as a benefit. In February 1868 a real attempt was made to use the land, but on account of the state of the municipal finances and the fear of contractors and heavy expenditure, the project was defeated. In 1870 effective action was at last taken. On the initiative of the Chairman of the Estates Committee, plans were ordered for town buildings fronting Ann Street and Congreve Street and for Assize Courts in Edmund Street. The well-known architect Waterhouse was engaged to advise the Council on them. In July 1870 the plans of H. R. Yeoville Thomason were selected, and the foundation-stone of the new building was laid in June 1874 by the Mayor, Joseph Chamberlain. It was not until 1879 that the new building was opened, and there was a final burst of controversy about what it should be called. The Estates Committee favoured the name 'Municipal Hall' and Alderman Avery 'Guildhall', but the title 'Council House' finally prevailed by thirty-four votes to twenty-six.

The building of the new Council House marked the beginning of a period of extensive development in its immediate neighbourhood. The course of building was often difficult, because of the increasing value of the property and the tangled mesh of interests of freeholders, lessees, and sub-tenants. Thus, although Sir Josiah Mason worked out the idea of a Mason Science College before 1870, it was not until 1872 that he succeeded in obtaining a large enough site in the neighbourhood, and not until February 1875 that the foundation-stone was laid, on his eightieth birthday. In 1881 the foundation-stone of a new School of Art was laid, and in the same year an extension of the Midland Institute was erected after a design by its secretary, John Henry Chamberlain. New reference and lending libraries were opened in 1882. Finally, in October 1889, the Chamberlain Memorial was inaugurated—the Gothic fountain of Portland stone, with its columns, arches, and water-jets. The present shape of the central block of public buildings was complete.

While these developments were transforming the Town Hall area, the building of Corporation Street revolutionized the topography of the whole central district. 'The old order has gradually changed in the streets cutting through the centre of

PLATE VII

The Council House
An Artist's Impression

PLATE VIII

Corporation Street about 1880

our town', wrote a local journalist, 'Corporation Street has completely eclipsed New Street as the premier street of the city.' The political and administrative implications of Chamberlain's Improvement Scheme are dealt with in a subsequent chapter:[1] the way in which it changed the face of the city is equally important.

Chamberlain looked across the Channel to France and talked of constructing 'a great street, as broad as a Parisian boulevard, from New Street to the Aston Road'. Paris provided the obvious model. 'Anyone who has been there', said Councillor White, 'must have noted the leafy verdure to be seen everywhere, its healthy look, and its broad streets and boulevards, and charming flowery open spaces in every direction.' It was not only a broad street, with traffic facilities for a busy community, which was required. Shops were necessary too. Despite the previous changes Chamberlain still considered the city 'under-shopped', and planned to make it 'the retail shop of the whole of the midland counties of England'.[2]

By the Act of 1876 the Council secured 43½ acres of land in the centre of the city. Much of the area was a rookery of crime and wretchedness, 'a sort of place which was shown to visiting philanthropists as a specimen of our slums'.[3] Lichfield Street, which ran almost parallel with the Victoria Courts, bore a none too reputable name, nor did the thoroughfare connecting it with Coleshill Street and Dale End on the one side, and Steelhouse Lane on the other. Stafford Street and Dale End were totally inadequate arteries to deal with the mass of traffic from Aston and Perry Barr.

Building operations in the scheduled area began in August 1878, but it was not until April 1879 that the first portion of the new Corporation Street—that between New Street and Cherry Street—was opened. The policy of the Improvement Committee was to proceed slowly, so as not to throw too much property on the market at any one time. The subsequent fortunes of the scheme were not always encouraging. It was a long-term project, and cut right across building boom years over into times of slump, its local popularity fluctuating with local prosperity.

[1] See below, pp. 77–82.
[2] The Artisans' and Labourers' Dwellings Improvement Act, 1875. *Proceedings for the Adoption by the Council of a Scheme for Improvement of the Borough*, October 1875.
[3] *B.M.*, 22 April 1902.

The chart of economic progress is interesting. The years 1878 and 1879 were bad. In January 1879 land at the valuable site of the corner of New Street and Corporation Street was withdrawn at an auction, when the highest bids reached £4. 15s. a yard. Although some important lettings were made in July, two months later, when *The Dart* ran a competition for the best verses on the new Corporation Street, one of the published entries ran:

Where is the fierce contention for those eligible spots
They prophesied would come about? They do not let their lots. . . .
How can I sing about the street? You've done it, sir, to vex,
It is an unknown quantity just like the letter *x*.

Another competitor was even more gloomy:

One end's begun, but who shall see
The other end?—a mystery!
'Twill be a Herculean feat,
To make it so that both ends meet.[1]

Criticism continued in 1879 and in 1880, but in 1881, as the building of the street between New Street and Bull Street progressed more rapidly, there was greater optimism. 'Trade is certainly improving', wrote one commentator, and 'I fail to see any grounds for the fears of the croakers who are continually asserting that the Improvement Scheme will turn out a failure and will never be made to pay'.[2] 'We should scarcely need to take a nap as long as Rip Van Winkle's to wake up and find Corporation Street complete, bustling with life and activity', wrote another.[3] Despite the revival in trade and the improvement in prospects many critics still charged the Committee with working the scheme as a great land speculation unworthy of the city both in its aims and its methods.

In 1882, when the portions between Bull Street and the Priory and John Street and Aston Street were opened, the Committee reported that since the beginning of active operations 529 buildings had been thoroughly repaired, 2,263 dwelling-houses temporarily repaired, and 600 buildings, including 375 houses, demolished. A continuous thoroughfare had now been provided, which was considered 'a street which deserves to rank amongst the noblest in the kingdom'.

The financial success of the scheme was in doubt until 1892,[4]

[1] *The Dart*, 13 September 1879.　　[2] *B.W.P.*, 18 February 1881.
[3] Ibid., 18 January 1881.　　[4] See below, p. 81.

but the street continued to make progress. By 1892, 53,555 yards had been leased, with a yearly rental of £36,696. By the beginning of the new century only one plot of land in Corporation Street—450 yards at the corner of Steelhouse Lane— remained unlet. A lease of this site at a rental of 10s. a yard was granted in May 1900.

Although all the available sites had been built upon, the problem remained of deciding whether to add 633 yards to the 850-yard-long street—as had been originally planned—by extending it beyond Lancaster Street as far as Aston Road, near the Bagot Street Canal Bridge. The issue was not a straight one. Although the property belonged to the Council and was let on short tenancies, it was clear that business premises in this area would not command the same rents as in the older portions of the street near Stephenson Place. To counterbalance this, the attractiveness of the scheme had increased since 1876 with the growth of the tramway system, and the possibilities of a direct service from Colmore Row to Aston, and possibly to Sutton Coldfield. In April 1902 the Estates Committeee of the Council agreed to recommend that the original plan, envisaging a street almost a mile in length, should be followed. But its recommendation was turned down by the Council in May. The refusal of the Council to sanction the work was brought before the notice of the Local Government Board, and in October the Council deferred consideration of the proposal until the Estates Committee had consulted with the Local Government Board about it. A letter from the Local Government Board in February 1903 stated that the continuation was part of the original scheme which had been approved, and should be proceeded with without delay. The only alternative to this procedure was an official application for the modification of the original scheme. At the same time that this letter was received, the Council learnt that ratepayers at the far end of Corporation Street intended to bring pressure to bear to have the continuation started. It was only after many months of discussion and delay that in March 1903 the Council authorized the Estates Committee to proceed with the final completion of Corporation Street.

One of the most important new public buildings at the lower end of Corporation Street was the Victoria Law Courts, built between 1887 and 1891. The architects were Aston Webb and E. Ingress Bell, and their work, conceived in the Renaissance style of Francis I, immediately created a good impression. 'The interesting windows, with their Gothic arches of buff terra-cotta,' wrote the *Birmingham Daily Post* in 1889, 'already afford a series of delightful cathedral-like vistas, and a nearer view of the ornamentation of the arches and capitals is an artistic treat.'[1] The great hall with its lofty timber-framed roof, enriched by sculptured walls and lighted by stained-glass windows, was much admired. The building was visited by the Art Congress in 1890, and was highly praised, particularly for the beauty of its turrets. In a letter to Sir Thomas Martineau in 1891, Mr. Justice Wills described the building as 'almost without a rival in its combination of artistic beauty and practical adaptation in almost every detail to the purposes to which it is destined'.[2]

While in these new plans and buildings the Corporation was attempting to create a worthy city, it also employed other methods to improve the face of the central district. Plane-trees, poplars, and limes were planted in Stephenson Place in 1875, and in other streets a little later. The event was recognized to be of importance. 'Some forty or fifty curious passers-by witnessed the proceedings, and thus unconsciously assisted the commencement of a new aesthetic era in municipal matters.'[3] The gesture was to herald many more ambitious projects in later years.

### III

The vigour of private interests and the widening scope of public policy did not produce a planned urban landscape. The varied architectural styles of the new buildings reflected the diffusion of ownership and leaseholding. There was no common city plan behind the shops and streets. 'Birmingham is an oddly laid out town,' wrote the *Builder* in 1897, 'or rather it is not laid out at all.' 'The streets in the central portion of the town wander about at all kinds of unexpected curves and angles, so that the stranger within the gates never quite knows in what direction he is going, and finds himself coming round unexpectedly, every now and then, to the point he had left a short time before.'[4] Residents found the shape of the town far less difficult. By the end of the century the shopping areas were fairly clearly defined —the smallest and probably the busiest of any large town in England. The administrative buildings were conveniently

---

[1] *B.P.*, 17 April 1889.   [2] *Birmingham Mercury*, 15 August 1891.
[3] *B.P.*, 30 November 1875.   [4] *The Builder*, 27 November 1897.

PLATE IX

The Victoria Law Courts

PLATE X

Victoria Square before 1897

centralized at the western end of Colmore Row, and there were still highly specialized industrial areas near the centre of the city, like the Jewellers' Quarter, near St. Paul's Square.

Opportunities had not been taken to subordinate individual buildings to any general design, nor to build squares of a spacious and unified character. A design for the new Council House, submitted by Lynn of Belfast, had suggested a closed square and a corrected frontage line, which would have given the city a more impressive central block of buildings, but it was turned down, while the opportunity was missed in the construction of the Law Courts to fit the new buildings into the framework of the Old Square, before it was built over.

If there was a lack of a common design, there was also a lack of anything like a common style of expression. Birmingham architects in the formative years of reconstruction, like architects elsewhere, reacted against Georgian building, 'the ugly classic period in architecture, which flourished at the beginning of the century'.[1] The public followed, and in some cases led, condemning a style which gave 'no projections to break up the dull flatness and give light and shade; no attempt to relieve the unmitigated square, hut-like appearance of the building'.[2] J. H. Chamberlain introduced Gothic houses into Edgbaston, houses 'with gabled roofs, pointed arch windows, red tiles instead of dull-coloured slates, and attractive detail and ornamentation'. Although at first 'some square-toed, un-compromising, old-fashioned folks' asked 'what next?—pointed arch windows for an ordinary dwelling house, who ever heard of such a thing?'— 'people began to like the style, or their architects told them they must like it, and after some time, residences of the new order began to be seen in many directions'.[3]

The new style became increasingly popular in the centre of the city, although before long it got rather lost in an architectural confusion. Shopkeepers and officials looked for showiness and conspicuous display and showed an exuberance which knew few restraints. The most favourable criticism that could be made of the new city was that of Joseph Hatton in 1887—'taken in detail, the Birmingham buildings are as magnificent as are her institutions, but en masse the effect is an architectural jungle'.[4]

---

[1] *Allday's Gossiping Guide to Birmingham* (1893).
[2] T. Anderton, *A Tale of One City* (1900), p. 92.
[3] Ibid., p. 96.　　　　　　　　　　　[4] *B.G.*, 16 March 1887.

The least favourable criticism was that made by *The Builder*, which compared Corporation Street unfavourably with Colmore Row, civic and commercial 'Renaissance' with 'the quiet and broadly-treated late Gothic of Barry's King Edward's School', and the confusion of central city architecture with the 'delights of Edgbaston'.[1]

The elaboration of the 70's and 80's was in part a protest against the hurried building of the 60's, when garish stuccoed buildings of what has been aptly termed 'pilasterish' style appeared to be the general model of street architecture, and the use of honest stone and brick was rejected for colourless and vapid cemented fronts. Birmingham became a city of terra-cotta, used more frequently than anywhere else in the country, and the favourite style amid a welter of styles became 'Italian Renaissance, treated however somewhat freely',[2] or less frequently 'French Renaissance', with shops designed to look like *châteaux* on the Loire. Eventually even these wide enough categories became blurred. One hotel was envisaged as 'Gothic, with detail somewhat French in character', while a shop designed to contain stock worth £25,000 was built 'in no particular style, but inclining if anything to the Italian'.[3] By the end of the century buildings were being raised 'in the free Renaissance style in terra cotta with an ornamental gable as a set-off'.[4] There were some buildings done in ornate classical style, like Lloyds Bank, designed by a local architect in 1871, but in general Italy and France were preferred to Greece and Rome.

The buildings were designed by various architects. Cubitt designed the Baptist Church of the Redeemer. The celebrated Waterhouse, 'whose smile was worth ten thousand pounds a year to him', was employed as consulting architect to the Corporation in the choice of the Council House plans. He was responsible himself for the design of the Prudential Office in Corporation Street, which can be compared with his Prudential Building in Holborn in London. Aston Webb and Ingress Bell, choosing 'a kind of Renaissance style, but Gothic in spirit and grouping', won the prize for the Law Courts in face of powerful competition, and did much to influence architectural style in the town. W. H. Ward, a local figure, was responsible for much of

---

[1] *The Builder*, 27 November 1897. See also ibid., 1 May 1914.
[2] A description is given in *B.W.P.*, 25 October 1889.
[3] *B.P.* 28 April 1886.                              [4] *B.M.*, 1 November 1897.

the commercial building, and his name was considered 'a guarantee that the creation will be something worthy of the town,
and that the style employed will be both handsome and effective'.[1]
Among his designs were the Great Western Arcade, 'resembling
to a great extent the light and graceful work of the *galeries* in
some of the principal thoroughfares of Paris', and the Board of
Guardians' office in Edmund Street, for which he chose a characteristic 'adaptation of a severe phase of the modern school of
the French Renaissance'. J. H. Chamberlain was another local
architect, whose work was characteristic of the standards of the
times. At the end of the century, in 1900, Lethaby and Ball designed the forward-looking Eagle Insurance Buildings.

Sometimes there were reactions against the prevailing architects and fashions.

It may be a stupid prejudice (wrote a wise critic in 1882), but
I regret the too-too epidemic in Birmingham. There was something
I liked about the Old Square, for at present I am not equal to Gothic
fire engine offices, and Early-English carpet shops. I rather preferred
the old inconvenient Bull Street, complete in itself, to the same street
sliced up. I have a prejudice in favour of stone fronts rather than brick,
even though the bricks be pressed into pretty patterns, and I cannot
take kindly to tinsel mural ornaments.[2]

The 'stupid prejudices' of yesterday often correspond to most
twentieth-century opinions of late-Victorian Birmingham, and
despite still changing fashions and taste, few would deny that
it is unfortunate that more of the old Birmingham before 1870
has not been preserved.

IV

The rate of building and demolition was far from constant.
Statistics collected by the City Surveyor show a sharp rise in the
number of plans registered for houses and small house-shops in
the years 1875, 1876, and 1877. The average for the years
1867–75 was 1,347; in 1875, 3,395 house plans were registered;
in 1876, 2,903; and in 1877, 2,700. The figure for 1875 was not
exceeded until 1926. These three years marked the peak of a
building boom, which was in progress in other parts of the
country as well. When foreign investment slackened off, as it did
after 1873, and funds were available, house-building investment
rose. Building provided a balancing make-weight to fluctuations

---

[1] *B.P.*, 20 February 1874.      [2] *The Dart*, 23 June 1882.

in foreign investment. More than private house-building was involved. A general impetus was given to local improvement. 'Money is cheap and that is a great advantage in our favour,' said one Councillor in supporting the municipal improvement scheme in 1875, 'and there are many capitalists waiting for good investments.'[1]

The boom broke in 1878 and 1879, black years when there was much local unemployment. While the Brassworkers' Society was paying £8,860 in unemployment relief between 1879 and 1880 as compared with a sum of £2,300 between 1872 and 1877, the Improvement Committee was reporting that no satisfactory bids had been received for land offered by auction in Corporation Street. The average number of house plans submitted in the years 1878–86 was down to 1,023. The 'speculative mania', as some local people envisaged it, had worked itself out, and a steady 1,000 houses were built each year, corresponding to an annual population increase of 5,000. There was an increase again in the 1890's, and 2,308 plans were submitted in the peak year 1898. In the period from 1900 to 1914 the annual number of completed houses and house-shops averaged 1,288. The years 1909 to 1914 were years of slump in the local building industry. They coincided with a great burst of foreign investment, unfavourable to building enterprise. A solicitor told the Housing Inquiry Committee in 1913 that his clients, who had invested £300,000 in local mortgages, had almost all called them in and invested overseas.[2] While there was a shortage of home capital at this time, caused by the prospect of greater returns from foreign investment, there were also rising costs both of labour and materials in the building industry, which made home prospects of profit even less favourable. By 1914 there was for the first time in Birmingham a serious housing shortage, the number of empty working-class houses having fallen to as low a figure as 1·35 per cent.[3] Only 1,396 houses were built in 1914 against an estimated net demand of 2,000 a year to accommodate the rising population.

The submission of plans for warehouses, workshops, and business premises was very regular and steady in the period from

[1] The Artisans' and Labourers' Dwellings Improvement Act, 1875. *Proceedings for the Adoption by the Council of a Scheme for Improvement of the Borough*, October 1875.

[2] City of Birmingham, *Report of the Select Committee on Housing*, 1914.

[3] City of Birmingham, *Report of the Medical Officer of Health*, 1914.

1865 to 1888, and reached peak figures in 1871, 1876, and 1879. From 1888 to 1899 there was a steady demand at a greatly increased figure, but for the years after 1902–3 there was a fall to figures well below the average for the 1870's. The year 1904–5 was particularly bad as far as figures of buildings completed were concerned. The explanation of these figures is to be found in the general economic history of the city. The fluctuations corresponded to fluctuations in economic activity in 'the workshop of the world'. To understand some of the changes described in this chapter, we must pass from the shops and the streets first to the warehouses and the factories, and then into the Council Chamber, where the civic gospel itself was being manufactured.

# III
# 'THE WORKSHOP OF THE WORLD'

## I

THE industrial structure of Birmingham in the mid-nine-teenth century was the result of a century of vigorous economic development. When in 1866 Samuel Timmins collected 'a large and important mass of facts' about Birmingham and the Midland Hardware District for the visit of the British Association to the city, he was able to present the picture of a town of many trades satisfying a wide range of consumers' and business men's needs. His book was a composite product. 'The productions of Birmingham are so numerous and so varied', he wrote, 'that no one could be found who would undertake to describe them all, and it has, therefore, been found necessary to make the sub-division of labour in this volume almost as exten-sive and minute as in the various trades of the town.'[1]

During the eighteenth century Birmingham had become re-nowned for the variety of its enterprises, and in particular for its production of finished brass goods, guns, buttons, and jewellery. Its metal-finishing trades—in various forms—remained the basis of its industrial activity. 'She writes her name in brass and iron, and in her normal condition her face is sooty and her sinewy arms are bare', wrote a visitor in 1893.[2] In the twentieth century, in addition to the thousands of tons of steel and the precious ounces of gold, silver, and platinum, new metals like aluminium have been exploited. 'There can be scarcely a kitchen where this aspect of Birmingham's vast production is not repre-sented—kettles and saucepans, frying pans and small domestic utensils are all made in Birmingham.'[3]

At the beginning of the nineteenth century Birmingham was not only an industrial centre, but the hub of the commercial life of the mining and manufacturing district of south Staffordshire and an increasingly important centre providing services and

---

[1] S. Timmins, *The Resources, Products and Industrial History of Birmingham and the Midland Hardware District* (1866), p. 208.

[2] J. A. Stuart, 'The Rt. Hon. Joseph Chamberlain, M.P., and Birmingham', in the *Ludgate Monthly*, November 1893.

[3] *The City of Birmingham Official Handbook* (1950), ed. F. W. Bradnock, p. 45.

trading facilities for a widening region.[1] The growth of the region as a whole was founded on iron. It was iron which acted as a key commodity of the industrial revolution. People slept in iron beds and washed in iron wash-bowls, travelled on iron rails pulled by iron locomotives over iron bridges towards iron railway stations, worked with iron machines, and fought with iron weapons. The growth of the west Midlands was based on the rich coal and iron deposits of south Staffordshire, which made it rich while turning it into a 'Black Country'.

Birmingham always remained distinct and different from the Black Country. The skill and versatility of the city enabled it to respond to changing technical and market conditions. Many of its oldest trades, like nail-making, bridle-cutting, and cutlery, had for the most part disappeared by 1914, but new ones had taken their place. Through times of changing technique and changing fashion, Birmingham stayed in the industrial limelight. It was becoming important before the local Iron Age, and it remained so after the south Staffordshire Iron Age had come to an end. So varied were its industries that, in 1832, leaders of the Birmingham Political Union had proclaimed that the state of employment in the town mirrored the economic fortunes of the country as a whole; while a modern economic historian has said that because of the vigour of its engineering industry and the unchallenged contribution of its special trades, Birmingham 'could not have fallen into a general decline, unless the whole of England had declined with it'.[2]

The economic fortunes of the Black Country were more mixed, for south Staffordshire felt the main impact of the waning of the Iron Age. When Timmins wrote in 1866 there was a depression in the iron industry, brought about chiefly by a contraction in the home demand for iron rails. The clouds were lifted during the roaring boom of 1870-3, which provided the optimistic economic setting for the municipal revolution of Joseph Chamberlain. The Birmingham trades underwent a vigorous expansion, the number of factories in the tube trade, for example, doubling between 1868 and 1873.[3] The munitions industries

[1] See W. H. B. Court, *The Rise of the Midland Industries* (1938); M. J. Wise and B. L. C. Johnson, 'The Changing Regional Pattern during the Eighteenth Century', in *Birmingham and its Regional Setting* (1950).

[2] C. R. Fay, *English Economic History, mainly since 1700* (1940), p. 181.

[3] G. C. Allen, *The Industrial Development of Birmingham and the Black Country* (1929), p. 197.

were working at full pressure to satisfy orders for the continental market and the British government. As a result of this stimulus, iron prices and production rocketed. The output of pig-iron in 1871 was the highest at any period in the history of south Staffordshire and amounted to nearly 11 per cent. of the total British supply.[1]

This was the biggest boom of the nineteenth century, in which both city and region shared. In March 1872 the statistician Giffen sensed 'a less prosperous period' ahead, but the peak of the expansion was not reached until 1873. In the summer of that year, iron bars were selling at £2 a ton less than in the spring.[2] A further fall in iron and coal prices and output followed. By the beginning of 1874 blast furnaces, forges, and mills were being closed down. There was a time-lag before the Birmingham trades shared in the downward trend. As late as 1875 the brass trade was still active, important locally because Birmingham was to brass what Manchester was to cotton, or Bradford to wool. It was not until the autumn of that year that the depression became general. By 1876 most local industry was hit, and there was a severe fall both in prices and in employment.

The boom that thus came to an end had been based on a tremendous burst of capital expansion, particularly railway construction, on a world-wide scale. Britain's part in the years of prosperity had been an important one, and Birmingham had led the way. The Black Country had done so too, but at a heavy price. The sustained pressure on declining supplies of mineral deposits led to decreasing returns and increases in costs. The reserves of raw materials on which the export of *real* capital had been based were wearing out in the west Midlands. This was a more serious long-term problem for the region than the cessation of foreign demand and lending, which brought the boom to an end. Birmingham, with its active supply of skilled labour and its wide range of products, could adapt itself to a changing world. The region as a whole, with diminishing supplies of local raw materials, found the process of adaptation more difficult.

The crisis in the Black Country was more than the periodically recurring problem of a regular business cycle. It was an historical crisis, which marked the end of a crowded chapter in economic history. The crisis had three features—first, the increasing ex-

[1] R. Hunt, *Mineral Statistics of Great Britain and Ireland* (1871).
[2] *Newspaper Cuttings on Birmingham Industries*, vol. ii (Birmingham Collection), p. 200.

haustion of materials; second, the substitution of steel for iron as a working material; and third, the challenge of foreign competition. Birmingham was affected by all these problems, and by problems of its own in addition, but as a result of its special advantages it contrived to look busy and was busy through all the years of the so-called 'Great Depression'. If some trades were depressed and slack, others were active and prosperous. 'There is generally business doing somewhere', wrote a commentator in 1900.[1] In any case, in the role of the city not as a manufacturing centre but as a distributor of goods for the whole region, Birmingham, the commercial capital of the Midlands, had gained rather than lost in importance by the end of the century.

II

The exhaustion of local resources led to the regional decline first of the coal trade and the mining of iron-stone, and second to a fall in the production of pig-iron itself. By 1900 coal production dropped to about half of what it had been in 1865: after 1900 the rate of decline became even more rapid. By 1913 output had fallen to 3 million tons, as compared with $7\frac{1}{2}$ million tons in the 1860's. The pig-iron industry, despite the shortage of complementary materials, had more vitality, and although the number of furnaces fell between 1880 and 1914, output did not fall correspondingly. Improvements in technique were making for bigger and more efficient plants. The result was that the output of pig-iron in 1907 was as high as it had been in 1875, and the industry was on the upgrade in the three years which preceded the outbreak of the First World War.

In addition to the problem of the exhaustion of local raw materials a further factor influencing the decline of south Staffordshire was the expansion of other steel-making districts following the development of the Bessemer process, and the displacement of the older wrought-iron industry. The Black Country remained the premier producer of high-grade wrought iron, but the challenge of steel affected the demand for the older product in many sectors of the economy. From 1878 onwards, for instance, steel became increasingly important in the shipbuilding industry, although as late as 1880 nine iron ships were built for every one of steel. At the same time, steel was super-

[1] T. Anderton, *A Tale of One City* (1900), p. 141.

seding iron as rail material. The first steel railway lines were laid down by the London and North Western Railway at Crewe as early as 1861, but the general switch-over did not come until the 70's. By the 90's, steel was displacing iron in the manufacture of tinplates, galvanized sheets, and constructional engineering.

Although the light engineering trades and the finishing trades of Birmingham turned over to steel on account of its technical and economic advantages, the Black Country itself did not become an important steel-producing centre. It is true that the first two basic Bessemer plants in England were opened at Wednesbury in 1882, and that in 1893 the Earl of Dudley set up his enormous open-hearth steel plant at Round Oak, but these were exceptions to the rule. New districts, some of them located near the coast, where imported iron-ore could be worked at low cost, were in a far more advantageous position.

The result of this change in industrial geography was that Birmingham finishing trades had to turn to the north or to south Wales for their supplies of crude steel. The tables were turned in the story of the west Midlands. 'The basic industries, which had originally called into being the finished-metal trades of the district, now owed their survival, not to the proximity of local materials, but to the existence of a large local demand for metal.'[1] The pull of the market had so tightened that local deficiencies in raw materials were overcome, and the survival of the whole area was guaranteed.

By the 90's, Birmingham had to turn, although on a relatively small scale, not only to other English sources of supply, but to German and Belgian producers. These foreign-placed orders were signposts to a new world. In the Iron Age, England had led the way, with Birmingham as its capital. In the Steel Age, the Germans and Americans soon outstripped all competitors as far as production figures went. By 1886 the United States surpassed Great Britain in the output of iron and steel, and in 1901 Germany likewise passed her. They were more important as producers than as exporters, however, and down to 1912, when Germany took the lead, Great Britain remained the principal exporter, judged by value, of iron and steel products.

Birmingham and the Black Country had always been sensitive to foreign competition. Local manufacturers had more to lose from foreign competition in the home market than they stood

[1] G. C. Allen, op. cit., p. 282.

to gain from building up overseas demand. In 1829 the *Birming-ham Argus* had complained

that the Swedish iron merchant is our competitor in all and every part of the continent. The German wire drawers glut our home and foreign markets with the best steel and brass wire. In France . . . they are our rivals in price and quality; excelling us in most ironmongery goods. They are using machinery made in this country, and are improving in the manufacture of machinery and hardware goods every year.[1]

The *Argus* always was a moaner, but the line that it took showed the complete contrast in outlook between the views of the iron interest and the cotton interest, at a time when the latter was beginning to stand for free trade. Manchester triumphed, but by the last quarter of the nineteenth century the bogy of foreign competition began to take real shape for the manufacturers of Birmingham.

It was at the turn of the new century that Joseph Chamberlain, who had made eloquent free-trade speeches in the 1880's, began to put forward his programme of tariff reform as an answer to national economic needs. His first statement of the programme stressed the value of the protective tariff as an instrument to give the colonies preferential treatment in the British market. Later the campaign developed into a drive for the general protection of home industries. Birmingham became the spear-head of the agitation, and its vigorous leadership was just as important as had been the leadership of Manchester in the battle for free trade in the 'hungry forties'. Indeed the city acquired that symbolical significance in the national history of the later nineteenth century which Manchester had possessed thirty years before.[2]

The case for tariff reform was argued at first in terms of Birmingham statistics. Just as the statement of Attwood's currency theses after the end of the Napoleonic wars had owed much to local conditions and grievances, so Chamberlain's arguments focused attention on the special problems of Birmingham and the Black Country as evidence of wider national problems. In his explanations, politics and economics were inextricably entangled.

The advance of foreign countries in face of Britain's early

[1] *The Birmingham Monthly Argus and Public Censor*, August 1829.
[2] W. K. Hancock, *Survey of British Commonwealth Affairs*, vol. ii, 'Problems of Economic Policy' (1940), p. 92.

leadership had been accomplished with the aid of protective devices of various kinds. Germany raised her duties on manufactured imports to a much higher level in 1870, and increased them still further six years later. The United States adopted a policy of protection with the McKinley tariff of 1890, and extended duties on imports still further in 1897.

The first reaction to the spread of protectionism abroad came in isolated protests from English business men in the 60's. Their voices were quietened in the boom of 1870 to 1873, but not silenced. During the 70's Fred Blood, a Birmingham button and jewellery merchant who claimed that he turned protectionist because his business began to suffer as a result of foreign competition, founded, with the support of P. H. Muntz, the Birmingham Reciprocity League. Local demands from other parts of the country for a policy of reciprocity and retaliation led to a nationwide 'fair trade' agitation, which came to a climax in 1881 with the setting up of the Fair Trade League. Its first president was S. S. Lloyd of Birmingham, a well-known manufacturer and banker. Another Birmingham member of the Executive was Henry Hawkes.[1] It was not surprising that in the general election of 1885 fair-trade propaganda played a big part in Birmingham, among workers as well as business men. 'Fair trade—you have no idea what a hold it has on the artisans', wrote Chamberlain,[2] while to Russell he admitted that it required all his energies to win each of the seats for the Liberal party.[3]

At that time Chamberlain was a vigorous opponent of any form of protectionism. At a Cobden Club Dinner in June 1885 he boasted with pride that 'the depression which has prevailed here as elsewhere throughout the world has not been intensified and accentuated by all kinds of artificial restrictions or by unjust, and injurious tariffs'.[4] In May 1887 he refused to accept election as chairman of the Birmingham Chamber of Commerce on the grounds that the Chamber had recently adopted a resolution in favour of fair trade, to which he expressed himself opposed in every shape or form.[5]

Despite Chamberlain's criticism, the protectionist movement

---

[1] See B. H. Brown, *The Tariff Reform Movement in Great Britain* (1943).
[2] J. L. Garvin, *The Life of Joseph Chamberlain*, vol. ii (1932), pp. 121–2.
[3] G. W. E. Russell, 'Joseph Chamberlain', in the *Contemporary Review*, vol. xxxvii, p. 317.
[4] L. Creswicke, *Life of Joseph Chamberlain*, vol. iv (1904), p. 44.
[5] G. H. Wright, *Chronicles of the Birmingham Chamber of Commerce* (1913), p. 328.

by no means died out in Birmingham, although the appeal of its arguments fluctuated somewhat as bad years gave way to good ones. In general the national movement lacked a leader with the vigour and the drive to turn the campaign into a cause. Despite his earlier statements Chamberlain was well fitted to lead such a crusade. He understood and represented business grievances more effectively than any other important figure in English politics. In March 1896 he called for an Imperial Zollverein, a call which far-sighted critics interpreted rightly as an advance demand for protection. In raising this cry, Chamberlain followed Birmingham rather than led it. As early as 1885, while Chamberlain was addressing the Cobden Club, the Birmingham Chamber of Commerce addressed a memorandum to the Colonial Secretary, the Earl of Derby, urging a 'well-considered scheme of Imperial Federation'.[1] They did not talk of imperial free trade or even of preferential tariffs, but what they said pointed towards an inevitable conclusion. 'Protection will not be Protection', wrote one shrewd commentator in 1902 before Chamberlain began his spectacular campaign, 'but Free Trade within the Empire.'[2] This was to be the central thesis of the Birmingham men who directed the tariff reform movement. In its earlier advocacy of free trade in the 1840's, Manchester had hoisted the banner of universal peace: Chamberlain and Birmingham now raised the flag of the Empire.

Chamberlain's tariff reform campaign began with a celebrated speech in Birmingham on 15 May 1903. Soon battle royal was joined, particularly on the thorny question of taxes on food. Statistics were hurled at opponents, as they had never been hurled before, even in the hungry forties.[3] The Tariff Reform League, with Professor W. A. Hewins as economic adviser, kept up a running commentary on the economic grievances of the day. 'Investigation is the order of the day,' observed the report of the Birmingham Conservative Association, 'commercial statistics, Blue Books, Board of Trade Returns and similar publications have never had so many readers.'[4]

On the general level, the case for tariff reform was urged on the grounds that it would increase the solidarity of the Empire;

[1] Ibid., pp. 316–17.
[2] J. A. Hobson, *Imperialism* (1901), p. 6.
[3] It is probable that the phrase 'hungry forties' goes back to this early-twentieth-century agitation. See T. Fisher Unwin, *The Hungry Forties* (1904).
[4] *Report of the Birmingham Conservative Association* (1903–4).

in practice the campaign consisted primarily of appeals *ad hominem* and *ad locum*, ingeniously varied to suit the background and needs of different parts of the country. In Birmingham, the home of the movement, the case for protection was argued in terms of metal manufacture. It was urged that the protective duties of Germany and the United States had enabled them not only to protect their own markets but to discriminate in their export prices, and so to capture English markets as well.

We are the one open market of the world. We are the one dumping-ground of the world (said Chamberlain in the House of Commons in May 1903). The moment trade is bad . . . it is perfectly certain that large quantities of iron would be put down in this country or in the countries that we supply at prices that we could not possibly contend with. The consequence of that would be that, inasmuch as no manufacturer here could possibly stand a loss of that description for many years together, his business would be ruined, and the whole of the capital lost as well as the profit. Of one thing I am certain. If there should be a depression in some of our greatest industries, and the result which I predict should follow, nothing on earth would prevent the people of this country from imposing a duty which would defend them against such unfair competition.

The kernel of the tariff reform proposals was put forward in the Reports of the Tariff Reform Commission, a body of Chamberlain's supporters who, at his own request, examined his suggestions. The Commission first met in January 1904, and it is significant that its first *Report*, published in July, dealt with the Iron and Steel Industry. It concluded that 'the relative decline of the British Iron and Steel Industry is not due to any natural British disadvantages, or want of skill and enterprise on the part either of British manufacturers or British workmen', but to the fact 'that the manufacturers of the United States and Germany, having secured control of their home markets by high tariffs and an organised system of their export trade, are in a position to dump their surplus products upon British and other markets, irrespective of cost'. It advocated a threefold system of tariffs—first, general tariffs, with a low scale of duties for those foreign countries which accepted British wares on fair terms; second, preferential tariffs on imperial trade; third, maximum tariffs, consisting of comparatively higher duties, but subject to reduction by negotiation to the level of the general tariff. A provisional scale of duties for the general tariff was drawn up. Iron-

ores, by now a necessary import, were to be free. Five per cent.
was to be charged on pig-iron, $6\frac{1}{4}$ per cent. on partly manufactured iron and steel materials, including rails, sleepers, and
girders, $7\frac{1}{2}$ per cent. on wire rods and plates, and 10 per cent. on
sheets.[1]

There were many differences among economists about the
wisdom of these proposals.[2] Although the protectionist arguments often overlooked the large volume of trade which Great
Britain continued to enjoy with protectionist countries and the
benefits it secured from the operation of the most-favoured-
nation clause, they were calculated to secure the support of
important interests in Birmingham and the Midlands. The
effects of foreign tariffs were felt not only by large-scale iron and
steel manufacturers but also by traditional Birmingham small
men, particularly the jewellers. Chamberlain always made a
point, wherever he possibly could, of attending the annual
dinner of the Birmingham Jewellers' and Silversmiths' Association, set up in 1887. During the 90's German jewellery began to
drive out Birmingham wares in foreign markets. The slump was
cumulative. 'In 1900 we sold to foreigners £50,000 worth, we
imported from foreigners £137,000 worth, and we were £87,000
to the bad. That was in 1900, but in 1902 we were £170,000 to
the bad. . . . There are tariffs, which prevent you from sending
your jewellery into those foreign countries, and which range up to
45 per cent.', Chamberlain told an audience of 10,000 in Bingley
Hall in November 1903.[3] What applied to jewellery applied
also to nut-and-bolt making, needle manufacture, pearl-button
production, the gun trade, and the bedstead-makers. In all
these instances it was the cheaper classes of goods which were
most seriously affected,[4] and producers were having to concentrate more and more on high-grade quality lines and finishing.
Even after such adaptation, and an increase in the demand from
the colonies, there was a fall in Birmingham's total receipts from
the export trade. Chamberlain's arguments seemed natural and
incontrovertible to local business men at the beginning of the
new century.

[1] *First Report of the Tariff Commission* (July 1904).
[2] See D. L. Burn, *The Economic History of Steelmaking, 1867–1939* (1940), ch. xii.
[3] L. Creswicke, op. cit., p. 316.
[4] G. C. Allen, op. cit., p. 277. Part IV, ch. 1 sketches the fortunes of the older
manufacturers during this period.

### III

It would be misleading and incomplete to allow the dark shadows of foreign competition to hide many other important features of the economic life of Birmingham in the twenty-five years before the outbreak of the First World War. The most important changes in Birmingham production were dictated either by changes in technique or by changes in taste. Both were important during this period. The declining profits of business men and their fears of foreign undercutting led them to seek more efficient and more varied machinery. In Birmingham, as elsewhere, machine tools superseded skilled artisans, although the extent of the substitution was not as great or as drastic as it might have been. Some industries, like the edge-tool and iron-mongery trades, still clung as long as they could to old methods, while others, like the jewellery trade, were by their nature un-suited for wholesale mechanization.

The key material in the late nineteenth-century burst of mechanization was steel. The uses of various types of steel were studied and tested in a metallurgical revolution, which has given to the world many of its most important twentieth-century materials. The greatest achievement was the development of special alloy steels, which combine very small quantities of cer-tain special elements with steel itself. The first alloy to be in-vented was manganese steel in 1888. With its remarkable tensile strength, elongation, and hardness, it was an ideal material for all machinery and plant subject to abrasive action, such as railway crossings and tires. Silicon steel soon followed. It was first used as a cutting steel, but after its magnetic qualities had been appreciated, it became one of the basic materials of the electrical engineering industry. These two discoveries were only the prelude to a whole series of further changes, which have laid the technical foundations of twentieth-century social develop-ment. The motor-car, for instance, which was one of the new products which the Midlands pushed into the market, would have remained a dream but for the production of metals suitable for making a high-speed engine and also of special alloy steels, which permitted more rapid production and a consequent lower-ing of costs.

If steel was the key material, it was increasing standardization which conditioned most of the advances in mechanization in the

Birmingham trades. The new engineering trade demanded large numbers of small standardized parts. The result was the growth of a flourishing machine-tool industry. Great accuracy in the manufacture by machines of further machine parts was made possible by the introduction of milling and grinding machines and turret and automatic lathes, and by the use of precision measurements. The technical implications of these advances took time to sort themselves out, but in the new motor, cycle, and electrical-apparatus factories, well-equipped and extensive machine shops became a regular feature.

The effects of mechanization on the older trades were also important. Small units were made more efficient by increasing their use of new power-machinery, in the form first of gas- and oil-engines, and later of electric motors or of electricity supplied by local power stations. It has been said that 'the great extension in the use of gas-engines played a part in the history of the small metal trades analogous to that of the steam-engine during the early years of the modern industrial era'.[1] Power made the use of machinery possible. The power-press took the place of the hand-press, and drilling machinery the place of punching. In the jewellery trades power could now be applied to stamping, wire-drawing, rolling, and polishing, while electroplating, which first began to use power to any extent about 1880, was making general use of power-presses and stamps in 1914. In the hollow-ware industry the substitution of mild steel for wrought iron made possible the employment of the power-press, while in the ena-melled-steel sector of the trade machines were introduced for spraying the coating. In the manufacture of edge-tools, first steam-hammers and then, just before the First World War, pneumatic hammers replaced the old tilt-hammers of earlier times.

In all these cases, improved technique transformed what had been originally handicraft trades. Power machines, steel accessories, standardized equipment, tools, and finished products brought the industrial Birmingham of the late nineteenth century closer to the Birmingham of today. In consequence many of the units grew in size, old industries like the lock trade as well as new ones, and industries which had previously been conducted in small shops or, as in the case of the button trade, even in garrets. With a few surviving exceptions, like leather and gun-

[1] G. C. Allen, op. cit., p. 316.

making, the factory became the typical production unit. By 1900 one old-established button firm was giving employment to over a thousand hands.

In the case of jewellery two systems existed side by side. There were no 'large factories with tall towering stacks, powerful steam engines, &c.',[1] but there were big workshops catering for new mass markets for standardized products. The jewellery trades were largely localized in Hockley, round St. Paul's Church. While some working jewellers still sat at their benches, playing their blowpipes and with delicate appliances and deft hands putting together works of art, others were producing 'gilt jewellery'—products by the gross, not necessarily of a shoddy character. Brooches of this second type sold at 12s. a dozen and even less, and watch-chains at about 10d. each. The social implications of these plentiful supplies were important in the history of taste.

If the changes in production methods and scale of operations, induced partly by the need to reduce costs, partly by the need to discover means of meeting hostile competition, remoulded the social structure of the city, it was equally true that the changing social structure of England as a whole helped to remould the economy of the Birmingham trades. Changes in society changed individual and group tastes, and consequently the shape and size of Birmingham's markets. Taste as well as technique always played an important role.

It was sometimes possible for changes in taste to blot out a local industry. Such was the case with the buckle trade, which, after reaching its peak about 1770, was destroyed after the introduction of the shoe-string. Such decline and fall of old industries were accompanied, however, by the rise and expansion of new ones. The competition of new German aluminium ware at the beginning of the new century, or at that time the more important increase in the use of wrought-enamelled ware, might imperil the prosperity of the hollow-ware foundries, but makers could turn over to the manufacture of different products, like oil- and gas-stoves or enamelled sanitary cast wares, for which there was an increasing demand.

A study of the markets for Birmingham wares throws a great deal of light on the course of English social history, particularly the history of everyday things. A future archaeologist, medi-

[1] T. Anderton, op. cit., p. 156.

tating on the excavated remnants of Victorian and twentieth-century daily life, would be compelled to note, as one of his most important clues, the label 'Made in Birmingham'. It would be an important starting-point in the task of historical reconstruction. Birmingham goods were used by all classes in all walks of life, and were produced to suit all income groups. Gillott's steel-pen factory, for instance, and more than ten other workshops offered dainty gold pens for the aristocracy, silver pens for the waistcoat pockets of the middle classes, and cheap steel pens for the masses. It was claimed with pride that Charles Reade, the Victorian novelist, wrote the whole of his book *It is Never too Late to Mend* with a single steel pen presented to him by the maker. For customers in distant markets, who were not neglected in an age which had a keen eye for business openings, Birmingham occasionally continued to produce articles which were no longer in current use in England. Thus as late as the twentieth century, snuffers and powder-flasks, which were not in everyday demand in England, were still made for travellers and for the citizens of remote countries who lacked cartridges, the electric light, and even incandescent gas within their reach.

Many of the changes of national taste are reflected in the history of the Birmingham tin-plate, japanned-ware, and papier mâché trades. The eighteenth-century tin-plate and japanned-iron trade produced a wide range of commodities, from trays to cash-boxes. It was challenged by the rise of the electroplating industry, which was based on a series of scientific experiments which did not lead to commercial exploitation until 1838. At first Elkington and Mason, the pioneers, were looked upon as wild, unpractical men, but from the time of the Great Exhibition of 1851 onwards, they both became influential directors of an expanding industry, producing not only magnificent vases, shields, and gold and silver services, but staple productions, like spoons and forks, for a wide mass market.

The japanned-iron industry was able to hold its own for a time by increasing its production of coal-scuttles and baths. Victorian demands for warmth and cleanliness kept the trade alive, although in the 60's there was a decline.[1] The growth of the holiday resort was reflected in an increased demand for japanned travelling-trunks about 1870, and the industry prospered

[1] See W. H. Jones, *The Story of Japan, Tinplate Working, Bicycle and Galvanising Trades in Wolverhampton* (1900), chs. vii–viii.

in the great boom, which lasted until 1874. Exports also went up, and the number of people engaged in the trade increased from 3,400 in 1871 to 4,800 ten years later. The trade kept pace with new needs down to the outbreak of the First World War. It made steel office furniture for the new age of business management, and provided cycle gear-cases for the office clerks to use, when their day's work was done. The japanning side of the trade was eventually by-passed with the new exploitation of sheet-metal, copper, and aluminium.

The papier mâché trade, which had been associated with japanning from the time when Henry Clay, a japanning apprentice, brought out his patent in 1772, was far less successful in adapting itself to social changes. Clay expected to see an age of papier mâché tea-trays, mantelpieces, card- and dressing-tables, and even ships' cabins. In 1793 he introduced his new material to the royal family, claiming that 'it was infinitely superior to any substance hitherto used for its surface and durability'.[1] The new material was associated not only with japanning but also with the use of pearl-shell, and in the first half of the nineteenth century a whole wealth of ornamental objects was turned out by the local trade. Although in the late 60's a new mother-of-pearl was obtained from the coasts round Australia demand did not keep pace with supply. Fashions changed, and in the last half of the nineteenth century the trade withered away, disappearing completely by 1900.

Other local industries which mirrored the continued diversity of the trading structure were the manufacture of ships' logs—in a city whose only suggestion of maritime operations was the canal; the making of skates—McCulloch has suggested earlier in the century that they were once sent, when home trade was bad, to Rio de Janeiro; and what W. C. Aitken described in Timmins's survey as 'the Revised Art of Metal-Working in the Precious Metals, Brass and Iron, on Mediaeval, or True Principles'.

If the ingenuity employed in these trades was remarkable, so too was the willingness to experiment with all types of material. One important brush-manufacturer told a visitor how he first learned the commercial use of *kiltool* from Ceylon. 'The first shipment came to me. I put it aside in some stables at my house in Coventry Road, intending to sell it for putting under ripe

[1] *Aris's Birmingham Gazette*, 27 May 1793.

strawberries, but by accident I found that by putting it into hot oil it took a beautiful black colour.'[1] From that time its use in his brush trade was assured. On another occasion Thomas Anderton asked J. S. Manton of what materials 'button dough' —a kind of paste that could be made into buttons useful for all sorts of purposes—was made. The comprehensive reply was 'Anything'.[2]

### IV

In the last decade of the nineteenth century the stage was set for the dramatic rise of what have since become, after very humble beginnings, the great new industries of the twentieth century. Three in particular deserve special attention—the electrical trades, the motor-car industry, and cycle manufacture.

Experiments were made with electrical dynamos and motors in the 1870's, but there was little commercial exploitation until after Swan invented the carbon filament lamp in 1880, and generating apparatus was improved. Before 1900 electricity was being used to an increasing degree both for light and power. The variety of subsidiary manufactures in Birmingham and the availability of a skilled labouring population made the city a centre of the new electrical trades. Engineering and allied firms were well equipped to turn over to the production of electrical apparatus. As early as 1862 arc-lamps for lighthouse purposes were manufactured at West Bromwich, and incandescent electric lamps appeared locally on a large scale in the 1880's. It was during this period that the first dynamos were produced in Birmingham.

In 1889 the earliest power station in the area to operate on a large scale, the Birmingham Electric Supply Company, was established, and in 1896 small premises were opened in Great Hampton Street for the manufacture of electric fittings. Five years later the newly-set-up General Electric Company opened its 240-acre factory at Witton, a site to the north of Birmingham, where at that time there were no industrial premises. Witton has subsequently become one of the world's largest centres of electrical engineering, and in 1911 about 7,000 people were employed in electrical trades alone in Birmingham and district.

[1] *Handbook of Birmingham*, prepared for Members of the British Association (1886), p. 168.
[2] T. Anderton, op. cit., p. 147.

The local demand for industrial equipment had made the neighbourhood a leading centre in the production of dynamos, motor-magnetos, pumps, meters, and transformers. Some of these goods were exported overseas, and on the outbreak of war in 1914 Britain came second only to Germany, although far behind her, in its exports of electrical manufactures. At that time British output was worth little more than a third of that of Germany.[1]

The motor-car industry also made great strides. Although French and German inventors were primarily responsible for the invention of the internal-combustion engine, Birmingham had for many years produced men who were interested in new methods of road transport. As early as 1834 a Birmingham man built a steam carriage, which carried forty passengers at a rate of ten miles an hour. The *Birmingham Gazette* gleefully commented that 'the hills appeared to offer no impediment, and the driver is of opinion that no hills to be found on the turn-pike roads would offer any considerable resistance to its progress. Not the slightest inconvenience was experienced from steam or smoke, and many horses were passed on the road without occasioning any alarm'.[2] It was not steam but the internal-combustion engine which was to revolutionize road transport, and here France took the lead. As early as 1893 France had an output of about 500 motor-cars a year, and British pioneers either had to carry out individual experiments in face of great difficulties, or to copy continental models.

Coventry took first place in the English industry in 1896, the year when the important Act of Parliament was passed removing the restrictions imposed in 1865 on the passage of road traffic. Birmingham men were, however, very active in experimental enterprise. H. W. Austin turned his attention to mechanical transport, because he was jaded with the labour of propelling a bicycle. As early as 1896 F. W. Lanchester was at work on the plans which were to produce the first full-sized British petrol-driven motor-car, the Lanchester.

Some of the new motor-car firms grew out of older concerns engaged in other types of industry, illustrating once again the adaptability of Birmingham manufacturers. The story of Wolseley Motors, for instance, goes back to 1895. Their first two-horse-power car, with its horizontal water-cooled engine and three

---

[1] J. H. Clapham, *An Economic History of Modern Britain*, vol. iii (1938), p. 124.
[2] *B.G.*, 6 October 1834. See C. Gill, *History of Birmingham*, vol. i (1952), p. 291.

wheels, was built in that year in the shops of the Wolseley Sheep Shearing Machine Company. The aboriginal model soon gave way to more elegant types, and the small factory to the large works at Adderley Park. By the time of the outbreak of the First World War, the works were manufacturing not only motor-cars but also marine engines, petrol buses, and aero-engines.

In 1905 Herbert Austin had set up his own motor-car factory at Longbridge, with high hopes of 'motorising the masses'. Longbridge was to become the model of a large-scale twentieth-century production unit, employing mass methods. Its beginnings were modest. The original site covered $2\frac{1}{2}$ acres, and Austin's capital consisted of £15,000. The first car was built there in 1906, and the first Austin Seven with a single-cylinder engine appeared four years later. At that time the output of the Austin works was 576 a year, and by 1914, when they employed 2,000 workers, annual production had increased to 1,500.

About 5,400 people were directly employed in the motor-car industry as a whole in Birmingham in 1914. In addition thousands of people were given indirect employment in the industries producing accessories, such as tubular frames, laminated and coil springs, coach-making and pneumatic tires, and electrical accessories. Some of these odd parts were manufactured in tiny workshops as side-lines, alongside more traditional products. In such an atmosphere the industry expanded. Although imports of cars into Great Britain still exceeded exports in 1914, the adverse balance was almost offset by a favourable balance on cycles and motor-cycles.

The cycle industry was a most successful enterprise. Once again it was in Coventry that the first steps were taken to produce the modern bicycle. In 1868 a Coventry firm switched over from the production of sewing-machines to the more risky production of bicycles. At first it catered for sportsmen rather than for members of the general public. The 'boneshakers' of the 70's were extremely uncomfortable, and it is not surprising that the 'high bicycles' and tricycles which succeeded them had only a limited appeal. The man who made the bicycle look much more like what it does today was J. K. Starley, who introduced the safety model in 1885. For the first time a bicycle appeared with two wheels of more or less equal size, and the rider was so placed that he was less likely to be thrown over the handle-bars.

Other improvements followed, and the cycle industry boomed, particularly between 1894 and 1897. Designs were improved. Pneumatic tires replaced the earlier 'cushion' tires, far less comfortable than the name suggests; the free wheel was adopted after 1897; and three-speed gears were introduced in 1903.[1]

Coventry was the most important centre of the industry in 1891, although Birmingham came a good second. By 1914 Birmingham and Aston had become the chief centres of the trade, employing nearly 10,000 workers. As in the case of motor-cars, just as important for the city economically as the trade itself was the production by the light metal and engineering trades of all sorts of composite parts and accessories, from tubes to leather saddles, and the extension of sales organization. Cycle depots were set up in many English towns, one chain of 112 shops in 1914 having its origins in a Birmingham enterprise. In addition foreign markets were tapped very successfully.

The motor-cycle industry also made rapid strides, particularly after 1900. At that time frames were little if any stronger than those of the ordinary cycle, and enthusiasts had become quite hardened to discomfort. Since there were also no spring forks, journeys demanded nerves of iron on the part of the riders. The battery ignition system was unreliable, and in busy traffic it was virtually impossible to travel at less than ten to twelve miles an hour, unless the exhaust-valve was lifted and an alarming amount of pedalling employed. In fact, riders had to be willing pedallers, since when there was a strong head wind pedalling had to be resorted to even on the level.

In motor-cycle as well as in motor-car design there was a remarkable improvement by 1914. The first side-car, a Birmingham product, made its appearance in 1903. Two years later the introduction of the high-tension magneto led to an improvement in the ignition system, and the addition of variable gears and all-chain drive greatly increased the technical efficiency of the machines. While in Coventry the motor-car and cycling indus-tries tended to become integrated, in Birmingham there was a broad distinction between them. It was in 1898 that James Norton set up a small Birmingham factory producing the Norton 'Energette', and nine years later manufactured the machine which won the first Tourist Trophy Race. From that time on-wards, the future of the machine and the industry was secure.

[1] See H. O. Duncan, *The World on Wheels* (1926).

The emergence of these three great new industries, each conspicuous not only for its own employment and production but also for its routine demand for complementary goods and component parts, transformed in a revolutionary way the industrial structure of Birmingham. The older specialized trades, like the manufacture of hardware or weighing-machines, often continued to expand in size and output, but they no longer dominated the economic life of the city. Light and medium engineering took their place. Machine tools were needed in increasing quantities, and the Midlands supplied them itself. In economics as well as politics Birmingham was representative of the changed structure of British industry in the bridge years between the nineteenth and twentieth centuries.

Although there were grave structural weaknesses in the general British response to the needs of a new age,[1] the Midlands were ahead relatively to other parts of the country in the manufacture and use of automatic machinery, capable of turning out a wide range and an increasing quantity of finished products. Birmingham supplanted the cities of the industrial north, which had been the most important centres of machine manufacture in the middle of the nineteenth century, and although Lancashire cotton still headed the list of export industries in 1914, steel and engineering products had increased enormously both in relative and in absolute importance since 1860.

Through all this great transformation from hardware to engineering, the basic distinction between Birmingham and the surrounding Black Country remained unchanged. As in the eighteenth century, Birmingham tended to remain the main centre for finished manufactures of all types, from tin trays to railway coaches, while the Black Country concerned itself chiefly with the making of component parts for the finishing processes and with the manufacture of cruder products which demanded less labour skill.[2] The big difference from the earlier period of history was that the new finished products were far more composite in character than the old ones. They were on the whole products of the new age of steel, which had taken the place of the old age of iron and brass. They were products of an age of precision and measurement, which depended on Birmingham

---

[1] G. C. Allen, *British Industries and their Organization* (2nd edition 1935), pp. 101–2, 117–21; A. E. Kahn, *Great Britain in the World Economy* (1946), ch. vii.
[2] G. C. Allen, *The Industrial Development of Birmingham*, p. 302.

and district for many of its instruments, from the balance to the micrometer screw-gauge.

V

It is interesting to put side by side, first, the facts of this necessary concentration on minute detail and, second, the increasing size of the normal business plant in the city. As industrial measurements grew more minute, business organization depended more and more on large-scale production. In the story of the rise of large-scale production in Birmingham, steel again provides the background.

In the age of iron and brass, although primary processes were organized in comparatively large units, Birmingham was renowned for its small industrial units, which contrasted markedly with the textiles factories of the north of England. 'The industry of this town,' wrote a French visitor to Birmingham in the late 30's, 'like French agriculture, has got into a state of parcellation. You meet . . . hardly any big establishments.'[1] When Timmins wrote in 1866, this still remained broadly true. The economic reasons for it were quite simple. The economies of large-scale production were less important in small metal trades, producing specialized products, than in textiles or heavy industry. Furthermore, in trades like the brass trade, different processes of production could be carried out in separate workshops. There were some exceptions to the general rule of small-scale production in the case of individual firms, like that of Robert Winfield in the brass foundry and brass-products industry which employed 700 to 800 people in the 1860's, or of special industries, like the heavy branch of the glass industry, run by Chance Brothers and employing 1,700 people in 1868. There existed also a few new factory industries, for the production of steel pens, machine-made nails, wire, and wooden screws, although even in some of these trades and their subsidiary operations, there were still opportunities for little masters, running very small concerns. As late as 1914 Norman Chamberlain wrote that 'the majority of masters in Birmingham are probably still "small men", and it will take more than a generation for the old order to pass'.[2]

From the 60's to the 90's, as a result of the introduction of

[1] L. Faucher, *Études sur l'Angleterre*, vol. ii (1845), p. 147.
[2] Norman Chamberlain, 'Municipal Government in Birmingham', in the *Political Quarterly*, no. 1, February 1914.

PLATE XI

ELECTRO AND SILVER PLATING

SKETCHED AT THE WORKS OF MESSRS. ELKINGTON AND CO., VISITED BY H.R.H. THE PRINCE OF WALES

MODELLING

GOLD PLATING

SMALL STAMP

ENTRANCE TO THE WORKS

SOLDERING

STEAM STAMPING

ENAMELLING

Elkington's Electro-plating Shop

PLATE XII

Workshop with House

mechanical methods and new forms of power, there was a gradual increase in the size of the typical producing units.

The first industry where standardized engineering led to increased scale of plant was the rifle industry. The Birmingham Small Arms Company was the first local factory to turn out complicated finished products by mass-production methods. The factory grew up out of the needs of the Crimean War, when only four Birmingham gun-makers produced military guns, and the government's development of the Enfield Rifle, for which they insisted on 'an interchangeable system'. In 1862 the Small Heath building was begun on a site consisting of 26 acres of land. Although certain parts of the guns were made by small masters outside, who handed them on to the B.S.A. in an unfinished stage—the process adopted later by the motor-car manufacturers —the 'interchangeable system' inside the factory was carried out 'in its full integrity'.[1] On the visit of the British Association in 1865, a newspaper compared the production of guns during the Napoleonic wars with the position in the second half of the century. 'During the war, with which this century opened,' it wrote, 'the men of Birmingham signalized themselves by the rapid introduction of arms, and, it is said, made muskets at the rate of one a minute. Now the single manufactory at Small Heath would probably, if called on to do so, soon be in a condition even to exceed that rate of production.'[2]

Small Heath was a portent. The really big change came with the general substitution of steel for iron. Wrought iron had been produced on a comparatively small scale. Steel demanded large plants and very heavy capital outlay. Furthermore, after steel had become the normal working material, beyond the primary processes the scale of production became greater at every stage of manufacturing and finishing. In engineering trades, like welded tube manufacture and edge-tool making, a few large firms had gained a dominating position by 1914. Finally, in the new industries like motor-car manufacture, large and not small firms were representative.

It was not only technical considerations which led to the increasing importance of the large firm. During the last quarter of the nineteenth century there were widespread attempts in the

---

[1] J. D. Goodman, 'The Birmingham Gun Trade', in S. Timmins's *Birmingham and the Midland Hardware District* (1868); also *B.M.*, 30 December 1897.
[2] *Leisure Hour*, September 1865.

Midlands to limit competition between manufacturers, and to amalgamate and combine existing separate enterprises. The social aspects of this movement were important. They remoulded the character of the Midlands business man, or, more frequently perhaps, a new type of Midlands manufacturer remoulded his economic environment. Joseph Chamberlain, for example, managed the commercial and sales organization of John Nettlefold's with such skill that in five years, from 1865 to 1870, new works were built, iron-mills were added, and a link-up with collieries was contrived. Realizing the importance of eliminating competition, he absorbed the businesses of his two largest competitors, and laid the foundations of an enormous combine, which, after beginning with vertical integration from screws back to steel, ended with horizontal combination to cover a wide range of products. In 1900 Guests & Dowlais Iron Company joined the Patent Nut and Bolt Company of Birmingham, two years later amalgamated with Nettlefolds, and subsequently absorbed Crowshays of Merthyr to form a new combine with an issued capital of £4½ million.

'No industry', it has been said, 'has so much syndicated and combined in all the great industrial countries as that of iron.'[1] Vertical integration had always been a characteristic feature of the industry, but it was not until the Victorians evolved the limited joint-stock company form that the financial conditions for large-scale mergers were afforded. Birmingham played an important role in a national movement. In the same year that Guest, Keen & Nettlefold was set up, H. & J. Stewarts & Menzies of Scotland, which had been built up on the basis of a Coatbridge local merger eight years before, and Lloyd & Lloyd of Birmingham also amalgamated with a capital of £1¾ million. By 1914 there were many similar amalgamations. The Birmingham Small Arms Company, for instance, absorbed the Edie Manufacturing Company in 1907, and the Daimler Motor Company of Coventry three years later. In 1914 the concern had an issued capital of £1 million. As a result of most of these and similar mergers, Birmingham and the Midlands were linked with other parts of Great Britain in a network of nation-wide industrial enterprises.

These giant concerns were not, however, the only products of an age of increasing combination. While big groups carved out

[1] H. W. Macrosty, *The Trust Movement in British Industry* (1907), p. 24.

monopolies, small men sought association. In some trades, like button manufacture, facing strong foreign competition, loss of markets, and a drop in profit margins, there was a strong tendency towards amalgamation, particularly in the late 90's and at the turn of the century. This grouping together of firms was accompanied by changes in business organization. The functions of capital provision on the one hand and of control of policy on the other, which had previously been linked together by the owners of small private firms, now began to be separated. The tendency continued into the twentieth century.

In addition to cases of capital fusion, there were other examples of the growth of contractual organizations to limit competition between producers by joint agreement. Association was an alternative to amalgamation, and appealed to many of the smaller firms. The degree of formality and tightness in the structure of the new associations varied. In some industries pools were organized, in others loose forms of price leadership. Most of the organizations in the 90's were informal price-agreement associations, like the Unmarked Bar Association in high-grade iron and the National Galvanized Sheet Association. Later, pools were more common and more binding, as in the case of the Gas Strip Association, set up in 1901, and the Bedstead Federation, established in 1911. By 1914 there were about eighty associations of one kind and another in the various iron and steel trades.

The Bedstead Federation had previously been organized in 1893 in what was called an 'alliance'. The 'alliance' examined the books of local bedstead manufacturers, calculated the average cost of production in the trade, added a uniform profit margin, and fixed prices for the industry. The alliance was consolidated by the association reaching an understanding with the trade unions. This 'alliance' type of organization was copied by other trades, but it led to considerable difficulties, particularly concerning freedom of entry and calculation of costs. In the case of bedstead manufacture, the system in practice at the outbreak of the First World War was highly complex. In 1911 the producers had drawn up a set of rules, assigning themselves quotas, fixing shares of total output, compensating manufacturers for producing less, and fining them for producing more. Minimum selling prices were fixed for the group for dealings both in home and foreign markets, and conditions of sale were laid down, including the offer of a deferred rebate to those clients who agreed to buy only from their members. This complex organization went as far in the use of compulsion and the consolidation of its administration as any other association of the time. Among other contractual bodies at the beginning of the First World War were the British National Light Castings Association, the Steel Sheet Makers' Association, and the Cable Makers' Association, founded in 1895.

Some of the bodies had international ramifications and agreements to limit marketing areas and control output. Local horizons had widened, and although Birmingham remained more preoccupied with the home market than most English cities, some of its business men were now beginning to take the whole world for their economic province. From the 1860's onwards new marketing methods had emphasized the importance of international contacts. The Tangyes set the example for direct selling abroad when they created depots in Melbourne and Sydney. Other firms soon appointed foreign agents and travellers and external selling organizations, and the rapid expansion of colonial engineering in the last years of the century led to a great increase in the number of representatives of local firms on the spot in far-away corners of the world.

Something of this world outlook was revealed in the intellectual and political development of Joseph Chamberlain. 'Let the little Englanders say what they like', he proclaimed in 1897, 'we are a great governing race, predestined by our defects as well as our virtues to spread over the habitable globe and to enter into relations with all the countries of the earth.'[1] Birmingham windows opened out on to world markets and world sources of supply. The city played a leading part in the conscious formulation of a theory of Imperialism.

## VI

Many of the most interesting aspects of this story are brought out from a study not of metals but of two other commodities of the late nineteenth century, both of which were to be leading commodities of the century which followed. The first was cocoa, and the second rubber. Neither was new in 1890. As early as 1887 a pneumatic tire had been invented, but it was never perfected or produced on a commercial scale because there was

[1] *The Times*, 30 January 1897.

no demand for it. Similarly, as early as 1824 John Cadbury opened his shop in Bull Street, where cocoa could be bought along with tea and coffee. In the cellar of his shop he experimented with the grinding of cocoa beans with a pestle and mortar, and in 1831 rented a small factory in Crooked Lane in which to develop the manufacturing side of his business. Eleven years later he was selling sixteen sorts of drinking chocolate and eleven sorts of cocoa powder. At that time there was a heavy duty on imported cocoa beans, and neither chocolate nor cocoa was in great public demand. The turning-point in the industry came in 1853, when Gladstone fixed the duty on imported beans at 1*d*. a pound. In the same year Cadbury Brothers were appointed makers to the Queen. In 1866 the firm, now established in Bridge Street, took a momentous step which had a great bearing on its future prosperity. It began to make a 'pure' cocoa, Cadbury's cocoa essence, and after the passing of the Adulteration Act in 1872 this beverage was firmly established, and with it the fortunes of the industry. The 1866 change-over was the prelude to the remarkable expansion of the firm in the late nineteenth century. In 1879 Bournville was built. In the 1880's the world market was tapped, and foreign monopolies broken.

The story of both rubber and cocoa links up Birmingham with distant corners of the world. Birmingham was renowned for the far-flung sources of its raw materials. Cryolite from Greenland was used in making glass globes, carnubin wax from Brazil in making tapers, and caroza nuts from Venezuela for making toys. Cocoa and rubber were in line with existing tradition. By 1914 the cocoa industry had developed far more rapidly than the rubber industry. The total world's supply of rubber in 1901 amounted to only about 55,000 tons,[1] and it was not until after 1910, by which time plantations of rubber had been developed, that the industry was properly established. Malaya, Ceylon, and Java were the key centres, and by 1914 plantation exports amounted to 76,000 tons.

The most important consumer of rubber in England was Dunlops, one of the great industrial giants of the twentieth century, holding a capital of £16 million in 1939. It was in 1888 that Dunlop took out a patent for his pneumatic tire. Two years

---

[1] J. W. F. Rowe, *Studies in the Artificial Control of Raw Material Supplies*, No. 2, '*Rubber*'.

later the cycle tire was perfected. In November 1889 the Dunlop Company began factory operations with an authorized capital of £25,000. The first Dunlop factory was in Ireland, at Dublin, but Coventry and Birmingham, with their obvious advantages as industrial centres, offering plentiful supplies of skilled labour, became the main headquarters after 1910. By 1914 the factory in Birmingham was employing about 4,000 people, and rubber was being used in the manufacture of a variety of different articles in addition to the component parts of the vehicle industry. The Dunlop Rubber Company owned plantations and factories in various countries—the first one in Malaya being bought in 1906—and supplied more than half of the domestic market.[1]

The growth of Cadburys' was equally striking. The story of the firm's activities outside England falls into two parts. First came the sale abroad of goods manufactured at Bournville, and second the buying of raw materials at first hand from producers in the country of origin, as well as through middlemen in the markets of London, or the other English ports. Early enterprise in selling led to the setting up of a shop in Paris as early as 1877, and during the same decade the company appointed agents in Chile and Canada. In 1881 an export representative was sent out to Australia and New Zealand with his first head office in Sydney, and later on new offices were opened at Melbourne, Adelaide, and Brisbane. In 1893 a resident representative was appointed for South Africa, and two years later a permanent representative for India. In 1897–8 one of the firm's travellers made a trip across the world which took him fifteen months, and led him to such far-flung ports of call as Lima, Smyrna, and Surinam.

The story of cocoa-growing is just as interesting as the story of sales developments. The first shipments of cocoa came from South America and the West Indies, but cocoa cultivation was later introduced into Ceylon, the East Indies, and after 1879 in tropical Africa. At first cocoa produced in the native-owned farms of the Gold Coast and Nigeria was not of good commercial quality, but Cadburys' sent out experts to instruct the small-holders in the methods of cultivation and preparation of beans. In 1908–9 the first buying agency with resident staff was set up in Accra. The first year's purchase, amounting to 690 lb., was a little more than one day's buying in any current season.

[1] See Dunlop, *Fifty Years of Growth* (1939).

Cadburys' were later associated with Frys' in setting up new agencies in the Gold Coast and with Rowntrees' and Frys' in Nigeria.[1]

The expansion of the cocoa and rubber industries illustrates the world-wide link-ups of twentieth-century industry. Birmingham had been called the 'toy-shop of Europe' in the eighteenth century. In the twentieth century it had become one of the economic capitals of the world.

## VII

The peculiar characteristics of Birmingham's industrial structure had important social consequences. Skilled craftsmen on the one hand and small masters on the other produced a state of society which Cobden described in 1857 as far more 'healthy and natural in a moral and political sense' than the capitalist oligarchy of Manchester, which has frequently been taken by contemporary and later writers as the industrial norm.[2] There was a high degree of social mobility in an environment where in George Eliot's phrase 'some slipped a little downward, some got higher footing'. These features of Birmingham life made for a local tradition of social co-operation and social peace. Timmins described the position in the mid-60's in very favourable terms, when he wrote that

Birmingham is in fact . . . the town of all others where the social and personal freedom is extreme. The large number of small manufacturers are practically independent of the numerous factors and merchants they supply. The workmen, mostly untrammelled by trades' unions, are paid according to their merits, and skilled labour of all sorts is nearly always in demand. The enormous variety of the trades renders general bad trade almost impossible, for if one branch is 'slack' another is usually working 'full' or even 'overtime'. In no town in England is comfort more common, or wealth more equally diffused. If millionaires are few, absolute poverty and wretchedness are also rare.[3]

The processes of economic and social change modified the shape of Birmingham society and the attitudes of both masters and men, but throughout the whole period to 1938 there was a marked difference between Birmingham and other English cities as a result of this basic nineteenth-century framework.

[1] I. A. Williams, *The Firm of Cadbury 1831–1931* (1931), especially ch. vi, 'Overseas Developments'.
[2] See J. Morley, *The Life of Richard Cobden* (1881), vol. ii, pp. 198–9.
[3] S. Timmins, op. cit., p. 223.

The small men of the mid-nineteenth century were often simple, unaffected people, revelling in the gospel of work and caring little about any form of ostentation. They fell into two groups—small factory owners, employing up to thirty or forty men, and 'garret masters', who used their own homes as places of work. The former group were 'well content, genial and hospitable. They did not give themselves any fine airs or pretensions; indeed they were often proud of their success and prosperity, and would sometimes delight in openly boasting of their humble beginnings, not always to the joy and delight of their children who might hear them.' They often regarded their workers as being members of 'quite a family', and would hold Christmas parties and social gatherings for them. Some of these business men would continue to spend one or two hours in the evenings in the respectable inns and hotels in the middle of the town, which they had frequented in their less wealthy days, and 'smoke their long clay pipes' and have a chat with 'old friends and kindred spirits'.[1] They cared little for fine clothes, and in face of the taunts of outsiders boasted that 'it is quite impossible to distinguish one man from another in Birmingham, and that it is not compulsory to wear a chimney pot hat and a black coat on a broiling July day'.[2]

A French visitor in 1895 described a typical workshop he had visited where a small master employed between ten and twenty-two skilled men, according to the state of the market. The manufacturer had begun life as a worker himself—his father had been a mechanic and his sister was a nurse—and he had become prosperous as a result of his own self-help and perseverance. He was proud of his independence, and boasted that 'he was ready for any emergency'. He would work alongside his men on a fifty-five-hour week, from seven in the morning until seven in the evening, and since his house and workshop were in the same building, he could put in overtime without difficulty, whenever it was necessary. In his spare time he still pursued his mechanical interests, and, in addition to owning his own horse and cart, had built himself a bicycle. His son, aged fifteen, was employed in the works.[3] Although he was a harder master, having been a

---

[1] T. Anderton, op. cit., p. 101.

[2] 'A Defence of Birmingham', by a Town Councillor's son in the *B.M.*, 3 July 1884, in reply to an article in the *St. James's Gazette*, 'A Tory View of Modern Birmingham'.

[3] P. de Rousiers, *La Question ouvrière en Angleterre* (1895), ch. i.

worker himself, than some big masters, he knew all his men by their names, and social relationships were direct and personal. Despite all the changes in the structure of Birmingham's industry, some such small men survived into the twentieth century.

The skilled mechanics and artisans were not separated from them by a wide gulf. It is true that their social position depended on whether they were employed in factories or not, and whether or not they were mere machine-tenders, but they were often independent enough not to wish to join trade unions or to look outside their craft for political and social slogans. The trades which set up the Birmingham Trades Council in 1866 were skilled groups, like the cordwainers and the mill sawyers, proud of their traditions and not unlike the gilds of the middle ages. There was pride in skill and in accomplishment, and Bunce in 1865 remarked on the large number of artisans in Birmingham who owned their own houses. It was not accidental that Birmingham was the home of the building-society movement. The artisans 'earn good wages, and by moderate thrift can afford to lay something by. That they do so is abundantly proved by the large deposits in the savings bank; by the existence of innumerable sick and benefit clubs, in connection with numerous churches and chapels, with various "Orders" such as Odd Fellows and Foresters, and, unfortunately, in connection with almost every public house.'[1] Hutton had noticed the same features in the eighteenth century.

The attitude of a skilled worker in an organized group can well be illustrated from the flint glass makers. The United Flint Glass Makers' Society was set up in 1845, and was recognized four years later under the title Flint Glass Makers' Friendly Society of Great Britain and Ireland. Its periodical, *The Flint Glass Makers' Magazine*, published in Birmingham, advocated as its main aim 'the education of every man in our trade, beginning at the oldest and coming down to the youngest'. 'Get intelligence instead of alcohol,' it urged, 'it is sweeter and more lasting.'[2] The flint glass makers disliked strikes and preferred peaceful methods of trade-union action. 'We believe', wrote the editor of their magazine in 1855, 'that strikes have been the bane of Trades Unions.'[3] Although the flint glass makers had to fight

[1] S. Timmins, op. cit., p. 687.
[2] *Address to the Glass Makers of England, Scotland and Ireland*, no. 1.
[3] *Fortnightly Circular*, January 1855.

many hard struggles in the nineteenth century, this mid-century attitude survived in many corners down to 1914. The French observer who had visited the workshop of a small employer also visited the home of a prominent member of the Flint Glass Makers' Friendly Society in the 1890's. Eli Bloor impressed him as a sympathetic and understanding man, who was both worker and magistrate, and the strength of whose union depended on a skilled labour *élite*, 'rather like a corporation of a pre-mechanized age'. Bloor was a local preacher as well as a trade unionist, proud of the twin facts that he had never known a blackleg in forty years' experience and that a great many working men, whom he had influenced, were now regular churchgoers, who never attended before. The French visitor contrasted Bloor with the typical trade-union officials he knew inside his own country, and pointed out that he was genuinely anxious to raise the general condition of labour. Bloor did, indeed, help in the setting up of other unions like the Amalgamated Society of Gas Workers, Brickmakers, and General Labourers, and by sitting on the Town Council he helped to secure an eight-hour working day for Council employees.

Before examining the dynamics of social change in Birmingham in the sixty years before 1914, it is necessary to discuss two other important features in the local social structure—the continued existence of large numbers of outworkers, and the key importance of middlemen—factors and merchants.

In many trades, in the middle years of the century, there were large numbers of specialized outworkers carrying out the orders of manufacturers or middlemen. The gun trade and the pearl-button trade, for example, were industries where factory production played a small part. In the gun trade the outworkers included women engaged in 'making off' or giving the final sand-papering and polish to the stocks, and boys who were often employed 'too young for the burdens they are called upon to bear'.[1] In both occupations and in many other Birmingham trades employment was casual, and it is difficult to estimate the number of workers employed. 'Probably no master can tell how many hands he is employing at any given time, and the number varies, from month to month, with the demand.' Even after the introduction of factory methods in old industries and the development of new industries, outworkers did not entirely disappear.

[1] S. Timmins, op. cit., p. 393.

Although the lock trade passed into factories, for instance, the manufacture of keys remained in the hands of outworkers, while the new trades depended on parts being produced by small men. In the case of the pearl-button workers, there was even a late-nineteenth-century attempt by the 500-strong trade union, the Operative Pearl Button and Stud Workers' Protection Society, to prohibit machinery altogether. Their 'Rules and Regulations' in 1887 stated peremptorily that 'the system of centering by the engine be annihilated *in toto*, and any member countenancing the system direct or indirect shall be subject to a fine of two pounds. Any member of the Society working at the trade by means of mill-power either direct or indirect, shall be subject to a fine of five pounds.'[1] This regulation marked a continued attempt to preserve independent craftsmanship against the challenge of the machine and the factory. It was coupled with extreme restriction of apprentices and an attempted ban on women's work.

The second feature which distinguished Birmingham from many other parts of the country was the middleman or factor system. There were two types of factor, those who were concerned only with the collection and distribution of products, and those who because they exercised a regular contact with workers and their materials began to co-ordinate the labour of dependent craftsmen. Without both types, Birmingham industry would have fallen apart. They acted as essential links not only in industrial processes, but also in the supply of credit, for they often served as intermediaries between banks and small masters. They hired out tools and equipment, and because they had low overhead charges they could pass the burden of industrial fluctuations on to the shoulders of the outworkers, whereas factory owners would have been obliged during depressions to face the problems of maintaining idle plant. None the less those factors who directed processes, as in gun-making, were compelled to become embryonic factory chiefs, interested in co-ordination as well as in collection and distribution.

By 1914 the industrial organization of the mid-nineteenth century had been radically transformed as a result of the increase in the scale of local enterprises and changes in their location. The growth of bigger units, employing over 1,000 people, created new-style business men and employers: the organization of production itself at the factory level produced

[1] See S. and B. Webb, *Industrial Democracy*, vol. i (1897), p. 395.

new conditions of work. The shift in location of factories from
the centre of the city to the suburbs enabled firms to expand
their factory space, to cease having to rely upon outworkers for
many technical operations, and to improve the amenities of their
plant. At the same time as workers were faced with increasingly
lengthy journeys to work and the separation of houses and workshops, social relations with employers became less intimate.
While the number of outworkers diminished, the hold of factors
diminished too, and the large-scale units in the new industries,
like electricity and motor-making, set a model with regard to
methods of factory layout and industrial organization.

The bigger units themselves were managed on new lines. The
factories became more or less self-contained, growing as the
years went by, adding new departments designed to secure both
vertical and horizontal integration. As overhead costs increased,
firms attempted to arrange a regular flow of work through their
plants and to cut down the amount of casual labour. Inside the
factories employers became more business-like in their methods,
ceasing to rely on intermediary figures like sub-contractors, who
had hitherto dealt out work to their underhands, and depending
increasingly on highly-trained office and technical staff as a co-
ordinating force, and on foremen supervising production in the
departments. Although some sub-contracting persisted and was
noted, for instance, by a deputation in 1910 as a marked distinction between brass-working in Birmingham and Berlin,[1] the
system was becoming archaic, and to counterbalance it other
firms were beginning to experiment with new methods of organization, which pointed not to the past but to the future. Flow
production on mass lines in the motor-car industry was to provide
the work pattern for thousands of people in the twentieth century.

As the factories changed so, too, did the business men. Some
of the changes in their economic outlook have already been
described. They had important social consequences. In 1904 a
local journalist commented that

in these days of big combines, the small employer who in the past
worked with or personally supervised his men, knew them all by name,
and felt a personal interest in their welfare, has given place to the
limited company, with directors, shareholders, and a works manager,
under whom the employees are merely so many 'hands'. . . . Under

[1] R. H. Best, W. J. Davis, C. Perks, *The Brassworkers of Berlin and Birmingham*
(1910), p. 40.

these large companies the work is specialised and divided into sections and sub-sections, with foremen and heads of departments, whose main concern with the workmen is to see that not less than a stated quantity of finished work of a certain standard of quality is turned out.[1]

The 'strenuous individualists' of older times gave way to new business men depending on managers, who were in turn, as Professor G. C. Allen has said, sometimes more concerned with the regularization and continued existence of their firms than with the size of their profit margins. Timmins's 'social and personal freedom' was being crushed and refined by the pressure of new forces.

While the business men were changing with the advent of mechanization in the old trades, the pattern of skills was modified, and the Birmingham labour force became divided into two groups—on the one hand skilled workers engaged in making and adjusting tools, on the other hand semi-skilled machine opera-tives. Among both groups there was a greater opportunity for trade unionism to expand than in the mid-nineteenth-century world, although Birmingham trade unionism always maintained its own special colouring. Some unions like the Amalgamated Society of Gas Workers, Brickmakers and General Labourers, set up in 1889, were designed to 'protest against managerial tyranny',[2] but most Birmingham unions stressed the importance of conciliation and co-operation in industry. They agreed with Arnold Toynbee, the first historian of the 'Industrial Revolution', that 'we should do all that in us lies to establish Boards of Conciliation in every trade when the circumstances—economic or moral—are not entirely unfavourable. . . . Notwithstanding failures and obstacles, I believe these Boards will last; and more than that, I believe that they have in them possibilities of a great future.'[3] They agreed with Mundella, who introduced the principle of arbitration into the hosiery trade of Nottingham as early as 1860, or Kettle, closer at hand in Wolverhampton, where he organized a board of arbitration in the building trades in 1865. In 1876 Joseph Chamberlain himself was first President of the South Staffordshire Mill and Forges Wage Board for the iron industry, and he also acted as an arbitrator in the nut-and-bolt and the coal industries.

[1] *T.P.'s Weekly*, 9 January 1904.   [2] *E.D.*, 30 January 1908.
[3] A. J. Toynbee, *Lectures on Industry and Democracy* (1881); H. Crompton, *Industrial Peace* (1876); A. Marshall, Preface to L. L. F. R. Price, *Industrial Peace* (1887).

Apart from Birmingham branches of big national unions like the Amalgamated Society of Engineers, which had over 500 members in 1870 and Alderman Cook (later Sir William Cook) as secretary of its largest branch, the Associated Society of Railway Servants which began its activities in Birmingham in 1872, and the National Union of Clerks, which was built up by Tom Mann who had been born in Birmingham, there were three unions of great local strength which are of special interest —the National Society of Amalgamated Brassworkers, the Tinplate Workers' Society, and the Bedstead Workmen's Association. The first two of these unions produced prominent local personalities, who, in addition to active local lives in bodies like the Council and the School Board, played a bigger role in national life—the former producing W. J. Davis, who later became the secretary and historian of the Trades Union Congress, the latter producing J. V. Stevens, who was president of the Trades Union Conference in 1897 and chairman of the Labour Group on the City Council between 1919 and 1923.

The National Society of Amalgamated Brassworkers was set up in 1872. It grew out of boom conditions, the men demanding and securing a 15 per cent. increase in wages all round. Between 1872 and 1883 when Davis, its secretary, left Birmingham to become a factory inspector in Sheffield, the Union made striking advances. Thereafter it shrank until in 1889 its very existence was threatened. Davis was induced to return and its membership and fortunes revived. In the early years of the twentieth century it had over 7,000 members.

The ideals of the brassworkers reflected Birmingham's tradition of industrial peace. The members prided themselves on their system of benefits—out-of-work pay, sick pay, superannuation, funeral payments, dividend grants, and benevolent and legal services—and on their advocacy of industrial conciliation. Davis himself always urged the building of a system which would 'establish and make secure a lasting friendship between employers and workmen'.[1] In 1891 he was responsible for the first active steps taken to develop 'mutual intercourse between employers and employed', both sides represented by their respective organizations. 'What is wanted', he said—and it was to be the basis of a whole philosophy of industrial alliance, which Birmingham came to stand for—'is union among the manufacturers as well as

[1] W. A. Dalley, *The Life Story of W. J. Davis* (1914), p. 33.

among the men, and this union is just as necessary in resisting undue encroachments by the latter as it is in enforcing good faith among the former.'[1] A Brass Trades Manufacturing Council was set up representing both sides, and a Conciliation Board began to operate. In their annual report for 1894 the Brassworkers pointed out with pride how 'disputes have been amicably adjusted by conciliation, and during the year have worked to the advantage of employers and workmen. Differences which might have led to abstentions from work, when discussed on both sides, have resulted in happy solution, and on no occasion have such means been unequal to the task of arriving at a mutual settlement.' Working through the existing conciliation machinery, the Union made an attempt in 1900 to secure a minimum rate in the industry, and although this failed and arbitration was necessary, the conciliation ideal was maintained. 'It has been my object in life', Davis later said, 'to minimize the number of disputes in trades with which I have been concerned.' Through all the disputes there was a recognizable 'community of interest' between master and men, sometimes vis-à-vis the consumer.

The tin-plate workers created a purely Birmingham organization, which could trace back its ancestry to 1812, when a society had been founded to protest against low wages. The late-nineteenth-century organization had a continuous history back to 1857. From 1874 its horizons widened, for in that year it realized that its attempts to secure a 10 per cent. increase in wages would be unsuccessful unless it could form a working front with the tin-plate workers of Wolverhampton. Together the two independent organizations secured their objective. The Tin-plate Workers' Society, like that of the brassworkers, stressed the provident side of its activities and the fact that it had saved workers from being compelled to go to the workhouse, which had become known among the local industrial community as the 'Tinman's Rest'. Welfare work was considered more important than militant action, and the organization struck only once, when the employers tried to reduce wages by 5 per cent. in 1898, and then the strike lasted only one day.

Like the brassworkers, the tin-plate workers recognized the importance of co-operation with employers. A price-list for government work was drawn up by the Society and the Employers' Association. It ran to 135 pages and fixed prices for

[1] Ibid., p. 171.

every conceivable article which tin-plate workers might be called upon to make. Whenever government tenders were offered, a meeting of the union's committee was held in conjunction with the employers, and set prices from the list were agreed upon. This system of co-operation, it was claimed, helped employers, by preventing under-cutting, and workers, by preventing starvation wages. If a firm was known to be paying less than standard wages, the case was reported by the union authorities to the government department affected.

The most advanced form of industrial understanding between masters and men was expressed in the organization of the Bedstead Workmen's Association. Three-quarters of the bedsteads made in England came from Birmingham, and workers and employers shared a keen desire to limit competition. Two early attempts to set up trade unions failed and it was not until 1889 that, as the result of the initiative of an employer, the Association was formed. The career of W. Mills, its founder, reflected the high degree of social mobility of the city—he was first employed in an office, then later as a manager, and finally became a manufacturer. He saw no essential antagonism in worker–master relationships, and by December 1889 he had built up a union of 600 members. The men struck for two weeks to secure a wage advance of 15 per cent., which was confirmed after arbitration. The bedstead masters set up their own organization to counterbalance that of the men, and in 1893 an Industrial Alliance was formed on the basis of virtually closed-shop union membership, an agreed price-list, and the use of conciliation machinery. 'The object of the Alliance', it was stated, 'shall be the improvement of selling prices, and the regulation of wages upon the basis of such selling prices, . . . thereby securing better profits to manufacturers and better wages to workpeople.' To make such a policy possible, the manufacturers had to pledge themselves 'not to employ any but association work people (over 21 years of age) excepting by special arrangement with the Operatives' Association', while the workmen had to promise 'not to work for any but those manufacturers who sell their goods at such prices as are from time to time decided upon by "a Wages Board", to be formed of an equal number of employers and employed'. As a result of the signing of the Alliance, which the Webbs described as 'an exceptionally developed manifestation of the doctrine that the conditions of employment . . . shall correspond to the relative strategic position of the parties to the bargain',[1] co-operation was maintained until about 1900. In 1901 the Alliance broke down, according to Mills, to the disadvantage of both sides. Cut-throat competition, forcing prices down to prime costs, superseded the monopolistic practices of the 90's, which men like Mills and E. J. Smith had seen as the necessary basis for a new social policy.[2] Mills's picture of a self-regulated industry did not completely disappear in Birmingham, but the immediate effect of its implementation was, as Clapham has said, not to ensure perpetual industrial peace, but to make Englishmen sleep again in wooden, or part wooden, bedsteads. 'The great furniture retailers, faced by undesirable monopoly policies, "directed and developed" the new public taste for wood',[3] and it was in face of this challenge rather than because of master–man conflicts that the Alliance system broke down.

Close relations between masters and men continued to exist in other trades in Birmingham like the flint glass trade, in which the employers went to the unions to find workers, and there was an agreed price and wage structure, allowing for a uniform grading of skills. In case of disputes a mixed committee of masters and men attempted to reach agreement. In the jewellery trades individual rather than collective bargaining persisted, and masters and men shared a common interest in 'the joint protection of the trade'.

In its Report for 1898 the Trades Council as a whole underlined the special features of the industrial atmosphere of Birmingham and the contrast with other parts of the country.

There has been an entire absence of any serious labour disputes (it stated), a spirit of conciliation having prevailed, which has enabled organized workmen to meet organized employers; and thus by reasoning and reciprocity, decisions have been arrived at which have maintained an honourable peace, beneficial to workmen, employers and the community. However, what may be said in this respect of Birmingham cannot be said of the whole country.

Although there were strikes in Birmingham between 1898 and 1914, this statement of the Trades Council continued with few

---

[1] S. and B. Webb, *Industrial Democracy*, vol. ii (1897), p. 579.
[2] See E. J. Smith, *The New Trades Co-ordination Movement* (1895).
[3] J. H. Clapham, op. cit., p. 304.

qualifications to mirror labour relations in 'the workshop of the world'. The ideal of conciliation persisted during and after the First World War, and even when social relationships were strained, most Birmingham manufacturers, like Neville Chamberlain, were proud of never having had a strike in their business concerns and deplored the loss of personal contact in the bigger industrial organizations. Birmingham still retained the essentials of a social philosophy which grew out of local conditions in the formative years of the nineteenth century.

# IV

# 'THE BEST-GOVERNED CITY IN THE WORLD'

WHILE Birmingham maintained its position as 'the work-shop of the world', it made striking advances in the sphere of government. The middle years of the century were years of municipal torpor. In the 60's and 70's the forces of inertia were overcome, and much of the vigour which had previously been devoted to business was applied to administration and to politics. In an age when the basis of political power was being widened in the country as a whole, and a larger electorate was demanding new programmes of social advance, Birmingham took up a position of leadership, not unlike that which it had assumed more than forty years before in the franchise struggle, which secured the passing of the Great Reform Bill. Birmingham was transformed from a badly-administered city into what an American observer called 'the best-governed city in the world'.[1] Social improvements completely altered the appearance of the town, working alongside the natural changes described in a previous chapter, and at times speeding them up. The death rate was lowered, the administrative departments were built up and rendered efficient, and above all the interest of citizens was captured and their horizons extended. In the process Birmingham not only reformed itself, but set a model for the nation and even for other communities overseas, and Chamberlain, the great architect of change, could write after he had become a Cabinet Minister in 1880 that unless he could secure for the nation the same social improvements he had already secured in Birmingham, 'it will have been a sorry exchange to give up the Town Council for the Cabinet'.[2]

The civic revolution was not the work of one man, but of whole groups of men who had the vision and the determination to push forward large schemes of city improvement. Already, long before Chamberlain became Mayor in 1873, a new social gospel had been proclaimed. The contemporary word 'gospel'

[1] J. Ralph, 'The Best-Governed City in the World', in *Harper's Monthly Magazine*, June 1890.
[2] Quoted by J. L. Garvin, *The Life of Joseph Chamberlain*, vol. i (1932), p. 385.

is an appropriate one, for the most important pioneers of the message were nonconformist ministers. As early as the 1850's, when the Town Council was refusing to spend any money on civic development, Dawson at the Church of the Saviour, Dale at Carr's Lane Chapel, Crosskey at the Unitarian Church of the Messiah, and Charles Vince at Graham Street Chapel, were all urging from their pulpits the need for Christians to take a keener interest in civic affairs. They were all powerful personalities and used their pulpits as platforms to rally public opinion.

Dawson was the pioneer. When Dale arrived in Birmingham in 1854, Dawson was already a radical leader, preaching radicalism and something more, for at a time when many radicals were content to ask for merely cheap government, Dawson pressed for direct legislation on social topics, and for governmental and municipal interference in the interests of general welfare. Dale, who remained minister at Carr's Lane until 1895, was always a politician as well as a preacher. Without being diverted from the other tasks of his ministry, he combated jobbery and corruption in municipal life with great vigour, and took an active part in the routine work of local committees like the School Board. 'In a country like this,' he would say, 'where the public business of the state is the private duty of every citizen, those who decline to use their political power are guilty of treachery both to God and to man.'[1] Dale not only worked hard himself to influence local politics, but looked around for business men to promote his gospel. From the time of his arrival he set out to study the organization of shops, offices, and factories in the neighbourhood. He saw that business could be useful to religion, and he believed that religion could work through business men to make them better citizens. 'The eleventh commandment', he would say, 'is that thou shalt keep a balance-sheet',[2] but he did not forget the other ten. Organization and vision needed to be harnessed together.

Chamberlain and others of his type and generation looked like good disciples. Dale himself has described the rise of a set of men who engineered the civic revolution.

Towards the end of the 'sixties, a few Birmingham men made the discovery that perhaps a strong and able Town Council might do almost as much to improve the conditions of life in the town as Parlia-

---

[1] Quoted by A. W. W. Dale, *The Life of R. W. Dale of Birmingham* (1899), p. 250.
[2] Ibid., p. 145.

ment itself. I have called it a 'discovery'; for it had all the freshness
and charm of a discovery. One of its first effects was to invest the
Council with a new attractiveness and dignity. . . . Weaker and less
effective members of the Corporation were gradually dropped, and their
places filled by men of quite a new type. The November Ward meetings
assumed a new character. The speakers, instead of discussing small
questions of administration and of economy, dwelt with glowing enthusiasm on what a great and prosperous town like Birmingham might do
for its people. They spoke of sweeping away streets in which it was not
possible to live a healthy and decent life; of making the town cleaner,
sweeter and brighter; of providing gardens and parks and music; of
erecting baths and free libraries, an art gallery and a museum; they
insisted that great monopolies like the gas and water supply should be
in the hands of the corporation; that good water should be supplied
without stint at the lowest possible prices; that the profits of the gas
supply should relieve the pressure of the rates. Sometimes an adventurous orator would excite his audience by dwelling on the glories of
Florence, and of the other cities of Italy in the middle ages, and suggest
that Birmingham too might become the home of a noble literature
and art.[1]

Many of these dreams were realized during the energetic
period of town government which reached its climax during
the mayoralty of Joseph Chamberlain between 1873 and 1876.
Dawson had been a prophet; Chamberlain was to be the
triumphant leader. When he arrived in Birmingham in 1854—
the same year as Dale—at the age of eighteen, he already had
the makings not only of a business man but also of a natural
leader. He served his political apprenticeship in the Birmingham
and Edgbaston Debating Society and the Working Men's Institute
of his Smethwick firm, and entered local politics in 1869 as a
militant Liberal Councillor. He was exactly the sort of person
for whom Dawson and Dale had been seeking. The committee
which promoted his candidature recommended him as 'a large
ratepayer, a man of thorough business habits, enlarged views
and marked ability, belonging indeed to precisely the class of
burgesses most desirable to the Council'. But he was far more
than a representative figure. Although there had been enlightened and able exponents of better government like George
Dixon and eloquent speakers like Hawkes, Chamberlain stood
out among his contemporaries. He caught the spirit of the times
and hurried it forward, revelling in the exhilaration of respon-

[1] Quoted by R. A. Armstrong, *Henry William Crosskey* (1895), pp. 245 ff.

sible power. He acted, it was said, 'like a small providence'. Within four years of entering the Council, when his name had already become nationally known as the driving force behind the Education League, he became Mayor of Birmingham, and began his three years of office, which transformed municipal government to such an extent that within a few years—to quote a contemporary—'municipal reformers were looking to Birmingham as the eyes of the faithful are turned towards Mecca'.[1]

The task of transforming dreams into realities was made possible because behind Chamberlain was a powerful Liberal party and great untapped reserves of business ability. Public duties required money, time, and energy if they were to be the driving forces of civil reconstruction. Many of Chamberlain's collaborators were business men like him who were prepared to devote an enormous amount of voluntary labour to direct the increasingly complex machinery of local administration. Chamberlain himself set them an example of service by retiring from business altogether in 1874. 'Municipal life completely swallowed up commercial life.' This sacrifice impressed Americans as much as it impressed Englishmen. 'Birmingham is above all else', Ralph wrote, 'a business city, run by business men on business principles.'[2] Religion provided the inspiration, and business sense the practical driving force, of the civic transformation.

The leadership of business men depended on many different factors, some of which have been examined in previous chapters. There was no wide gap between the small business man and the skilled worker. As for the bigger business men, they still were on the offensive in politics, their militant nonconformity issuing out naturally into a wider radicalism. Many of them saw the openings in politics as clearly as Chamberlain, with his theories of 'ransom' and his zest for a social policy. Large numbers of Birmingham merchants and industrialists lived at Edgbaston, only one mile away from the centre of the city, and there were few 'absentee capitalists', content merely to regard the town as a workshop.

Civic expansion needed not only men but money, and, more important in civic affairs, the willingness to spend money. The Economy party which had ruled the Council since 1853 had made lack of funds the main excuse for complete municipal

---

[1] Quoted by A. Shaw, *Municipal Government in Great Britain* (1898), p. 169.
[2] J. Ralph, loc. cit.

PLATE XIII

Joseph Chamberlain

PLATE XIV

The Wizard of the Gas

stagnation. Money was always forthcoming in the early 1870's. The golden age of business prosperity between 1867 and 1873, described by Disraeli as 'a convulsion of prosperity', warmed the hearts and lined the pockets of local business men. The year 1872 'was rarely equalled and never surpassed', wrote one local business man waxing lyrical at the state of the markets. It was in such bright weather, when Gladstone was seriously considering—and was indeed about to advocate—the total abolition of the income-tax, that Chamberlain was launched into administration. Even when the industrial and commercial skies grew darker, building continued to boom in Birmingham as in other parts of the country at least as late as 1877. After the fall in foreign investment the rate of interest for public investment was favourable, and there were plenty of available funds.

Birmingham was ready for a period of civic spending. There was much work waiting to be carried out in the city, for it was behind the times, not ahead of them, in 1873. In many cities there were large municipal undertakings dealing with public services like gas and water. Municipal gas was manufactured by thirty-three municipalities in England and Wales before 1870,[1] and the Manchester Gas Works went back to 1817, when they were opened on the grounds that 'a general establishment conducted under an effective public control' was better for the consumer of gas and the town as a whole than 'any private establishment founded for immediate gain'.[2] Many of the issues fought out in Birmingham in the 1870's had been anticipated in the Manchester controversies of the 1820's, and when in 1823 Parliament sanctioned the use of Manchester rates for trading purposes, it was laying the foundations of municipal trading. The argument was even used that profits made on the sale of gas could be applied for general improvement purposes.

The experience of Manchester in the early nineteenth century may have been somewhat precocious, but by 1870 municipal action was already far advanced in other parts of the country in other spheres of civic policy. Many municipalities, including Manchester, Leeds, Dublin, and Cardiff, owned their own water-supply, and twenty-six of them had acquired it for the first time between 1860 and 1870. At Liverpool there had been

---

[1] See H. Finer, *Municipal Trading* (1941), p. 46.
[2] Ibid., p. 39; S. D. Simon, *A Century of City Government* (1938); L. S. Marshall, *Development of Public Opinion in Manchester, 1780–1820* (1946).

a Medical Officer of Health since 1847, and in Manchester since 1868. In other towns there were large schemes of city improvement in progress, particularly in Glasgow, where the City Improvement Trust, set up by a pioneer local Act of 1866, was engaged in pulling down the pestilential Frying Pan Alleys. Birmingham in the 70's was behindhand, Chamberlain and his friends knew it, and by making others realize it they were able to transform municipal progress into a kind of moral crusade.

II

The three big measures of Chamberlain's mayoralty, from 1873 to 1876, were the municipalization of gas, the taking over of the water-supplies, and the city improvement scheme.

The gas proposal came first. In January 1874 Chamberlain moved that the General Purposes Committee of the Council be authorized to negotiate terms with the two existing private companies, the first of which had been set up in 1819 and the second in 1825. The proposal meant raising the borough debt from £500,000 to £2½ million. Chamberlain did not worry about that. He followed the maxim that 'a Corporation that is afraid to borrow is too timid to do its duty'. In 1873 he claimed that he had thought of the possibility of municipalizing gas from the moment he got on the Council, for two reasons—first, that all monopolies in any way sustained by the State should be in the hands of the elected representatives of the people, to whom their profits should go; and second, that such a measure would increase the power and influence of the local Council, which should be encouraged to become a real local parliament, supreme in its own special jurisdiction. He urged an additional and very persuasive argument, not dissimilar to that advanced in Manchester in 1823, that despite the increased debt charges, the municipalization of gas would in the long run prove a most lucrative undertaking. Birmingham's financial power rested at that time entirely on sums raised from rates. The city had no landed property, dock dues, or profits. Income received from running the gas-works would make it possible to finance other schemes of social development. When asked to say why he had chosen to deal with gas first rather than with water, he gave it as his reason that additional civic income had to come before additional civic responsibilities. 'When the purchase of the water works comes before you, it will be a question concerning the health of the town; the acquisition of the gas-works concerns the profits of the town, and its financial resources. Both are matters of absolute public necessity.'

Fifty-four members of the Council supported the gas resolution, and only two voted against it, but Chamberlain soon had his first lesson concerning the power to delay, if not to prevent, of vested interests working outside the elected bodies. Various local boards and large consumers of gas opposed the Bill when it came before a Special Committee of the House of Commons, which included Mr. Gladstone. The opposition was unsuccessful and the Bill was finally passed in July 1875, and a Gas Committee appointed in Birmingham.

Throughout the whole gas agitation, Chamberlain fought the issue in terms of costs, interest rates, and profits. His basic calculation was that if the Corporation had to pay 5 per cent. on the purchase money for the Birmingham undertaking, they would immediately begin making an annual profit of £14,800. In point of fact, the first yearly statement of accounts showed a profit of over £34,000. By 1880, when Chamberlain resigned from his chairmanship of the committee, this had risen to £57,000. In 1881 the *Birmingham Mail* could write that it was very easy for the members of the Gas Committee to present their annual statistical reports, 'for the figures always sounded to be part of some fairy tale'. They had about them a 'sound which is musical, and a sound which is captivating'.[1] In 1882, during an inquiry held on the Birmingham Corporation Consolidation Bill, it was conclusively shown that during the seven years' working of the scheme, after allowing for considerable reserve, a sum of £182,500 had been set aside for the borough improvement fund. This meant a reduction of the rates by over 4d. in the pound.

Chamberlain's boast at a local meeting in 1875 had been fulfilled. He had been asked by a member of the audience whether he would himself have given to the companies the sum they had asked for, to which he replied that if the Corporation would take the offer and farm it out to him, he would pay them £20,000 a year for it, and at the end of fourteen years would have 'a snug little fortune of his own, worth about £200,000'. At the same time, he dealt with a point of economics, which in some ways is more relevant to 1950 than to 1875. A ratepayer asked if the gas

[1] *B.M.*, 2 March 1881.

concern would be made to pay merely by increasing the price of gas, to which he retorted that 'such methods would be mere juggles'.[1]

The municipalization of gas in Birmingham was one of the best examples in the nineteenth century of business energies being turned successfully from individual self-help to collective local government. It was this undertaking more than any other which made Ralph describe Birmingham as 'the best-governed city in the world'. Business men revelled in the work of the Gas Committee. Norman Chamberlain wrote in 1914 that membership of this and the Electricity Committee was sought after more than any of the others, 'as is natural in a large business community'. Joseph Chamberlain himself saw local government in business terms.

The leading idea of the English system of municipal government (he wrote in 1892), may be that of a joint stock or co-operative enterprise in which every citizen is a shareholder, and of which the dividends are received in the improved health and the increase of the comfort and happiness of the community. The members of the Council are the directors of this great business, and their fees consist in the confidence, the consideration, and the gratitude of those amongst whom they live. In no other undertaking, whether philanthropic or commercial, are the returns more speedy, more manifest, or more beneficial.[2]

In point of fact the advantages of the new gas monopoly were felt in many other directions besides increased profits. The Corporation secured a lower rate of interest than that obtainable by private firms. The plant was increased and modernized. The price of gas was twice lowered during the first five years of municipal ownership. The working conditions of the employees in the gas-works were improved. A plan of selling gas-stoves on a system of deferred payments was introduced, and prepayment meters were issued on a large scale.

The municipalization of water was argued out in different terms, and Chamberlain always emphasized the sanitary rather than the economic aspects of the question. The question was by no means a new one. The main source of supply was controlled by the Birmingham Water Works Company, incorporated in

[1] N. M. Marris, *The Rt. Hon. Joseph Chamberlain, the Man and the Statesman* (1900), p. 213. See also A. Mackintosh, *Joseph Chamberlain, an Honest Biography* (1906).

[2] Joseph Chamberlain, 'Municipal Institutions in America and England', in *The Forum* (New York), vol. xiv, November 1892.

1826, but because this concern could not meet all local needs, 150,000 people were dependent on wells for their water in 1869. As early as 1850 the Birmingham Improvement Act had contemplated 'the purchase and conduct of the water-works', and three years later the General Purposes Committee of the Council took steps, in vain, to buy the works, local opinion being opposed to change on the grounds that 'the necessary increase in the taxation of the kingdom, the depression of trade, scarcity of labour, and dearness of provisions, together with the pressure on the money market' all made it 'unpolitic and unwise' to buy the works and to levy local water-rates.[1] The Bill was dropped, and the matter remained in abeyance until Avery raised it again in 1869 and 1871. In 1874 Chamberlain reopened the question in far more eloquent terms, knowing that he could rely upon a wide measure of public support. 'What do you think of the inhabitants being compelled to drink water which is as bad as sewage before clarification?' he asked. He used statistics to compare Birmingham's experience with that of other towns, and declared that in many cases poorer folk were so destitute of water that they were compelled to steal it from the Company's taps in their neighbourhoods.

He laid down two general principles, both of them of interest in the history not only of local government but of public ownership—first, that 'all regulated monopolies, sustained by the State, in the interests of the inhabitants generally, should be controlled by the representatives of the people, and not left in the hands of private speculators', and second, that 'whereas there should be a profit made on the gas undertaking, the water-works should never be a source of profit, as all profit should go in the reduction of the price of water'. He did not take credit for discovering these two principles, but referred them back to John Stuart Mill, 'the greatest political thinker of our age'.[2]

There was a long fight between the Council and the Company, for the property was increasing in value, and more than good health was at stake. In the House of Lords the Bill was bitterly opposed, Lord Hampton among others arguing that it was without precedent, and full of injustice to the shareholders. The

---

[1] Quoted by J. T. Bunce, *History of the Corporation of Birmingham*, vol. ii (1885), p. 403.
[2] *A Short History of the Passing of the Birmingham (Corporation) Gas Act and the Birmingham (Corporation) Water Act* (1875).

Company argued that water management would be inefficient under the Corporation, since the stimulus of private interest was necessary to business efficiency. Chamberlain claimed that the Council would make its profit indirectly in the comfort of the town and the health of the inhabitants. The Bill eventually went through the House of Lords and received the Royal Assent in August 1875. The works were transferred on 1 January 1876, and soon afterwards extended and the supply of water increased. 'Without the additions which have been made', the *Birmingham Mail* wrote in 1889, 'the town would have been a desert of Sahara, while the Edgbaston horticulturalists would have been reduced to the necessity of moistening their lawns with beer.'

A more serious consideration was that without the water scheme, Birmingham would have been a less healthy city. In the improvement of local health standards, Chamberlain was helped by national policy. The Public Health Act of 1872 required all urban sanitary authorities with a population of more than 25,000 to appoint a full-time Medical Officer of Health, and in that year Dr. Alfred Hill was given the post in Birmingham. The Council could now secure valuable expert advice on all health problems. It needed to supplement expert assistance with collective action. In 1875 it responded to the new opportunity by setting up a Health Committee, charged with many tasks—the disposal of sewage and refuse; the inspection of houses and the removal of nuisances; the maintenance of epidemic hospitals and disinfection facilities; and milk and food inspection. A vigorous period of enlightened administration followed, the annual reports of the Medical Officer of Health reflecting the energy and drive of extended social action. The number of inspectors was increased to bring Birmingham into line with other cities, for it had only one inspector for every 30,000 inhabitants, while Manchester had one in 8,000 and Leeds one in 13,000. More inspectors meant more reported nuisances, and these increased to 20,000–30,000 a year, 1878 and 1879 being peak years. Within seven or eight years more than 3,000 wells, used by 60,000 people, were condemned on the ground of serious contamination by sewage and permanently closed. Domestic cleanliness was enforced, zymotic diseases attacked, and the death-rate, which had been 25·2 per 1,000 for the years 1871–5, 3·2 per cent. above the national rate, was reduced to 20·7 per 1,000 for the years 1881–5, only 1·3 per cent. above the national rate.[1] The averages for the whole city do not express the full measure of benefit reaped by those streets and districts which were black spots in 1870, and where the death-rate was as high as 60–80 per 1,000 inhabitants. Although Birmingham was naturally a more healthy town than many other large centres of population in England, these improvements were the fruits of policy and administration, and not of good fortune.

The third great undertaking of Chamberlain's mayoralty, the Improvement Scheme, raised these problems of public health along with other interesting questions. The motives behind the scheme were mixed, and the economics at times complicated. The idea of town improvement itself was not new, and as was shown in a previous chapter, there was a high 'natural' rate of demolition in the 1870's which was transforming the face of the city. What was new was a large-scale civic policy, an all-out drive to make the Council itself an active participant in the building of a new central district. From the first mooting of the scheme Chamberlain stressed that it would cost the ratepayers money, 'but it would not involve nearly so much expense as the bit-by-bit improvements, which they were making in the town, and which never repaid the town in proportion to their cost'.

The Improvement Scheme was made possible by the passing of a piece of national legislation, the Artisans' Dwellings Act of 1875, a Conservative measure which Cross, the Home Secretary, referred to Chamberlain for his approval during the course of its passage through Parliament. Indeed, Chamberlain stated before the Royal Commission on Housing in 1885 that he considered Cross's Act the most important contribution which had been made to the settlement of the improvement question. The 1875 Act provided for the acquisition by certain types of local authorities of insanitary areas within the limits of their towns. The land could be brought compulsorily without paying an extra price for the compulsory sale, and, after its acquisition, the local authorities were authorized to remove buildings unsuitable for habitation, to arrange for the building of dwellings, and to carry out other improvements. They were not allowed to build working-class houses themselves without the special authority of the Local Government Board. The Act itself was

[1] See J. T. Bunce, *History of the Corporation of Birmingham*, vol. ii (1885), chapter iv, 'Public Health'.

a landmark. Parliament, in making it, Chamberlain claimed, had 'recognized something higher than property'.

The legislation was no sooner passed than steps were taken to put it into effect in Birmingham. Chamberlain moved the appointment of a committee to be called the Improvement Committee, and drafted a preliminary description of an area in Birmingham suitable for complete transformation. He pointed out how behind the wealthiest and most prosperous parts of the city there existed a strange world which was not always known to local citizens. 'Some would even lose themselves in New Street. There are people who do not know that there is an existence on the other side of the Town Hall.' Councillor White, who represented the particular ward in question, filled in the outlines of the picture. 'It is not easy to describe or imagine the dreary desolation which acre after acre of the town presents to anyone who will take the trouble to visit it. . . . The rubbish and dilapidation of whole quarters have reminded me of Strasbourg, which I saw soon after the bombardment.'

In such a setting, sanitary improvement was extremely difficult. 'As long as there is a wall, like Bull Street, dividing the town east and west and cutting off the air from those quarters, so long shall we be unable to make a perfect plan of sanitary reform.' The death rate in St. Mary's Ward in the scheduled area was double that in Edgbaston and the healthier parts of the city. Eighteen thousand people in the condemned area were sick for at least six weeks each year, and this meant a total loss in wages and medical attendance of £54,000 each year. 'The town must pay for this state of things in meal or in malt,' Chamberlain said, with health or with money.

The first report of the Improvement Committee confirmed the gloomy picture of the scheduled site. Hill, the Medical Officer of Health, reported on the 'narrow streets, houses without back doors or windows, situated both in and out of courts; confined yards, courts opening at one end only, and this small and narrow; the impossibility in many cases of providing sufficient privy accommodation; housing and shopping so dilapidated as to be in imminent danger of falling, and incapable of proper repair'. The evils following from this state of affairs were 'want of ventilation, want of light, want of proper and decent accommodation, resulting in dirty habits, low health and debased morals on the part of the tenants'. Quite apart from these issues

PLATE XV

Slum Property, 1876

PLATE XVI

THE LOCAL OBSTRUCTIONISTS.

The Local Obstructionists

of sanitation and housing, the principal thoroughfares of the city, the Report went on, were quite insufficient to meet immediate traffic problems, let alone to allow for the growth of the city.

The committee worked out a project which applied in all to 93 acres of land. Of this area, the Corporation was to acquire about 43½ acres, at a total cost of £1,310,000. The proposed new streets would absorb nearly 8 acres, and would cost £34,000 to build. The estimated improved value of the surplus land was £794,000. This left the estimated net cost of carrying out the Improvement Scheme at £550,000. Some modifications were made to these initial proposals, but they formed the basis of all subsequent calculations. The financial variables were complicated, particularly in so far as they involved estimates of future land values. Money could be borrowed by the Corporation at 3½ per cent. repayable in fifty years, which gave the town an immediate advantage as compared with private building, for which 5 per cent. was being charged by the building societies. The low figure of 4½ per cent., then, would cover both repayment and interest. For the 50 years of the loan, the annual cost to the borough would be £18,000, and at the end of the 50 years the property would belong to the borough itself.

In working out these estimated costs of improvement, there was a further factor to introduce—rateable value. The rateable value of the scheduled property amounted to £32,000. Chamberlain claimed that this figure would rise three times over, and 'assuming a rate of two shillings in the pound, which I take as the normal rate', this would mean an annual increase in revenue of £6,000 per annum to set against cost. This reduced the estimated net cost of the scheme to £12,000 a year, although until all the sites were occupied the estimates of increased rateable value would have to be scaled down.

When he presented these calculations to the Council, Chamberlain finished his recital of statistics with a characteristic peroration. '£12,000 a year will be the average cost of the whole of the scheme. Is that too heavy a burden for the town of Birmingham to contemplate for such an improvement as that proposed? I believe the town, and above all, the next generation will have cause to bless the Town Council of Birmingham if it carries the scheme before it, and exercises what I venture to call a sagacious audacity.'

The scheme was approved by the Council on 16 October 1875, and without waiting for the Local Government Board Inquiry, opened in March 1876, the committee at once went into the property market, obtaining ready funds to do so through an Improvement Trust consisting of prominent local people. Chamberlain himself guaranteed £10,000. Before Harrison opened his inquiry for the government, the Trust had actually bought properties worth over £50,000.

The inquiry was continued over six sittings and there was vigorous criticism of the Council's proposals. Some owners whose properties were affected by the scheme opposed compulsory purchase, while the Birmingham Tories fought the proposals on party grounds as a wild Liberal measure. 'They fought the scheme tooth and nail', said Sir William Bowater. 'They racked their brains for arguments against it; they contrived and schemed at every turn to wreck it. The town echoed with the noise of wordy combat. . . . For it was a Chamberlain scheme, and must, therefore, be vile and ruinous and pernicious and wicked and against the constitution and the scriptures, and—well, it was a damnable scheme.'[1]

Eventually Harrison reported to the Local Government Board in favour of the scheme, a provisional order was made, and later, after continued opposition, a Bill was drawn up to confirm it, which received the Royal Assent on 15 August 1876, the day on which Parliament was prorogued.

The course of building operations, which did not begin until 1878, has been described in a previous chapter. The project was a long-term one, and its financial fortunes varied. Although the Council had planned to let out sites bit by bit to secure a steady market and to avoid too sharp a fall in immediate income from rents, it was obvious from the start that the business value of the premises erected at the New Street end depended considerably on the thoroughfare being continued to Bull Street. The financial stability of the enterprise depended on (i) income from premises already standing, (ii) ground-rents for new sites, the demand for which fluctuated with good and bad times, and (iii) a continued vote from the rates in aid of the project. If ratepayers were to consider the third of those three sets of figures as too high, the success of the whole project would be threatened.

[1] Quoted in *B.G.*, Special Number, *Birmingham Charter Centenary Celebrations* (1938).

The borrowing side of the scheme also had its financial difficulties, particularly in 1877. The Corporation found the first terms offered it by the Public Works Loan Commissioners too onerous, and it met with no success in an attempt to issue sufficient debenture stock. It was only after it had obtained a short-term loan of £500,000 from the Bank of England that a more satisfactory agreement was reached with the Public Works Commissioners, and £1½ million was borrowed for thirty years at 3½ per cent. In 1881 an additional £100,000 had to be borrowed, and further loans of £50,000 in 1887 and £10,000 in 1888 were necessary.

There was much criticism at moments of crisis. As Chamberlain said in 1877, 'there were some of our political opponents who actually rejoiced at the prospect of a financial failure, which might have plunged the town and the Council into severe embarrassment'.[1] The year 1881 was a critical year, but complaints had not disappeared when in 1883 the general oversight of the Scheme as a whole was transferred from a separate office to the other Corporation departments. Long-continued depression of trade led to annual deficits on the revenue account, even when the municipal grant from the rates had been made, and the deficit was as high as £18,995 in 1883, as against the £14,000 anticipated only one year before. As late as 1888 the deficiency estimated (in 1881) at £500 actually amounted to £5,708. But the position was about to improve, and at last in 1892 the Committee had the satisfaction, after taking a grant of £25,000 from the rates, of reporting a surplus for the first time. As one newspaper put it, 'the corner has at last been turned in the Improvement Scheme'. There were then 15,000 yards of property cleared for letting, 'and when the Committee have managed to attract tenants for this, the finances of the scheme ought, as the saying is, to go swimmingly'.[2] Although it was not until 1937–8 that income from rents was sufficient to meet capital charges as well as current expenses and a net profit was made, the Scheme had conferred enormous advantages on the city, which were generally recognized right at the beginning of the new century. And as the loan from the Public Works Commissioners was being gradually redeemed, the city could look forward with anticipation to the falling in of the original leases,

[1] Quoted by J. T. Bunce, op. cit., p. 473.
[2] B.M., 28 April 1892.

and give grateful thanks to Chamberlain for insisting in face of powerful opposition that they should be made not for ninety-nine but for seventy-five years.

### III

If there were few critics left in 1900 to attack the basic idea of Corporation Street, there were growing numbers of critics who were following up an old line of attack, claiming that the big improvements of the Chamberlain era had not paid sufficient attention to the housing of the working classes, the main purpose for which the 1875 Act had been passed.

In 1882 the committee had tried to answer this line of attack by saying that it had tried to let sites in the middle of the town for artisans' dwellings, but with no success, there being so many dwellings of this type unlet as to prevent any further speculative building. The committee itself could not build without leave of the Local Government Board, and did not wish to ask for such permission. Although it had bought 14,250 square yards for private working-class house-building, no houses had been built. 'May I ask whether any workmen's houses have been built,' asked Henry Hawkes in 1882, 'or whether the shops and houses created are not in the occupation of master tradesmen or other middle-class residents?'[1]

The position was obviously unsatisfactory, particularly since the prosecution of the Improvement Scheme involved the ejection of families living in the scheduled areas. In December 1883 the Council resolved unanimously to set up a committee of inquiry to 'ascertain how far the dwelling-house accommodation for the artisan and labouring classes in the Borough is sanitary and adequate, and the amelioration, if any, that it is in the power of the Town Council to effect'. The committee reported in June 1884 that there was quite adequate dwelling-house accommodation for the artisan and labouring classes in Birmingham, that the percentage of houses unlet was highest in the cheapest houses—14·6 per cent. of the houses let at 2s. 6d. a week or less— that there had been no examples of 'jerry building' since the new building by-laws of 1876, and that there was no appreciable over-crowding. Certain improvements were necessary, however, and it was advisable, first, that all new houses should be certified by

[1] B.M., 22 May 1882.

some competent official before they were allowed to be inhabited, and second, that model dwellings for the working classes should be erected by private enterprise.

This reassuring report, accepted by the Council, was, as Vince has pointed out, 'strangely at variance with the representations by which the Council had been persuaded to embark upon the Improvement Scheme'.[1] It did little to blanket criticism or to stifle further controversy. Critics still went on to attack the administration of the Improvement Scheme, and their complaints circulated far outside Birmingham. 'It is little to the credit of the men who have managed the municipal affairs of Birmingham', wrote the Conservative *St. James's Gazette* in 1885, 'that not one artisan's dwelling has been built out of the £1,800,000 which has been spent on the new street, and therefore that wretched and unwholesome dwellings, which still remain standing, are overcrowded to a fearful extent.'[2]

In June 1885 the Improvement Committee, under the chairmanship of Richard Chamberlain, prepared a scheme for the erection of working-class houses on the flat system in James Watt Street. Twenty thousand pounds was to be borrowed from the Local Government Board for the purpose. The scheme was advocated with great vigour—Richard Chamberlain offering to guarantee the undertaking for three years against loss—but it met with a great deal of opposition both inside and outside the Council Chamber, and, after a spirited debate, was defeated, an amendment being carried that the matter be left to private enterprise. Political issues were involved. Alderman Kenrick pointed out that the amendment had been supported by the very people who had blamed the Council 'for pulling down workmen's houses to make a Chamberlain boulevard'.

Four years later, in 1889, the committee brought forward a new proposal, based on an older idea. As early as 1883 a Local Government Board Order had been obtained appropriating a plot of land in what was later called Ryder Street for the building of workmen's houses. Although the land was offered to private enterprise at the low rental of 8d. a yard, it was still lying unused in 1889. The committee proposed building on the site twenty-two two-story cottages, costing £182 each, and, in face of considerable opposition, carried its scheme. The houses were

[1] C. A. Vince, *History of the Corporation of Birmingham*, vol. iii (1902), p. 353.
[2] *St. James's Gazette*, June 1885. See *B.M.*, 3 July 1884.

finished in September 1890 and were at once let without difficulty at 5s. 6d. a week.

The eagerness of the working classes to get into the Ryder
Street houses led the committee in 1891 to bring forward a more
extensive plan, involving the building of eighty-two houses,
costing £172 each, and similar in size and in character to the
Ryder Street dwellings. The scheme was approved and put into
effect, and eighty-one houses were built. The implementation of
the two schemes did not solve Birmingham's housing problems.
Five shillings was a high rent for many tenants to pay, for in
1884 there were 27,000 houses let at 3s. 6d. a week or less. Municipal building had not shown how families turned out of cheap
insanitary houses by the progress of the Improvement Scheme
could be housed at such new rents as they had been accustomed
to pay in the past. In addition the Scheme ran at a financial loss,
for the relatively high rents did not cover full capital charges.
The Ryder Street houses involved a subsidy from the rates of
£3. 5s. per house, while those in Lawrence Street—where the
land had cost more to buy—involved a contribution from the
rates of £4. 10s. per house each year.[1] These subsidies were not
reckless by post-1918 standards, but any subsidies at all were
objectionable to most councils before the First World War, and
it was clear from the rents charged that the Birmingham subsidies were going not to the poorest elements in the local community, but to relatively well-off workers.

The Council's distrust for a more active Council building
policy was reinforced by actual experiences in the planning of a
further building scheme in 1895. The Housing of the Working
Classes Act of 1890 empowered the Council to prepare schemes
outside the Improvement Area, and in 1894, after representations from the Medical Officer of Health, a block of property in
Milk Street was scheduled as insanitary. In July 1895 the Council
was empowered to purchase the unhealthy area, consisting of
sixty-five dwelling-houses and a few workshops, and to demolish
the buildings. One half of the site was cleared for the building of
sixty-four three-room dwellings on a dual-house system, with
rents at 4s. 3d. for the lower and 3s. 9d. for the upper houses. It
was calculated that the net revenue from rents would cover the
interest and sinking fund, but would leave no surplus to meet
charges upon capital borrowed for the purchase of the site.

[1] *Report of the Finance Committee*, 1904.

There was fierce opposition to the proposals, led by the chairman of the Health Committee, and the scheme was withdrawn, but in 1898 it was taken up again in a modified form—tenements being erected, and not dual houses. Even then the plans entailed upon the community the sacrifice of £4 each year in respect of every tenement provided. This was the consequence of the terms of the Act of 1890, which, as Nettlefold said, ensured that 'property owners were handsomely rewarded for owning insanitary property'.[1] The Council had accepted as a duty the carrying out of the intentions of the Acts of Parliament to 'provide some accommodation for the class of persons displaced in the interest of Public Health', but it did it with no enthusiasm. The difficulties in working out the Milk Street Scheme hardened opinion still further, so that the president of the Birmingham and District Trade and Property Association could claim in 1907 that 'for ten years the 1890 Act was practically a dead letter in Birmingham, indeed, as it has been in most of our cities and towns to this day'.[2]

Although a housing policy worthy of a great city seemed impossible to secure, and Vince could write in 1902 that 'we still seem to be as far as ever from the possession of any acceptable philosophy of municipal duty in housing matters',[3] it was becoming clear that vigorous action was necessary. The Medical Officer of Health in his annual reports continually focused the spotlight on the problem. A pamphlet by Fallows quoted evidence from many other sources—including newspapers, the coroner, two bishops, and the Church Army. Finally, in 1901 the *Birmingham Daily Gazette* sent a special correspondent, J. C. Walters, into the slums to report on local conditions, and his articles, reprinted in pamphlet form,[4] led to a sustained agitation culminating in 1901 in an acrimonious debate on the setting up of a Housing Committee of the Council, during which the Lord Mayor tried to cool the temper of the contestants by reminding them that it was the anniversary of the Battle of Waterloo.[5]

By thirty-two votes to thirty the Council decided to set up a new Housing Committee, which would take over from the Estates and Health Committees all powers exercised under the

[1] J. S. Nettlefold, *A Housing Policy* (1907).  [2] *B.P.*, 18 September 1907.
[3] C. A. Vince, op. cit., pp. 351–2.
[4] J. C. Walters, *Scenes in Slumland* (1902).  [5] *B.P.*, 19 June 1901.

Housing Acts, and such powers under the Public Health Acts as might be thought desirable. With men like Nettlefold to direct it, the committee worked with great determination. It refused to recommend a large-scale programme of municipal building on the grounds that such a scheme would check private enterprise and require a means test to make it work fairly. Council policy remained unchanged down to 1914, when a Special Housing Committee still reported that 'it is doubtful whether a public body could build as cheaply as a private individual, whose whole life has been devoted to a study of his business, and who in his own interest would be sure to watch every detail with a view to keeping down the cost'. Municipal building was only a measure of last resort. 'In the last resort, if private enterprise failed, the Corporation must step in, but they feel very strongly that the public money can be used to much greater advantage than in building houses.'[1] Nor was large-scale demolition suggested. The Council pinned its faith on private building in the suburbs, along with a cheap transport policy—that was where housing questions were mixed with tramway questions—and what came to be known as the Hull method of compelling owners thoroughly to repair their property. The policy of clearance which was challenged both in the Council and in the courts in 1905 reached its peak in 1913, when 28,265 houses were completely repaired. From 1905 onwards the Council also advocated a policy of town planning and the purchase of land, claiming in language reminiscent of Chamberlain that 'a corporation cannot own too much land, provided that it is judiciously purchased'.[2]

The housing policy of the Council down to 1914 had by no means solved Birmingham's housing problems. The Special Committee, set up in July 1913, with Neville Chamberlain as chairman, reported bluntly that 'a large proportion of the poor in Birmingham are living under conditions of housing detrimental to both health and morals'. Two hundred thousand people were still housed in 43,366 dwellings of a back-to-back type, when there were only 2,881 of this type in Liverpool and none in Manchester. In the six worst wards of the city from 51 to 76 per cent. of the houses were of this type. Over 42,000 dwellings had no separate water-supply, no sinks, and no drains,

[1] City of Birmingham, *Report of the Housing Enquiry Committee* (1914).
[2] City of Birmingham, *Report of the Housing Committee* (1906).

and over 58,000 had no separate sanitary facilities. In addition to the problems of these black spots, there was a general housing shortage in the city, and the rate of private building was slow.[1]

The continued challenge of housing questions showed that the sphere of municipal duty could never be fixed for all time. The policy bequeathed by Chamberlain was not in itself an all-comprehensive creed, satisfactory in itself for each new generation. What Chamberlain and his associates had done in the 70's was not to set the mould of municipal action for even a quarter of a century but to light the fires of zeal in local government, and to infuse collective vigour into municipal affairs.

It was the energy and the spirit which were most important. Chamberlain set the standard. Even before he changed his gospel songs from local to imperial themes, he conceived of the building of a city as an objective as adventurous and noble as the building of an empire. He was proud of the advance made in Birmingham. In January 1876 he compared the expenditure on the Improvement Scheme with the buying of the Suez Canal shares, and claimed that the Birmingham Town Council in twelve months had carried to a successful issue an undertaking considerably larger and more secure than the purchase of a controlling interest in the Suez Canal.[2] A year later, still in the same vein, he contrasted his local achievements with the imperial achievements of Disraeli, and claimed that he was so parochially minded that he looked with 'greater satisfaction to the annexation of our gas and water, to our scientific frontier in the improvement area', than he did 'to that imperial policy which has given us Cyprus and the Transvaal; and I am prouder of having been engaged with you in warring against ignorance and disease and crime in Birmingham than if I had been the author of the Zulu War, or had instigated the invasion of Afghanistan'.[3]

After he had become a leader in the upsurge of imperial expansionism, Chamberlain could never forget the lessons he had learnt as an architect of Birmingham government. He began with the parish pump and ended with the consolidation of an Empire, but he followed the same basic approach to both sets of problems. There were echoes of gas and water throughout the whole of his later career. The Hammonds have said not unjustly

[1] See above, p. 26.  [2] *B.P.*, 28 January 1876.
[3] C. W. Boyd (ed.), *Mr. Chamberlain's Speeches*, vol. i (1914), p. 77.

that he believed in his approach to Irish problems that the fires
which were smouldering in Irish minds could be put out by
a bucket of the best Birmingham water,[1] while later on in South
Africa his advocacy of Home Rule for the Rand through the granting of modified local autonomy to the citizens of Johannesburg
recalled his earlier attempts to offer good government along
with the maximum amount of civic independence to the people
of Birmingham.[2] In such ways, as through more direct economic
channels, Birmingham contributed to a new theory of empire.

IV

The forceful personality of Chamberlain left its mark—an
indelible mark—on English and imperial history. It could
hardly have failed to leave its mark on Birmingham. But after
Chamberlain's retirement from Council politics, the range of
problems in local government was widened, and the answers to
them could not be worked out in a purely derivative way. Local
government was developing into a complex machine, which had
to move effortlessly and with almost automatic regularity in the
performance of its daily routines. Birmingham needed not only
a civic gospel but new techniques of city management.

The operative powers of the Town Council were codified and
unified by the Birmingham Corporation Consolidation Act of
1883. This comprehensive measure was proposed by the Town
Clerk in a Report of 1882, but it met with great opposition from
the Conservatives on the Council, who demanded a poll of ratepayers. When that went against them—by a small majority on
a low poll—they applied to the Court of Queen's Bench to have
the proceedings declared illegal. Queen's Bench decided unanimously in favour of the Corporation, and the Act came into
force on 1 January 1884. It provided ample powers for the town
to extend and tighten up its administrative authority, and from
1883 onwards a mass of further legislation, consisting both of
national and local Acts, and of Provisional Orders, added new
contributions to the scope and functions of local government.

Birmingham's position as 'capital of the Midlands' was being
advanced step by step. In 1884, by Order in Council, Birmingham became an assize town, and three years later Queen
Victoria in person, during her Jubilee year, laid the foundation-

---

[1] J. L. and B. Hammond, *Gladstone and the Irish Nation* (1938), p. 521.
[2] J. L. Garvin, *The Life of Joseph Chamberlain*, vol. iii (1934), p. 129.

PLATE XVII

Sir James Smith, the first Lord Mayor

PLATE XVIII

The Making of the Elan Valley Scheme

stone of the new Law Courts. In 1885 the Redistribution Act, following the Reform Bill of 1884, divided the multi-member parliamentary borough into seven single-member constituencies. In 1888 the County Councils Act turned Birmingham into a county borough, and a year later Royal Decree made it a city. The modern seal and arms were adopted, based on the de Bermingham arms, with figures of Industry and Art as supporters. In 1896 the status of the mayoralty was raised by Letters Patent, and Sir James Smith became the first Lord Mayor of the city. Other favours followed. In 1900 a Royal Charter was granted founding the University, and in 1905 the city became the seat of a Bishop.

As the prestige of the city was enhanced, civic responsibilities eagerly sought after in the Chamberlain era were either deliberately extended or almost automatically accumulated. The most spectacular advance was made by the Water Committee. At first it had been thought possible to supply Birmingham's needs along the lines laid down by Chamberlain after the purchase of the Water Company. By the Act of 1875 the Council had been authorized to raise £250,000. When this became exhausted a further Act of 1879 authorized the raising of a further £300,000. Important new local developments were carried out. Reservoir and filter-beds were completed at Plant's Brook, a large reservoir with a capacity of 420 million gallons was constructed at Shustoke, and a conduit to take the waters of the River Bourne to the filter-beds at Whitacre was built. In the 1880's the city had fourteen reservoirs at its disposal with a total capacity of nearly 630 million gallons, and Gray, the engineer, hoped that the opening of the Shustoke Reservoir 'would make an ample provision for the water supply of the borough and the surrounding districts for many years to come'.

The hope was not fulfilled. Increasing population, area and mileage of sewers, and improving sanitary standards made it essential to find new sources of water-supply, if need be far from the city itself. As early as 1870 a report had been presented to the Corporation, recommending a scheme for taking water from the Rivers Teme and Ithon in mid-Wales, and in the following year Rawlinson urged the Council to secure water from the upper reaches of the Elan and Claerwen Rivers and bring it to Birmingham by conduit, supplying the towns *en route*. There was nothing new now about finding water for cities from miles away.

Before Birmingham adopted a Welsh water scheme, Liverpool led the way in 1877, securing a Bill in 1881, and receiving its first supplies of Welsh water from Vyrnwy, seventy-seven miles away, in 1892. By that time the cry of *Welsh Water* had been raised again at Birmingham in 1890, for supplies were totally inadequate, and new borrowing powers were needed from Parliament. A scheme was devised by James Mansergh, based on Rawlinson's proposals of twenty years before, and in 1892, after considerable opposition, the ratepayers approved it and a Bill embodying the project became law. Mansergh was entrusted with carrying out the scheme and his sons became joint engineers.

The Bill authorized the acquisition of gathering-grounds in the upper reaches of the Elan and Claerwen Rivers, covering a total area of 70 square miles, the building of three reservoirs on each of the rivers, together with an aqueduct for conveying the water over seventy-three miles to Birmingham, a receiving reservoir, filtration works, and pumping-station at Frankley, trunk mains, and other subsidiary operations.

The project was an extremely ambitious one, planned to cost over five million pounds. The city had to buy a vast estate, bigger than the existing boundaries of Birmingham itself. The lonely tract of wild Wales, dotted with hill-side farmsteads, was very remote from the streets and workshops of Birmingham. 'Rhayader is so far out of the way', wrote the *Birmingham Mail*, 'that you won't find it in any of the railway time-tables, and the Railway officials are not at all too sure about the best way to get to it.'[1]

Not only was the chosen site a remote one, but the actual course of negotiations to secure it was not easy. The catchment area fell within the boundaries of four counties—Radnor, Brecknock, Cardigan, and Montgomery. Skilful diplomacy was necessary on the part of the City Engineer, the Town Clerk, and the chairmen of the Water Committee, first Sir Thomas Martineau and then after his death in 1893 Alderman Edward Lawley Parker. The County Surveyor of Radnorshire acted as an intermediary between the landowners and the Corporation. Sometimes the Council itself took an active part in the operations. In July 1894, for example, an impressive municipal delegation left Snow Hill by special train to inspect the site, 'a second

[1] *B.M.*, 4 December 1893.

Niagara' as one of the Councillors called it. They were impressed by the rainfall—69·4 inches a year. 'Rainless days', it was said, 'are like angels' visits, few and far between.'[1]

On 21 July 1904 the waterworks were opened by King Edward VII and Queen Alexandra. The tiny Welsh site was crowded with people, including a contingent of 150 metropolitan police sent down from London. The first supplies of water came through to the city on 21 September 1904, and by 1905 the whole city was supplied from the Elan valley. The average daily consumption of water had reached a figure of 23 million gallons, as compared with 8 million gallons in 1875 and 16 million gallons in 1895. And the new Welsh water was much softer than that previously provided, and as a beverage so superior to the old town supply that wise men said that it would no longer be necessary to put whisky in it.[2]

Naturally there were complaints about the inevitably high cost of the scheme, and some critics doubted the value of Chamberlain's policy of not allowing profits to be made on water. 'Had the profits been allowed to accumulate, even in part, and had the charges been kept at a higher figure, it might have been possible to mitigate somewhat the heavy burdens on the present, if not the next generation.'[3] The most telling argument to meet this criticism was that which had been supplied by Chamberlain thirty years before, that water was a necessity, which should always be as cheap as possible. Still considering this to be the right approach to the problem, the city subsidized the Water Undertaking from the rates between 1904 and 1930 in order to meet the heavy expenditure begun in 1892. The expenditure continued to increase as the service extended. In 1912, for instance, powers were obtained to borrow money to effect an extension of the Elan aqueduct to increase its capacity, but the First World War interrupted the progress of the new scheme.

The growth of the giant water enterprise was a magnificent sequel to the administrative progress of the age of Chamberlain. Between 1880 and 1914 there were two other developments in municipal policy, which raised new issues and posed new sets of problems. The first and by far the more controversial of the two was the introduction and expansion of tramways, the second the growth of the electricity department.

[1] B.M., 19 June 1903.    [2] Ibid., 13 March 1905.
[3] The Times, 25 September 1902.

The tramways question raised problems both of ownership and of control. Not only did the big question of private versus municipal ownership loom behind all the debates, but there were, in addition, keen struggles between different groups of promoters and frequent bickering about the best form of traction and the ideal routes and schedules. Although the tramway system developed as a result of private initiative, almost from the start the Corporation interested itself in the problem. A detailed set of requirements touching the duties and conduct of drivers and conductors and the furnishing and lighting of cars was imposed. Furthermore, the Corporation showed a modified initiative in constructing tram-lines and letting them out to operating companies upon terms which repaid the capital outlay within the periods of the leases. It was thus possible for the Corporation to begin operations itself when the leases expired without the expensive procedure of having to buy out the companies' interests.

It would be a mistake, however, to imagine that there was anything like a long-term city transport policy. There were shifts and vacillations, decisions and reversals of decisions, and a considerable amount of purely accidental progress. It was clear by 1900 that under private initiative, as it had expressed itself, there was a lack of system and of continuity which not only militated against the interests of the passengers but also reflected on the outlook and enterprise of the city authorities. But just as there had been no immediate answer to the problems raised by the railways for the country as a whole fifty years before, so there was no immediate answer to the problem of the tramways within the smaller community of the city.

The story of the actual building of the tramways is an interesting and at times an amusing one. The first tramway was projected as early as 1860, when a licence was granted to an enterprising but reckless American inventor, George Francis Train, to lay a tramway along Paradise Street, Easy Row, and Broad Street to Five Ways, with an extension up the Hagley Road to the corner of Monument Lane. This experimental concession, made ten years before the National Tramways Act, was never taken advantage of, and although in 1861 the Corporation itself obtained parliamentary authority to build tramways, nothing was done until 1873. In that year the Council built a local line, costing £15,000, from Hockley to Colmore

Row, and leased the track at an annual rent of £910 to the Birmingham and District Tramway Company, managed at that time by Busby, who some years previously had introduced into the town a system of light omnibuses. The new tramway used horses and not electricity. The Company enjoyed mixed fortunes, but after early hazards the city began to enjoy a tramway boom. Many companies were floated, including the Western Districts Company, the Birmingham and Suburban, and the South Birmingham—and a tramway syndicate, the Birmingham Central Tramways Company, was formed, attracting a large number of local investors. The same procedure was followed as before. The Council built the track: the companies worked the lines on leases.

As a result of these speculations, many new lines were built, the first tramways being worked by steam. The steam-cars were often regarded by visitors as being particularly unpleasant. Ralph, who had so many good things to say about Birmingham, called the cars 'hideous, cumbrous and dangerous', and claimed that 'no American city would tolerate them'.[1] The Council itself regarded steam-power as merely a temporary experiment, and from the start only consented to the use of steam for limited periods, renewing the sanction from time to time, but rarely for more than six months. In 1884 the first steps were taken to reform tramway traction. The Patent Cable Tramway Company offered, in conjunction with the Central Tramways Company, to introduce the system of cable propulsion driven by a stationary engine—a system already in use in San Francisco, Dunedin, and Chicago. The Council accepted, and a cable was constructed from the bottom of Hockley Hill to Colmore Row. The new method was financially unsuccessful and seemed technically inferior to electric traction. As a result, in 1890 self-contained electric cars, driven by accumulators, were introduced on the Bristol Road route. Unfortunately there was a great leakage of energy, which resulted in the power frequently running out, leaving cars and passengers stranded on their journeys. An attempt in 1894 by Joseph Smith and Carruthers Wain to erect overhead electric wires in Bristol Road, similar to those already in use in Walsall, was unsuccessful because of the opposition of the Corporation. When, two years later, after the overhead system was working smoothly in Dublin, Bristol, and Leeds, the Council gave

[1] J. Ralph, loc. cit.

permission for its introduction locally on the Nechells route, the concession was not taken up.

It was about this time, in 1896, when the tramway question was one of the lively questions of the day, that Ross and Mackenzie, two Canadian tramway experts, directors of the Toronto and Montreal Street Railroads Company, arrived in the city, having heard tales of the possibilities of making their fortunes in Birmingham. They came, in their own words, 'to wake things up'. Birmingham had long complained of the nuisance of steam tramway engines and the lack of enterprise on the part of the Central Tramways Company, which had not sufficient capital to make changes, and had few prospects of acquiring new capital because of the shortness of its leases. Ross and Mackenzie formed a new City of Birmingham Tramways Company, which bought up the interests of the old Central and planned large schemes of reconstruction, involving the utilization of an improved system of traction and building of new radiating lines to provide through-routes across the city. They proposed to the city that they should surrender the leases which they had just bought—which on an average had only about ten years to run— and in return negotiate new leases of twenty-one years. They promised to pay a rent which would guarantee the municipality against any loss and which would make it possible to abolish steam traction altogether.

In July 1896 the Public Works Committee discussed this offer, and decided to recommend its acceptance. They considered seriously for the first time the possible municipalization of the service, which had already been adopted in Leeds, Blackpool, Huddersfield, Plymouth, and Glasgow, but rejected it on the grounds that possibly long-run advantages were less important to the city than the immediate advantages offered by the Company of abolition of steam, reduction of fares, shortening of working hours, and an immediate increase of rental to the Corporation. The full Council supported the committee, an amendment in favour of municipalization being defeated by thirty-three votes to twenty-three. As a result of this division the City of Birmingham Tramways Company took steps in 1897 to promote a private Bill for the extension of its powers. This was not the end of the story. A quarrel ensued between the Company and the Corporation concerning not the terms of transfer but the suggested method of traction. The Company wanted to use overhead wires, but the Corporation, advised by Hopkinson of Manchester, first preferred the surface contact and later, after a city deputation had travelled to the Continent, the conduit system which they had admired in Budapest and Blackpool. The disagreement between the Company and the Corporation led to much bitterness and recrimination, and eventually the Public Works Committee presented an ultimatum to the Company to withdraw their Bill. No satisfactory compromise could be reached and in June 1898, in an atmosphere of mutual indignation, the Council, by the narrow margin of twenty-eight votes to twenty-seven, gave instructions to the Committee not to re-open negotiations. The awkward position had thus been reached, where, after many high hopes, the new Company was left with nothing but the remnants of its leases and the cars, engines, and depots bought from its predecessors.

In the meantime opinion was veering round towards municipalization, on the lines already developed in some other cities —indeed, in six of the sixteen British cities with a population of more than 200,000. In 1899 a resolution was passed by the Council, with only one dissentient, proposing that parliamentary powers should be sought to enable the Council itself to work the lines when the leases fell in, and a new Tramways Committee was appointed in 1900 to take the place of what had hitherto been a Tramways Sub-Committee of the Public Works Committee.

Despite these changes in policy, it took a long time to secure the necessary municipal powers to run the tramways. The General Powers Bill of 1902, which would have provided them, was, for various other reasons, rejected by a vote of ratepayers. By the time a second General Powers Bill, of a more acceptable character, had been drawn up, a new tramway contestant had entered the fray. In 1902 Emil Garcke, the guiding spirit of the British Electric Traction Company, succeeded in obtaining a dominating interest in the City of Birmingham Tramways Company, and nearly all the other tramway companies in the district. He endeavoured, and very nearly succeeded, in inducing the Corporation to go back on its decision to municipalize. He made a much more tempting offer to the city than had ever been made before by any private concern, and in addition suggested extremely attractive terms to the outside suburban authorities, who preferred the high rents he waved before their eyes to the plans of the City Council of Birmingham. At the instigation of the British Electric Traction Company the surrounding local authorities promoted a rival Bill to obtain compulsory powers over lines running in the city. Their campaign was supported by a series of articles in *The Times*, which attacked the dangerous implications of municipalization.

Despite the vigour of the anti-municipalization party, a new General Powers Bill of 1903 survived both a ratepayers' poll and a passage through a parliamentary committee. It was passed just in time for the Corporation to take over the Aston route, the lease of which expired in December 1903. On 4 January 1904 the first municipal tram-cars were running merrily between the top of Bull Street and the municipal boundary in Aston Road. Alfred Baker, who had been manager of the London County Council Tramways, took over the new Birmingham municipal concern.

By July 1911 the city had gained complete control over the tramway system. An Act of 1905 permitted the reconstruction of the existing unconverted steam routes, the building of terminal lines, and the provision of new services. As a result, at long last, on 1 January 1907, Birmingham passed over entirely from steam to electricity. A cold winter's night on 31 December 1906 marked the last performance of the old steam trams. This did not go without mourning. On their last journeys they were covered with black flags, some of them bearing the eloquent text—'Brief Life is here our Portion: Funeral at Midnight'. As one old engine made its way to the depot for the last time a band played the 'Dead March' from *Saul*, and the passengers sang 'Should auld acquaintance be forgot'. The Corporation started its new all-electric services with a rolling stock of 220 cars and a staff of about 1,000 municipal employees. Within three years the Council was running 300 cars on thirty-four miles of track in the city. It had made profits amounting to over £75,000 for the relief of the rates. This was a nest-egg which had been long awaited. As early as 1902 the *Birmingham Daily Post* had written that 'the city is looking to the tramways to relieve it of the enormous increase of rates growing out of the Welsh Water Scheme'. But more than profits were involved. Over £80,000 was placed in a Special Reserve Fund, and, as in the case of Chamberlain's gas reforms, the wages of employees were raised, their conditions of work improved, and their hours shortened.

With the falling in of the last leases, and the skilful policy of transferring private routes to public management without dislocation of services, Birmingham had secured an efficient tramway system. The guarantee of cheap tram fares to the suburbs made possible the growth of a greater and more healthy city.

The tramway system had scarcely been consolidated when the development of omnibus services provided a new form of competition. As early as 1905 some cities, like Leeds, were running their own bus services. In 1913 the City of Birmingham bought ten omnibuses, and a year later acquired by purchase the interests of the Birmingham and Midland Motor Omnibus Company. The way was prepared for Birmingham to build up after the War its enormous transport system, the second largest in the country.

The third branch of municipal trading—electricity—was closely bound up with the fortunes of the tramways, and some of the features in the story of its municipalization are not unlike those already related. The supply of electricity in Birmingham began in the year 1882, shortly after the passing of Chamberlain's national Electric Lighting Act. A Select Committee of the House of Commons set up in 1878 had recommended that while no uniform national pattern should be laid down, electricity provision could be municipalized by local Acts, and in the case where private firms began to operate they should be subject to being bought out by the local authorities at the end of twenty-one years. The Act of 1882, modified slightly by a later Act of 1888, realized some of these suggestions. No private firm was allowed to supply electricity without consent of the local authority, and the authority had power to purchase compulsorily at the end of twenty-one years.

In Birmingham a Provisional Order was granted to the Incandescent Electric Lighting Company for the lighting of a small portion of the middle of the city, but owing to the non-fulfilment by the Company of certain statutory obligations, the Order was cancelled in 1889, and the responsibility for supplying local electricity was handed over to the Birmingham Electric Supply Company. The Corporation refused itself to take over what it regarded as an experimental venture, and maintained the attitude taken up by the Gas Committee in 1882, when it advocated private electricity concessions in the city for limited areas only. The 1889 concession to the Birmingham Electric

Supply Company allowed them to operate only in a very small business area in the centre of the city, where they began their service in 1891.

The prospect of municipalization could never be relegated far into the background, and in 1893, after the Company gave notice of its intention to apply for a new Order extending its area in three directions, the General Purposes Committee considered the question of local ownership more thoroughly than before. In July 1895 they reported that they were still unable to recommend the Council to engage in such an undertaking. Although a minority argued that it would be wiser to take over the undertaking in its infancy, as it might have done more profitably in the case of gas and water, the Council agreed with the majority, and the opinion was freely expressed that electricity, unlike water, was neither a monopoly nor a necessity. The Company was given authority to extend the area it covered, and although the number of its customers remained small, its profits rose substantially each year.

Municipal interest in acquiring electricity undertakings was keenest in those towns where the local authorities did not themselves own a gas undertaking, and where they were anxious to force down the Company's price of gas. It was the weakest in those cities, like Birmingham, where there was a firmly entrenched and extremely efficient Gas Department, and where the authorities attempted to limit electricity development, while retaining it in private hands. The issue of municipalization came to a head in Birmingham, as in some other cities, when the companies supplying electricity began to make assured profits. In 1897 the Electric Supply Company in Birmingham made profits of £12,962, more than double the profits of two years before, and on 4 May that year the Council unanimously decided to instruct the General Purposes Committee to report on the desirability of purchasing the undertaking. The immediate result of the passing of the resolution was that the £5 shares of the Company, already at a premium, rose to £12.

In 1898 the Council and the Company came to provisional agreement upon terms of purchase, the city paying the considerable sum of £420,000, which was recognized to be more than the market value of the Company. Municipalization was considered essential, even if the bargain struck was not a perfect one, and it was felt that further delay would merely increase the future price. A private Bill was drafted, which received the Royal Assent in August 1899.

The area of supply was extended to the whole city, the system was converted to a higher voltage, and a large new station at Summer Lane was erected in 1906.

The tramways were the most important customer, and the plans for the construction of the generating station had to be modified to fit in with the complete switch-over to municipal control of an entirely electric system. This was an early example of the co-ordination of public undertakings. The new power station was the symbol of a new age. 'It is of gigantic dimensions, and in some respects it will be unique', wrote one local newspaper. 'To give some idea of the size of the engine room, it is necessary only to point out that the Town Hall, could it be moved, might be placed within its walls.'

Although an attempt was made by the municipal undertaking to increase the number of its customers, they were still few in number by more recent standards. At the time of transfer in 1900 there were only 1,742 of them, and the total consumers' load amounted to the equivalent of 4,400 kilowatts for all purposes—only half the monthly average for the 1930's. The price of electricity was high, higher in Birmingham than in some other areas in the district, although there was a reduction in the range of lighting charges from 1899 to 1909 of 7d.–4d. per unit down to 4d.–2d. per unit and of power charges down from 2d. per unit to 0·7d. per unit. The cheaper power charges encouraged the increasing use of municipal electricity in local industry. The demand increased so much that the city found it difficult to build sufficient plant. In 1912 steps were taken to acquire a new site for a generating station at Nechells, and although this was held up by the First World War, electricity had become so important to local industry that the government agreed in 1915 to permit the creation of a new temporary station with an initial capacity of 10,000 kilowatts. That such a station was erected in war-time shows how far electricity had developed since the days of the 1890's, only twenty years before, when the Council had refused to regard it as a necessity, and had considered it mainly as a means of lighting shops in the crowded streets of the centre of the city. Electricity had established itself as an essential part of Birmingham's municipal enterprise.

V

The story of water, tramways, gas, and electricity covers only one-half of the civic progress of the city, the trading half. The other half was equally important. Birmingham boasted that the title 'best-governed city in the world' meant something bigger than an efficient business-like control of essential services. 'A great town', George Dawson had said, 'is a solemn organism through which should flow, and in which should be shaped, all the highest, loftiest, and truest ends of man's intellectual and moral nature.' Alongside gas and water, the city had to take account of libraries and art gallery, parks and schools. Sometimes trading and cultural activities were not separated by that wide gap which made the ratepayers in 1852 turn down a proposal to set up a free library under the terms of the Public Libraries Act of 1850. In 1881 there was fruitful co-operation between private benefaction, municipal trading, and the search for beauty. When the Gas Committee needed new offices, it served its own purposes, and those of the Art Gallery Committee at the same time, by allowing a Public Museum and Art Gallery to be built over the top of its premises. 'Acquisition of gas supply had a consequence apparently as far removed as Tenterden Steeple from Goodwin Sands—the provision of the present commodious Art Gallery.'[1] The motto on the memorial stone in the entrance hall bore the appropriate words, 'By the gains of Industry we promote Art', a perpetual reminder of the circumstances in which the Art Gallery was erected and equipped. The profits on the gas undertaking furnished the building, and local industrialists contributed its contents, the only direct charge upon the rates being the sum necessary for its maintenance and the insurance of its collections.

Before examining the subsequent history of the Art Gallery, it is important to take stock of Birmingham's educational policy and administration, which not only acted as an instrument of local cultural and technical expansion, but also stimulated widespread interest in the rest of the country. Indeed, Birmingham played an important part in the evolution of national educational policy. In 1870 educational topics produced some of the sharpest political conflicts and controversies of the day: by 1914 a sound

---

[1] British Association, *Handbook of Birmingham* (1886), p. xiii.

educational structure had been evolved, which depended on teachers and administrators for its smooth routine working.

The demand for a new educational system had become vociferous in the 1860's, when education was still in the hands of denominational bodies. Birmingham was one of the cities which took the lead in demanding 'the establishment of a system which shall secure the education of every child in the country'. Dixon, who was Mayor of Birmingham in 1867, had long taken an active interest in the question, and he was responsible for the setting up of an independent, non-sectarian Education Aid Society, on the model of a similar organization founded in Manchester in 1864. The Society undertook, as a part of its duty, the investigation of the educational conditions of the town. A house-to-house canvass produced interesting statistics, which demonstrated the inability of many parents to pay school fees, the absence of proper school facilities, and the weakness of arrangements which did not provide compulsion to secure school attendance. Discussing the education question, even in statistical terms, meant raising religious differences, and these were important at the 1868 General Election, when non-conformists were sharply alined against churchmen. It was a year after the election that Birmingham became the centre of the National Education League, a highly organized political body, which struggled for eight years both inside and outside Parliament to press for a programme of educational reform. Its principles were important in the renaissance of local government as a whole. It urged that local authorities should be compelled by law to see that sufficient school accommodation was provided for every child in their district; that one-third of the cost of founding and maintaining such schools as might be required should be provided out of local rates, the rest out of government grants; that all schools aided by local rates should be under the management of local authorities, and subject to government inspection; that admission to such schools should be free, and that teaching should be unsectarian; and that after facilities had been provided, the state or the local authorities should have the power to compel the attendance of children of suitable age not otherwise receiving education.

The organization of the League was extremely efficient and its financial resources considerable. It provided a training course and a model of management for the National Liberal Federation which grew out of it. Birmingham men were its directors. Its chairman was Dixon, the head of its Executive Committee and acting chairman was Chamberlain, its secretary was Collings, its propaganda organizer was J. T. Bunce, the editor of the *Birmingham Daily Post*. Martineau organized its Branches Committee, and its treasurer was first Jaffray and then Mathews. Men of the calibre of Timmins, Dale, Vince, and Dawson were members of its Executive. Within four months of its creation the League had built up a guarantee fund amounting to £60,000, 113 town branch committees were in existence, and a quarter of a million copies of different educational publications had been circulated.

While the League was growing in importance, the government introduced Forster's Education Bill of 1870, which made education for the first time the direct concern of the nation. The Act divided up the country into school districts, and set up School Boards where denominational school accommodation was considered inadequate or unsatisfactory. These Boards, to be elected by the Town Council in boroughs, were granted the power to remit school fees in cases of poverty, and to frame by-laws to compel the attendance of children up to thirteen years of age. No restrictions were placed on School Boards with regard to religious instruction, except the observance of a conscience clause. Forster's Bill, though framed by a well-known Liberal, fell far short of the full Birmingham programme. Forster, indeed, had written in a memorandum as early as October 1869 that he considered the 'complete logical machinery' of the Birmingham League would quickly undermine the existing schools, would relieve the parents of all payment, would entail upon the country an enormous expense, and would drive out of the field most of those who cared for education.[1] None the less the first Birmingham reaction to the Bill was not unfavourable, and Dixon gave a general consent to the principles which it enunciated.

The quiet was short-lived. When the members of the Birmingham League saw that as a result of the new measure the old denominational schools, instead of being swept away or left to wither away, were to be maintained and even to be offered the possibility of further strengthening, they were goaded into vigorous denunciation. Ill feeling persisted and grew. 'There is

[1] T. Wemyss Reid, *Life of the Rt. Hon. William Forster*, vol. i (1881), p. 465.

much hot water in Birmingham on the education question', Bright wrote to Forster in March 1871.[1] The League claimed that Forster's Bill left the election of School Boards to bodies which in many cases would merely represent the land and the Church; that it did not offer completely free schools; that it contemplated an extension not an abolition of the denominational principle, and that it meant unnecessary delay in implementation. These and other failings in the 'feeble, hesitatory and tentative bill' were 'exposed' in a series of suggested important amendments, which the League took direct to Gladstone, the Prime Minister, in March 1870. At the same time that the League objected to the Bill, an even more militant Central Nonconformist Committee was founded in Birmingham, with Dale and Crosskey as honorary secretaries and Schnadhorst, then an unknown draper, as paid secretary. It attacked that side of the measure which seemed to favour the Church, and above all it strongly urged the Prime Minister to reconsider the proposal to give local boards unrestricted power to determine the religious character of schools supported by local rates. Although the government amended its original proposals in May and June 1870, the amendments were still felt to be inadequate, and the League raised a special fund of £10,000 to increase the volume of its pressure and the scope of its activities. During the passing of the Bill many Liberal M.P.s voted against the government in the House on important clauses, 62 of them on one motion and 132 on another, in the second case with 133 abstaining as well. On a League amendment to extend School Boards to all districts, 112 Liberals voted against the ministry. The ministry made some concessions. Dilke's proposal that the School Boards should be elected by the ratepayers instead of by town councils and vestries was rejected by the narrow majority of 150 to 145, but the government later accepted the suggestion. The use of the ballot in School Board elections was carried by a large majority. When Gladstone closed the debates it was clear that the gulf between Birmingham and Hawarden was very wide.

The immediate local effect of the Education Act in Birmingham was to generate the great excitement of the School Board election contests of 1870 and 1873. No time was lost in preparing for a School Board election in Birmingham, but it produced a

[1] Ibid., p. 527.

result far different from that which had been expected. Parliament had laid down that School Board elections should be based on the cumulative vote—that is to say, that electors could distribute their votes as they pleased and give them all to one candidate if they so wished. Minorities could thus buttress themselves against majorities, if the majority group were foolish enough to run too many candidates at the elections. In the first School Board election in 1870 in Birmingham, the Church party, by putting up fewer candidates than the Liberal nonconformists, won eight seats out of fifteen, while the Roman Catholics topped the poll with their one candidate. Although the fifteen Liberal candidates secured a majority of 4,462 voters and of 46,934 votes on the total poll, they failed to secure a majority on the Board. It was their failure on this occasion, as much as any other single factor, which led to the tightening up of the Liberal caucus organization. Indeed, Francis Adams has gone so far as to say that the caucus was simply 'the offspring of the cumulative and the minority vote'.[1]

The Liberals did not make the same mistake at the next election in 1873. The defeat of 1870 had not been entirely due to the cumulative vote: it had sprung also from an unsatisfactory voting system and a good deal of apathy and indifference. After the 1870 result had been announced the *Birmingham Post* remarked that the Liberals might 'profitably occupy themselves with self-examination and reorganization.... Uninterrupted success is not wholesome for parties any more than for individuals. ... The "cumulative vote" was against them, but this difficulty may be overcome if the Liberal organization is perfectly worked, and if the party polls a full proportion of their strength.'[2] In 1873 the tables were reversed, and a great Liberal victory returned the Liberal Eight, who now secured control of local educational policy.

Between 1870 and 1873 a Conservative School Board had come into headlong collision with the Liberal-Radical Town Council. The School Board had no power to levy a rate, but was empowered to issue to the Town Council a precept requiring payment of the amount estimated as the outlay for the following year. The Council paid the first precept for £3,000, but refused to pay the 1872 precept, on the grounds that the School Board

[1] F. Adams, *History of the Elementary School Contest in England* (1882), p. 251.
[2] *B.P.*, 2 December 1870.

was buttressing denominationalism. The same trouble arose again a year later. In consequence of the dispute, the fortnightly School Board debates reached a high standard of eloquence. They were 'looked forward to with the greatest interest and zest, partly because of the principles at stake, partly no doubt also because of the intellectual enjoyment they afforded. They were always inconveniently crowded by the public.'[1] The Conservative majority, led by the Rev. F. S. Dale, urged the payment of money out of the rates to cover fees to the existing denominational schools—all the schools that were then in existence in Birmingham: Chamberlain retaliated by a nation-wide campaign against School Board grants to strengthen denominationalism. This bitter issue was fought at every level between 1870 and 1873 —in the Board itself, in the Town Council, in Parliament, in the Education Department, and in the Queen's Bench—and when at last the School Board majority, by writ of mandamus from the Queen's Bench, compelled the Town Council to honour the Board's majority support of the Rev. F. S. Dale's policy, the Board did not dare to enforce the by-law they had made, 'since it was well understood that the levies would have been resisted in the homes of the ratepayers, and that distraints, on a scale wholesale and unparalleled, would have been necessary to collect the rate'.

During and after these first three years of conflict, which reflected the deadlock between a Liberal Council and a Conservative Board, the first beginnings were made in the organization of non-denominational elementary education in Birmingham. The practical educational problems facing the new non-denominational system in the 70's were enormous—the status of the teachers was low, facilities for their training were inadequate, pupil teachers had to be used to fill responsible posts, and scholars were irregular in their attendance and little used to learning. Above all there was still complete disagreement about the forms and place of religious teaching. At first dissenters tried to arrange voluntary religious instruction in the new Board Schools through a Religious Education Society, which organized a pool of volunteer teachers, but the numbers were not sufficient, and in 1879 the Board laid down that the Bible should be read in schools by the ordinary full-time teachers, without note or comment. This became the basis of the twentieth-century compromise. As far as general education was concerned, the three R's—reading,

[1] F. Adams, op. cit., p. 256.

writing, and arithmetic—formed the basic content of the curriculum or code which qualified the school for the receipt of educational grants from the government, but in addition grammar, history, and geography were taught to older children and needlework to the girls.

The first Birmingham School Board calculated that accommodation was required in elementary schools for 59,710 children, and that the existing denominational and private schools catered only for 37,442. A census of children taken in 1874 confirmed this figure. The first Board School built to meet the deficiency was at Bloomsbury, designed to accommodate 1,059 children. It was opened on 24 March 1873 with few formalities. By 1880 there were twenty-eight Board Schools, providing accommodation for 28,787 children. They began to follow a common pattern of design—central hall with classrooms—and a more highly developed curriculum.

Before the local educational system could run smoothly it had to ensure compulsory attendance and free places. As far as the former was concerned, the Board made by-laws as early as July 1871 compelling attendance at school from five to thirteen, but providing that Standard IV should be the standard for total exemption from attendance, and Standard III for half-time exemption. The first School Board attendance officer was appointed in 1872. National legislation made his work more straightforward. Sandon's Education Act of 1876 laid down the important principle that all parents were under the legal obligation to have their children instructed, and could be subjected to penalties if they defaulted, and a further Act in 1890 made it obligatory instead of optional for School Boards to compel attendance. Free schools came later. The fees charged in the first Board Schools were 3d. a week for children over seven years of age, and 2d. a week for infants below the age of seven. Disraeli's government protested when the Council tried to lower these fees, on the grounds that the proposal was an attempt to discriminate against the denominational schools, but the School Board was able none the less to establish 1d. schools throughout the city. In September 1891 all school fees were abolished.

Under the twenty-year chairmanship of George Dixon, who replaced Chamberlain in 1876, the Birmingham School Board became a model for educational authorities everywhere. Dixon 'followed his ideals in determined fashion, never discouraged by

PLATE XIX

An Early Board School

PLATE XX

Sir George Kenrick

momentary failure, never unduly elated by temporary success'.[1] He and his colleagues were responsible, among the first Boards in the country, for improving the training of a new corps of adult teachers, and for requiring pupil teachers to attend half-time at special classes for the continuation of their own education. In the schools themselves the beginning of a welfare policy can be traced back to the provision of free meals and health services for poor children, while as early as 1894 'special educational treatment' was devised for various types of backward children. Equally important was the provision of further education, for although the Act of 1870, which set up the School Boards, was concerned only with the provision of elementary schools, Birmingham built its own higher grade schools, the first of them in Bridge Street and Waverley Road. Later on one of the schools was named after George Dixon. In addition to setting up these schools, Birmingham adopted the wise policy of providing scholarships from the elementary schools to the King Edward VI Schools, thereby building a bridge between compulsory elementary education and traditional secondary education, as it had been evolved in Birmingham since the golden age of Tudor education. To extend the new educational system of the city to meet the needs of the untaught masses, who had not been given the benefit of a formal education, evening classes were arranged, for which a curriculum was designed to suit local needs.

The Birmingham School Board was so successful in its work, and had designed an educational apparatus so worthy of a great city, that it came as a bitter disappointment to many local people when the Education Act of 1902 abolished School Boards altogether, and handed over the administration of education to the general local authorities. Disappointment at the loss of the Board was increased by suspicion and fear, once more aroused among nonconformists, that the new Act was designed to strengthen the hold of the Church of England on national education. Chamberlain, who had thrown all his energies into the National Education League of the early 70's, was now a member of the Cabinet, and he had the irritating experience of seeing his colleagues prepare a Bill which offended many of his principles and which he feared would lose him much support. His position was an awkward one, for he could make no public protest, and he tried to explain the reasons

[1] *B.M.*, 5 January 1898.

for the Bill to old nonconformist allies like Dr. J. G. Glover,[1] but behind the scenes he was writing frankly to the Liberal Unionist Duke of Devonshire, who had introduced the measure, that 'the political future seems to me—an optimist by profession—most gloomy. I told you that your Education Bill would destroy your own party. It has done so. Our best friends are leaving us by scores and hundreds, and they will not come back.'[2] Chamberlain attempted to persuade the government to accept an optional clause, under which no local authority need adopt the Bill unless it liked, but this clause was thrown out by the Commons on a free vote in July 1902 by 271 to 102, while Chamberlain was out of action as the result of a cab accident. Birmingham thus had to accept a set of new administrative managements, which were uniform for the whole country.

The 1902 Act, despite all the political problems which it raised, had real merits. The new education committees did not simply take over the functions previously exercised by the School Boards: they were given full control over all types of education in their neighbourhoods, below the university level, and including voluntary schools (with their own managers) as well as board schools, and both technical schools and general schools. A unified educational policy could now be developed by the local authorities, without fear of exceeding their powers.

Despite the nonconformist opposition in Birmingham, the new Act worked well. Religious divergences faded into the background, and by 1914 most of the controversial fires had burned down. The new Education Committee cared little for rhetoric and relied on sound administration. Its chairman was George Kenrick, later Sir George Kenrick, who had been a member of the old School Board for more than twenty-two years, and was elected a City Councillor for Edgbaston by the general agreement of all parties. He provided experience and continuity. By 1914 there were more than sixty Council schools, attended by 70,000 children.

While the Council developed the outlines of a comprehensive educational policy, there were important developments in other fields of education. King Edward VI School secured a revised

---

[1] See his letter to Glover, 22 April 1902, printed in L. Creswicke, *The Life of the Rt. Hon. Joseph Chamberlain*, vol. iii, pp. 181–4.

[2] Chamberlain to the Duke of Devonshire, 23 September 1902, printed in B. Holland, *The Life of Spencer Compton, Duke of Devonshire*, vol. ii (1913), p. 284.

constitution, which brought it into closer touch with the city as a whole. In the 1860's it had been extremely unpopular with Liberal reformers, partly on the grounds that admittance was by individual nomination, partly on the grounds that its governing body was unrepresentative of local interests. 'No Dissenter, within the memory of man, has been a governor', reported the Endowed Schools Commission of 1868; 'no Mayor of the town has till the present year been a Governor; no member for the borough, except one, a Conservative; not one Town Councillor.' Reform schemes in 1875, 1878, and 1883 modified the old structure, and eight branch schools of the central institution were converted into secondary schools under the name of grammar schools. The 1885 constitution provided for twenty-one governors, eight nominated by the Town Council, one each by the Universities of Oxford, Cambridge, and London, eight by co-option, and one elected by the teachers of the foundation. Admittance rules were changed, and nomination gave way to competitive examination, one-third of the pupils holding foundation scholarships which exempted them from tuition fees. A somewhat irksome outside control, enjoyed by the Charity Commissioners, was abolished by a further Act of 1900, promoted by the governors and backed by Chamberlain. King Edward's School and the town finally made peace with each other.

The 1900 Act allowed for a place on the Board of Governors for a representative of Birmingham's newest educational institution, the University. It was the setting up of the University in 1900 that crowned Birmingham's educational aspirations. The enterprise had more than one root. The Midland Institute, set up in 1854, was in some sense the mother of the School of Art, the Technical College, the School of Music, and the University, while Queen's College, a theological college, had existed since 1843. Mason College was built in 1880 as a result of the munificence of Sir Josiah Mason, whose career, from the time that he entered Birmingham as a poor lad at the age of twenty to the laying of the College's foundation-stone on his eightieth birthday in 1875, well illustrates the adaptability and vigour of the Midlands.[1] The new College was designed to be 'as liberal as possible in the character and extent of the teaching, the system of management, and the mode and terms of admission'.[2] Fifteen years after

---

[1] See C. Gill, *History of Birmingham*, vol. i (1952), pp. 301–2.
[2] J. T. Bunce, *Josiah Mason, a Biography* (1882), p. 101.

Mason's death in 1881, the trustees incorporated Mason College as a university college, with Joseph Chamberlain as President. A year later a movement began for converting the College into a university; in November 1898 a petition was drawn up, praying for the granting of a Royal Charter; and after a final bout of enthusiastic benefactions, the new University was opened. It was fortunate in securing Sir Oliver Lodge, the scientist and philosopher, as its first principal.

The University had been conceived of by Joseph Chamberlain as the crowning glory of a new democratic educational system, 'enabling the poorest amongst us, if he has but the ability, if God has given him these gifts, to rise to the greatest height of culture'.[1] 'Chamberlain's power and the boldness of his ideas'[2] played a large part in the ultimate success of the venture. He had a clear vision of what he wished to accomplish—the creation of a new place of learning, where men of outstanding ability could find assistants and interpreters, who would carry across their ideas to the masses, and where scholarship would not be divorced from practical living. Chamberlain was not alone in his vision. A list of benefactors to the University, among whom George Dixon is to be counted, reveals the extent to which local business helped to create the conditions for educational progress in Birmingham.

The story runs parallel with the story told previously, of business energies turning to civic reform. There was pride in the search for something more than technique. 'Not only is the craftsman considered,' wrote the *Birmingham Mail* in December 1898, 'but the schoolboy whom the exigencies of life force into the workshops, when he could continue his education, has facilities now-a-days which his father before him never possessed.' Technical education, which was being promoted energetically by the Technical School set up in Suffolk Street with its three branch schools, was fitted into a comprehensive framework. That the framework was so comprehensive shows how securely founded were the social strivings of an expanding community.

VI

The development of educational policy and administration was accompanied by other important developments in the provision of artistic and recreational amenities.

[1] *B.P.*, 29 May 1888.
[2] See J. Amery, *The Life of Joseph Chamberlain*, vol. iv (1951), ch. lxxxiv.

PLATE XXI

Sir Oliver Lodge

PLATE XXII

Jesse Collings

The history of the Public Library itself illustrates the change-over from a policy of economy at all costs to a policy of civic enterprise. In 1850 the first permissive Free Libraries and Museums Act was passed, but Birmingham, unlike Manchester, failed to find sufficient local support to implement its provisions. It was not until 1860 that the Act was adopted, and although a branch library was set up a year later in a rented building on Constitution Hill, it was not until 1865, on the occasion of the visit of the British Association, that the Central Library was opened in Ratcliff Place. The opening of the Library was indeed the beginning of the new age, trumpeted by Dale and Dawson. 'I am glad the Corporation has given itself an officer, who represents intellect,' Dawson said in his impressive opening address. The Reference Library was opened in 1866, with its first aim to secure books which would represent, 'as far as practicable, every phase of human thought, and every variety of opinion'. This ideal represented the basic value of Birmingham's rising democracy. From the start it set itself the standards of encouraging critical thought in an atmosphere of tolerance and free discussion. On the day that the Reference Library was opened, Deritend Branch Library was also opened and the foundation-stone of Gosta Green Library laid. Two years later, in April 1868, the Shakespeare Memorial Library was opened in a room at the Central Library, set aside specially for the purpose.

The library project made great progress, and in 1878 a scheme for the extension of the central building was sanctioned. While work was in progress, the great day-time fire of 11 January 1879 interrupted the programme of expansion. Within a quarter of an hour of its outbreak the heat was so great that it proved impossible to get into the Reference Library, and although help was provided from all sides—Jesse Collings, then Mayor of the town, hurrying from the Council House to try to save some of the treasures—by the end of the day the Library had been ruined. Only about 1,000 books out of 50,000 in the Reference Library were saved, although 15,000 of the 17,000 volumes in the Lending Library were undamaged.

The Free Libraries Committee soon took action to try to deal with this unexpected calamity. The fire took place on a Saturday: on the following Monday the committee met and passed a resolution urging that it was a public duty immediately to repair the loss, and proposing the establishment of a special fund for the purpose. At the same time they appointed a sub-committee to confer with the architects about plans for a new building. By the end of 1879 a sum of £14,000 had been collected by public subscription, and this amount, along with £25,000 from the insurance companies, provided the necessary funds to set up a new Library. It was opened on 1 June 1882, John Bright delivering the opening address.

In 1883 the Free Libraries and the Art Gallery Committees of the Council were separated, and in the same year the Birmingham Consolidation Act removed the limit of the penny library rate, which had acted as a curb on buying. Six years later the Local Government Act of 1888 gave the committee an additional source of revenue, and work went ahead on the task of building branch libraries in the city and the suburbs. Balsall Heath and Harborne made it a condition of joining the city in 1891 that free libraries should be provided in their districts, and Saltley stipulated that the branch at Adderley Park already in existence should be enlarged and reorganized. Five new branch libraries were set up between 1888 and 1898, and the six existing libraries were enlarged, and in some cases entirely rebuilt.

While this work was going on in the outer districts, the work of the Central Library was improved and extended. In 1909 work began on the building of a storehouse for books under the floor of the News Room capable of holding from 100,000 to 150,000 volumes, and accessible by a lift from the Reference Library. In 1915 the invaluable Boulton and Watt collection, presented to the city four years before by George Tangye, was opened to the public. A further aspect of library work linking it up with education was the provision of free lectures on subjects connected with books and similar topics.

While the Library was catering both for experts—often coming from great distances to use it—and for the general public of the city itself, the Art Gallery, too, set itself the same ideal. 'Art must not be the perquisite of a few,' urged Jesse Collings, 'but must permeate the whole people with its blessings and advantages.' Between 1886 and 1910, over fifteen million people passed through the turnstiles of the Art Gallery which had been opened in 1885.

Birmingham's Art Gallery came late, for although there had been a scheme to include a 'Gallery of Art' in the Midland Institute building in 1854, like much else at the time it was 'deferred', and until 1885 what few pictures the city owned were kept in the Free Library building and in Aston Hall.

The new Art Gallery of 1885 had the Gas Committee as its landlord, but from the start it relied on private munificence for its exhibits. There were no rate-aided funds available for the purchase of pictures, and the basis of the collection was a gift of £10,000 from Richard and George Tangye, other money gifts amounting to £13,000, and numerous gifts of pictures, including Nettlefold's collection of twenty-six paintings by David Cox, the Birmingham artist who died in 1859. The Art Gallery Purchase Fund, advised by (Sir) Whitworth Wallis as Keeper, who held the post for forty-two years, built up a magnificent collection, which made Birmingham Art Gallery the finest in the provinces. It began to be known far and wide, particularly for its unsurpassed collection of pre-Raphaelite drawings and paintings, and alongside the works of Cox were those of another famous Birmingham artist, Sir Edward Burne-Jones. To emphasize the relationship of art to its local background, the Gallery set up an industrial art section, which included many exhibits having a direct bearing on the industrial activities of the city.

Such was the pressure on the space of the Art Gallery that in 1905 the City Council authorized plans for additional rooms over the new Gas Offices on the north side of Edmund Street, but before they were begun, John Feeney, who had already been a generous donor, died, and in his will left £50,000 to build a new Art Gallery. In July 1912 the first set of Feeney Galleries was opened, and a year later a Natural History Museum was added. The Feeney Galleries as a whole were finally opened immediately after the end of the First World War.

By 1914 Birmingham had not only developed its indoor artistic amenities but had improved its outdoor recreational facilities by the provision of parks and open spaces. The need was recognized to be a pressing one. After they had been provided, the people 'were not slow to realise their advantages, and it is a storm indeed that sees the parks deserted; while during the day Mamas, nursemaids and little folks hold well-pleased possession'.[1]

The provision of parks and open spaces was, like the provision of libraries and art galleries, partly a result of private benefaction, partly a result of civic policy. Birmingham's first park

[1] *B.M.*, 1 September 1886.

was offered to the Corporation in 1856 for a nominal rent by the Hon. Charles Bowyer Adderley, afterwards Lord Norton. By 1865 the city had two other parks—Calthorpe Park, opened by the Duke of Cambridge in 1857, and Aston Hall and Park.

It was not until 1873 that the next addition was made, when Miss Louisa Anne Ryland presented Cannon Hill Fields, now Cannon Hill Park, to the town. By 1914 Highgate Park, Summerfield Park, Small Heath Park (provided by another generous gift of Miss Ryland), Handsworth Park, and Queen's Park, Harborne, had been added. By the beginning of the twentieth century the approach to the acquisition of public parks was changing. Cities were beginning to pay more vigilant attention not only to the setting up of new parks but to the preservation and improvement of open spaces. The idea that every district ought to have its private park, every ward its recreation ground, was propounded as early as 1876,[1] while Chamberlain claimed that beautiful gardens and parks were as much a part of the education of the people as any other means to which they could devote their attention.[2] Birmingham played an important part in the movement to protect open spaces, the Birmingham Association for the Preservation of Open Spaces and Public Footpaths, with T. Grosvenor Lee as secretary, doing much to awaken opinion and to carry out actual purchases of property. It was this Association which saved Rednal Hill from the private builders, the Corporation acquiring 32 acres of delightful country-side in 1889. At the same time, Lord Windsor leased the adjoining hill, Bilberry Hill, to the city, and in 1913 sold it for £3,385. A third hill, Beacon Hill, came into the possession of the city through the liberality of Edward Cadbury and George Cadbury, Junior.

The safeguarding of open spaces was accompanied by the improvement of conditions in various ways in the middle of the city. The Birmingham Closed Burial Grounds Act of 1878 enabled eighteen graveyards to be turned into public gardens, the first of them, the old Park Street burial-ground, in 1880. At the same time, from 1887 onwards, recreation and playgrounds were acquired in built-up areas, the first of them being the Burbury Street Recreation Ground. Once again it was a voluntary body which did much to popularize the need for public places of

---

[1] *B.M.*, 1 June 1876.              [2] *B.G.*, 3 June 1876.

recreation. J. S. Nettlefold organized the Birmingham Playgrounds, Open Spaces, and Playing Fields Association in 1906 on the model of a Chicago organization, which stressed that the organization of playgrounds was 'in no sense a charity. It is a municipal function. Children must have playgrounds if they are to become decent citizens.'[1] The Birmingham Association was responsible for the opening of the Garrison Lane Recreation Ground, a large open space on the site of demolished slum property at the corner of Watery Lane and Garrison Lane, which was equipped for gymnastics and open-air games.

The provision of these services—Art Gallery, Libraries, and Parks—had already gone far by 1914. They marked an important step forward from the mid-nineteenth-century extension of environmental services to the ideal of more elaborate civic services in the twentieth century. In every case, their success could not have been assured had it not been for the willing co-operation of private individuals and of voluntary bodies: the services grew out of a society, which was itself growing up. Birmingham had become more mature, and had secured a lead over towns with less experience and a shorter history. One writer wrote in 1900 that when he visited a 'newly-risen manufacturing town which has lately blossomed out into a state of thriving progress' he was forcibly reminded of what Birmingham had been some years before.[2] There was of course still plenty of room left for improvement. Horizons were always changing. In a lecture given in 1910, W. H. Bidlake looked forward to 'Birmingham as it Might Be', and envisaged the transformation of the city, with the great radial streets by which men reached their offices and workshops widened and planted with trees, 'carrying something of the country into the heart of the city'.[3] This was the civic gospel of the leaders of Birmingham life and thought on the eve of the First World War. Out of a great metropolis of industry, they believed it might still be possible to create a modern Utopia.

## VII

The chief instrument of civic development in Birmingham throughout these years was the Council, and it was the Town

[1] Dunne, the Mayor of Chicago, to Nettlefold, 18 May 1907.
[2] T. Anderton, *A Tale of One City* (1900), pp. 106–7.
[3] W. H. Bidlake, 'Birmingham as it Might Be', in *Birmingham Institutions* (ed. J. H. Muirhead, 1911).

(later the City) Council which made the most important decisions which gave Birmingham the reputation of being 'the best-governed city in the world'.

The prestige of the Council grew out of all recognition from the days of the discredited régime in the 1850's and 60's, when the Councillors used to meet in the old Woodman Tavern in Easy Row. In the middle years of the century Birmingham was under the influence of men of 'the unprogressive tradesmen class —many of them worthy men in their way, but of limited ideas. In their private businesses they were not accustomed to deal with big transactions and high figures, so that spending large sums of money, if proposed, filled the brewer, the baker, and the candlestick maker with alarm.'[1] Not only was an undue emphasis laid on a narrow policy of economy in civic affairs—on the single objective of keeping down the current rates, even if, as part of the price, it meant increasing them in the future—but council methods and procedure were cumbrous, undignified, and at times disorderly. Debates were long and turbulent, personal feuds were considered more important than the pursuit of public interests, and local politics consisted largely of bargains and scandals, frequently and often maliciously drawn into the limelight for all to see. Alderman Manton recalled that 'there was nothing to attract those days in the position of a Town Councillor, or to lead the people to suppose that there was any dignity attached to the position; or any sacrifices made in serving them by filling it'.[2]

The Council Chamber in Moor Street was dingy and inadequate, a small room hidden away down an entry with room for about a dozen of the public to stand and watch the frequently sordid proceedings. Most of the business of the borough was carried on in a small private office. The Mayor had no parlour until he secured a room in Temple Street on the first floor of Unity Chambers, and for a long time he had no mace, no chain of office, and little dignity.

It is possible to over-draw the picture, and to forget that similar conditions prevailed in many other parts of the country, but it is undeniable that the difference between the 'Old Woodman' Council and the Council of Joseph Chamberlain's time was greater by far than that between the unreformed House of Commons before 1832 and its successor, elected on a broader-

[1] T. Anderton, op. cit. (1900), p. 6.    [2] B.W.P., 7 February 1903.

based franchise. And just as the full effect of the Great Reform Bill of 1832 was not felt until a new type of member was chosen by the constituencies, so the reform of the Birmingham Town Council was a gradual and difficult process, which could not go very far until a new type of councillor was elected by the wards.

The full Council in 1869 consisted of 48 Councillors, 3 for each of the 16 wards, and 16 Aldermen, chosen by the members of the Council for a period of 6 years. In 1891, when Saltley and Balsall Heath were added to the city, the size of the Council increased to 72. The Greater Birmingham created in 1911 had 30 wards and a Council of 120, consisting of 90 Councillors and 30 Aldermen. The Aldermen differed little in character from the Councillors, although one local writer claimed that their 'freedom from the sword of Damocles', which overhung their less venerable neighbours, made them 'less susceptible to the vagaries of popular sentiment and interest, less anxious to press for $\frac{1}{2}d.$ tram fares, or wood paving, the *panem et circenses* of modern Rome: certainly more often on the side of established authority, and less often in a hurry to move amendments'.[1] That statement was made in 1914. Before 1900 the aldermanic system, despite some local criticism, did provide an important element of continuity in Birmingham, which was not unimportant in a body shaped and moulded by the political controversies and cleavages of the day.

Aldermen and Councillors together constituted a sort of local parliament meeting each month. They prided themselves on the fact that they were a parliament, particularly after the opening of the new Council House in 1874. 'Instead of the Town Council being a by-word,' E. V. Hiley said in 1909, 'it has been the pivot upon which the whole life of the community has turned.'[2] The members could feel a real link with Parliament at Westminster too, for as early as 1888 Chamberlain could point out that eleven Mayors of Birmingham had become Members of Parliament, and many ordinary members of the Council as well. Some local personalities with experience of both institutions preferred Birmingham to Westminster. 'I sometimes comfort

---

[1] Norman Chamberlain, 'Municipal Government in Birmingham', in the *Political Quarterly* (1914).

[2] E. V. Hiley, 'Birmingham City Government', in *Birmingham Institutions* (ed. J. H. Muirhead, 1910).

myself', Kenrick said when he was made a Freeman of the City in 1911, 'when I compare our little parliament with the big parliament at Westminster. I compare the briskness of our pace with the slowness or—if I wished to be complimentary—the deliberateness, the tardy progress which characterises the proceedings of the Great Parliament.'[1]

The procedure of the full Council was simple and straightforward. After the formal business of acknowledging communications—such as announcements of gifts, petitions, or statements of changes in the membership of committees—the reports of the committees were taken in succession. Notices of motion concluded the business. The Council went into Committee of the Whole Council for the approval of estimates, the formal making of a rate, or the discussion of a Bill to go before Parliament. The Council as a body had to give its consent to the appointment of all chief officials and subordinates receiving over £300 a year, and to approve of any increases of salary of £50 upwards, any measures necessitating a loan, or any measures involving an expenditure of £100 not in the current year's estimates.

The real work of the Council, far more than in most cities, was carried out at committee level. The committee system had been introduced in the town in 1851 when an important clause in the Improvement Act not only authorized the appointment of committees to deal with problems 'which in the Discretion of the Council should be better regulated and managed by means of such Committees', but also laid it down that 'the Acts of every such Committee shall in case the Council shall so order, but not otherwise, be submitted to the Council for their approval'. The qualification 'but not otherwise' saved long discussion of points of minor importance in full Council and from the start enhanced the responsibility of the committees in their regular tasks. The committees met monthly and were required to report to the Council at least twice each year. Their reports formed the basis of the Council's debates.

When a committee wished to bring a matter before the Council, a report was circulated among members of the Council about a week before the meeting, giving explanations or setting out plans, and the chairman of the committee opened the debate. No member was allowed to speak more than once on any single resolution, except that the chairman had the right of

[1] B.P., 14 July 1911.

reply. There was no rule about the length of speeches, although twenty minutes was the usual period for an opening speaker and ten minutes for the rest. On the eve of the First World War, owing to the long debates which followed the making of Greater Birmingham, the Council adopted the rule of allowing the motion, 'that the question be now put', and this checked long discussions. The change in procedure was a matter of convenience and not of discipline, for there had never been any attempts at obstruction, talking against time, or turning the rules of procedure into weapons of political warfare, as had been the case in the House of Commons.

The chairman of the Council was the Mayor, after 1896 the Lord Mayor. He was elected each year on 9 November by the Aldermen and Councillors, and could if desired be re-elected for a second year. Between 1870 and 1899 thirteen Mayors served for one year, four for two years, and three for three years.

The Mayor was more than the chairman of the Council. He attended each meeting of the committees of the Council, and either he or later the Deputy Mayor was chairman of the General Purposes Committee. He was thus the chief co-ordinating influence in the Council's work. He alone of officials and members was entitled to attend all meetings of committees, and could thus act as a carrier of information, an adviser, and if need be a mediator or a referee. If he were a man with a dominating presence, like Chamberlain, he could become a sort of Prime Minister, but by 1914 one factor alone, the increasing complexity of the Council's work, made this role a difficult one to assume. Furthermore the increase in the number of his official engagements made it impossible for him to engage in continuous committee work.

The successful development of the committee system was by far the most important feature of the constitutional history of Birmingham between 1865 and 1914. 'Every effort is made to ensure the very best results from it', it was said in 1896. 'No precedents require the appointment of old members even to important committees, and a new member, known to be capable and interested in some special work, has no difficulty in obtaining an assignment that may enable him to do his best. But in practice the experienced men are re-appointed.'[1] Wise chairmen, like

---

[1] *B.M.*, 31 October 1896, referring to an article by G. F. Parker in the *Century Magazine*, 'An Object Lesson in Municipal Government'.

William Kenrick of the Art Committee and his cousin George, the Chairman of the Education Committee after 1902, provided a deep experience and an essential continuity in local administration.

Although the committee system had been introduced in 1851, it underwent considerable changes between 1869 and 1914. In 1869 there were thirteen committees—Baths and Parks; Estates and Buildings; Finance, Rate, and Appeal; Markets and Fairs; Borough Inspection; Public Works; Watch; Lunatic Asylum; Burial Board; Free Libraries; Industrial School; Grammar School; and, most important of all, General Purposes. The General Purposes Committee was already beginning to act as a co-ordinating committee of the whole Council. It was required 'to attend to all business and matters referred to it by the Council, of a general character, not entrusted to the various other committees, and to suggest to the Council, from time to time, any new business which, in its opinion, is important to the public interest'.

As early as 1869 the committees sometimes employed sub-committees to deal with specific problems. Delegation of work went down to the lowest levels. The Public Works Committee, for instance, with its varied functions and responsibilities, had three sub-committees concerned with Finance and Stores, Sewage and Night Soil (passed over first to the Sewage Committee and then after 1876 to the Health Committee), and Lamps and Paving. All these tasks, which involved personal inspection of work and visiting of sites, were well suited to small sub-committees of three or four. The Markets and Fairs Committee, as well as having sub-committees to deal with the General Market and Smithfield, had a special sub-committee to deal with Weights and Measures. Both the Finance Committee and the General Purposes Committee had important sub-committees to deal with the examination of accounts.

With the exception of Public Works (12), Watch (12), Free Libraries (12), and General Purposes, which had one member from each of the other committees and the Mayor as chairman, each of the committees until 1911 had eight members. The Free Libraries Committee and the Art Gallery Committee differed from the rest in that they included co-opted members. The idea of co-option met with fierce opposition when it was first mooted in 1860, Alderman Hawkes, one of the most influential men on the Council before Chamberlain, arguing that 'if the Council votes its own incompetency for this duty, it will degrade itself in the eyes of those who sent it here'. Co-option was carried none the less, amid considerable tumult, by thirty-two votes to seventeen. It was frequently attacked again before 1914, but it proved such a useful method of augmenting the experience and talents of the Council that it was difficult to dispense with it.

The committee system of 1869 was merely the primitive shell out of which highly developed city government developed. The civic gospel of the 70's made new trading committees essential, and the Water and Gas Committees were set up. With the addition of the Improvement Committee and the substitution of the Public Health Committee for the older Borough Inspection Committee, there were sixteen committees at work when Joseph Chamberlain retired from the Council in 1880. The development of the later trading concerns of Electric Supply and Tramways added two new committees, and by 1914 there were other important changes bringing the total number up to twenty-one. The most important additions were Education, Town Planning, and Distress. The Education Committee came into existence as a result of the Education Act of 1902, abolishing the old School Board. The Town Planning and Distress Committees showed Birmingham's willingness to explore new problems of social policy. Local interest in town planning ante-dated the Town-Planning Act of 1909, which gave the city limited but useful powers, and the committee led the way. The Distress Committee was appointed under a permissive Act, the Unemployed Workmen Act of 1905.

The Education and Distress Committees relied like the Free Libraries and Art Gallery Committees on the help of members drawn from outside the Council, and in the case of the Distress Committee, the co-opted members were in the majority. The Education Committee, constituted under a scheme subject to the approval of the Board of Education, consisted in 1914 of thirty members of the Council, fifteen persons of experience in education (of whom seven had to be women), and one representative nominated by various local bodies—the University, the Grammar School, the Birmingham Church Education Society, the Birmingham Roman Catholic School Association, the Midland Institute, the National Union of Teachers, and the Trades

Council. The Distress Committee included eighteen members of the Council, thirteen representatives of the Birmingham Guardians, and eight co-opted members from local voluntary relief societies, the most important of which was the Birmingham City Aid Society set up in 1906. In the case of both of these committees, the principle of co-option was important not only because it brought in men of experience and knowledge, but also because it softened the line of demarcation between private and public bodies and between official and voluntary workers, an important task in a society where much was still left to local effort and where the main targets of social advance were imperfectly defined. As early as 1890 Julian Ralph had claimed that the plan of local government in the city was 'to distribute the power among as many persons as possible, even outside the Council, to interest and make responsible as many citizens as possible'.[1] Between 1900 and 1914 this ideal was put into practice on a far larger scale than ever before.

By 1914 the committee system was extremely highly organized. The extension of the city itself enlarged the size of the committees and at the same time led to longer debates in the Council and closer scrutiny of committee reports. In the last year of the smaller Council, fourteen meetings were held, with a total duration of just over thirty-four hours: in the first year of the enlarged Council twenty-one meetings took place, lasting over ninety-one hours. Yet, despite this increased activity, the Council apparently did not cease to repose confidence in its committees.[2]

There were four distinct types of committee. The first group consisted of those committees mainly concerned with carrying out the various Public Health Acts—Baths and Wash-houses, Lighting, Markets and Fairs, Parks, Health and Housing, Public Works, and Town Planning. These were all environmental committees, some of them going back to 1851, with the services which they offered going back even earlier. The second group consisted of committees deriving their powers from separate Acts of Parliament, whether compulsory or permissive—Watch, Lunatic Asylums, Pensions, Education, Free Libraries, Distress, and Museum and Art Gallery. This group catered for some tasks which were very old, such as Watch, and some which

[1] J. Ralph, loc. cit.
[2] C. A. Vince, *History of the Corporation of Birmingham*, vol. iv (1923), p. 3.

represented the latest moves in civic policy, such as Distress. The third group consisted of trading committees—Electric Supply, Gas, Tramways, and Water. In an industrial community like Birmingham, membership of these committees was more eagerly sought after than that of any of the others.

The fourth group consisted of what might be called co-ordinating committees—Finance, General Purposes, and Estates. The Estates Committee, the main business of which was Allotments, Cemeteries, and the collection of Corporation rents, dealt with all sites or houses under the control of any of the other committees, for which they ceased to have any use. If no other committee wanted the site, the Estates Committee tried to sell it. The General Purposes Committee collected under its wing all matters, other than financial, not handled by other committees. It dealt with problems of town planning, for instance, before the setting up of the Town Planning Committee. It considered special matters of temporary importance, such as the building of the Council House and its subsequent extension. It prepared private Bills and issued general instructions to committees. Finally it provided a co-ordinating apparatus for such general matters as Council motor-cars and, more important, labour questions. After the successful implementation of the Greater Birmingham Scheme, a special sub-committee of the General Purposes Committee investigated all problems concerning the number and composition of committees, and worked out the scheme whereby each member of the Council was expected to serve on two committees.

The Finance Committee was the keystone of the whole arch. The decision to appoint a Finance Committee, divorced from the administration of separate services, had been taken long before the need for independent control was generally recognized by local authorities, and long before the amounts spent by the Council were large enough to make careful vigilance essential. By Joseph Chamberlain's time, Birmingham could boast that it had the revenues—and the commitments—of a small continental state.[1]

The cardinal principles of the city's financial policy were laid down in his time—that capital expenditure should be defrayed out of moneys borrowed by the issue of stock or by mortgages, these constituting a prior charge on all the property of the

[1] *A Short History of the Passing of the Birmingham Corporation Gas Act* (1875).

Corporation and on its rates (the first issue of stock was made in 1881); and that all other expenditure should be defrayed out of the revenues of the Corporation, that is to say, from profits of trading undertakings, grants from the Exchequer, rents of Corporation properties, charges for special services, and rates levied on occupiers of property; that the revenue-producing undertakings, with the exception of Water, should always be self-supporting; that the accounts of the separate departments should be kept quite distinct; and that each specific new investment should be provided with a sinking fund that would extinguish the debt within a prescribed period. The emphasis on borrowing, although it was often criticized, meant that the cost of ambitious schemes did not fall on one year's rates, and thus it prevented undue fluctuations in rates and allowed the charge to fall partly on those who would benefit from it in later years.

As far as financial control was concerned, until 1912 the practice was for each committee to send to the Finance Committee its estimate of the income and expenditure for the ensuing year. From these individual estimates the Finance Committee made up the Council's total estimates for the year and brought them up before the Council. Occasionally the chairman of the Finance Committee would personally suggest to the chairman of a committee the advisability of cutting down his estimates, generally arranged by agreement. Otherwise, within its broad framework, the Finance Committee had no further influence on the general policy of the Council.

With the realization of the Greater Birmingham Scheme, new principles were introduced into city finance, and the powers of the Finance Committee were increased. As regards estimates, a Consultative Committee of the Chairmen of the chief spending committees was constituted, to be consulted formally by the Finance Committee as to the final form of the estimates. Still more important was the instruction to the Finance Committee 'to consider the financial bearings of proposals made by committees, which might involve new loans or income and expenditure other than that provided for in the current rate estimates'. After 1912 every such proposal in a committee's report was accompanied by a report of the Finance Committee, which not only set out how much the scheme would cost, then and later on, but also offered an expression of opinion as to whether it was extravagant or not. In addition the Council attempted to restrict expenditure by deciding neither to apply for a loan of less than £500 nor to allow the grouping together of a number of lesser items with a loan to cover them all.

Behind the committees was the permanent staff. The Finance Committee could not have carried out its work but for the assistance of a growing City Treasurer's Department. The General Purposes Committee would have been paralysed in its task of co-ordination had it not included the Town Clerk, who also attended one or two other committees, and any of them if specially required. The administrative departments grew in size and scope. The City Treasurer's Department, under the direction of W. R. Hughes, who in 1867 was appointed to the post at the age of thirty-seven, in face of fierce competition, grew in numbers from a book-keeper and a youth in 1867 to a Deputy Treasurer and about twenty clerks in 1898, when Hughes retired. The Town Clerk's Department was expanded and reconstructed. Until Hayes became Town Clerk, in 1868, the Town Clerks carried on their own business as solicitors, but it was arranged with him that he should devote himself exclusively to the services of the borough, his clerks and office expenses being paid by the Council. By the end of the century his department contained eight committee clerks, who acted as clerks for the various city committees, as well as a Deputy Town Clerk, a Chief Clerk, and two Assistant Solicitors, the whole office acting as a co-ordinating influence on the legal and constitutional side of the city's work just as the Treasurer's Department did on the financial side.

If the committees provided the policy-making core of the Council, the permanent staff of officials provided continuity of administration. In the Council, as well as in private industry, Birmingham was passing into a managerial age by the beginning of the twentieth century.[1] From their offices the permanent staff of officials became increasingly responsible for the day-to-day work of the departments, the trading departments included. Along with the chairmen of the committees, who often held their chairmanships for very long periods, they provided an element of continuity in the development of the city. Their increasing importance did not go unchallenged. There were sometimes complaints that officials in the trading departments lacked the sense of competitive enterprise, and were unsuited for the control

[1] See above, p. 61.

of large concerns. From the opposite angle there were occasional complaints that the city did not pay sufficiently large salaries to secure the best men, although it was generally acknowledged that the early introduction of a superannuation scheme on the Liverpool model in 1897 was a useful step to attract younger men from outside. The growth of local administrative services must necessarily be described more in terms of trends than in terms of personalities, but Birmingham was fortunate in most of its officials, and recognized their importance from the early days of Birmingham's civic gospel. When Chamberlain carried through the purchase of the gas and water-works, he told the Council that if they were not prepared to be generous in their salaries to their experts, they had better not enter upon a policy of municipal ownership. In 1897, in a speech at Glasgow, he argued that if ever corruption crept into the cities of Great Britain, it would be when the higher officials were paid less and the lower employees more than the market value of their services.[1] This statement summed up Birmingham's municipal experience.

The role of the officials was limited to the working out of satisfactory administrative methods. When Hughes became City Treasurer, the arrangement of civic accounts was in a chaotic state. There were two books of accounts, called respectively the White Book and the Yellow Book, each made up to different dates and containing overlapping matter. In 1870 Hughes thoroughly revised the system of accounts, and substituted one Blue Book. Later he introduced a very effective system for distinguishing the account books, cheques, and receipts of the various Corporation departments by binding them in distinctive colours—the Borough Fund Account, for instance, being bound and printed in black, the Gas Department in blue, the Water Department in violet, and so on. The city 'blue books', presenting the general accounts, increased from being pamphlets to large volumes. Yet despite these essential reforms, the control of financial policy lay in the hands of committee members, particularly brilliant chairmen like Powell Williams, so that when in 1900 the Town Clerk, E. O. Smith, was asked by the House of Commons Committee on Municipal Trading to state the City Treasurer's powers, he replied: 'The treasurer of a borough has no duty except to pay on the orders of three members of the

---

[1] *Local Government Journal*, 13 November 1897.

Council, countersigned by the Town Clerk . . . the treasurer is a mere machine as regards finance.'[1]

The 'machine' was indispensable throughout the whole of city administration, and if the permanent officials did not always go uncriticized in the early years of the twentieth century, neither did the councillors themselves. There were natural enough complaints in some quarters that the standard of the Council had deteriorated in comparison with the golden age of the 1870's. *The Times* doubted in 1902—a year when the Birmingham Council was in danger for the first time of being counted out— whether the high standard of efficiency had been maintained. It pointed out that many of the leading merchants and others carrying on business in Birmingham no longer lived within the city boundaries, and consequently did not feel the same degree of concern for local affairs as before. 'There is also a disposition to think', it went on, 'that the same degree of credit can no longer be got out of local administration by the leisured or aspiring citizen, as was the case especially in Birmingham a few years ago.' On the other hand, 'there seems to be an in- creasing desire on the part of small manufacturers, professional men, especially solicitors, tradesmen and others, to secure municipal honours. . . . For rising professional or business men desirous of keeping their names before the public, a seat on the Town Council is found to be a very practical way of achieving local fame.'[2]

*The Times*'s attack was mixed up with a partisan attempt in 1902 to pit Council and people in opposition to each other. In December 1901 the General Purposes Committee had prepared a draft General Powers Bill, which was accepted unanimously, with minor adjustments, by the Council. The statutory Town's Meeting, however, to which the Bill had to be referred, rejected it on a show of hands, and a subsequent three-day poll of rate- payers defeated it by 15,419 votes (6,982 voters) to 2,097 votes (1,461 voters). 'This was the most serious rebuff ever inflicted on the Council by its constituents.'[3] The Consolidation Bill of 1883, which had been bitterly opposed, had been approved by the ratepayers, although only by a small majority. The causes of the rebuff were mixed, but they reflected a considerable volume of criticism of the Council as such. The Council had to take great

---

[1] Committee on Municipal Trading, *Commons Papers* (1900), vii. 183, Q. 1819–20.
[2] *The Times*, 25 September 1902.     [3] C. A. Vince, op. cit., vol. iv, p. 21.

care with its redrafting of the Bill in 1903, and it was finally accepted at a Town's Meeting and after a ratepayers' poll.

The *Birmingham Mail* returned to the question four years later. 'Has the personnel of the Birmingham City Council deteriorated? This is a question which is frequently asked among all classes of citizens. The answer is invariably that there is a deterioration, and that the process has been going on steadily for some years.' It suggested that the unfavourable verdict was unfair, because it was based on a comparison of the average men of the 1900's with the great men of the 1870's. In point of fact, it went on, 'during Mr. Chamberlain's regime, the proportion of men (to say the least of it) of distinctly moderate calibre was much larger than is generally imagined'. What had happened since the 1870's was not a decline in civic virtue or in ordinary council membership, but in leadership. 'Given another leader of great personality and influence, the old reputation of the Council would be speedily restored. Mr. Chamberlain's great success, of course, lay largely in his genius for electing the right men to do the work.'

TABLE I. *Functional Composition of the Council*

|  | *1865–6* | *1875–6* | *1885–6* | *1895–6* | *1905–6* |
|---|---|---|---|---|---|
| Gentlemen | 6 | 9 | 14 | 6 | 7 |
| Manufacturers | 23 | 26 | 20 | 29 | 25 |
| Tradesmen | 10 | 5 | 7 | 10 | 5 |
| Banking, Commerce, Merchanting | 15 | 16 | 8 | 7 | 13 |
| Professional | 8 | 5 | 12 | 16 | 16 |
| Working men | 2 | 3 | 3 | 4 | 6 |
| Totals | 64 | 64 | 64 | 72 | 72 |

Certainly down to 1914 the same social groups retained control of the Council. Business men, particularly manufacturers, predominated, but they tended to join the Council later, or even after retirement. The reason was not far to seek. 'A quarter of a century ago the manufacturer made his money more easily than his successor of today. Competition is keener: the business man works longer hours, often his profits are smaller, and he does not consolidate his position at such an early age.'[1] For some younger men, motoring and golf were taking the place of the local politics of their fathers' time. As a counterbalancing influence it was

[1] *B.M.*, 27 April 1907.

true that the number of professional men on the Council had greatly increased, but the day of large numbers of 'working men' councillors was yet to come, and although the first woman was elected to the Council in 1911, the day of large numbers of women councillors is still to come. On the eve of the First World War the Council consisted of 42 manufacturers, 5 merchants, 14 lawyers, 13 other professional men, 15 retailers, 10 working men, 5 builders, 2 farmers, 2 women, and 12 others of miscellaneous occupations. This was the full Council of Greater Birmingham. The changes in the smaller Council in the forty years after 1865 are summarized in the table opposite.

Perhaps before 1900 a religious and kinship analysis would be more revealing than a functional analysis, for the Council still to a great extent relied in its municipal life on the service of families and on the inspiration of nonconformity, particularly on the driving force of Unitarians and the conscientious service of Quakers. Between 1872 and 1900 Quakers and Unitarians provided more Mayors of the city than any other two bodies, and in 1900, according to one estimate, accounted for one-quarter of the seats on the Council. They set a standard of diligence which was remarkable, as Vince showed from a study of the attendance statistics of members from 1885 to 1899. In no year was the percentage of attendance to summons less than 81.[1]

In the light of these figures and of other evidence it is difficult to accept the thesis that the calibre of the Council deteriorated between 1877 and 1900. What had occurred, however, was a loss of faith in an adventurous policy of civic development. Politics became more cautious and horizons narrowed. The reasons for the change in atmosphere were in large measure financial. Even in Chamberlain's time there was an undercurrent of criticism of the policy of large-scale spending and borrowing.

Unless there was a determination on the part of the Town Council and its Liberal majority, to stop capital expenditure (argued a Liberal councillor on the eve of the split in 1886), the rates would go up to an extent that Birmingham shopkeepers and traders could not stand . . . the expenditure meant a larger outlay year by year for interest and for sinking fund than the town could afford. Money had been spent in the Council to an extent that was simply appalling. He had all along disapproved of it.[2]

[1] C. A. Vince, op. cit., vol. iii, p. 398.    [2] B.P., 20 January 1886.

These cries became more common during periods of trade recession, and as government taxation increased. They were affected, too, by the greater financial stringency, which raised the cost of borrowing in the late 1890's. The Corporation had been fortunate that the civic gospel had been implemented during a period when money was cheap. From 1881, the year of the first issue of Corporation Stock, to 1897 the rate of interest fell steadily from 3½ to 2½ per cent. The Water Stock of 1898 and of 1902 was offered at a higher rate of interest, and the second issue even then was only just successful. From 1902 to 1914 no favourable opportunity for floating new stock presented itself, and although powers were obtained for raising money by means of bills, this sort of borrowing proved uneconomical and it was discontinued after a short experiment between 1904 and 1907, although taken up again on a small scale in 1914.

While financial stringency curbed the rate of investment, the organized pressure of ratepayers modified civic policy. In 1907, for instance, ratepayers were strong enough to defeat the proposals of the Public Works Committee to construct a new thoroughfare from Paradise Street to Broad Street and to embark upon a new central demolition scheme, which would have added ½d. in the £ to the yearly rates. It was an attractive scheme from a planning point of view. There had long been complaints that Birmingham lacked worthy direct thoroughfares linking the middle of the city with the open country. As the roads in, like the Hagley Road or the Bristol Road, approached the heart of Birmingham, they either lost themselves in an intricate maze of narrow and tortuous streets, or stopped short at abrupt corners. It was said by critics that Birmingham had only two important streets, and that neither of them led anywhere. The Paradise Street scheme was a sensible attempt to deal with this problem, but there was much local opposition, not only from shopkeepers directly affected, but also from ratepayers in general. On the day that the Council considered the report of its committee, the streets were packed with sandwich-men, and the strangers' gallery thronged by angry ratepayers protesting against 'reckless expenditure'. In face of this barrage, the Council turned down the Committee's proposals by forty votes to eighteen. 'Should the Council with the city's present obligations and future necessities indulge in what was largely in the nature of

PLATE XXIII

The Council in Session, 1903

PLATE XXIV

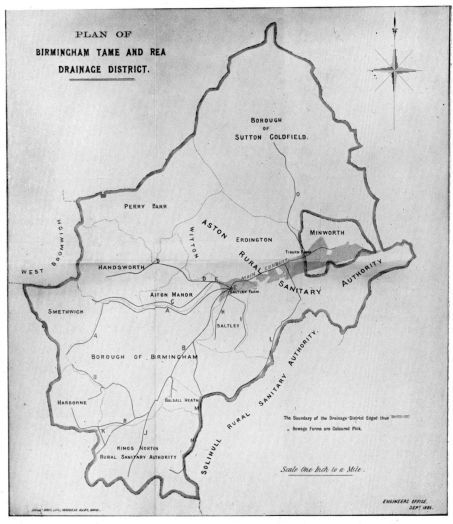

The Birmingham Tame and Rea Drainage District, 1886

a luxury?' the main opponent of the scheme asked,[1] while a correspondent of the *Birmingham Post* complained that he knew dozens besides himself crippled beyond endurance by the past few years of municipal extravagance.[2] The Chamber of Commerce urged that the city had reached its taxable limit, and pointed not only to the increase in rates, but also to the sharp rise in national taxation. Neville Chamberlain supported the scheme on exactly the same grounds as his father would have done, and said that the present generation was just as capable of bearing the burden as their fathers had been, while Chance argued that Birmingham could not afford to stagnate or 'to lapse into the languid indifference of the pre-Chamberlain era',[3] but the voice of 1907 was not that of the civic reformer but of the unknown ratepayer. 'One must cut one's coat according to the cloth at one's disposal. My grandfather did not spend five-twelfths of his income for my benefit, and I for one would strongly object to paying 8s. 4d. in the £ rates for the benefit of posterity.'[4]

It was the gospel of Greater Birmingham which transformed this cautious and negative attitude into a positive crusade to make Birmingham a worthy Second City of the Empire. Quite apart from the momentum of the cause itself, and the energies it liberated, the Greater Birmingham scheme brought back into the turmoil of city politics many men who were really citizens of Birmingham at heart, but who had been forced into the backwaters of suburban life. It could not bring them all back, for things had changed irrevocably. Greater Birmingham was more than the vigorous, relatively small community of the later nineteenth century writ large. It was a new phenomenon, a centre of a 'conurbation', to use Patrick Geddes's now familiar word. By its size it lost some of the intimacy and colour of Birmingham politics in the Chamberlain era, and its problems were bigger, and needed more planning, than those of 'the best-governed city in the world'. Though a civic gospel was still needed, or at least a civic loyalty, which would knit men together into one community, a gospel by itself would not have been enough. And the sources of inspiration required more and more to be canalized in expert channels, if life was to run smoothly and progress be maintained.

[1] *Birmingham Mercury*, 20 July 1907.    [2] *B.P.*, 6 April 1907.
[3] *B.M.*, 10 July, 12 July 1907.    [4] *B.P.*, 13 July 1907.

## VIII

A new body, which reflected both the increased importance of expert solutions to technical problems and the need for administering not only Birmingham but the region around it, was the Birmingham, Tame, and Rea District Drainage Board, set up in 1877.

In 1871 the Birmingham Town Council appointed a Sewage Inquiry Committee to report on the best way of disposing of the sewage of the borough. There was widespread discontent with the Public Works Committee, which was the weakest link in the civic structure before Chamberlain and his friends raised the cry of reform. As early as 1865 there had been an attempt to take the sewage question out of the hands of the Public Works Committee. Sewage, which today is treated as a technical question for specialists, was then regarded as a political question both by Councillors and by men in the street. The Sewage Inquiry Committee reported that, if possible with Government co-operation, a Drainage Commission should be founded, elected by ratepayers of the whole district. It would provide a joint organization for all the local authorities whose drainage system linked up with the River Tame.

In 1865 it would have been necessary to have a local Act to carry this proposal, an Act which would have been costly to promote and doubtful in its result. Just as the Artisans' Dwellings Act proved invaluable in affording opportunities to the city to embark upon its scheme of local improvement, so the Public Health Act of 1875 offered a solution of the sanitary question. Section 279 provided that where it appeared that it would be to the advantage of interested local authorities to create a United District for specified sanitary purposes, the Local Government Board might by Provisional Order form such a District. For the first time the principle of co-operation between authorities for the administration of a particular service had been given statutory recognition.

In consequence, a meeting of local authorities was convened in March 1876 by the Sewage Committee of Birmingham 'for the purpose of obtaining the foundation of a United District'. Chamberlain was in the chair. A joint committee was set up to manage a drainage area of 34,343 acres, the Local Government Board and Parliament gave their blessings, and the Board began to operate in 1877. At first it had two *ex-officio* and twenty other members, of which Birmingham itself sent twelve, a working majority, although not proportionate to the share of the town in the cost of running the undertaking. Birmingham accounted for most of the population of the district, but only one-quarter of the area. The other authorities represented were Aston Manor, Balsall Heath, Handsworth, Harborne, Saltley, Smethwick, Aston Union, King's Norton Union, and West Bromwich Union. Of these authorities some subsequently joined the city, either in 1891 or in 1911, while other new authorities have been added since.

The Board had plenty to do, particularly to add to the various existing sewage plants and estates of the constituent authorities by acquiring land for its own works. It received sanction from the Local Government Board to borrow £164,000 to pay for the works, the land taken over, and new constructions, and it proceeded to consider the best methods of treatment and disposal of the sewage of the combined districts. The Saltley sewage works, which already existed in 1877, were extended and modernized, and new sewers designed, including one in 1881 about 6¼ miles in length between Sparkbrook and Ashold, partly in tunnel near Hodge Hill Common and in syphon under the River Tame. In 1897, with increasing population, another £400,000 scheme was authorized by Act of Parliament. The total acreage of the works, which had been as little as 260 acres in 1877, rose to 1,792 acres by 1895, and to over 2,000 acres in the new century.[1]

In the early stages of the Drainage Board, a large sewage farm was run under very high cultivation, and yielded rich crops, but in 1898 a joint report by Professor Dewar, the scientist, and Hawksley, Consulting Engineer to the Board, recommended that simple experimental filters should be constructed to test the expediency of adopting artificial filtration. The death-knell of the sewage farm had been rung, and soon afterwards the system of treatment of sewage in bacterial filters instead of by irrigation was adopted. In subsequent years Watson, Engineer to the Board, designed and carried out a complete system of treatment by bacteriological processes. The Board was able as a result of these technical improvements to sell and lease large parcels of land for industrial purposes and farm holdings. The farming operations of the Board, which Ralph had described as more perfect than those in any other city, were abandoned; and

---

[1] J. D. Watson, *The Works of the Birmingham, Tame, and Rea District Drainage Board* (1912).

bacteria filter-beds took their place. The new methods were in advance of those adopted in most other cities, particularly in the use of waste products. It proved possible, for instance, to work a 150-horse-power internal combustion engine generating electricity by sludge gas collected in concrete containers, which floated on the surface of the sludge-digestion tanks.

The technical improvements introduced by the Drainage Board illustrate the scientific basis of twentieth-century city management, but the achievement of the Board had wider implications than the discovery of new techniques. The Board was a model of co-operation between local authorities. It emerged successfully from many complicated legal proceedings, and it maintained its independence in face of frequent attempts by some of the Birmingham Councillors to take over its duties. Fifty years after its formation, Neville Chamberlain wrote that it had set the standard for 'harmonious and successful co-operation between adjacent local authorities, widely dissimilar in size, wealth and population, but working together for common interests and with common benefits to all concerned'.[1] It did indeed point forward to the future—to the integrated development of Birmingham and its region in the interests of a wider community. The extent to which the community was growing can best be understood by a more detailed study of the background of the Greater Birmingham Act of 1911.

[1] City of Birmingham, *Birmingham and its Civic Managers* (1928), p. 144.

# V

## GREATER BIRMINGHAM

### I

By the early years of the nineteenth century, Birmingham had fully emerged as the leading industrial and commercial centre of a region. While throughout the nineteenth century the town itself was expanding and changing from 'a great village' into a city of suburbs, its relations with the surrounding region were never static. It not only maintained its position as a financial and trading metropolis, but also attracted increasing numbers of visitors as a centre of amenities and political and social activities. It was swallowing up to an increasing extent the life of the area around the town, so that in 1870 a local writer could describe how each year with new expansion 'the neighbouring hamlets are approached by Birmingham's streets and ere long will merge in her arms . . . the great and multitudinous assemblage of one people—one vast manufacturing community—one Birmingham'.[1]

But the story of the city growth is less simple than the mere filling in of unused spaces on the map. Indeed, many of the spaces were left unfilled. There is no one single factor which explains the spreading out of the city. One form of expansion— new industrial development—was similar to that of the early nineteenth century. New factories, often on a scale unknown in the older Birmingham, attracted new settlement. Between 1861 and 1871, for example, the increase in the population of Witton can be attributed to the establishment of a large works for the manufacture of fog-signals and cartridges, that of Northfield to the setting up of metal works. There were four main lines of industrial expansion—to the north-west, beyond Ladywood; to the south and south-west around Selly Oak and Stirchley and eventually Bournville, which grew up around Cadbury's factory after it had moved out of the city in 1879; to the south-east along the Warwick Canal and the Birmingham–Oxford Railway, the Birmingham Small Arms Company's factory, built at Small Heath in 1861, acting as a magnet; and to the north-east along the line of the Fazeley Canal to Aston and

[1] L. W. Clarke, *The History of Birmingham* (1870), MS., p. 1.

the Rea valley, the two 'tongues' of development meeting at Salford Bridge.

In these new waves of industrialization, transport facilities played an important part. There were good railway and canal facilities which opened up new areas. Saltley, for instance, was conveniently placed in relation to both the Birmingham and Derby and the Birmingham and Coventry lines, and to both the

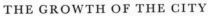

THE GROWTH OF THE CITY

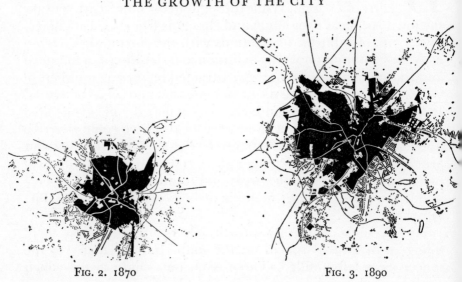

FIG. 2. 1870                              FIG. 3. 1890

Grand Junction and the Fazeley Canals. Another extremely important consideration was cheapness of sites for new industrial concerns. The wastes of Birmingham Heath to the north-west and of the hitherto undrained Rea valley were very attractive from this point of view.

When the process of industrialization begins in completely virgin territory, it produces mushroom towns. When it develops on the fringe of an earlier agglomeration, it sets up a cycle of changes, frequently altering, as in the case of Birmingham, the balance of homes and workshops and the geography of amenities and services. In short, it changes the character of the city rather than adds cumulatively to existing features and problems. The new Birmingham of the twentieth century was more than the old town of the nineteenth century writ large: it was a different sort of social unit from the old.

Industrialization was only one form of growth. In addition

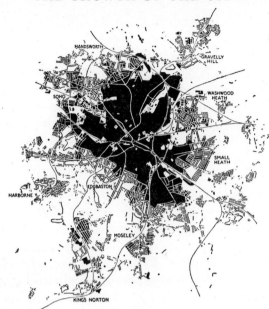

FIG. 4. 1918

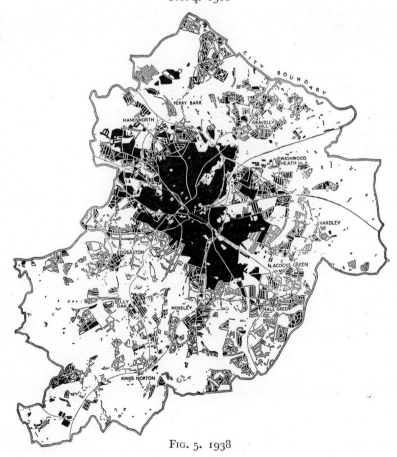

FIG. 5. 1938

there was continual overspilling of the old central city core, the gradual lapping up of adjacent areas.

Districts hardly more than a mile or so from the centre of the city (wrote a Birmingham man in 1900), which in my boyhood were fields and meadows are now laid out into streets and covered with houses and shops. Indeed I sometimes feel very aged when I look upon places where as a boy I went fishing for small fry, and now find the river that afforded me such juvenile sport is, owing to the enhanced value of land, compressed into the dimensions of a fair-sized gutter, with houses and small factories closely packed on its margin covering every foot of ground.[1]

A similar nostalgia can be traced in the comments of other Birmingham men of the late nineteenth and early twentieth centuries on the transformation of their city environment.

Along with overspilling and the building of houses to serve the new industrial areas—often, like those at Sparkbrook, 'rows and rows of anaemic looking houses, depressingly uniform in pattern, effacing the picturesque delights of lane and meadow'—went the deliberate attempt to escape the noise and smoke of Birmingham itself, first by business men and then by working men. As early as 1797 an observer had declared that 'Birmingham is not a place a gentleman would chuse to make a residence. Its continual noise and smoke prevent it from being desirable in that respect',[2] and the more wealthy local manufacturers and merchants were sometimes beginning to live a mile or two away. By 1860 business men were moving farther and farther from the centre. They would settle in a suburb, as they settled in Yardley from 1861 to 1871, and then move out again as the city expanded, leaving better-paid working men to come in. Many factors increased the pace of change in the last quarter of the nineteenth century. Improved transport, a reduction in working hours, a rise in real incomes, and an upward movement in central land values all extended the area of migration. There were thus ripples of expansion, farther and farther away from the city core. The way was prepared for the large-scale twentieth-century separation of homes and work, perhaps the most important social feature of our age, so that daily journeys provide a new framework for routine living.

The pace of change varied in different areas around the city: in some cases it was spectacular. Within the brief space of a

[1] T. Anderton, *A Tale of One City* (1900), pp. 112–13.
[2] *A Brief History of Birmingham* (1797), p. 4.

generation Small Heath, for example, changed from a scattered hamlet into a town as big as the Oxford or Worcester of its day. As late as the 1860's it really was a heath, dotted with stray cottages and farms. The building of the B.S.A. factory and the opening of Victoria Park in 1879 encouraged rapid urbanization, and the whole area was swallowed up in built-up Birmingham. As late as 1860 there were only three or four 'bus' journeys into Birmingham each day from the Malt Shovel Inn with its little flat windows and swing sign: by 1900, it was in direct and regular contact with the city.

The story of Handsworth is equally striking. Even though James Watt lived in Heathfield Hall and Matthew Boulton constructed his factory there 'on one of the most barren commons in England', Handsworth grew slowly in the nineteenth century. At the top of Soho Hill there were some large and important residences, occupied by Birmingham business men, who regarded this part of Handsworth as being right out in the country. Until the setting up of the Local Board there was no properly constructed sewer in the district. The subsequent growth was rapid, the population of Handsworth increasing from about 11,000 in 1861 to 70,000 in 1911. The oldest inhabitant could recall in 1903 that in his youth there was hardly a single house on the main road and that Handsworth Wood had rivalled Sutton Park, but bricks and mortar had swept away most of the survivals of the past.

The growth of the residential areas was often equally striking. In the middle of the nineteenth century, Moseley was a pretty little village with a green, low-roofed old-fashioned houses, and a parish church tower dominating the landscape. It changed from a village into an exclusive suburb with large villas of red brick, regular train services into Birmingham, and trams. Erdington to the north-east began to develop into a residential area from the opening of the Sutton Railway Line in 1862. At the 1881 Census its population was still only 2,599. By 1891 it had risen to 9,629. In the next ten years it had increased to 16,368, and when it was absorbed in the Greater Birmingham of 1911 it had a population of 32,500.

Many of the residential areas changed in character. Acock's Green and Olton were comfortable residential areas with semi-detached villas and winding lanes until at the beginning of the twentieth century small householders for the first time gained control of the area. The wealthy residents were moving farther out. 'Like the Arab', wrote one local newspaper, 'they are folding their tents and stealing silently away in the direction of Knowle or Solihull, where the octopus tentacles of expanding Birmingham are as yet in the distance. Silently and without any show of ostentation a little revolution is in progress.'[1] The revolution had begun in 1878 when the Widney Manor and Dorridge Park estates at Knowle, belonging to G. F. Muntz, were laid out for the building of villa residences, and the Great Western Railway arranged special express trains from Knowle not only to Birmingham but also to Paddington.[2]

If the motor-car was the most important factor determining the limits of the outer migration of the business man, the tram and the bicycle were the chief agencies which enabled the working man to live farther from his work. From the 1860's onwards the tramway systems spread outwards from the centre of Birmingham, following the long ribbons of settlement and encouraging workers to push out farther to the terminal points. Penny fares were introduced by 1890. The opening up of Yardley, one of the first suburbs to attract business men, owed much to the extension of the tram service from Small Heath to the Swan Hotel, which brought along a more differentiated population. Some places resented the intrusion of the tramway, Edgbaston in particular, and each new development led to renewed fear and anxiety. One of the elements in the public opposition to the General Powers Bill of 1902 was the Edgbaston protest against clauses authorizing the laying of tramways there, and even though the clauses were dropped in the 1903 Bill, fear persisted. 'Whisper it quietly, lest Edgbaston may hear', commented a local paper in 1903, but 'Harborne is hankering after tram lines from the city.'

As the services developed, the distribution of Birmingham's population changed. From 1896 to 1911, the number of occupied houses in the twelve innermost wards of Birmingham fell by $9\frac{1}{2}$ per cent., while the number in the six outer wards rose by nearly 30 per cent.

As the city grew in size, two problems loomed larger than the rest—first, the adaptation of the anachronistic structure of local government to meet the requirements of the enormous area of Greater Birmingham; and second, the control of the direction of

[1] B.M., 26 November 1903.      [2] B.P., 23 May 1878.

the process of expansion itself, the attempt to plan growth rather than to leave it haphazard. Neither problem has reached any final solution, although without the successful implementation of the Greater Birmingham Scheme in 1911 it would have been impossible effectively to plan at all. A new administrative framework was required, and there were men big enough to secure it.

II

The boundaries of the borough of Birmingham even in 1880 were far from coterminous with the natural drainage area or the 'true lines' of Birmingham population. 'Balsall Heath, and the suburban district beyond it, Saltley and Washwood Heath, a great part of the populous manor of Aston, Smethwick, and Handsworth,' wrote a local journalist, 'are all populated by a people connected with Birmingham trade, or thrown off, so to speak, from the Birmingham centre, and legitimately belonging to the population of Birmingham.'[1]

The first change in the existing framework was the extension of the parliamentary borough of Birmingham by the Redistribution of Seats Act of 1885, which added Harborne, Balsall Heath, Saltley, and Little Bromwich to the city. The municipal borough was left untouched.

In 1887 the General Purposes Committee of the Council recommended the inclusion within the municipal borough of those districts which had recently been added to it in 1885 for parliamentary representation, along with the Local Board districts of Handsworth and Aston Manor, the hamlets of Witton and Erdington, the parish of Yardley, and as much of the districts of Moseley, King's Heath, and Selly Oak as was included in the Birmingham, Tame, and Rea District Drainage Board. These changes would have increased the total area of the borough to 33,000 acres and the population to 600,000. The scheme aimed at including within the future County Borough of Birmingham 'all persons who might reasonably be supposed to be connected in any way with the trade and manufactures of the town, and who were residing in areas outside the borough, but yet within a distance not too far removed from it for the purposes of efficient and economical municipal government'.

In January 1888 the Council discussed the report, and accepted it practically unanimously by fifty-one votes to one.

[1] *B.M.*, 29 April 1881.

'The proceeding appealed so directly to the amour-propre of the Assembly that no-one except Mr. Lowe, whose intrepidity is undoubted, had the inclination or the hardihood to raise a discordant voice.'[1] To assist the deliberations, a large map showing the area proposed to be included was spread to the right of the mayoral chair; 'the invitation to look and lingeringly admire was irresistible'. The Mayor said that it was a serious question whether Birmingham was to be hemmed in for ever by a ring of small Local Boards which had nestled round its confines, or whether these outlying but now continuous districts should join hands with, and become part of, a larger authority.

In April 1888 the Local Government Board opened an inquiry by Chambers, one of the commissioners, into the Birmingham Scheme. Although Chambers sympathized with the city authorities, he made it clear that the government did not wish municipal extension to be pushed forward very far at that moment. His report, published in April 1889, merely recommended the amalgamation of Edgbaston Parish and part of Aston Parish within the borough with the Parish of Birmingham, but this reform was not carried out. The bigger scheme was shelved, but not dropped, and in December 1889 the City of Birmingham communicated with outlying authorities to test their reactions to union with the city, with a view to asking for a local inquiry under the provision of the new Local Government Act of 1888.

Apart from a favourable reply from Balsall Heath, where rates were considerably higher than in Edgbaston, there was fierce opposition from Harborne, which later came over, King's Norton, Handsworth, Aston, and Saltley. Apart from local pride, which was strong, particularly in Aston, which had been seeking to secure its own incorporation since 1876, there were material reasons for the refusal of the outlying authorities to consider union with Birmingham. The chief inducement to bring them in—drainage—had already been dealt with by the institution of the Birmingham, Tame, and Rea District Drainage Board. The chief deterrent was the high poor-rate in the parish of Birmingham, which made them reluctant to enter the borough, fearing that this might be a step towards their ultimate inclusion in the parish. Finally, and this factor was even more important on the eve of 1911, the new County Councils set up by

[1] *B.G.*, 4 January 1888.

the Act of 1888 were reluctant to part with populous districts of comparatively high rateable value.

After a second government inquiry held in March 1891, Saltley, Balsall Heath, and Harborne were added to the city, the first outlying districts to join Birmingham. New wards were created at Saltley and Balsall Heath, while Edgbaston was amalgamated with Harborne. 'The blameless inanity characteristic of local life at Harborne', commented the *Birmingham Daily Mail*, 'will be changed for the fierce and purifying excitement of municipal warfare.' More than a mere militant spirit could be expected: good government also would follow. 'Hitherto their melancholy fate has been to be governed by a Local Board, a form of government no greater than that of small villages in the heart of the Black Country, or the most beknighted [*sic*] agricultural district.' They would now help to govern 'the best-governed city in the world', and would even have a chance of controlling it. 'When the Romans conquered a country, the advantage was on the side of the conquered, who learnt manners, discipline and improvement from the conquerors. May not the bulk of the advantage here be on the side of the annexed?'[1]

With the incorporation of Balsall Heath, Harborne, and Saltley in 1891, 4,000 acres were added to the city, and the strength of the Council was increased to seventy-two. For nearly sixteen years afterwards the boundaries question remained dormant, although the advocates of a Greater Birmingham, like Councillor H. J. Manton, J. V. Morton, the Editor of the *Birmingham Gazette*, and above all J. S. Nettlefold, never lost sight of the vision. Nettlefold was the most important guardian of the Chamberlain tradition of the city. 'Of all Mr. Chamberlain's disciples', an observer wrote in 1909, 'he is the only one who within very recent times has shown what the Chamberlain traditions mean. He is an enthusiast, a masterful man, with an immense stock of driving power.'[2] This was the quality which was most needed if vision were to turn into accomplishment.

By the time the boundaries question was again raised, the issue had become more urgent. New problems had arisen, particularly the questions of town-planning and tramways, although some old difficulties, like the differences in School Board rates, had disappeared. It was in December 1906 that a proposal was brought forward in the City Council that the General Purposes

[1] *B.M.*, 7 November 1891.  [2] *B.G.*, 20 October 1909.

Committee should be instructed to consider and report their re-commendations as to the expediency and necessity for an altera-tion of the boundaries of the wards of the city. In January 1907 city extension was proposed by Councillor Walthall, and referred to a sub-committee; but before the Town Clerk, the Medical Officer of Health, the Treasurer, and the Surveyor had had time to report, the question of city extension was brought before the Council in a new way.

The tiny outlying village of Quinton proved to be the spear-head of the successful expansion campaign. The question of the annexation of Quinton by Birmingham was originated by the people of Quinton themselves. In 1907 the Halesowen Rural District Council brought forward a scheme for the disposal of the sewage of Quinton. The Quinton Parish Council, under the chairmanship of the Rev. James Jones, protested and passed a nearly unanimous resolution in favour of incorporation with Birmingham and of opening communications with its powerful neighbour. In July 1908 the Birmingham General Purposes Committee advised the Council to turn down the idea of unifica-tion on the grounds that the reform desired could be secured more easily by the inclusion of Quinton in the area controlled by the Drainage Board, but in full Council an amendment pro-posed by Nettlefold was carried by forty-four votes to eighteen, urging expansion as a means of securing housing areas and plan-ning future suburban growth. A representation to the Local Government Board was prepared and approved by the Council in October, and on the same day it was resolved by forty-two votes to ten to entrust further proceedings to a Boundaries Com-mittee of eight people. A month later Nettlefold, the vigorous chairman of the Housing Committee, was appointed chairman of the new body.

In February 1909 the Local Government Board held an in-quiry into the Quinton case, after 180 out of 224 electors in Quinton had sent a memorial in favour of unification. The Town Clerk of Birmingham gave four reasons why Quinton should be incorporated in the city—a community of interests; the future development of the district; the desire of the inhabitants; and sewage disposal. The community of interests was stressed. One hundred and eleven Quinton people worked in Birmingham, as against only 128 in Quinton itself. The whole of the Quinton food supplies came from the city. While the washing from Edgbaston was sent to the laundresses of Quinton, Quinton men and women went into Birmingham for their shops and entertainment. These were powerful arguments, more powerful than the chairman of the Worcestershire County Council, Willis Bund's, talk of 'plunder and robbery'. The inquiry favoured Birmingham, and a Provisional Order Bill came before the Local Legislation Committee of the House of Commons in June 1909. Quinton was incorporated and the first stage in the policy of city extension was accomplished.

It was impossible to treat Quinton in isolation. Indeed Councillor Napier Clavering showed wise judgement when he advocated the policy of Quinton first, and the rest later. The Boundaries Committee, upon whom the task of securing a Greater Birmingham depended, were now supported by nearly all the Council and public opinion in the city, but their work was difficult. Their predecessors in the 1880's had been attacked for being timid where they ought to have been bold and dictatorial where they ought to have been conciliatory. The committee of 1908 had to show real statesmanship in negotiations that were often difficult and delicate, and required both vision and diplomacy.

The Boundaries Committee published its first Report in February 1909 and it was unanimously accepted by the Council. It proposed that the borough of Aston Manor, the urban districts of Erdington, Handsworth, and King's Norton and Northfield, and the rural district of Yardley should be added to the city. All these places already fell within the physical area of the town's development, and if they were unified in one great city, Birmingham would cover 40,000 acres, about three times its existing size, and its population would rise to about 850,000 to make it the second city in England.

The proposals seemed so far-reaching at the time that it is worth while taking the districts one by one and examining more closely their relationship to the existing city of Birmingham.

1. The Borough of Aston Manor in the County of Warwick and the Aston Poor Law Union had an area of 943 acres, a population of 82,000 in 1908, and had just been incorporated in 1903, after two previous applications in 1876 and 1888 had failed. It was almost entirely a built-up area, covered with factories and business premises, most of them built in a rapid spurt of expansion between 1851 and 1881, and although it owned its own tramways, free libraries, technical school, baths,

fire-station, refuse destructors, and electricity generating-station, it was already dependent on Birmingham for its supply of gas and water, and on the Birmingham, Tame, and Rea District Drainage Board for its sewage disposal. In addition Birmingham trams ran into and through Aston. Indeed it was difficult to see where Birmingham ended and Aston began. The amalgamation of Aston and Birmingham had frequently been discussed, but it had never succeeded in appealing to the leading figures in Aston's local life, despite the limited scope for separate local development. With rates at 8s. 4½d. in the pound in 1908, it was in a worse position than Birmingham, and with a poorer population to pay them.

2. The Urban District of Handsworth in the County of Stafford and the West Bromwich Poor Law Union had an area of 3,667 acres and a population of 68,000 in 1908.

It was an almost entirely residential district, which had grown with the growth of Birmingham. There were few large works in the district, most of the residents being employed in Birmingham and Aston. Its population had increased from 14,359 in 1871 to 68,000, but the north part of the area was still undeveloped or in the course of transformation. Over 4,000 new houses—mainly artisans' dwellings—were built in the ten years between 1901 and 1911.

Although Handsworth was part of the Drainage Board and received its gas and water from Birmingham, it did possess several local amenities. It had its own public offices, free library, technical school, baths, refuse destructor, and electric power-station. There were good shopping facilities and one of the finest parks in the suburbs of Birmingham. It was joined by two tramway services to Birmingham.

3. The Urban District of Erdington in the County of Warwick and the Aston Poor Law Union had an area of 4,550 acres and a population of 29,000 in 1908.

It was a rapidly developing area, which had a population of under 10,000 in 1891, when it was a rural residential district just beginning to be popular. In 1908 it was five times as big as its neighbour Aston and had 50,000 fewer inhabitants—an ideal site for town-planning, the more so since it lacked local amenities, particularly for recreation and entertainment.

The Urban District Council, set up in 1894, was an extremely canny local authority. When it was created it did not own, so the records state, either a pick or a shovel. It retained a healthy distrust of capital expenditure for the provision of public services, and rather than supply its own requirements it preferred to treat with neighbouring and more powerful authorities to supply its needs on terms which subsequently proved most advantageous. It took gas and water from Birmingham, and went to Aston for electricity, fire-brigade services, and hospital treatment for infectious cases. Although it had no cemetery, one of Birmingham's cemeteries at Witton actually fell in its area. Only in the laying and equipment of the tramways did the Council embark on a project for which it could have got an outside contract from a municipality or a private firm, and even then the tramways were worked by the Birmingham City Corporation.

The Urban District had two distinctions. It was the healthiest in the Birmingham area, the death-rate being as low as 8.72 per 1,000; and it was the lowest rated, the general rate, including the poor-rate, standing, and having stood for some years, at 6s. 6d. in the pound. With a high rateable value of £152,466, which had risen in eight years by nearly £50,000, Erdington was a very useful acquisition to the city.

4. The Urban District of King's Norton and Northfield in the County of Worcester and the King's Norton Poor Law Union had an area of 22,453 acres and a population of 78,608 in 1908.

It was by far the largest of the new districts scheduled in the Greater Birmingham Plan, and it covered one of the most important 'development areas' in the making of the region. The suburbs of Moseley, King's Heath, King's Norton, Cotteridge, and Bournville fell within the King's Norton and Northfield area, which also included the partly industrial district of Selly Oak. The development of the area had been spectacular, much of the district having been open country twenty years before. The population had increased by 200 per cent. in the twenty years from 1881 to 1901, the rise being principally due to overflow from Birmingham, following the introduction of good tramway and rail facilities. The areas farthest away from the city, like Rednal, Rubery, Bartley Green, and Northfield, were, for the most part, agricultural in character. The suggested boundary divided Rednal in two, since it marked the limit of the Drainage Board area, rain falling on one side of the boundary flowing to the Bristol Channel, rain on the other side to the Humber.

The Urban District Council was facing an administrative

problem bigger than it could reasonably tackle, and there had been some talk of incorporating part of the more populous district as a municipal borough. Although it had its own industrial units at Selly Oak, Stirchley, Bournville, and King's Norton, the area had no organic centre. The seat of its poor-law administration was at Selly Oak Workhouse, situated on the edge of the district, while the District Council offices were in the heart of Birmingham. It had reasonable library facilities, recreation grounds, cemetery accommodation, an infectious diseases hospital, a refuse destructor, public baths, and schools, but the services were widely scattered, and the dependence on Birmingham was strong. Each year the District Council paid Birmingham £1,737 for the use of the city's sewers. Tramway routes followed continuous built-up areas from Edgbaston to Selly Oak and from Balsall Heath to King's Heath. Outside the Birmingham boundaries the tramway to Moseley and King's Heath belonged to the Urban District Council, but an arrangement had been reached whereby it was worked on profit-sharing terms by the Birmingham Corporation with Birmingham rolling stock and electric current. Other lines were run by the District Council, and the Bristol Road line by the Birmingham and Midland Tramways Company until the expiration of its lease in 1911. The District Council had obtained a Provisional Order in 1898 authorizing them to generate and supply electric light within their area, but nothing had been done by 1908.

The rateable value of the area was £409,800, over £300,000 of this pertaining to the 9,000 acres contiguous to Birmingham, and the rates in 1909 were 6s. 6d. in the pound. The financial importance of the district to the Worcestershire County Council was considerable.

5. The Rural District of Yardley in the County of Worcester and the Solihull Poor Law Union had an area of 7,589 acres and a population of 60,000.

The population of the district had grown rapidly: at the census of 1881 there were only 9,745 people living there. The increase was due largely to overflowing pressure from the city, although there were many workers at Greet employed at the Small Arms factory near by. New houses were being built at a considerable rate—736 in 1905, 813 in 1906, and 832 in 1907. Eight separate centres, more or less well defined, made up the rural district—Greet, Sparkhill (the centre of administration),

Hay Mills, Yardley village, Stechford, Hall Green, Acock's Green, and Tyseley.

Local government was most inadequate. In none of the population centres was there a public library, public baths, or a refuse destructor. Government of such an urban area by a Rural District Council was admitted to be unsatisfactory, and the ideal of the authority was low rating rather than a well-equipped community.

The district was supplied with gas and water from Birmingham, but was the one area covered in the extension proposals which did not form part of the Drainage Board. Tramway facilities were provided by the Birmingham Corporation but there was no provision of electricity. One thousand three hundred and twenty-five Yardley children were attending Birmingham Council schools.

The rateable value of the area was £207,965, and its rates in 1908 were 6s. 8d. in the pound.

The publication of the extension proposals led to immediate opposition on the part of the scheduled authorities. Aston Town Council and Handsworth Urban District Council led the way on 4 July 1909. While Aston affirmed with only one dissentient that from time immemorial it had had a well-defined boundary, and that no case had been made by Birmingham, Handsworth decided by seventeen votes to one that the Birmingham proposals were unfair and should not be accepted. These meetings started the ball rolling: there were private conferences and public debates everywhere, while the local press kept the controversy at fierce heat, and gave voluminous illustrations of the advantages or disadvantages of unification both from local lore and the examples of other areas, such as Stoke and Dewsbury.

It soon became clear that in many of the suburbs there was a real conflict of interests between large numbers of ratepayers, who began to organize themselves into unification committees, and the existing local authorities, who were equally active in stirring up anti-Incorporation rallies. The first attempt to reconcile these differences was taken in Erdington, where the District Council decided to hold a poll of ratepayers. It took place on 12 November 1909 and, to the annoyance of the Incorporationists, 1,529 people voted against union with Birmingham to 1,174 for. Nearly 2,000 ratepayers were indifferent and did not bother to record their votes. At King's Norton only 38 per cent. bothered to vote in a ratepayers' poll, the anti-annexationists securing 3,628 votes to 1,764. At Aston, in February 1910, for the first time a poll went the other way, 3,782 voting for union with Birmingham and 2,401 against. On all these occasions the method and the procedure of the polls were criticized by the losing sides. The figures seemed to prove nothing. As the *Birmingham Mail* put it—and it was thinking of the national General Election as well as the local ratepayers' polls—'there is no machinery yet devised by which the will of the people can be discovered. Petitions, polls and even elections are evidenced, but each in turn is shown to be hopelessly misleading. The will of the people is shown to be inscrutable, and yet it is that sovereign will which is to shape our national destiny.'[1]

If the attempt to find the will of the people proved nothing, the attempt to negotiate quietly behind closed doors proved equally unsatisfactory. In December 1908 and in January 1909 the Birmingham Boundaries Committee wrote in turn to the five Councils inviting them to confer on terms, without necessarily committing themselves to the project, but little progress was made. Private conferences with Birmingham broke down and various local authorities tried to amalgamate their forces from October 1909 onwards to form a common front against the city.

The case for the amalgamation of the scheduled areas was on all counts a very strong one. Quite apart from questions of prestige—the desire to raise the status of Birmingham—the proposals merely attempted to relate administrative machinery to the functional structure of the area. Of 69,973 householders and other male workers in the districts suggested for incorporation, no less than 38,269, or over 54 per cent., were employed within the city. The limitation of the area of Birmingham had prevented the normal internal increase of population and rate-able value. At the same time there was no dividing line in the shape of a rural zone between most of the new suburbs and the city boundaries. 'Our little kingdom is not like a great Empire', said William Kenrick. 'Wide seas do not divide us, and I hope no separatist counsels will ever divide us from one another. Our lives interweave. We are all Birmingham men.'

There were some signs of a conflict of interests. While middle-

[1] *B.M.*, 21 January 1910.

class residents of new suburbs who feared that they would be adversely affected by higher Birmingham rates complained of the financial impact of a Greater Birmingham, working men were more directly concerned with cheap and efficient tramway services, which could better be provided by a uniform administration. From the start, Labour organizations along with the Birmingham Liberal and Conservative Associations supported the proposal. As Fathers said at Yardley: 'The Labour Party did not believe in talking a lot about the independence of the Kingdom of Yardley. Their anxiety was to get the best possible conditions for the working class population of the city.'[1] But while Labour was pushing the scheme most business men rallied to it as well. The Birmingham Chamber of Commerce held a poll between July and October 1909, and out of 281 replies 209 (74 per cent.) were in favour of the scheme as a whole. Only 32 (11·9 per cent.) were against the scheme in its entirety.[2] A Chamber of Commerce Report stressed the need for seeing 'the great industrial district' to which they belonged 'developing as a commercial and trade centre under the best possible conditions'. The Lord Mayor of Birmingham said that if the Chamber of Commerce had been briefed by the City Council, it could not have done its work better.[3] Other bodies like the Birmingham and Midland Counties Grocers' Association took the same line.

The opposition to the scheme from the representative authorities of all the scheduled areas raised some issues of general principle. They were mainly concerned with the cry of decentralization, although centralization presupposed a directing centre, which did not exist in the conditions before 1911— George Cadbury argued at one time in favour of federation with devolution of powers, a system which had worked most unsatisfactorily in the relations between Manchester and Withington.[4] Willis Bund, the chairman of the Worcestershire County Council, argued that the counties could not stand without the support of valuable revenue-yielding districts, and from the middle of 1910 onwards he had the support of the County Councils Association.

More important to the opposition than issues of principle were the psychological barriers of local pride and in some cases the

---

[1] *B.G.*, 22 March 1909.   [2] *B.P.*, 21 October 1909.   [3] Ibid., 28 October 1909.
[4] Cadbury wrote to the *B.P.*, 23 October 1909. Nettlefold replied on 25 October 1909.

material difficulties of finance. A Handsworth speaker said that
their motto, 'Handsworth for Handsworth people', was better
than being a part of the second city in the kingdom. Before
Birmingham came Soho: before Chamberlain, Murdock. 'He
could imagine a thrush addressing an objective worm upon the
advantages of losing its humble form and becoming part of the
anatomy of a beautiful bird. There might be worms in Handsworth, but they preferred to retain their humble identity than
be part of the magnificent anatomy of Birmingham.'[1] A Yardley
speaker said that he was not willing to barter Yardley's liberty
or sell his birthright for a mess of pottage,[2] while Willis Bund
said once that he thought Birmingham was suffering from too
big ideas. Its citizens, he said, did a great trade with the United
States, and seemed to have assimilated their ideas as to boundaries from across the Atlantic. They were not bounded on the
north by the Pole, but extended to the Aurora Borealis. On
the south they took possession of the equinoxes, on the east the
rising sun and on the west the day of judgement. It was a pity
that with their big ideas Birmingham did not agree to wipe out
the County of Worcester altogether.[3]

These impassioned exercises in rhetoric were much more
exciting than the difficulties about finance, yet the success of the
city's proposals depended a great deal on this factor. There were
two reasons for this: first, the ratepayers of each scheduled
district stood on a different footing from the rest, and second,
the possibilities of future changes meant that it was difficult
to accept the existing structure of local accounts as a basis of
negotiation.

In an attempt to deal with these difficulties Clare, the City
Treasurer, worked out an impressive set of calculations, com-
paring (i) the actual 1908–9 rates in the scheduled areas,
(ii) the estimated rates for 1913–14, assuming that the scheduled
areas remained under the control of independent authorities,
and (iii) the estimated Birmingham figures, with and without
the scheduled areas, for the period 1913–14. On the basis
of these figures, differential rating allowances were suggested
for Erdington, the most favoured area, and Aston Manor, the
least. As far as Birmingham itself was concerned, it was estimated
that the effect of the proposals would be to raise the Council
rates by 1*d.* in the pound by 1913–14.

[1] *B.G.*, 11 November 1909.    [2] *B.G.*, 20 January 1909.    [3] *B.P.*, 5 October 1909.

The issues had already been stated very clearly, and the battle was joined when the Local Government Board inquiry into Birmingham's claims opened in the Council House on 14 December 1909. It was conducted by Major Norton and lasted for more than three weeks. The atmosphere was exciting at the time, for the inquiry took place on the eve of a general election, and Balfour Browne, the leader for the Corporation, had to dash off to Yorkshire to fight a campaign in Bradford before the sittings ended. Nettlefold, who had been one of the most active sponsors of the scheme, was prevented by illness from attending. The inquiry was a thorough one, and worthy of the magnitude of the enterprise. Thirty-eight witnesses were called by the Corporation, sixteen by the County Councils, and five by other bodies. In all 24,000 questions were asked, and the printed record of the proceedings fills 2,000 pages. At the end of this detailed interrogation, Major Norton submitted a confidential report favourable to the claims of Birmingham, and on 26 May 1910 the Local Government Board issued a Provisional Order, upholding in almost every detail the Birmingham City scheme, and referring it to the local authorities concerned for observations and suggestions. By this time, the opposition had been so carefully organized that it was reluctant to give way, and was determined to oppose the measure in Parliament, if necessary to the last. It was unfortunate for the recalcitrant opponents of the scheme that the façade of resistance crumbled about the time that the first reading of the Bill took place in the House of Commons on 22 June 1910.

Erdington was the first suburb to announce its intention of joining hands with Birmingham. Its Council had spent £2,000 in attacking unification at the December inquiry, and having failed to convince the Local Government Board of the wisdom of leaving it out of the Order, it philosophically reviewed the state of affairs. In June 1910 it decided to withdraw its opposition. Strategically this 'submission' was of great importance to Birmingham, because with Erdington willing to be absorbed on the terms offered, the Aston Town Council realized that its position was practically untenable, particularly since it was out of sympathy with what was probably a majority of the ratepayers. In the circumstances it would have been foolish to persist in opposition, and as the result of a conference at the Birmingham Council House in July terms of settlement were agreed upon.

Aston gained something by starting its negotiations so early. The differential rating figures were adjusted in its favour, and other points with regard to the Free Library were settled on satisfactory terms.

Before the Aston arrangement was arrived at, the Greater Birmingham Bill had been read in Parliament for the first time. It was the most important measure relating to local administration since the Government of London Bill of 1900, which had advocated a very different solution from that applied to Birmingham. The second reading of the Greater Birmingham Bill was carried without a division on 7 July. In committee it met with vigorous opposition and it soon became clear that the discontinuation of opposition by Erdington and Aston had merely made the opposition of Handsworth, King's Norton, and Yardley all the more fierce. In committee the Bill was opposed by Stanley Baldwin, the Member for Bewdley—an interesting case of a local problem overshadowing a national identity of interests with the Chamberlains—but it was vigorously backed by John Burns, the Liberal president of the Local Government Board, and by Sir Arthur Steel-Maitland, one of the Conservative Members for Birmingham. As Nettlefold, who had some experience of being independent, remarked, it was a good augury when a Liberal and a Conservative had worked so well and so loyally together for the creation of a Greater Birmingham. The Bill was opposed by Irish Home Rulers, to whom Birmingham was anathema not only because of Chamberlain's action in 1886 but because, some years before, Birmingham Members had opposed a Bill to add certain new townships to the city of Dublin.

In August 1910 the Bill passed the committee stage of the House of Commons, almost intact, the only effect of the vigorous opposition being to leave the Handsworth Poor Law area just as it was before. This decision of the House of Commons led to an inevitable reaction in those districts where opposition still lingered. King's Norton and Northfield entered into negotiations and eventually, after disagreements about differential rating figures, reached agreement in October 1910. The agreement undoubtedly favoured King's Norton. It secured for the first ten years a differential rate of 1s. 8d. in the pound less than Birmingham, 4d. more than Birmingham had originally suggested. In return for this and other concessions, King's Norton District Council agreed not to oppose any further the proposals

of the Birmingham Corporation, both parties promising to use
their best endeavours to obtain the inclusion in Birmingham of
the whole of the scheduled King's Norton area.

The securing of this agreement required great tact and diplo-
matic skill on the part of the Birmingham Boundaries Sub-
Committee, headed by Councillor Brooks and the Town Clerk.
Agreement with Yardley followed in November, Handsworth
now being left alone. The Handsworth District Council refused
to budge; it would neither negotiate with Birmingham nor take
a poll of its ratepayers. Its intransigence was supported by the
Worcestershire County Council, where Willis Bund on 12 December compared the districts which had already surrendered to
mackerel, which could always be caught by a bit of scarlet
cloth.[1] Handsworth was determined that there should be no
surrender.

The progress of the Bill through Parliament had been slow
as a result of the General Election of December 1910 and the
pressure of other business. It was not until 16 February 1911
that it came up again in the House of Commons, and was read
a third time on 20 February. Its passage through the Lords was
facilitated by a dramatic turn of events in Handsworth, which
eventually capitulated at a critical moment in the parliamentary
history of the Bill, not as a result of pressure from without, but
as a consequence of revolution from within—on 27 March 1911,
in elections for the Handsworth Council, annexationists were
returned in every ward. On the following day the Bill came before
the Lords, and Counsel for Handsworth admitted that as a
result of the elections, the matter had changed from a conflict
of principles to a bargain about terms. With Handsworth out of
the way, the only other opposition came from the Worcestershire County Council, and after Birmingham gave an undertaking
to offer compensation for loss of rateable value, the Bill went
through without further difficulty, finally passing the Lords on
19 May 1911 and going on to receive the Royal Assent.

With the passing of the Bill, Birmingham gained control of
a city area three times the size of Glasgow and twice the size
of Manchester, Liverpool, or Belfast. The length of Greater
Birmingham at its extreme points—Rubery or Rednal to Oscott
—was exactly thirteen miles. Although at the time there were
complaints of excessive ambition, this was in fact the minimum

[1] *B.P.*, 13 December 1910.

efficient working area of the city. Securing it at this stage gave
Birmingham an advantage over other English cities like Manchester, which remained hemmed in by a ring of rival authorities,

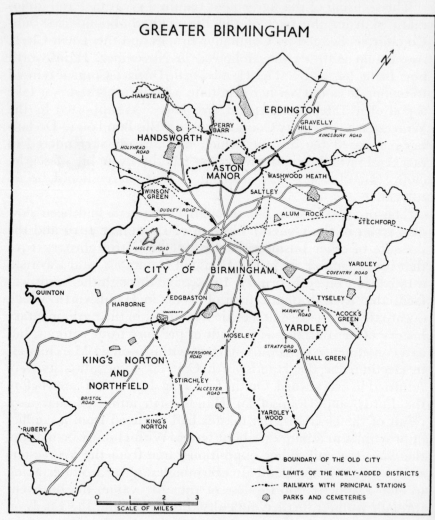

Fig. 6

but it by no means settled for all time the administrative geography of the region.

The successful passing of the Bill led to many congratulations
and many statements of future policy. One letter of congratula-
tion came from Chambers, the Inspector of the Local Government Board, who twenty-three years before had suggested that

the city should be extended on such lines. The local leaders who had taken part in the drawing up of the scheme stressed its value from different angles.[1] Councillor Walthall, an active member of the Boundaries Committee, talked in terms of increased efficiency of public administration and the removal of the disadvantages arising from the multiple control of one district. He looked forward to an improvement in the calibre of the Council and the attraction of men of ripe experience to city government. Councillor Brooks thought the chief point of the scheme—and this linked up with Walthall's hopes—was that it comprised within the city the whole of the population which might really be regarded as Birmingham's citizens. The chairman of the Tramways Committee said that the scheme would confer an inestimable boon on the city. 'The control by one authority of the whole of the routes of the enlarged city is bound to result in a more efficient service.'

All commentators agreed in regarding the Greater Birmingham scheme not as a final victory but as an opportunity. Brooks said that he hoped that the new city would be a great city in the best sense of the word, in municipal efficiency and in promoting the prosperity and happiness of its citizens. Better Birmingham was the ideal. Nettlefold, one of the main architects of the triumph, declared likewise that the victory would be a barren one unless Greater Birmingham resulted in Better Birmingham.

### III

One of the first results of the successful implementation of the Greater Birmingham scheme was the new impetus it gave to the town-planning movement—to the attempt to make 'the real town coincide more closely with the ideal'.

Social reformers in Birmingham, first of all the English cities, realized that isolated and spasmodic city growth was leading to very unsatisfactory results. 'It blights the countryside with dreary rows of bricks and mortar; it destroys imagination and the free play of child life; it compels men and women to live in an environment of sordid monotony unrelieved by any touch of nature.'[2] Town-planning was thought to provide the answer.

[1] *B.G.*, 20 May 1911.
[2] G. Cadbury, *Town Planning with Special Reference to the Birmingham Schemes* (1915), p. 18.

'The problem of town planning', wrote Nettlefold, a pioneer in this field also, 'is one of the latest of those great problems which are engaging the attention of social reformers, and it is beginning to be recognized as one of the most important, because it is concerned with the living conditions of the whole population.'[1]

Birmingham was fortunate in that it had within its borders two examples of enlightened 'estate development'. On the west of the city Edgbaston, exclusively in the possession of one owner and planned with much care, provided a large residential population with substantial houses, ample gardens, and open spaces. Restraints were placed upon the introduction of industry and commerce, and the 'Birmingham Belgravia' has retained its character until the present day.

Bournville was a far later development, a pioneer idea which has played an important part in the subsequent history of town planning, helping to inspire Ebenezer Howard in his dream of garden cities.

The germ of the idea of Bournville can be found in the decision of the Cadbury brothers in 1879 to remove their works from Birmingham, where they had been since 1824, to the open fields four miles away. The step was taken on the grounds that it would be better for the workpeople to live in the country. At first many of the workers continued to live in Birmingham, although it was clear that the pressure of economic necessity would take them nearer to the new factory. George Cadbury planned to make the factory a magnet to attract a new community, which would shape its own environment.

In 1895 he bought 120 acres of land in the neighbourhood of the works, an area which subsequently greatly increased. From the start he took a personal interest in the success of the venture, and although he employed the most competent professional advice and consulted anyone whose experience was valuable, he had clear and decisive views of his own which he advocated with great vigour. He began by building 143 houses, which he sold at cost price, on a lease of 999 years for the ground on which they stood. This lease condition made it impossible that the gardens should be destroyed or built over. He went on to advance half the purchase cost at a low rate of $2\frac{1}{2}$ per cent. interest, and charged 3 per cent. interest on loans in excess of this half. No single individual was to hold more than one acre or six houses.

[1] J. S. Nettlefold, *Practical Town Planning* (1914), p. 1.

PLATE XXV

George Cadbury

PLATE XXVI

Dame Geraldine Cadbury

In 1900 the management of the estate was changed, because some leaseholders were selling their houses at a profit, in one case as much as 30 per cent. Cadbury renounced financial interest in the undertaking and handed over the whole area, valued at £172,724, to the Bournville Village Trust on terms which ensured that all profits would be devoted to the further improvement and extension of the village. At the time of the outbreak of the First World War the total area of the estate had increased to 672 acres, and its population had gone up to 4,390.

George Cadbury resisted the temptation, if temptation there was, to become a kind of feudal magnate at Bournville, but although he himself wished to have trustees representing the Birmingham City Council, the District Councils, the County Council, and the Society of Friends, he was persuaded that for the first generation members of the Cadbury family should be the trustees. This was their only control over the estate. Preference was not even given to workers employed by the firm in the allocation of houses.

By the Trust Deed the income from rents and every other source had to be devoted to making full provision for repairs and maintenance. Full economic rents were charged and any surplus remaining had to be used in laying out the rest of the estate, in building houses, in buying additional estates, or in promoting by other means the better housing of the people. Thus in effect all the revenues, instead of going to George Cadbury personally, as they would have done under normal conditions of land ownership, were automatically reinvested in model housing.

Cadbury laid great stress on *model* houses. He insisted that each house should have a separate garden, and that no building should occupy more than one quarter of the land allotted to it. The roads had to be ample—42 feet wide—and bordered with trees, the houses set back at least 20 feet from the pavement. They were not placed in long straight rows, but irregularly. Design was simple. Expensive embellishments in architecture were discouraged, and for some time there were no separate bathrooms, Cadbury's first idea being to set the baths in the floor with boards to cover them. As an example of how to furnish simply and comfortably on a small sum one of the houses was set aside as a show-place. Cadbury took a detailed interest in gardening, and often provided the tenants with gardens which he had planted before the houses themselves were built.

Apart from houses and gardens, at least one-tenth of the land on the estate was reserved for parks and recreation grounds. There were plenty of open spaces, for only seven houses were built to the acre, and, although factories were allowed by the Trust Deed, they were restricted to one-fifteenth of the total area.

In this model community there were no public houses, but there was a village institute, Ruskin Hall, available for social and educational purposes, a church, and a Friends' meeting house. In 1906 a handsome school was provided, with clock-tower carillon, and spacious playgrounds, a model for village communities. Considerable scope was left for local self-government, and an elected village council was set up and endowed with substantial authority.

As a result of the Bournville scheme, there was a great improvement in health as compared with the city as a whole. In the five years before 1919 the average death-rate for Bournville was 7·7 per 1,000. In Birmingham it was 13·7 per 1,000, and in England and Wales as a whole 14·9. The scheme reduced infant mortality by nearly one-half.

The influence of Bournville on English thought was considerable, though of course it was a special case. Cadbury was his own capitalist. In the case of the Letchworth Garden City set up a few years later or the Hampstead Garden Suburb the additional problem was posed of raising the sums necessary to develop the property. There was thus no complete comparison between Bournville and these later developments. Other schemes like Lord Leverhulme's project, begun in 1888 at Port Sunlight, conceived of the village community as an integral part of the local industry, and related it to experiments in profit-sharing. Bournville remained a special venture, and from the time of the Deed of Gift in 1901 visitors came pouring into it from all sides. In September 1901 the recently founded Garden City Association, which was created to carry out the ideals of Ebenezer Howard, held its conference in Birmingham and made a memorable visit to Bournville. 'It is not possible', said Bishop Gore, in addressing the National Housing Reform Council in Birmingham in 1906, 'to measure the debt we owe to Mr. Cadbury.' Germany and France also offered tributes, while the *Melbourne Age* in 1910 wrote that 'Bournville is as important to England as a Dreadnought'.[1] In 1916 the Trades Union Con-

---

[1] A. G. Gardiner, *Life of George Cadbury* (1923), p. 142.

gress sent him a memorial calling him 'a pioneer of better conditions of life, both in the home and in the factory', and spoke
of his achievement as 'the work of a great Englishman filled
with a generous and noble desire to serve his fellow men'.[1] There
were of course national and local critics of the scheme, and
occasional tilts at its sponsor, including suggestions that George
Cadbury's descendants would become multi-millionaires when
the Bournville leases fell in, but Cadbury triumphed over all
these criticisms, and the scheme established his position as one
of the most important Englishmen of his time.

There was one further, less well-known example of planned
housing development in Birmingham—another Nettlefold enterprise—Harborne Tenants Limited. The Harborne Estate con-
sisted of about 54 acres situated $2\frac{1}{2}$ miles from the centre of the
city. There were about 500 houses in all, strictly serviceable
with every advantage taken of economy in building. The householders were co-partners as well as tenants, being to the extent of
their shares their own landlords, and they thus had a real interest
in taking care of their property. The estate prospered in healthy
conditions, and the high rate of infant mortality prevalent in
the centre of the city was 'fought and routed' in a battle where
the successful contestants were all volunteers.

Edgbaston, Bournville, and Harborne, each in its own way,
were models, but problems of town planning in the city as a
whole were much more complicated. Before the extension of
the city in 1911, housing and town planning were intimately
associated together. They were conceived of as parallel policies
in the drive towards social improvement.

The agencies responsible for policy-making at the end of
the nineteenth century were the Estates Committee and the Improvement Committee. Pursuing powers granted it by the
Housing of the Working Classes Act in 1890, the second of the
two bodies had built the tenements in Milk Street, which were
finished and let in the autumn of 1900. In 1899 the two committees merged to form the Estates Committee, but since there
was so much work to do that housing questions were still
left in an unsatisfactory state, a vigorous campaign led to the
appointment in 1901 of a new Housing Committee, of which
J. S. Nettlefold later became chairman. From the start the
committee realized that the problem of housing was mixed

---

[1] Ibid., p. 160.

up with that of town planning. It had to decide whether
to recondition and replace houses in the centre of the city or to
encourage people to move out to the suburbs. Although the
flavour of the word 'suburb' did not always commend itself,
the committee chose the second alternative, thereby falling into
line with 'natural' trends. After sending a delegation to Germany
in 1905 to study town extension plans in operation there, it
recomended a clear-cut town plan for the new suburbs on the
lines later laid down by the Housing and Town Planning Act
of 1909. The road, tram, and bus systems were to be deliberately
controlled so that city development could take place in the right
directions. Municipal land-ownership was advocated on a large
scale to smooth over difficulties. As Neville Chamberlain said in
1914:

A great many of the difficulties and much of the expense which is
at present involved in town planning would be avoided if the land
belonged to the Corporation. The allocation of sites, the direction of
streets, the density of houses to the acre—all these points are often
thwarted and checked in town planning, because we find that what
would be best for the community would involve injustice or hardship
to individuals.

The policy of land acquisition, which had made possible Calthorpe and Cadbury's successful ventures, was not implemented
by the city, but none the less it forged well ahead of other large
cities in its town plans. Indeed, the Quinton, Harborne, and Edgbaston Scheme, dealing with 2,320 acres, approved by the Local
Government Board in 1913, was the first in the country to be
accepted under the 1909 Housing and Planning Act. In 1914
there were three other schemes waiting to be developed—the
East Birmingham Scheme (1,673 acres), the North Yardley
Scheme (3,164 acres), and the South Birmingham Scheme
(8,400 acres).

The purposes of the various schemes differed. The Quinton,
Harborne, and Edgbaston Scheme scheduled a residential area
without factories, with ring and radial roads and open spaces.
The East Birmingham Scheme concerned an industrial area,
traversed by three main lines of railway. The North Yardley
Scheme, taken in hand soon after Greater Birmingham became
an accomplished fact, dealt with a completely rural area, isolated
by its lack of good road communications from the rest of the
city. The South Birmingham Scheme covered a mixed area,

largely residential, but with a northern industrial zone and some factories in the south-west. The problems to be faced were the provision of better communications north and south, the straightening and widening of many of the existing roads, the provision of ample open spaces, the creation of new factory areas, and the development of working-class accommodation. In short the problems covered in this enormous area were those of Birmingham in miniature—roads, many of which had been perfectly satisfactory before the age of motor traffic had begun; allocation of sites; the limitation of houses to the acre; the provision of train services; above all land values, and the so-called 'price gradient'.

The work of the Town Planning Committee was to be the basis of much subsequent work, not all of which realized the dream of the first pioneers, who imagined the spaces between the factories 'filled with garden villages and garden suburbs, where each house, quiet and homely in appearance, and standing in its own garden land, is grouped around the common green or borders the turf-edged and tree-planted road, the poor in association with the well-to-do, the employer and the worker, all inspired with a common aim, and that aim the maintenance of the beauty of their suburb'.[1] The dream was a characteristic dream of the Midlands—its language the language of co-operation and its symbols still rural rather than urban. Even while it was being formulated, giant factories, claiming the world as their market, were beginning to dominate the local scene. World war was a threatening shadow of a cloud in the sky. And the death of Joseph Chamberlain in July 1914 seemed to mark the end of a heroic period in Birmingham's history.

[1] W. H. Bidlake, 'Birmingham as it Might Be', in *Birmingham Institutions* (1911), p. 597.

# VI

## THE POLITICS OF THE CAUCUS

### I

In the last quarter of the nineteenth century, Birmingham was as renowned for the structure of organization of its political parties as it was for the vigour and efficiency of its local government. The two achievements were of course closely linked together. Without the assistance of a powerful Liberal Association, men like Chamberlain could never have secured control of the Town Council and turned it into a workable instrument of local action. It was a Liberal majority not only in the Town Council but also in the School Boards, which were captured amid tremendous enthusiasm in 1873, that made local reform possible.

So efficient was the machine which the local Liberals forged that it roused the continuous anger and jealousy of their opponents. The frequent attacks on the machine often concealed a more deep-seated hatred of the radical reforms themselves. When Chamberlain's opponents attacked the tyranny of a local machine, which denied them any civic influence, Chamberlain replied that the tyranny simply consisted in the fact that the majority of Birmingham people would not accept the political services of his opponents on the terms on which they offered them. When they talked of the need for a greater representation for themselves, they were merely disguising their real demand for power. The Liberal machine was contrived to get things done, and the real objection of the opponents of the machine was that things that they did not like to see were being done, and they could do nothing about them.

The sustained attack on the Liberal organization, which was known as the *caucus*, was characterized by the violence of its vituperation. Lord John Manners described the new party structure as 'the creature of a tyrannical oligarchy, crushing out all independence of thought and action, worse than that which destroyed the Venetian Republic'. Lord Sandon called it 'a new and terrible monster, swaying men's actions from his unfathomable caves'.[1] Some compared it not to a living monster, but to

[1] Quoted by F. Schnadhorst, *The Caucus and its Critics* (National Liberal Federation, 1884).

an inhuman machine, manufacturing public opinion on factory lines, and mechanically setting agitations in motion, not only in Birmingham but throughout the country. Others denounced it as an un-English product. Although it bore the Birmingham trade mark, it really marked the intrusion of American methods into English politics. Sound Members of Parliament, even of a Liberal persuasion, wrote that they considered it an honour to represent independent constituencies, but would not sit in Parliament for one month as 'dummy delegates of any caucus'. A close glimpse of Birmingham politics in the middle of the nineteenth century scatters the clouds of rhetoric that have gathered round the national controversy. The Liberal machine in Birmingham existed long before the days of Schnadhorst and Chamberlain. Far from being American in character, it drew its main strength from the memories of the local Liberal tradition of the city, which went back at least as far as the glorious May days of 1832. Then, as forty years later, victory had been associated not only with right principles but also with powerful organization. When John Bright first addressed his Birmingham constituents in 1858, he apologized for stressing the need for a new crusade for reform in a city which thirty years before had shaken the fabric of privilege to its base. Ten years later, after the passing of the Second Reform Bill, he endorsed the remarks of a Birmingham deputation, which had said that 'if you go to the sea, anywhere you like, and take up a spoonful of water, it will be salt, and if you will return any member from any district in Birmingham you like, he will be a Liberal'.[1]

It is sometimes said that the Reform Bill of 1867, which provided Birmingham with three seats in Parliament and Birmingham electors with only two votes each, was responsible for the establishment of a comprehensive Liberal party organization. Such a cause-and-effect explanation is too technical. In point of fact the Birmingham Liberal Association was set up three years before the 1868 General Election, and even as early as the 1850's there were various reform organizations in being. At the General Election of 1857, for instance, when the franchise was still restricted, an open meeting of all Birmingham Liberals, electors and non-electors, was held to support Bright's candidature. 'A new feeling had arisen', it was said, 'that the whole party, non-

---

[1] J. E. Thorold Rogers, *Public Addresses by John Bright* (1879), p. 103; G. B. Smith, *The Life and Speeches of John Bright*, vol. iii (1885), p. 325.

electors as well as electors, ought to have a voice in a matter so deeply affecting their interests.'[1] This wider interest in politics annoyed many of the old-fashioned Whigs, who felt a sense of disappointment at seeing the management of political affairs taken out of the hands of the 'influential citizens' and confided to a popular assembly in which the non-electors had their share of control. The caucus pushed democratic control farther, particularly after the widening of the franchise in 1867 had offered the additional assurance that the votes of all members of the party were of equal weight. 'The day had gone by', as Crosskey wrote, 'for attempting to control a large constituency by a clique composed of a few wealthy men. A whole suburb could be outvoted by a couple of streets.'[2]

It was the increasing size of the constituency and the cumulative development of the political consciousness of working men, as well as the more dramatic challenge of the 'two-votes three-members' clause of 1867, which stirred local Liberals to a new effort. Indeed, the new Liberal organization was more a major cause than a major consequence of the 1867 Reform Act.[3] Chamberlain was quite clear about the wide social changes which were responsible for the shift of emphasis and control.

It is no longer safe to attempt to secure the representation of a great constituency for the nominee of a few gentlemen sitting in private committee, and basing their claims to dictate the choice of the electors on the fact that they have been willing to subscribe something towards the expenses. The working class, who cannot contribute pecuniarily though they are often ready to sacrifice a more than proportionate amount of time and labour, are now the majority in most borough constituencies, and no candidate and no policy has a chance of success unless their good-will and active support can first be secured.[4]

Their goodwill and support were secured at the test elections of 1868. The Reform Bill of 1867 provided Birmingham as a whole with three seats in the House of Commons and Birmingham electors with only two votes each. The result was an obvious challenge. 'Every Liberal throughout the country is asking,

[1] The Bright Celebrations in Birmingham (National Liberal Federation, 1883).

[2] H. W. Crosskey, 'The Liberal Association—the 600 of Birmingham', in Macmillan's Magazine, February 1877.

[3] See F. H. Herrick, 'The Origins of the National Liberal Federation', in the Journal of Modern History, June 1945.

[4] J. Chamberlain, 'The Caucus, A New Political Organisation', in the Fortnightly Review, July 1877 and November 1878.

"What is Birmingham going to do with the minority clause?" ',
Bright declared. As a result of careful organization, the Liberals
secured enormous majorities of nearly three to one, and in the
final poll there was less than a thousand votes difference between
the first and the third Liberal victor. So great was the extent of
the triumph that in the autumn of 1868, Birmingham Liberals
were circulating to many of their friends and opponents a black-
edged card announcing that the mortal remains of 'OLD TORYISM'
would be consigned to their last resting-place on Tuesday, 17
November. 'A Man that is born a Tory hath but a short time to
live, and is full of Humbug: he springeth up like a fungus, and
withereth like a cauliflower; and is seen no more; in the midst
of life and hope he meets his death.' At the foot of the card, in
block capitals, were printed the words NO RESURRECTION.

The death was not entirely due to natural causes, and in some
ways it was more like a murder than a suicide. Liberal power
had been organized with remarkable tactical skill. During the
Election of 1868 Liberal voters had been given their marching
orders. In some wards they had been asked to vote for Bright
and Dixon, in others Dixon and Muntz, in the remainder
Muntz and Bright. This request, which saved a waste of good
Liberal votes, provided an example for constituencies in a
similar position in other parts of the country. The advice of the
successful Birmingham Liberals was eagerly sought after. Alderman Baker of Portsmouth thanked Birmingham for having set
the keynote for action in other constituencies, while Gladstone
himself admitted that Birmingham had acquired 'a kind of
primacy' in organizational leadership. Crosskey recounted the
rumour that a saloon railway carriage was always kept ready in
New Street Station 'to convey a few discontented agitators to the
remotest parts of the country, in order that the proper echoes
may speedily reply to the directives of a Birmingham committee'.
The leadership of Birmingham first in the National Education
League and then in the National Liberal Federation, both of
which were in a sense mere extensions of local Birmingham movements, confirmed the earlier and less tangible influence exerted
by Birmingham Liberals in the middle of the century.

The construction of an efficient Liberal caucus machine owed
much to a handful of men of outstanding organizing drive and
ability. The secretary of the remoulded Liberal Association,
which won the electoral victories of 1868, was William Harris,

the Abbé Sieyès of Birmingham, leader-writer for Bunce and a most active and intelligent wire-puller behind the scenes. Chamberlain admitted that he was the Father of the Caucus. 'The whole credit of having initiated and carried out this new machinery belongs to my friend, Mr Harris.'[1] Five years later, Francis Schnadhorst, a 'spectacled, sallow, sombre' Birmingham draper, who had been discovered by Dr. Dale and who made his way into Liberal politics through dissent, became secretary of the Liberal Association. He was an indefatigable worker, 'although he did not happen to be burdened with much originality',[2] and had great success in his efforts as secretary of the Central Nonconformist Committee created to resist the Education Act of 1870. He was later to play a national role as secretary of the National Liberal Federation set up in 1877.

The leaders were important, but so were the followers. The structure of the Birmingham Liberal Association was based on what has since been called 'democratic centralism'. At the base were the Liberal electors, choosing ward committees to organize the canvassing and routine business of their districts. It was the drilling of Liberals by wards which made possible the successful voting by instruction in 1868. Effective control began at the lowest level. In 1868 when a 'Liberal' canvasser called at a house and gave instructions to vote differently from the published ward instructions, the householder first asked him whether he really came from the Liberal Association, and after the canvasser had said 'Yes', he replied, 'Then I believe you're a liar.' The scene ended with two hundred angry Liberal electors chasing him out of the ward.[3]

The ward committees elected a central representative committee, which increased in size as the population of Birmingham grew. In 1868 it had 400 members, ten years later 600, subsequently 800, and finally 2,000. This committee, which hostile critics frequently compared with the Tammany General Committee in New York, met eight or nine times a year, usually on the summons of its Management Committee, sometimes by requisition of the members. A meeting could be summoned by any two ward committees or by any twenty members. Apart from the dissemination of propaganda, this General

---

[1] J. L. Garvin, *The Life of Joseph Chamberlain*, vol. i (1932), p. 261.
[2] T. Anderton, *A Tale of One City* (1900), pp. 84-5.
[3] The story is told in *Searchlight*, 13 November 1913.

Committee chose parliamentary candidates and Liberal candidates for the School Board elections. It was not, however, the central hub of the system. It was itself managed first by an executive committee of over 100 members, including twenty co-opted

FIG. 7. Municipal Ward Map, 1911

members, and second by a small management sub-committee of eleven. This was the inner cabinet of the new organization, working quietly but always anxious to proclaim the fact that it was acting democratically. While to save time and to avoid friction its proceedings were unreported, there were sufficient opportunities left for the bigger bodies to initiate general discussions.

'Ample opportunity was given to everyone for discussion', Chamberlain claimed, 'and even the humblest ward member was able to make his opinions known.'

It was indeed this opportunity offered to all electors, rich or poor, to play an active part in politics which frightened many of the opponents of the 'caucus principle'. The transfer of power inside the party from narrow party cliques to the masses of electors, all of whom participated directly in party work, offended traditional canons of party management. 'The aim of the caucus', Chamberlain urged, 'is essentially democratic. It is to provide for the full and efficient representation of the will of the majority, and for its definite expression in the government of the people.'

Three objections were raised against the new form of organization. It was argued first of all that the new machinery would disfranchise minorities, even inside the party, and crush individualism; second, that it would misrepresent the real opinion of electors and give effective power to a faction, which would work behind the cover of democratic forms; and third, that it would lead to political corruption.

Undoubtedly there were many local men, both Conservatives and men of a Liberal persuasion, who felt that the caucus was an instrument of party tyranny. George Dixon was aware of its threats to individual freedom, John Bright always defended it with important qualifications, and Satchell Hopkins, the Conservative leader, declared that, as a result of its sway, if a man ventured to call himself a Conservative he was disqualified from serving his fellow townsmen, either in the Town Council or on the Board of Guardians, whatever his other qualifications might be. Hopkins also claimed that at Council meetings there was a Whip to keep up communications between the leaders and the rank and file, and that the caucus had also taken control of the Council of the Birmingham and Midland Institute and the Board of Governors of the Grammar School.[1] William Lloyd told the Conservatives that the Liberals claimed that the red flag ruled over the whole city.

Chamberlain had little use for the argument that the caucus disfranchised minorities or crushed individualism. 'It is because minorities, and often very small minorities, have had such power in determining the course of English politics, that

[1] *B.G.*, 15 November 1882.

such deep hostility is shown to the new organization.' He believed that the new electorate wanted things to be done, and not merely to have its representatives argue interminably about every issue in local policy. 'The nice balance of parties which some people affect to desire', he said in 1877, 'means stagnation in public business', and those who believed in a new gospel of civic progress could not afford to miss their opportunities of putting their ideas into practice. The taunt of anti-individualism was usually a 'mere cloak for selfishness', and 'political liberty, if in one sense a sheer negative and a doctrine of rights, in another name is thoroughly positive and a gospel of duties'.

The second argument against the caucus, that it gave power to a faction operating behind the cover of democratic forms, leading to 'the iron rule of a little clique', had been publicized by Bagehot, and was freely exploited both by dissentient Liberals and by Conservatives. Marriott, a Liberal Member of Parliament, suggested that in the Birmingham system the wire-pullers were the men of power, and that in deciding upon candidates for general elections they first decided upon a man, foisted him on the General Committee, and then on to the constituency, and finally congratulated the people on the excellent candidate the people as a whole had selected.[1] The *Morning Post* extended the charge. The caucus had not only falsified the voice of public opinion, but had also revolutionized the working of the constitution. It had 'terrorized Parliament', paralysed the Opposition, and made members of it 'the slaves of the all-powerful dictator of the hour'.

Local Conservatives had no doubts about the identity of the all-powerful dictator of the hour. Chamberlain's Conservative opponent in St. Paul's Ward in the vital municipal election of 1872, the first year of voting by ballot, denounced him as 'a monopolizer and a modern dictator'.[2] In the municipal elections of the following year there were Liberal splits in St. Paul's Ward and Market Hall Ward about Chamberlain's choice as Mayor. At that time a cartoon depicted him haranguing a crowd in New Street with the words: 'Now, lads, let's be equal, and I will be your king.' Despite local criticism Chamberlain towered over his contemporaries. He was known to be the coming man. 'He far surpassed in ability any previous local leaders. . . . I remember

[1] Quoted by F. Schnadhorst, loc. cit.
[2] Quoted by W. J. Davis in the *Searchlight*, 13 November 1913.

him appearing at a meeting in a seal-skin top-coat. This made people gasp. A man daring enough to dress thus must be a Caesar or a Napoleon.'[1] When it was announced in 1877 that Gladstone would probably come to Birmingham for the first meeting of the National Liberal Federation, J. C. Stokes, a local Conservative, told his friends that he was perfectly confident 'that if the "people's William" came down to the "people's Joseph", there would be such a gathering of Joseph and brethren that the "people's William" would become eclipsed one of these days'.[2]

When faced with this line of attack, the supporters of the caucus pointed out quite rightly that the people as a whole played a far bigger part in political life in Birmingham than they did, for instance, in Marriott's constituency at Brighton. 'I cannot call to mind any other town outside Birmingham', said Crosskey, 'in which Democracy has been so largely interpreted as the *life of the people as an organized whole*.' The vigour of party enthusiasm prevented the caucus from becoming a mere device to manipulate public opinion. 'It cannot be too strongly insisted on', Chamberlain urged, 'that the caucus does not make opinion, it only expresses it. . . . It will not turn Conservatives into Liberals or secure for a Liberal minority a representation to which its numbers do not entitle it.' There were some who concluded that if a public meeting was tolerably unanimous, it was due to 'machinery', 'if hundreds of public meetings are held, it only shows the perfection of the arrangements'. 'They do not know what is known to every active politician in the country, that all the machinery in the world will not rouse any enthusiasm in England unless there is a solid foundation of genuine and earnest feeling to work upon.'

The truth was that the caucus organization succeeded in harmonizing, with some frictions but fewer than in any other system, many elements which might otherwise have come into collision. It secured, as Crosskey claimed, both complete confidence in its largest representative body and the power of prompt executive action. It connected local ward interests with the social and political life of the town as a whole, and in days of national crisis with those of the whole country.

Sometimes sweeping charges of corruption were made. For

[1] R. S. Kirk, 'Recollections of Chamberlain and his Times', in the *Searchlight*, 13 November 1913.  [2] *B.G.*, 21 May 1877.

instance, it was said that teachers, paid out of the rates, were employed as Liberal canvassers at elections, whereas 'anyone who had the hardihood to canvass for the Conservative party would be very speedily dismissed by the radical School Board', or that 'while the policemen and officials generally were supposed to be non-political, they must take care that they served the dominant party'.[1] Such complaints received wide publicity, particularly at a time when the Aston riots of October 1884 raised local animosities to a violent boiling-point. From the other side of the Atlantic American critics of their own caucus system prophesied that Birmingham would go the same way as the worst caucus-dominated cities in the United States. The *Nation* said that general interest in politics would soon flag, educated men would cease to take an interest in civic life, and all power would be left with a few, in the last resort a corrupt few. Chamberlain pointed out in rejoinder that there was no evidence of any flight from politics in Birmingham, while even Gladstone himself stressed Birmingham's dedication 'to the banner of a higher and holier principle' than the power of the purse.[2] The facts were equally eloquent. At the 1880 Election, for instance, there were 3,000 voluntary workers in the Liberal cause. 'Public spirit, the interest in local work, and the readiness to undertake its responsibilities have developed immensely in the last few years as a direct consequence of the caucus.' As for the taunt of corruption, 'no doubt there are instances, notably in connection with the municipal history of New York, in which the caucus has been the instrument of evil; but it would be as unreasonable thereupon to condemn the principle of the caucus, as to denounce all republican institutions because the French democracy indulged in lamentable excesses during the Great Revolution'.

The threat of corruption could hardly be great in a city where politics were conceived of by so many leaders and followers as the extension of a gospel. There was a prevalent sense of responsibility which led to a cleaning-up rather than to a dirtying of municipal life. The Birmingham caucus, unlike the caucuses of other towns such as Glasgow and Wolverhampton, interfered directly and continuously in municipal politics at a time when the intrusion of politics into municipal affairs was looked upon with widespread suspicion. Without the political spur it is doubtful

[1] *B.P.*, 14 January 1886.      [2] Ibid., 1 June 1878.

whether the improvements that led to Birmingham's becoming 'the best-governed city in the world' could have been achieved. 'The work which has been done in Birmingham has involved a heavy expenditure, and has necessarily touched many vested interests. It would have been absolutely impossible', said Chamberlain, 'to any but a strong and united party, backed by all the influence and authority of a great majority of the constituency.'

But the influence of the caucus on the life of the city was not all. Birmingham methods were not only copied by individual cities like Leeds[1] or Glasgow; they were projected into the National Liberal Federation, which was set up on the initiative of Birmingham. Already, in 1869, the National Education League had been set up in the city to mobilize nonconformist opinion in all parts of the country. By 1873 Chamberlain, under Harris's influence, was planning a more comprehensive organization. 'I have long felt that there is not force enough in the Education question to make it the sole fighting issue for our friends', he wrote to Morley.[2] The Liberal party 'will not be re-united until a programme has been elaborated which shall satisfy the just expectations of the representatives of labour as well as conciliate the Nonconformists who have been driven into rebellion'.[3] Four years later the bigger plan had matured. 'We are just going to issue the League dissolution circular,' he said in a letter to Morley in February 1877, 'announcing at the same time the formation of a Federation of Liberal Associations with headquarters in Birmingham and the League officers as chief cooks. I think this may become a very powerful organization, and proportionately detested by all Whigs and Whips.'[4] The prophecy was justified, just as the timing was opportune. The Federation was inaugurated in May 1877 at a meeting where 25,000 people were present, and glass had to be taken out of the roof of the building to admit more air. From 1877 to 1886 the National Liberal Federation, with a powerful Birmingham nucleus—keeping Leeds and Manchester out—including Schnadhorst as secretary, became a key factor in nation-wide

[1] Clark, the president of the Leeds Liberal Association, told the National Liberal Federation Conference how, 'since they had adopted the system of the Birmingham organisation, they had changed the representation very materially with regard to their municipal council'. [2] J. L. Garvin, op. cit., vol. i, p. 258.
[3] J. Chamberlain, 'The Liberal Party and its Leaders', in the Fortnightly Review, September 1873. [4] J. L. Garvin, loc. cit.

Liberal politics. By the early 80's it was so powerful that Hartington, the Whig leader, felt that Chamberlain had organized an outside power to belittle Parliament itself, while Gladstone wrote to Rosebery that 'what is outside Parliament seems to me to be fast mounting . . . to an importance much exceeding what is inside'.[1] This was an old complaint against a Birmingham political product—it had been raised against the Political Union in 1832—but it was now appreciated by a far wider public. Birmingham stood for the most powerful political machine in the kingdom and the most active and adventurous brand of English radical Liberalism.

## II

By 1886, when Gladstone's Irish Home Rule proposals led to the breaking-up of the Liberal party, the control of the Liberal caucus over the political life of the city was less strong than it had been ten years previously. 'The caucus has had a decided and supreme sway for some years,' wrote a local Conservative in 1883, 'but already its power is waning. Its intolerance has caused the reaction which ever attends upon tyranny.' There were signs of resistance to the long Liberal sway, signs which can be traced in the local press, in municipal election results, in pamphlets and political squibs, and in the School Board campaigns.

The most important counter-force to the Liberal caucus was the Conservative party machine, which was itself refashioned between 1874 and 1885 to meet the demands of a mass electorate. The improvement in the Conservative party machine between 1874 and 1886 was unmistakable. At the time when Disraeli came into power in 1874 Birmingham Conservatives were broken and disheartened. They had lost most of their seats on the Town Council, and faced a vastly superior organization. In the 1875 municipal elections twelve Liberals were returned unopposed, as against one Conservative, Stone, and in the three contested elections the Liberals had majorities of 634, 897, and 1,071, enormous victories by municipal standards. Almost the same story was repeated in 1876, when the Liberals swept the board and only one Conservative troubled to contest a ward. In 1877 there were no contests at all, and seventeen Liberals were returned unopposed. At a meeting in All Saints' Ward only

[1] J. Morley, *Life of Gladstone* (1903), vol. iii, p. 4.

three people were present, one of them the reporter of the *Gazette*. Chamberlain boasted that the Conservative group had become so small that it would have to import a few Conservatives from Handsworth or West Bromwich, 'or from other portions of the Black Country, where they still lingered, in order to impart some life into our local elections'. So powerful was the Liberal hold that a Conservative leader wrote at this time that it was 'no easy thing for a Conservative in Birmingham to occupy a position in the front. We should learn to be as thick-skinned as possible.'[1]

But 1877 was in some respects a Liberal peak year, and all the time Conservative organization was improving. From 1874 to 1880 J. B. Stone, later M.P. for East Birmingham, did much to stimulate the party to new life. Up to this time Conservative strength had been concentrated in the local Conservative clubs, of which there were several important ones in the middle 70's—including the Birmingham Conservative Club, the Birmingham Junior Conservative Club, and the Birmingham Conservative Association. These clubs were not forgotten in the reorganization—indeed, they were extended in the 1880's with the growth of working men's Conservative clubs—but they were supplemented and made more representative. In 1877 a sort of Conservative caucus emerged, one of the pioneer forms of 'democratic' Conservative organization in England. A Central Executive Committee was appointed consisting of representatives from each of the sixteen wards, thirty-six members of Conservative clubs, and the officers of the Association. Within this large body a Committee of Management, consisting of the secretary and treasurer and twelve members, acted as an inner directorate. It was claimed that the relationship between the Committee of Management and the Central Executive Committee was analogous to that between the Cabinet and the House of Commons.

These reforms in management were accompanied by a more vigorous canvassing of the borough. Over 6,000 objections were made to existing names on the register and new names were added. As a result of what Schnadhorst rather enviously called 'a gigantic fraud', a large net gain in names was reported. In 1878 a Conservative Union was founded and a Conservative evening paper, the *Daily Globe*, made its appearance. The

[1] *B.G.*, 21 May 1877.

PLATE XXVII

Frank Schnadhorst

PLATE XXVIII

Sir Benjamin Stone

result of all this activity was that the 1880 General Election was fought with a far more efficient Conservative party machine than any previous election in Birmingham. In 1874 the Liberal three, who had won the Election of 1868—Muntz, Dixon, and Bright—had been returned unopposed. Chamberlain himself had been returned unopposed at the by-election of 1876. Although in 1880 the Liberals secured a large majority, the two Conservative candidates polled 15,731 and 14,308 votes respectively.

The improvements in organization continued between 1880 and 1885. In 1880 Satchell Hopkins took the place of Stone as secretary of the Association, and a real attempt was made to produce a democratic form of local organization. Distinguished Conservative visitors arrived to address the local party, the most important of them Lord Salisbury, who began his speech in March 1883 by saying how glad he was to see 'evidence of so strong a Conservative feeling' in this 'good old town of Birmingham'. In that same year Birmingham was selected as the rendezvous for the Conference of the National Union of Conservative Associations. It was there that Lord Randolph Churchill appealed to the delegates to transfer Conservative policy-making from a self-elected body to an annually elected body. 'If you want to gain the confidence of the working classes,' he said, 'let them have a share and a large share—a real share and not a sham share—in your party Councils and in your party government.'[1] Later on he was even more explicit. 'The caucus may perhaps be a name of evil sound and omen in the ears of aristocratic or privileged classes, but it is undeniably the only form of political organization which can collect, guide, and control for common objects large masses of electors.'

So attractive was the appeal of Churchill's message that in 1884 the Birmingham Conservatives asked him to fight the city at the next election along with Colonel Burnaby, who had given Chamberlain a hard fight in 1880. Churchill opened his campaign by talking of the declining power and prestige of the local Liberal caucus. 'Parties, like empires and like all human combinations, wax and wane. The law of perpetual change, which is the motive principle of the Radical, exercised its fatal effect upon the Radical himself.'[2] He went on to advocate a popular Conservative policy for a large constituency and appealed to the electors to rally round a new banner.

[1] W. S. Churchill, *Lord Randolph Churchill* (1907), vol. i, p. 250.  [2] Ibid., p. 233.

It was not only dissatisfaction with the caucus which was the driving force behind the revival of Conservatism. In face of falling profits, local business men were beginning to be sceptical about the traditional Liberal programme of free trade. In the middle of the 1880's, as Howard Vincent, one of the leading fair-trade orators put it, 'Birmingham offered ample material for a study of depression'.[1] Conservatism caught up some of the discontents and canalized them, and before 1885 Lord Randolph encouraged not only business men to expect protectionist legislation from a Conservative government, but also working men to expect new forms of social legislation. 'At the present moment, the masses are crying out for work', wrote a Conservative in 1884, 'and the Radicals offer them a vote [a reference to the Reform Bill of 1884]. His lordship will boldly grapple with the "unemployed" question and find the people work.'[2] The issue was an important one in the elections of 1885.

The year 1885 was the climax of a period in local as well as in national history. The wave of Conservative revival had reached its highest point. Between 1882 and 1885 the Conservatives were winning far more votes in local elections, particularly in the centre of the town, and they could usually count on about 1,000 votes in each of the wards which they contested. The number of active Conservative workers increased too, so that during the General Election of 1885 there were 2,400 voluntary workers taking part in the campaign, fought in the seven new divisions set up by the Redistribution Act of 1885.

It was a very keenly contested election, and although the Liberals won all seven seats, they were hard pressed for much of the campaign. Lord Randolph Churchill, bearding them in their central den, made a most exciting fight of his contest with John Bright, which he lost by less than 800 votes; while Alderman Kenrick, the chairman of the National Liberal Federation, only saved his seat by about 600 votes from Matthews in North Birmingham. Although the Liberals could still say 'We are Seven', it could no longer be argued categorically that Birmingham was as Liberal as the sea is salt. Even Chamberlain had to concede that there was a working Conservative organization, although he still called it merely 'a servile copy of our machinery

[1] *B.P.*, 1 February 1888.
[2] The Sir Benjamin Stone Collection of Newspaper Cuttings, &c., in the Birmingham Reference Library.

without the life with which we have imbued it'. He was to find
this Conservative apparatus extremely useful to him after the
split of 1886, when it became abundantly clear that the Liberal
patent had expired.

The rising tide of Conservatism was important for other
reasons besides those of organization. Even before 1886 some of
the Birmingham business men were anticipating Chamberlain
in his switch-over from aggressive radicalism. They were men
who were ready to listen to Lord Randolph's account of the
limitations of the traditional radical programme, and at the
same time were glad to hear him paying tribute to their radical
heritage. Churchill conceded that among their other 'lofty
results' the radicals had 'enlarged the boundaries of freedom'
and had 'brought the Constitution into the home and the cottage
of the artisan',[1] but he claimed that in the making of the policy
of the future traditional radicalism would be found wanting.
Business men were increasingly ready to listen to such language,
for they were passing from the offensive to the defensive in
politics. 'Really the Liberal party are on the defensive', wrote a
special correspondent from Birmingham to the *Chicago Tribune*
in 1883. 'Almost for the first time in the history of the party it is
losing its hold.'[2] There is some truth in the view that the Home
Rule split, which severed Chamberlain from Gladstone, really
brought him back to the class and generation from which he
sprang. 'He lost the Liberal leadership, but he regained that of
the modern English bourgeoisie.'[3] After 1886 Conservatives and
Liberal Unionists were able to march together, and Birmingham
led the country yet again in its somewhat untidy advance into
the twentieth century.

### III

The immediate effect of the events of 1886 in Birmingham,
however, was not to inaugurate a new period, but to bring to
an end an old one amid great confusion. In particular, the
difference of opinion about Ireland subjected the Liberal party
to great strain. For a long time Birmingham Conservatives had
pinned their hopes on a division among their opponents as
much as on an augmentation of their own strength. Even in the
heyday of the caucus they liked to think that the days of the

[1] Quoted by W. S. Churchill, op. cit., p. 233.   [2] Quoted in *B.G.*, 2 July 1883.
[3] R. C. K. Ensor, 'Joseph Chamberlain', in the *Spectator*, 3 July 1936.

Liberal party were numbered. In 1877, for instance, one local Conservative described the Liberals as 'like that great planet which it was said once existed and bounded steadily in its orbit between Mars and Jupiter, but now has burst into more than 20 fragments which are even intercepting each other'.[1] The same point was hammered home by Salisbury on his visit in 1883, when he described the Liberals as 'not a united homogeneous party, but an alliance of parties'. These prognostications of Liberal collapse were sometimes coupled with an anticipation of a switch-over in Chamberlain's own outlook and loyalties. It would have been difficult to foresee the whole drama of 1886. What the split of that year did was to divide the Liberal party not between Whigs and Radicals, with Chamberlain securing a position of unrivalled leadership in a new Radical Liberal party, but between those in favour of continued union with Ireland and those against. 'No longer was Tory opposed to Whig and Whig to Tory alone, but Whig fought Whig, and Radical fought Radical. . . . In some of the political clubs it was said to have "rained black balls", and certainly in many socially inclined drawing-rooms the word Ireland was taboo.'[2]

In the town of Birmingham, where the Liberal caucus had ruled for so long, there was considerable reluctance at first to allow the Irish question to break up existing associations. 'It would be a national calamity if Mr. Chamberlain resigned in consequence of the miserable Irish question', said a prominent Liberal in March 1886.[3] Even as late as 1888 Osler, the president of the Gladstonian Birmingham Liberal Association, wrote that there was a general disposition among Liberals of all shades of opinion in Birmingham to ignore in local matters differences on the Irish question.[4] But however natural the disposition, it had proved impossible by that time to maintain a united Liberal Birmingham. The Irish Home Rulers and the Chamberlain Unionists were separated by an unbridgeable gulf. 'I want to show you', said Councillor Lancaster, a Gladstonian, in November 1887, 'that it is absolutely impossible that we can ever work together again.'[5]

The story of the split in Birmingham is an interesting one.

---

[1] The Stone Collection in the Birmingham Reference Library.
[2] L. Creswicke, *The Life of Joseph Chamberlain*, vol. ii (1904), p. 87.
[3] *B.P.*, 27 May 1886.                    [4] Ibid., 26 January 1888.
[5] *News Cuttings on the Liberal Split*, kept in the Headquarters of the Birmingham Unionist Association.

When Chamberlain resigned from Gladstone's government in March 1886 on the Home Rule proposals, and the Bill had passed through its first stages in the House of Commons, he went down to Birmingham to try to justify himself to his constituents. The visit was an important one. If he wished to maintain his national political influence, it was essential that he should maintain his hold on the city of Birmingham. On 21 April he explained to the Liberal Two Thousand the facts of his case. Schnadhorst had attempted to dissuade him from addressing the Birmingham Liberal Association, and there were ominous signs of a cleavage between the two men. On 13 February Schnadhorst had written to Chamberlain telling him that he wanted a bold and thorough policy for Ireland. By 7 April Chamberlain believed that Schnadhorst was working against him and could no longer be regarded as 'a safe or a friendly guide'. But Chamberlain had influential allies in Birmingham, and Arthur Chamberlain, the Kenricks, and Bunce forced the Birmingham Liberal Association to give Chamberlain a hearing on 21 April.

The meeting was a turning-point in Chamberlain's career. Opinion was very excited in the city, but the peace-loving and well-respected Dr. Dale was in the chair. Chamberlain objected to the Home Rule Bill as a symbol of separation, and said that he would sooner go out of politics altogether than give his vote to the Land Bill. He pointed out that his resignation, far from being unique, was not without precedents in the life of Gladstone himself, who had more than once separated himself from a government of which he disapproved. 'I have not changed', he said with pride, and went on to demand a vote of confidence. If for private interests or personal ambition he had been false to his convictions, and had disregarded the vital interests of his country, then he was worthy of condemnation. If not, then he could in no way be blamed. Schnadhorst, the secretary of the Liberal Association, had the difficult task of proposing a vote of 'unabated confidence', which was carried amid acclamation. Although it was 10 o'clock, and both Schnadhorst and Dale, the chairman, were in favour of adjourning the meeting, Chamberlain realized that he must press his case to its conclusion and ask for a vote of confidence, not only in himself but also in his policy. He got this too. Dale moved a second resolution practically committing Birmingham to Unionist policy. While restating its unchanged confidence in Gladstone, and its belief in the general principle of Home Rule, it demanded that the Irish Members should be retained at Westminster. The resolution was carried. In effect the Two Thousand had pledged themselves to follow Chamberlain, to reject Gladstone's proposed Land Bill, and to entertain only a Home Rule Bill so revised that Chamberlain himself would approve of it.

Chamberlain was naturally elated. To Harcourt he wrote that he was very pleased with his Two Thousand yesterday. 'They answered splendidly to the call.' There had been only one fly in the ointment—Schnadhorst, who had been doing everything to thwart him. To Bunce Chamberlain wrote: 'Schnadhorst behaved badly last night. It was evident that he had done and was doing everything in his power to postpone a decision.'

Schnadhorst's power may have been restricted in Birmingham, where he had himself followed his political apprenticeship, but it still remained powerful in the National Liberal Federation itself, the national caucus, which Chamberlain had reared and taught himself. At its meeting on 5 May a resolution by William Harris of Birmingham requesting Gladstone to maintain Irish representation at Westminster was defeated, and an amendment proclaiming unconditional confidence in the Prime Minister and his policy was carried by a large majority. Schnadhorst himself threw the whole of his own influence behind Gladstone. The result was what proved to be a final break; Chamberlain and many of the Birmingham group resigned from the Federation, and soon afterwards it transferred its headquarters from Birmingham to London.

As a substitute for the old organization, Chamberlain built up a new body called the National Radical Union. He was anxious to maintain the word 'radical' in the title, for most of his Birmingham supporters had little sympathy with Hartington, the leader of the Whigs, who were united with Chamberlain in opposition to Home Rule. Indeed Hartington's name had been greeted with hisses at the 21 April meeting in Birmingham. The National Radical Union was founded a few days before the General Election of 1886 with the purpose of promoting a system of local government—an extension of the Birmingham model—applicable to England, Scotland, Wales, and Ireland under the supreme authority of one parliament for the whole of the United Kingdom. The treasurer of the new organization was George

Dixon, its hon. secretary was Arthur Chamberlain, and its chairman of the Executive Committee was Jesse Collings. It was thus a Chamberlainite body through and through. Like all Chamberlain's other political progeny it laid great stress on organization, which it claimed was rendered more imperative than ever 'by the unfortunate and intolerant action of the older Liberal Associations'.[1]

But the hastily improvised Radical Union could not secure the unanimous support of all Liberals anywhere in England, not even in Birmingham itself. Of the seven Birmingham Liberal Members of Parliament elected in 1885 one, Cook, was a Gladstonian, and another, Broadhurst, chose to leave Bordesley for Nottingham, thus opening the way to political bickering in his old constituency. The Gladstonian Liberals chose Tait as their candidate, while the Liberal Unionists put up Jesse Collings. In the 1886 Election, five Liberal Unionists were returned unopposed, and in a straight fight in Bordesley Collings got in without difficulty. In East Birmingham, in the fight between Matthews, standing as a Conservative Unionist, and Cook, standing as a Gladstonian Liberal, the Conservative candidate was elected. Cook's Liberal poll fell from 4,277 in 1885 to 2,552 in 1886, although Matthews only increased his poll by 216 votes. The figures indicate that in the awkward political situation many Liberals abstained. Some, like Dale, who occupied a half-way position, supported Cook, and did their best to heal the split in the party.

In 1886 and early 1887 there was some possibility of a *rapprochement* between the two groups of Liberals. In the municipal elections of 1886 and 1887 there were no fights between Liberal Unionists and Liberals. There were not even two distinct local organizations. Trouble came to a head when the Gladstonian Liberals tried to capture all the places in the Birmingham Liberal Association. They aimed at controlling the ward committees at the base of the whole organization and thereby changing the composition of the divisional councils. Ward meetings were extremely stormy, epithets were hurled about from side to side, windows were broken, and tempers ran high. The fight went on not only in the wards but also in all sorts of local bodies. The Allotments and Small Holdings Association, for instance, removed Collings as president in February 1888,

[1] *First Report of the National Radical Union*, 1887.

although he had been one of the pioneers of the movement. 'If ever there was a question upon which the two sections of the Liberal party might advantageously have co-operated, it was on this question of allotments', said the *Birmingham Daily Post*.[1]

Chamberlain had hoped that it would be possible to work within the framework of the old caucus. 'We have no reason whatever for interfering with the old organization', he told the Executive Committee of the National Radical Union in March 1887.[2] A year later, on his return from America, where he had been serving on the Fisheries Commission between November 1887 and February 1888, he wrote that the Gladstonians were 'much more malignant' than when he had gone away. 'Last night they secured a large majority of the Liberal Association at the primary elections even in my division.'[3] From that time onwards he determined to set up an entirely new Liberal Unionist Association of his own in the city. In April 1888 the new caucus emerged. It worked through divisional associations with subsidiary polling district committees, each divisional body having an elected council. Together the Councils made up a Grand Committee for the whole city. This committee had an inner Executive Committee and a small Management Committee of seven, not counting the officers. By Easter Chamberlain reported that the organization was 'going like wildfire', and a few weeks later he declared that he would not be satisfied until he had purged the Council of every Gladstonian. 'Je tiens ferme.'[4]

In the meantime, with Schnadhorst still behind the scenes and Harris returned to the fold, the older Liberal Association maintained its vigorous organization. An attempt was made in February 1888 to reduce the importance of the Two Thousand on the grounds first that it had become too unwieldy for deliberation or debate, and secondly, that to call a meeting of it cost £20 at least. Osler proposed that an Executive Committee of 400 should be given power to elect the officers, and the members of the Management Committee, and to lay down policy. The proposed change was rejected and it was agreed that the Two Thousand should remain in being, meet at least once a year, and continue to elect the officers of the organization. The

[1] *B.P.*, 6 February 1888.
[2] 12 March 1887, in *Circulars, Leaflets, &c., of the Radical Union and Liberal Unionist Association.*          [3] Quoted by J. L. Garvin, op. cit., vol. ii, p. 355.
[4] Ibid., p. 356.

caucus forms were thus retained in their entirety. The Liberal Association staged a gigantic rally of Liberals from all parts of the country in November 1888 at Bingley Hall, where over 15,000 people heard Gladstone himself make one of the finest platform speeches of his old age. 'The scene at the close was absolutely indescribable and incomparable, overwhelming like the sea', wrote Morley.[1] It was perfectly clear, even if it had not been clear before, that there were two Liberal Birminghams divided by an unbridgeable gulf. There was a feud of families as well as of individuals—the Chamberlains and the Kenricks were on one side, the Tangyes and the Cadburys on the other. In the municipal elections of 1888 Liberals and Liberal Unionists came face to face for the first time. In the four wards where they met, the Liberal Unionists won three.

If relations between Liberals caused difficulties, so too did relations between Liberal Unionists and Conservative Unionists. The roots of animosity went deep into the past on both sides. 'It is almost impossible to get Tories to vote for Liberals or for Liberals to vote for Tories', said Chamberlain in March 1887.[2] Later on in the year, before he went to America, Chamberlain was taking a stronger line. 'We shall be taunted', he said, 'by our alliance with the Tories. At least our allies will be English gentlemen and not the subsidised agents of a foreign conspiracy.' He quoted Burke that when bad men combined it was time for good men to associate.[3] A little later the Liberal Unionist, Councillor Baldwin, was declaring that if he had to take his choice and either go over to the Tories or to the Parnellites, he would sooner go over to the Tories, but he went on to say that he failed to see the necessity for doing either.[4]

At least until 1888 the Radical Union laid great stress on its radicalism. It was wary of the Conservative government and stated in its first report that one of the most important political facts of the time was that the Conservatives would be in a minority in the House of Commons, their continued tenure of office depending on the Radical Unionists. Later on, in January 1888, Dixon expressed himself satisfied with the results of this political balance. The Conservative party, having recognized

---

[1] *The Life of Gladstone*, vol. iii, pp. 387–9.
[2] Chamberlain was speaking to the Executive Committee of the National Radical Union. See *Circulars, Leaflets, &c., of the Radical Union and Liberal Unionist Association.*
[3] Ibid., June 1887.　　　　　　　　　　[4] *B.P.*, 21 November 1887.

that Democracy was in power, were playing to the gallery and had shown themselves eager to pass measures which would have set their own hair on end twenty years before.[1]

Sometimes the Radical Unionists could flaunt their radicalism in the faces of the Gladstonians. In a by-election for All Saints Ward, for instance, in January 1888, Jacobs, a Conservative, was elected against Smith, a Radical Unionist, on a very small poll, and the Radicals claimed that Jacobs had been returned with Gladstonian help in one of the most radical wards in the city, where there had not been a municipal election since 1878.[2] No wonder that in May 1888, after Chamberlain had changed his policy and a Gladstonian and a Conservative were fighting another by-election, Chamberlain wrote that 'the difficulty is to get the rank and file to vote for a "tory". . . . The issue is doubtful at present, and we are risking a good deal by thus burning our boats and throwing in our lot with the Conservatives.'[3]

The difficulties of *rapprochement* between Liberal and Conservative Unionists did not all lie on the radical side. The Conservatives, too, were often frightened of their new allies. Some of them strongly objected to Jesse Collings in the General Election of 1886. 'Many Conservatives abstained from voting in Bordesley owing to the candidate's personal popularity, but a greater number, placing their patriotism before their private feelings, recorded their votes in his favour', said the Conservative party report.[4] It required all Lord Randolph Churchill's persuasion to prevent the Conservatives from running their own candidates, and taking advantage of the Liberal split to gain control of the town. Lord Randolph visited Birmingham on 19 June 1886, to appeal to local Conservatives not to oppose Liberal Unionist candidates. He was successful, and wrote to Chamberlain on his return that 'we shall run no other candidates except Matthews, and we shall give all our support to the Liberal Unionists, asking for no return and making no boast or taunt'.[5]

The terms of the limited compact were vaguer than they seemed, and although from 1888 onwards Chamberlain's policy was to maintain and strengthen the Unionist alliance, there were

[1] *B.P.*, 27 January 1888.                    [2] Ibid., 17 January 1888.
[3] J. L. Garvin, op. cit., vol. ii, p. 356.
[4] *Annual Report of the Conservative Association*, 1886.
[5] W. S. Churchill, op. cit., vol. ii, p. 527.

occasional misunderstandings and crises. In 1889 there was a major crisis, which had repercussions on national as well as on local politics. On the death of John Bright the Birmingham Conservatives proposed that Lord Randolph should be adopted as the Unionist candidate. He already had a close connexion with the constituency, having polled 4,216 Conservative votes there against Bright in 1885. He was idolized by local Conservatives and respected by some Liberal Unionists too. On the day after the vacancy was declared the *Birmingham Daily Post*, Liberal Unionist in politics, published an article supporting his candidature. But Chamberlain and many of the Liberal Unionist leaders were opposed to the idea of having a Conservative representative for Bright's old constituency. Chamberlain, it was widely thought, did not want any rival figure in the town to divide his popularity with him. As Jennings wrote: 'Chamberlain is boss in Birmingham and means to remain so.'[1] Although Lord Randolph decided not to stand, the situation remained bitter and involved. When John Albert Bright was brought forward as a Liberal Unionist candidate, the Conservative leaders, including Rowlands, Sawyer, Satchell Hopkins, and Moore Bayley, refused to support him. So violent was their opposition that it seemed likely that the Gladstonian candidate, Beale, would carry the seat. It was only the direct intervention first of Sir Michael Hicks Beach and then of Balfour, who came down to talk to the Birmingham Conservatives 'almost at an hour's notice', which persuaded them to accept J. A. Bright and restore peace in the constituency. Balfour urged them to oppose the return of a Gladstonian at all costs, and carried the meeting with him. John Albert Bright was accepted as Unionist candidate by a large majority, and won the election against a Gladstonian Liberal without any difficulty.[2] None the less, relations between the Conservative party and the Liberal Unionists were not

---

[1] Ibid., p. 741.

[2] The total poll in 1889 was less than it had been in 1885, but was bigger than it was to be in 1892. For statisticians of election results, the figures are interesting.

November 1885: John Bright (Lib.) 4,989; Lord Randolph Churchill (Cons.) 4,216.

1889: J. A. Bright (Lib. Unionist) 5,621; Beale (Gladstonian Lib.) 2,561.

1892: J. A. Bright (Lib. Unionist) 5,525; Herbert (Gladstonian Lib.) 1,522.

The next election in the Central Ward was not until 1906, when the figures were: Parkes (Lib. Unionist) 5,684; Lee (Lib.) 2,075.

improved when the Liberal Unionist party went on to pass a
resolution affirming that the election had proved their 'prepon-
derance of power' in the Central Division. There was trouble
again in the same constituency in 1895, when J. A. Bright resigned. The secretary of the Conservative Association wrote to
Vince, the secretary of the Liberal Unionist Association, stating
that Lord John Beresford had written to him saying that he
wished to stand as a Unionist candidate at the forthcoming
General Election. The Liberal Unionists would hear nothing of
such a proposal, and the Conservatives in turn would not support
the suggested candidature of the Liberal Unionist, T. Grosvenor
Lee. Meetings between the two Unionist wings ended without
agreement being reached. Whereas in 1889 it was the Conservatives who claimed that the compact of 1886 had been broken by
the Liberals, in 1895 it was the Liberal Unionists who passed a
resolution protesting against Conservative action as 'a flagrant
and unprecedented violation of the terms of alliance' between
the two parties. Finally Parkes, the chairman of the Liberal
Unionist Association, was chosen as candidate, and was returned
unopposed.

Although the Liberal Unionists remained the dominant
political group in general elections, the Conservative party in
Birmingham could not fail to gain ground in municipal affairs
as a result of the Liberal split of 1886. They won 2 seats immediately from Gladstonians, and by 1891 had 19 seats on the
Council as against 29 Liberal Unionists and 24 Liberals, a great
advance on the low-water days of the 1870's.

Conservative organization continued to improve. The Reform
Bill of 1884 had provided them with a final challenge to refit
their organization to the requirements of a mass electorate. They
set about completely reorganizing their party in 1886, and
accepted with enthusiasm 'the extension of the representative
principle'. A small Executive Committee was formed, consisting
of the representatives of the committees of the seven new parliamentary divisions created by the Reform Act, along with one
member elected by the two senior Conservative clubs, and two
members sent by the combined working-men's clubs. In addition
a large General Committee was established, consisting of the
members of the Executive Committee, four representatives of
each ward, four each from the two Conservative clubs, and two
each from working men's clubs. Other agencies like the Primrose

League gained ground in the neighbourhood. There were ten habitations of the League, and over 250 members in Lady-wood alone.[1] In 1886 the Midland Union was created to organize Conservative strength throughout the whole area. The trend was towards a new brand of industrial Conservatism adapted to the political requirements of a new age. The new spirit was revealed in the burst of pride which greeted the choice of Matthews as Home Secretary in the Conservative government of 1886. 'Birmingham is the first of the large towns of the kingdom with a Home Secretary as one of its representatives.'[2]

As the years went by, the Conservatives and Liberal Unionists drew much closer together. A working machinery of co-opera-tion was set in motion in the 1890's. In 1890 Chamberlain suggested a Joint Committee of the two bodies to deal with motions affecting Unionists generally. It received Salisbury's blessing. A letter from Hatfield to the Conservatives told them: 'It is almost certain that unless both parties heartily co-operate in support of the Unionist candidate in each division, from which ever side of the combined party he may be drawn, the victory of the separatists will be an inevitable result.'[3] The first meeting of a Joint Committee was held on 27 December 1890. It staged its first demonstration of strength in March 1891, when Salisbury and Chamberlain appeared on the same platform in the town. In 1893 there was effective common action against the proposed new Home Rule Bill. In 1898 the 'long-standing difference' about ward representation was settled by 'the concession' to Conservatives of the right to nominate the Unionist candidate for the Edgbaston division, and on the death of Dixon the Con-servative, Sir Francis Lowe, was returned at a by-election, al-though at the same time the Conservatives took no part in the School Board elections because, among other things, 'they could not count on the support of the Liberal Unionist party'.[4] In the same year the committee agreed that the selection of municipal candidates by either wing of the Unionist party should be reasonably acceptable to the other wing, that there should be a conference in case of disputes, and more frequent routine meetings. In 1899 co-operation was pushed farther than before, and as the fiscal question burst into English politics in 1903, the two wings were drawn even closer together. In the 1906 Election,

---

[1] *Report of the Conservative Association*, 1888.      [2] Ibid., 1886.
[3] Ibid., 1892.                                          [4] Ibid., 1898.

although there were some dissidents on the fiscal question like Arthur Chamberlain,[1] Birmingham remained 'an impregnable stronghold of Unionism', and Liberal Unionists and Conservatives celebrated the victory with a joint Election Banquet. The same story of increasing co-operation can be traced down to and throughout the Election of 1910.

By this time it was realized that the division caused considerable waste of energy and effort for two sets of independent organizations. There were not only two independent associations in Birmingham itself, but also in the west Midlands area—the Conservative Midland Union and the Midland Liberal Unionist Association. In 1912 a committee was set up to attempt to fuse together these two regional bodies, with Lord Dartmouth as Conservative chairman and Neville Chamberlain as Liberal Unionist vice-chairman. With the outbreak of the First World War, the scheme was laid on one side. So, too, were the schemes for fusion mooted within the city. In March 1914 the question of amalgamation had been discussed by the Liberal Unionists, who agreed to set up a sub-committee to consider the matter and to report to the next meeting of the executive, but the war brought all these hopes to an end.

The schemes were taken up again before the Armistice was signed. In June 1918 a Provisional Management Committee of the two parties was set up consisting of ten representatives of the Executive Committee of the Birmingham Conservative Association, headed by Sir Francis Lowe and Sir Arthur Steel-Maitland, and ten representatives of the Birmingham Liberal Unionist Association, headed by the Chamberlain brothers, Austen and Neville. Seven months later the important decision was taken to omit the words 'Liberal' and 'Conservative' from the new Unionist Association. Fusion had come at last, and as it came, effective power still lay with a member of the Chamberlain family. 'The decision to unite', Neville Chamberlain wrote, 'practically places the direction of Unionist politics in Birmingham in my hands. I am not quite sure whether all those present perceived this; I did not mention it.'[2] The way was prepared for the post-war period in English politics, and as if to draw an old chapter to its close

---

[1] See A. Chamberlain's powerful 'straight talk', *On Free Trade and Protection* (December 1905), with its advice to his work-people in Kynoch's to 'Vote Liberal for Free Trade and Spending Power'.

[2] K. Feiling, *The Life of Neville Chamberlain* (1946), p. 80.

Vince, who had been secretary of the Liberal Unionist Association since 1893, resigned after twenty-six years' service. The year 1919 was not so much the end of a chapter in Birmingham politics as the beginning of a new one.

## IV

In the inter-war years the main political opponents of the Unionists in Birmingham were no longer the Liberals but the members of the rising Labour party. It is necessary to go back in time to examine the growth of the Labour movement from the pioneer days of the late nineteenth century onwards.

Although Birmingham was far less important than many other parts of the country in the growth of a separate Labour movement, it is interesting to note that it was at conferences in Birmingham that two of the most important national political decisions in the rise of Labour were made. In 1869 the Trades Union Congress, holding its second annual meeting in Birmingham, decided to set up a 'Parliamentary Committee' to watch parliamentary proceedings affecting workers, send deputations to ministers, and lobby M.P.s. In 1902 the third annual conference of the Labour Representation Committee, also meeting in Birmingham, resolved that a scheme for raising a parliamentary levy should be adopted, and that the proposals should be placed before the trade unions. The adoption of this method of finance was of fundamental importance in laying the foundations of the Labour party.

The presence of large numbers of highly-skilled working men in Birmingham, a labour *élite*, was one of the most important features in local social history. It also influenced politics. At the Election of 1868, after the extension of the franchise, both Liberal and Conservative organizations made intelligent and vigorous attempts to capture the working men's vote. While the Liberals stressed abstract rights, mainly concerned with franchise and electoral reform, the Conservatives went out of their way to appeal to the local artisans in economic terms. Sebastian Evans stressed that he had been engaged for seven years as practical foreman in an important branch of local art manufacture, in 'continual contact with my fellow working men in all departments of labour', while both he and Lloyd placed reform of trade-union law—'the fullest legal recognition of Trade Unions'

—in the forefront of their electoral addresses.[1] Already a Conservative Working Men's Liberal Conservative Association had been set up in 1866, and at the end of the year it claimed 2,000 members.

With a Conservative organization conscious of the need for appealing to working men, and a powerful Liberal organization monopolizing local political power, there was little space left for the growth of independent Labour organizations. At the election of 1868 G. J. Holyoake had offered himself to the electors as a progressive working men's candidate and proclaimed that in the newly-founded 'political commonwealth', working men would sooner or later find their way into Parliament, but it was clear that, however eloquently he argued, the time was not ripe. 'The object of my being a candidate at Birmingham', Holyoake himself wrote, 'was to test and advocate the question of working-class representation. At that time there was no strong feeling on the part of the working class in favour of the representation of their order.'[2]

Some of the difficulties of building up an independent organization during the golden age of the caucus can be illustrated from the history of the radical groups like the Working Men's Reform League and the St. George's Reform League, which had been set up in the 1860's to push the claims of artisans to a share in parliamentary representation. The Leagues were persuaded to merge their fortunes with the Liberal Association. Some prominent local working-class figures, like G. Nuttall and W. Finnemore, went over with enthusiasm. Others held out against the merger, including W. J. Davis, who later on was to write *The History of the Trades Union Congress*. Some of the recalcitrant working men were persuaded to support W. M. Ellis, Chamberlain's Conservative opponent in the St. Paul's election of 1872. Twenty-one members of the Brassworkers' Society were only won over to Liberalism at the last moment, after Arthur Chamberlain had persuaded Davis to appeal to them not to vote for a Conservative candidate.[3] After Davis had been elected to the School Board in 1875 as an independent working men's candidate, although he had been opposed by both Conservatives and

[1] J. A. Langford, *Modern Birmingham and its Institutions* (1872), vol. ii, pp. 369–77, prints the addresses.
[2] G. J. Holyoake, *Sixty Years of an Agitator's Life*, vol. ii (1892), p. 151.
[3] *Searchlight*, 13 November 1913.

Liberals, Joseph Chamberlain told him to abandon independent action, throw in his lot with the Liberals, and find a place on the Town Council. 'As far as I can see', he said, 'your principles are the same as mine and you have a following which must eventually be recognized.' Davis refused and told Chamberlain that 'a Labour Party must and would exist', but he continued to give the Liberals his support, and the Birmingham Labour Association which he organized threw all its weight, numerically very small, behind Chamberlain's attack on private monopolies.

While these political developments were taking place, the Birmingham Trades Council was beginning to interfere to an increasing extent in local politics. It was a body set up in 1866, growing up out of the craft organizations of the town, and following the model of the London Trades Council set up six years earlier. Its beginnings were modest. The cost of postage to summon its first meeting amounted to 1s. and the Tamworth Arms was a big enough rendezvous to hold the delegates. The first convener and secretary was R. Bateson of the Carpenters' and Joiners' Society, while other founder unions were the Basket Makers, the Cabinet Makers, the Amalgamated Society of Carpenters and Joiners, the Cordwainers, the Lath Benders, the Mill Sawyers, the Painters, the Tailors, the Wood Turners, the Fire Iron Makers, and the Coachmakers. It was on this essentially craft basis that the venture started.

The first policy of the Trades Council was to follow and support 'those advanced and independent Liberals who believe that the broader the basis of our constitution, the firmer they will stand', and in 1873, for example, it passed a resolution thanking Joseph Chamberlain for 'his able exposition of the principles of Trade Unionism at Sheffield'.[1] As labour problems loomed larger in the 70's, it set up a parliamentary fund in 1873—with Chamberlain as a trustee—and adopted the policy of recommending some of the Liberal candidates in the municipal elections as 'suitable representatives of labour'.

There were several Labour nominations and successes in the 70's, not all of them Trades Council nominees. Heyden, an independent working man, represented Market Hall from 1867 —he first stood in 1866—until 1876. In 1873 he defeated the official Liberal Association candidate Scruton, but he was himself defeated by W. H. Dixon three years later. In the meantime

[1] See *An Historical Sketch of the Birmingham Trades Council 1866-1926* (1927).

Whateley, a working men's candidate, had won Hampton in 1871, although Osborne of the Labour Representation League was bottom of the poll in St. Mary's Ward a year later, with the dubious consolation of seeing Schnadhorst defeated alongside him in the same ward. Perhaps it was the obvious danger of letting Conservatives in which caused the Liberals to change their policy of opposing all non-Liberal candidates. Schnadhorst admitted to Davis that there had always been a minority of Liberals in favour of separate Labour representation, 'but now that minority is a majority'.[1] The Liberal Association recognized the Labour Association as an independent force, and agreed to consult with it as to anti-Conservative co-operation. In 1880 W. J. Davis, standing as an Independent, won Market Hall with a majority of over 500 from a candidate supported by the Conservatives.

During the 1880's there were various attempts in Birmingham, as elsewhere, to build up new and distinctive political labour movements. Each had its own sources of inspiration and its own set of loyalties. Some working men looked to the Liberals and began the 'Lib-Lab' alliance. One of their most important representatives was Henry Broadhurst, the stone-mason, who won Bordesley at the General Election of 1885. Broadhurst did not fight the 1886 Election in Birmingham, but six years later W. J. Davis stood as a Lib-Lab candidate in the same constituency, where he was defeated by Jesse Collings. In 1900 J. V. Stevens, the tin-plate worker, and the president of the T.U.C. in 1897 was defeated in Birmingham East. Bordesley and East Birmingham were the two most winnable seats, but although there were six other attempts by Lib-Labs or socialists before 1914, none of them was successful.

The Lib-Labs proclaimed working-class interests but they were not doctrinaire socialists, and were content to follow Liberal leadership. While they did not triumph in any of the Birmingham constituencies, they did succeed in winning several municipal elections, the first of them in 1889 when, in a spectacular election contest in St. Thomas's ward, J. V. Stevens beat young Austen Chamberlain by eleven votes. In 1901 Keegan captured St. Mary's Ward from a Liberal Unionist. He held the seat in 1904, but was defeated in 1907.

In the meantime there had been a remarkable growth of

[1] W. A. Dalley, *The Life Story of W. J. Davis* (1914), p. 53.

PLATE XXIX

The Chamberlain Family

PLATE XXX

W. J. Davis

Labour groups much farther to the left than the Lib-Labs, most of them advocating programmes of their own, many completely socialist in character. As early as 1887 Haddon had stood as a Social Democrat in St. Mary's Ward, where he had polled over 750 votes, and Tanner had stood as a Socialist in Ladywood. Tanner tried again in 1888 and 1889, being defeated on the second occasion in Nechells Ward by a candidate who enjoyed the combined support of both Gladstonians and Unionists. In 1893 the Trades Council sponsored two of its own candidates— Tanner in Ladywood and Eades in St. Martin's—but they were both heavily defeated. There was some consolation a year later when the Trades Council secured its first direct representative on the School Board, nominated, financed, and elected independently of any other party.

The 1890's were the pioneering days of the English socialist movement, and Birmingham had its share in the adventure. They were days of street-corner oratory, of collection boxes, and Merry England fairs. There were two bodies in Birmingham which kept a watchful eye on the various smaller organizations, some of them very small, which were spreading with evangelistic fervour what was conceived of as a new gospel. The first was the Joint Socialist Committee, which included representatives of the Independent Labour party, set up in 1893, the Social Democratic Federation to which Tanner belonged, the Co-operative Societies, the Fabian Society, and some of the trade unions. All these bodies shared in the first big Labour Day demonstration of 6 May 1894, which was advertised by 125 posters and 7,000 handbills.

The second co-ordinating force and the main centre of the Labour movement in the city was the Birmingham Labour Church, founded in September 1892. While the Liberals had their caucus, the Socialists had their church. It attracted not only Socialists, but social reformers of all shades of opinion, and aimed at bringing them together. In January 1895 it carried unanimously a resolution asking for the formation of 'ONE Socialist Party', based on the amalgamation of the existing bodies.[1] The Labour Church invited prominent Socialist speakers to Birmingham, such as Tom Mann, Ben Tillett, Stewart

---

[1] Minute Book of the Labour Church, 25 January 1895. The Minute Books of the Labour Church present a full picture of the tangled skein of labour activities in the 1890's.

Headlam, J. F. Oakshott, and Bruce Glasier. It sold copies of journals like the *Clarion*, and spread the message of Merry England. It encouraged the Clarion Cycling Club, which combined progressive politics and *joie de vivre* so successfully that Clarion Cycling Clubs soon flourished all over the country. Indoors it tried to avoid sectarian strife. It offered its rooms to the Social Democratic Federation, while continuing to correspond with the local I.L.P. It won over some of the intelligentsia, so that in 1895 the local Fabians asked to amalgamate with the Church. The fusion was accomplished and a Socialist Lecture Committee set up.

The Labour Church had its moments of shadow as well as of sunshine. Although it thought of socialism in terms of a crusade, it could not always maintain a firm crusaders' hold over its members. We read in the minutes, that 'between 1895 and 1901 some thirty of the original members of the Labour Church became Laodicean and showed the *lack of staying power in their characters*'. There was sometimes a falling off in attendance, while in 1898 'only one third of the members paid their subscriptions although every member had promised to pay at the end of each week or in advance'.

If the 1890's were the pioneer days, when the Labour movement in Birmingham was carried forward with religious fervour, and the Labour Church was a natural centre, the 1900's were the years of growing organization concentrated increasingly in a secretary's office. In 1900 the Labour Representation Committee was set up in London to try to secure a united front of working-class organizations. The national model was copied locally in Birmingham as elsewhere. A Birmingham and District Labour Representation Council was set up in 1902, which for the first time tried to build up an effective party organization. Among the bodies represented on it were the Birmingham Trades Council, the Labour Church, the Social Democratic Federation (only for a short time), the Independent Labour party, the National Women's Labour League, the Amalgamated Society of Engineers, the National Amalgamated Societies of Brassworkers and of Furnishing Trades, the Britannia Metal Workers' Association, and the Aston Manor Labour Association. According to the constitution of the Council, divisional committees were appointed 'open to all members of Socialist Societies, Trade Unions and Co-operative Societies which are represented in the Birmingham Labour Representation Council, and to all others in sympathy with the principles and objects of the national Labour Party, who declare that they are not members of any other political party'. Within the committees, small executive committees directed business. The executive, elected annually and meeting at least twice a year, consisted of the chairman, the secretary, the treasurer, the chairmen and secretaries of sub-committees, and three others. Among the sub-committees were ward organizers and a finance sub-committee to deal with the difficult problems of funds.

In 1906 the Council felt an increasing optimism about the future of the party in the country as a whole, if not in Birmingham. The newly elected Labour Member of Parliament, Philip Snowden, told a big rally in the city that the General Election of that year had 'discovered the Labour movement'. 'The Liberal party which half a century ago had a reason for its existence and had work to do was a disjointed party' and could not long continue to exist. 'They knew that just as sure as tomorrow's sun would rise, so sure would socialism become a reality.' Although even in 1914 the Labour movement in Birmingham was far from established, its main lines of future development had already been marked out.

In municipal matters, in particular, the members of the various Birmingham labour organizations could claim that they had a new message to offer, as distinctive a message as, though a different one from, the social gospel of Joseph Chamberlain twenty years before. There was a link between their programme and that of Chamberlain, for Sidney Webb confessed that the path to his town Utopia was that of Mr. Chamberlain's early career in Birmingham.[1] 'Since Mr. Chamberlain arose in Birmingham', wrote W. T. Stead in 1892, 'there has been no man so like him as Mr. Sidney Webb, who aspires to be Mr. Chamberlain of London—only more so.'[2] The Birmingham Socialists, like the London Socialists, stressed the 'more so'. The Trades Council led the way. In 1889 it was urging that 'all contracts given out by local governing bodies in this city should not be placed in the hands of any contractors who do not pay the recognized rate of wages'.[3] Ten years later it orga-

---

[1] Quoted by B. Webb, *Our Partnership* (1948), p. 105.
[2] *The Elector's Guide* (1892), edited by W. T. Stead, p. 50.
[3] *Twenty-fourth Annual Report of the Birmingham Trades Council*.

nized the Midlands Conference on Old Age Pensions. In 1902 and 1903, when fiscal reform was the main political talk of the day, it urged with Fallows 'that the workers will be equally exploited both under Protection and Free Trade until such time that nations shall produce for use and not for profit'.[1]

This was the long-range vision. The immediate objectives were a new social programme designed to invigorate town and nation. Its main headlines were: improved housing; an extension of the health departments of the city to include personal as well as environmental services—school meals as well as improved drainage; direct labour for municipal contracts; closer supervision of working conditions for municipal employees; control of tramways and town planning; and a more positive programme to deal with the 'unemployed question'. A Citizens' Committee was set up to try to secure some of these objectives. In pressing for them the local representatives of the Labour movement had the blessing and sometimes the financial support of George Cadbury. He had long sympathized with an independent Labour organization. 'We want a hundred working men in Parliament', he said at the time when John Burns was elected for Battersea.[2] Although he was anxious to keep in the background, he helped the Labour Church financially and wrote after 1906 that he had no interest in the Liberal party 'except in so far as it promotes the welfare of the millions of my fellow countrymen who are on or below the poverty line'.[3]

In the first few years of the twentieth century the number of Labour and Socialist candidates standing at municipal elections increased. The first man to get in on a distinctively Socialist ticket was J. A. Fallows in Bordesley in 1902. He polled 2,666 votes against the Conservative candidate's 2,485 but was heavily defeated by a Liberal Unionist in 1905. At the elections of 1907 there were three Socialist candidates, all of them defeated, and two Lib-Labs. A year later the Lib-Labs and Socialists came into open conflict for the first time, and in Saltley, Toller, the Lib-Lab candidate, beat Beard, a prominent local leader of the I.L.P., by nearly a thousand votes.

The reorganization of the city boundaries in 1911 gave Labour a real bridgehead in the Town Council for the first time. In the miniature 'general election' of 1911 there were fifteen Socialist

[1] *Twenty-seventh Annual Report of the Birmingham Trades Council.*
[2] A. G. Gardiner, *The Life of George Cadbury* (1923), p. 77.          [3] Ibid., p. 83.

candidates, of whom six were successful, four of them topping the poll, in Duddeston and Nechells, Saltley, and Washwood Heath. In Selly Oak, where George Cadbury, who later joined the Labour Party, came out head of the poll, Shann, a Socialist, was second. Although only one of the seven Socialist candidates in 1912 was successful, four out of seven got in a year later.

The young Labour party in Birmingham grew up in a different sort of environment from Labour parties in most other parts of England. While facing powerful established party organizations, it received frequent encouragement and help from outside. The result was that during the First World War Neville Chamberlain's best ally in pushing forward his scheme for a Municipal Bank, in itself an adventurous proposal, was a Labour councillor, Eldred Hallas. Chamberlain recognized the link. After welcoming the Trades Union Congress to Birmingham in 1916, he wrote, concerning labour relations in England as a whole, that the Midlands 'were the most likely part of the country for experiments to start in, and the moment may come when there will be work for me to do in smoothing the way'.[1] The local distinctness of Birmingham and its politics was to remain of great importance in national politics and economics throughout the inter-war years.

[1] K. Feiling, op. cit., p. 61.

# VII

## A CITY AT WAR

### I

ON 2 July 1914 Joseph Chamberlain died. His funeral in Birmingham on 6 July symbolized the end of an epoch. About a month later, on 4 August, Great Britain declared war on Germany. Europe was set on a still unfinished course, which was to destroy an old world for all time.

Between 1914 and 1918 all life in Birmingham was coloured by war—local government, politics, industry, and culture. The First World War differed from all previous wars in its total impact on daily life. Although Birmingham industries had boomed during the Crimean War and Birmingham soldiers had fought in the Boer War, the setting of these conflicts was so far removed from Birmingham itself that the wars left no deep imprint on municipal activities or on social organization. The First World War was different. Although men expected at first that the fighting would be all over in a few months, the war developed into a prolonged and exhausting struggle of attrition, 'life against life, purse against purse'. In that struggle Birmingham had an important part to play. An age of violence demands complex centres of industrial organization. Birmingham was one of these centres, the immensity of its effort 'beyond calculation'. 'You work here,' wrote a group of journalists who visited the city in March 1918, 'work night and day, without talk, with sleeves rolled up and your shoulders to the task. . . . The scale of Birmingham's war activities is colossal. The industrial epic will never be written, for the simple reason that no man is equal to the task.'[1] But the workshops were not everything. The war of 1914–18 demanded large-scale armies, and big centres of population like Birmingham had to help to provide them too. The city had its own military effort as well as its industrial effort, and a complete picture of Birmingham's share in the struggle of 1914–18 must take account of both.

While the effort was built up and directed towards the goal of victory, the atmosphere and conditions of Birmingham life

[1] Quoted by R. H. Brazier and E. Sandford, *Birmingham and the Great War* (1921), p. 123.

PLATE XXXI

Sir William Bowater

itself changed. Normal life was suspended. The political conflicts of the pre-war years came to an abrupt end, and there
were no contested elections either for the Council or for Parliament. Institutions found new functions and let slip old ones.
The Gas Department, for instance, placed its industrial labora-
tory at the disposal of local firms, and produced several war-time
inventions. Toluol was produced for the manufacture of high
explosives: chrome steel was developed as a substitute for rare
tungsten: a tube furnace was designed for hardening metals,
with temperatures under close and expert control: photomicro-
graphic apparatus was built which could show the state of the
various constituents of a given sample of steel or metal alloy.
The Municipal Technical College was used as the headquarters
of a scheme for training large numbers of munitions operatives
either how to make shells, the primary staple of war production,
or to become tool-setters and gauge-makers. The University at
Edgbaston was used as a military hospital. Tables, desks, and
apparatus gave way to rows of beds. The Feeney Art Gallery in
Great Charles Street was turned into a depot of the Lady
Mayoress's Committee, which arranged for the reception and
distribution of clothing and war comforts.

The contribution of Birmingham to the war effort depended
on the co-operation of both official and unofficial agencies.
Officially, the Council and the various Corporation departments
did much to carry out essential tasks—like food and fuel rationing, the raising of a force of special constables, the organization
of air-raid precautions, and the utilization of waste products and
salvage.

The war-time Lord Mayors set a high standard of service for
the Councillors and the officials to follow. Colonel Ernest Martineau, who was Lord Mayor when war broke out in 1914,
volunteered for active service abroad, and later received the
C.M.G. for his services. His successor, Sir William Bowater, who
had played a big part in the realization of the Greater Birmingham Scheme and had been Lord Mayor for three years during
and after the extension of the city, galvanized Birmingham into
war-time activity—raised the City Battalions, took the lead in
the setting up of the Citizens' Committee, collected large sums
of money for war purposes, and accompanied the King on his
visit to local munitions factories in July 1915. For his services
Bowater received the thanks of the Army Council and was made

an honorary Colonel, a Knight, and a Freeman of the City.
Neville Chamberlain was his successor, and so energetic and
successful was he in his local duties as First Citizen that, like his
father, he was translated from local to national administration,
and became Director-General of National Services in Lloyd
George's coalition government. Alderman A. D. Brooks, another
of the Greater Birmingham pioneers, replaced Chamberlain as
Lord Mayor of the City, and had the satisfaction of leading the
Armistice Day celebrations, at the end of four years of struggle,
and of acknowledging the signing of the Peace Treaty, which it
was hoped would mark the beginning of 'peace in our time'.

Official action was supplemented by voluntary action. The
two forms of initiative were conceived of not as competing, but
as complementary. Voluntary service had played a large part
in Birmingham life before the war—through bodies like the City
Aid Society: during the war, particularly through the Citizens'
Committee, a whole network of social activities was organized
by willing, unpaid workers. Indeed, in the last resort it was on
the foundations of this willing consent rather than on the pressure of the law that the whole war effort depended.

The Birmingham Citizens' Committee was set up at the Council House on 7 August 1914 by a representative gathering of
experienced social workers, convened by Sir William Bowater.
It acted as the pivotal local committee for the administration of
grants to meet problems of distress, and it distributed not only
the Prince of Wales's Fund—which met with a ready response
in Birmingham—but also the funds of the pre-war City Aid and
Charity Organisation Societies. In 1916 it was incorporated
and its Executive Committee acted as the local War Pensions
Committee to administer what was in fact official policy. Often its
action anticipated government intervention. It was responsible,
for instance, in the early stages of the war, for the relief of de-
pendants of soldiers and sailors, other than wives and children.
This task was subsequently taken over by the government. In
addition to the distribution of funds, the Citizens' Committee
did much to throw light on the social problems of a large city in
war-time. One of its first tasks in August 1914 was the collection
of information concerning local unemployment. As a result of
Professor Ashley's investigations, Birmingham secured its own
miniature war-time counterpart of Booth's great survey of
London life and labour.

It was paradoxical that out of the grim necessities of war the first beginnings of a welfare policy were evolved. The Citizens' Committee turned its attention, for example, to maternity care and child guidance. As part of its maternity service it offered a grant of 3s. a week for seven weeks to soldiers' wives to assist in providing extra nourishment, essential to mother and child before and after confinement. Neville Chamberlain emphasized the central importance of social welfare from an official as well as from a voluntary point of view. He encouraged schemes which would assist infant welfare, set up a committee to explore the price of milk and the possibility of its municipal distribution, and stored coal to be sold at cost price to the poor.[1] As a result of these often tentative explorations in welfare politics, Birmingham began to look forward to the broader social horizons of the later twentieth century. In Birmingham perhaps more than elsewhere 'the momentum of war spread and quickened a trend towards social altruism, and crystallised . . . demands for social justice'.[2]

## II

Apart from social advance towards welfare objectives, the war raised in Birmingham as in other large cities one central economic question, the problem of the feeding of a large and crowded population. The central task was not only that of maintaining an adequate total supply, but that of distributing scarce commodities fairly.

The immediate effect of the war was a sharp rise in retail prices. In the first week of the war the rush on tradesmen was so heavy that some of them had to close their premises for one day. Shortage of staff and stocks in face of large-scale panic buying was aggravated by arbitrary official measures leading to dislocation. For instance, forty-five of the best Co-operative Society horses were taken away for military purposes within two or three days of the outbreak of war, and although there was an attempt to substitute stationary bread-carts for them, it was difficult to maintain business as usual.[3] In such a situation prices rose. At the end of the first week of war the price of lard had risen from 7d.–8d. per lb. to 8d.–9d. per lb.; sugar had gone up

---

[1] See K. Feiling, *The Life of Neville Chamberlain* (1946), p. 57.
[2] See R. M. Titmuss, *Problems of Social Policy* (London, 1950), p. 54.
[3] T. Smith (ed.), *History of the Birmingham Co-operative Society* (1937), p. 31.

from $2\frac{1}{2}d$. per lb. to $5d.-6d$. per lb.; bacon had increased from $10d.-1s$. per lb. to $1s. 2d.-1s. 4d$. per lb. There was a fear that bread prices would reach unprecedented figures, for, as one con-

# FOOD.

# WEEKLY BULLETIN

## *Issued by the*

# BIRMINGHAM FOOD CONTROL COMMITTEE

These Bulletins appear in the *Birmingham Mail* and *Evening Despatch* every Saturday. They always contain information which Householders and Shop-keepers will find it to their advantage to read.

---

BIRMINGHAM WEEKLY FOOD
,BULLETIN, No. 107.
(LAST ISSUE).

(CUT THIS OUT FOR REFERENCE.)
RATIONS NEXT WEEK.—Sugar, 8oz.

SUGAR.—The allotment for the ration has to be made up by including Brown Sugar. The approved retail prices for the ration sugar are: Castor and Icing, 1s. 2¾d. per lb.; Class 1, Cubes, Loaf, 1s. 2¼d. per lb.; Class 2, White Granu. lated, etc., 1s. 2d. per lb; Class 3, Brown, etc., 1s. per lb. The approved retail price for sugar for domestic preserving obtained through the applications made in March last is 1s. 2d. per lb. "Free" Sugar may be supplied at 1s. 7½d. per lb. on a written undertaking being given by the purchaser that the sugar will only be used for domestic preserving of fruit.

GOVERNMENT BUTTER.—From Monday next the maximum retail price is 2s. 8d. per lb.

No further bulletins in this form will be issued.

OFFICE HOURS, 9 a.m. to 5 p.m.; Saturdays, 9 a.m. to 1 p.m.

H. RICHARDSON, Executive Officer.
Local Food Office, Margaret Street, Birmingham.
June 26, 1920.

FIG. 8

fectioner stated, 'the bakers cannot afford to be public philanthro-pists because the nation has got into difficulties'.[1]

Much of this early rush subsided after the government an-

[1] *B.P.*, 7 August 1914.

nounced that it had decided to fix twice weekly the retail prices of certain commodities, such as sugar, but even after the panic had disappeared, the problems of fair allocation persisted, and some commodities continued to be very scarce, particularly potatoes. A new feature of the war years was the long queue outside a greengrocer's shop. Demand bore no relationship to available supplies.

Before the local authorities or the government adopted state policies of control, many private retail firms had found it necessary to impose voluntary systems of limitation of supplies. A complex example of such a system was that introduced by the Birmingham Co-operative Society. In November 1916 the committee declared that it could only accept new members on condition that they were not entitled to sugar, bread, or coal, and in July 1917 it came to the conclusion that the only satisfactory way of ensuring a fair distribution of sugar to existing members was to introduce sugar cards. The introduction of these cards was six months ahead of governmental food policy.

The evolution of an official policy of control was slow, and it depended much on the initiative of local authorities. It was not until March 1917 that a provisional Food Committee was appointed in Birmingham to try to spread the belief in food economy as a means of obviating the necessity for compulsory rationing. The national position became more serious in the summer of 1917, and the appointment of Lord Rhondda as central Food Controller led to the pursuit of more drastic lines of action. In August 1917 he requested local authorities to appoint Food Control Committees, with special powers to regulate the distribution of sugar supplies. As a result the provisional food committee in Birmingham was converted into a statutory authority. Retailers of sugar were made to register—there were 4,586 of them—and to fill in regular returns of their stocks and the number of their customers. In September 1917 ration cards were introduced for the supply of sugar.

This was the beginning of a far more comprehensive system, for it soon became clear in the autumn of 1917 that the supply prospects for butter, margarine, tea, and bacon were deteriorating rapidly. In November 1917 the Midland Food Commissioner, Sir James Curtis, reported to the Food Ministry on the causes of local queues. A month later he was asked to ascertain whether a general rationing scheme could be inaugurated in Birmingham as an experiment. After conferences with local retailers and with the city authorities, he agreed, and on 12 December, after it had been approved by Lord Rhondda, a scheme was launched whereby each household received an official ration card for tea, sugar, butter, and margarine. By Christmas nearly 300,000 family cards had been issued. The scheme was so successful even before its twelve weeks' trial period had come to an end that it was copied by other municipalities and ultimately, after it had been slightly modified, by the government. In July 1918 the government, after experimenting with meat, introduced a general scheme with uniform national ration books: 870,885 of them were issued at once in Birmingham. They included not only ration tickets, but slogans telling customers to grow more food, or to note that 'if everyone in Great Britain ate only $2\frac{1}{2}d$. a day less than last year, this saving alone would enable 200,000 additional soldiers to be sent to France and maintained there'.

The development of food policy in Birmingham, which was one of the country's key industrial centres, illustrated the importance of close co-operation between retail dealers, local authorities, and government. The government worked out its policy last rather than first: it followed rather than initiated. Even after the end of the war in 1919, when there were widespread complaints of high food prices, the Birmingham Food Control Committee led the way by adopting a scheme designed to restrict profits of retailers of fish, fruit, and vegetables by the pooling of supplies and the co-ordination of transport.

Food was not the only article which had to be rationed. Fuel was equally essential for war purposes and equally difficult for domestic consumers to acquire. In 1916 Chamberlain set up a Corporation Coal Purchase Committee, and took the precaution of storing at the gas works a considerable quantity of coal, which would be ready for any emergency. When in April 1917 there was a cold winter and an epidemic of miners' absenteeism, 600 tons of this reserve stock were distributed among the smaller coal yards and the bags-wagon merchants, who sold coal to the poorest customers.

Rationing was developed in 1918, when the situation had become still more acute. In April a conference was held at the Council House, at which a representative of the Coal Controller issued a statement concerning future government policy; and the City Council set up a Fuel Committee with the Lord Mayor as chairman. Its first task was the reverse of that already adopted in the case of sugar: it was to register all local coal consumers. The complications of this registration involved the employment of a total staff of 200 officials. A list of coal merchants (226) and dealers (501) was also drawn up, and certificates and forms were prepared which provided statistics concerning the details of local trade. On the other side of the market, 400,000 certificates were issued to coal consumers, with special arrangements designed for hospitals and hotels.

Even after the development of the rationing system, the amount of coal available in Birmingham was insufficient to cover the regular rations, and particularly during the difficult winter of 1918 the committee had to issue special permits for emergency supplies of coal. The war did not end the emergency, and it was not until 1920 that it proved possible to disband the local Fuel Committee.

### III

Problems of allotting scarce supplies were not the only new questions that the Council had to face in war-time. The task of maintaining law and order with a depleted force of police involved grave difficulties. Before the war a police force of about 1,400 officers and men had been considered necessary to protect persons and property in Birmingham. The first effect of the outbreak of war was to rob the authorities of large numbers of reservists. Between 1914 and 1918, 450 other members of the police force joined the fighting services, making a total of 536. To deal with the gaps caused by this depletion of the regular police, the Chief Constable issued an advertisement inviting ex-policemen and ex-servicemen to rejoin under a temporary arrangement, what was called the 'First Police Reserve of Additional Constables'. Two hundred and fifty-seven men joined this emergency organization by the end of 1914. They were later supported by over 5,000 citizens who enrolled as unpaid special constables. At first the special constables were not a very highly organized body, but in 1917, as the regular police were released in increasing numbers for military duty, and as the number of duties to be carried out by the police increased rather than diminished, it became necessary to organize the special constables on a broader basis. The Lord Mayor convened a Town's

Meeting and made a strong appeal to citizens to take up
voluntary police service. J. E. Hill, a local solicitor, was appointed Head Special Constable, and, as a result of his first
publicity campaign, over 3,000 men enrolled themselves within
a month. Eventually a rota was drawn up and police jobs were
allocated according to age and physical fitness. One of the jobs
most eagerly sought after was that of joining the detachment of
twenty-five men and two officers on duty far away in the Elan
Valley.

By 1918 the war-time organization had become extremely
efficient, and after the building up of a volunteer motor transport service, employing about 100 cars placed at the disposal of
the authorities, between 700 and 800 men could be mobilized
at an hour's notice, while 90 per cent. of the force could be
called out if given a day's warning.

The most serious problem of law and order during the war
lay not in the internal threat to property, but in the danger of
German air raids on the city. Birmingham's importance as a
munitions centre made it a very likely target, although its distance from the coast appeared at first to give it some measure
of security. As early as November 1914 the Chief Constable
issued a notice ordering the dimming of lights visible from
above, and in January 1915 arrangements were made for air-
raid warnings to be sounded in case of impending attack. The
first order was much criticized at the time on the grounds that
it would have a damping and depressing effect on the routine
life of the city. It later proved very valuable.

It was not until January 1916 that the first attempt was made
by the Germans to bomb Birmingham, and on that occasion
no damage was done to the city, for the Zeppelin pilots were
attracted to Walsall, Wednesbury, Tipton, and Dudley by the
glare of the furnaces in the Black Country. Although no damage
was done in Birmingham itself, considerable indignation was
caused by the fact that no air-raid warning had been given, and
Chamberlain appealed to the authorities in London to organize
better precautions against attacks from the air. As a result of
his individual efforts and the convening of a meeting of mayors
and chief constables from towns around Birmingham, lighting
restrictions in the surrounding zone were brought into line with
those already adopted in Birmingham; anti-aircraft guns, of
which there were only four, were removed from the neighbour-

hood of the munitions factories to the outskirts of the city; and searchlight protection and signal inter-communication were developed. Despite these necessary precautions, when a second Zeppelin flew over parts of the city in 1917, no air-raid warning was received until after the Zeppelin had made its appearance, and although the darkness of the city saved Birmingham from damage, several bombs were dropped on the Austin works at Longbridge, which were brilliantly lighted. The third attack, in April 1918, when five Zeppelins set out to bomb the industrial towns of the Midlands, was dealt with far more successfully. The Zeppelins were followed along their course from the North Sea to Birmingham, and their movements charted on a large-scale map of the Midlands. Guns were trained on them to such effect that they dropped their bombs harmlessly in fields in the open country-side.

There were no dangers of an aeroplane attack on Birmingham, for the city was outside the range of the enemy planes which visited London and the coast towns. The only aeroplanes which Birmingham saw during the war were British, and later on American machines, operating from the aerodrome at Castle Bromwich.

Quite apart from these special war-time problems and the efforts made to deal with them, the Corporation found itself during the war compelled to modify many of its normal peace-time activities. Nearly 7,000 municipal employees joined the Services, of whom nearly 800 gave their lives. This high proportion of servicemen meant that many of the municipal departments had to run on a very depleted basis. The tramways and omnibus departments, for instance, provided 1,792 men for the forces—534 of them reservists who went very quickly—and women had to be employed in large numbers to fill their place. In July 1915 women began to be employed in large numbers as conductors and car-cleaners, and during peak hours about 450 Boy Scouts worked for a time as bell-boys on the trams.

The Public Works Department lost 828 men, and had to employ women for street-cleaning and in preparing road surfaces for tar-spraying. The shortage of equipment was almost as serious as the shortage of man-power, for many road-rollers and carts were transferred to the government for military purposes, and the city had to develop new mechanical appliances such as steam-wagons and petrol-driven road sweepers.

The Birmingham, Tame, and Rea District Drainage Board lost 44 men, half its normal establishment, and in order to maintain its works and normal extensions, 55 German prisoners of war and 70 conscientious objectors had to be employed by special arrangement with the War Office and the Home Office.

Not only were the departments depleted by the lack of men, but positive steps had to be taken to fit the city's services into a war-time mould. The assembly halls of various buildings—of the Baths Department, for instance—were used as recruiting stations, and at the end of the war as demobilization centres. The Parks Department encouraged the establishment of allotments to grow more food. In December 1916 the first Cultivation of Lands Order was issued, but it was not until after February 1917, when local authorities were enabled to acquire ground compulsorily, that the allotments movement really got under way. The Parks Committee divided the city into thirty areas and appointed an overseer in each to supervise the plots and to assist the users of them in various ways. There was such a big demand for land that it was impossible to meet all requirements, and by 1918 as much as 1,200 acres had been devoted to war-time food production under the management of between 11,000 and 12,000 allotment holders. This acreage figure compared with 400 acres of permanent Corporation allotments in 1914. The Parks Department not only disposed of land, it made an arrangement for war-time growers to secure seeds at reduced rates, and seed potatoes at cost price, and it offered such communal facilities as spraying of potato crops. All these developments were useful, particularly in 1917, when there was a serious shortage of potatoes and the city found itself compelled to set up communal kitchens in some of the working-class districts. Quite apart from these local efforts to bring land into cultivation, from the spring of 1916 onwards a committee was organized to try to enlist women workers for service on the land.

The most important war-time development in relation to the subsequent history of the city was much more controversial than these earlier schemes of war-time co-operation. The setting up of the Municipal Bank in 1916 marked an entirely new departure in civic policy, and it proved difficult to secure the necessary legislation to inaugurate it.

The idea was first mooted by Neville Chamberlain in 1915. 'The thought of a need of a bank, backed by the municipality,

flashed across my mind when crossing Chamberlain Place.'[1]
Chamberlain felt that the government's handling of the working-
class war savings was most unsatisfactory. 'I don't believe in Mc-
Kenna's bonds. . . . He is beginning at the wrong end', he wrote
in November 1915. 'The real problem is how to make a man save
who hasn't saved before. . . . My idea generally is to start a
municipal savings association, the town would guarantee the
interest . . . to lend the scheme the prestige and weight of the
local authorities. . . . You will never do any good unless you
save at the source.'[2] The scheme of a municipal bank appealed
to many members of the City Council, particularly to Labour
representatives, whom Chamberlain canvassed with great vigour.
It appealed less to the central authorities. The Treasury vetoed
Chamberlain's first draft, as bringing the city into competition
with the Exchequer; in March 1916 the Savings Advisory Committee 'began by heckling me and finished up by heckling each
other'; and in April, even after a Bill had been prepared with
the support of the Local Government Board, so strong was the
opposition from the joint-stock banks that it was abandoned.
Rumblings of opposition in Birmingham as well suggested that
the ambitious scheme would prove abortive, and in May 1916
Chamberlain could write: 'I am beat, and the Savings bank is
dead. The selfishness of the banks and the apathy of the Treasury
together make an inpenetrable entanglement, but what makes
it impossible to carry on the fighting is that I have been taken
in the rear.'[3] This was speaking too soon. A month later all the
difficulties had been surmounted, and a second Bill, brought
before the House of Commons in July 1916, passed through its
various stages without serious opposition and received the Royal
Assent on 23 August.

The Act permitted local authorities with a population of
250,000 or over to set up banks for a period up to three months
after the end of the war. Deposits could be accepted only from
employed persons by deductions from wages or some similar
arrangement. The maximum amount that could be accumulated
was fixed at £200, withdrawals on demand were limited to £1,
and control of investments was in the hands of the National
Debt Commissioners. Despite all these limitations, the Act

---

[1] Quoted by K. Feiling, op. cit., p. 60.
[2] Quoted by J. T. Jones, *History of the Corporation of Birmingham*, vol. v, pt. ii
(1940), p. 461.                                    [3] K. Feiling, loc. cit.

proved a useful means of collecting small contributions for the war effort on a large scale.

As soon as the Act had been secured, the city launched an active publicity campaign to interest workers in the project. Nearly a thousand meetings were held in factories, business premises, and warehouses. 'If it is really shown to meet a need,' Chamberlain declared, with exactly the same spirit as his father, 'not all the bankers in Lombard St. will prevent its becoming a permanent part of the municipal undertaking.'[1] Although the first premises of the bank were very small, in the basement of the Corporation Water Department, it soon became a going concern. Deposits in the bank were made by means of coupons paid to the workers as part wages, or purchased from the employers. The coupons were then gummed on a card. Completed cards were forwarded to the bank and the amounts entered into a book. Interest was paid at the rate of $3\frac{1}{2}$ per cent. and both principal and interest were guaranteed on the security of the funds of the Corporation. Prize schemes were introduced to try to make the bank popular.

The bank was opened on 29 September 1916. At the end of its first twenty months it had interested 30,000 depositors who had collected a sum of upwards of £500,000, 80 per cent. of which had been lent to the government. By 1918 the average number of transactions a week was about 3,000. So successful was the scheme that Chamberlain and many other civic leaders desired to make it permanent. Indeed, after Chamberlain returned to the city in June 1918, when his work as Director-General of National Service had come to an end, he stressed the possibilities of the bank encouraging thrift in post-war as well as in war-time conditions. The Savings Bank Committee reported that 'a remarkable feature is the stability of the accounts opened by the early depositors, showing that the desire to save is not a passing fancy, but the expression of a powerful instinct which will continue to act so long as the people are provided with facilities suited to their habits and conditions'.[2] It was in the light of this and other similar considerations that the city secured a permanent municipal bank by the Birmingham Corporation Act of July 1919.[3]

The continued existence of the municipal bank after the end

[1] K. Feiling, op. cit., p. 61.
[2] *Report of the Savings Bank Committee*, 29 July 1919.     [3] See below, p. 270.

of the war, because of its intrinsic merits, reflected the way in which the war could encourage the setting up of permanent institutions. Birmingham played an important part in the financing of the war in many other ways, through street collections and flag days, tank weeks, dreadnought weeks, big-guns weeks, and victory loans, but, when these were all forgotten, the bank remained.

IV

All these municipal activities of the city were superimposed on an industrial background, and in the sphere of industry, as in the sphere of administration, the war left permanent marks on both structure and outlook.

Birmingham's industry was essential from 1914 to 1918 to the whole national war effort. 'The country, the empire and the world owe to the skill, the ingenuity, the industry and the resources of Birmingham a deep debt of gratitude', Lloyd George told the city, speaking not only as Prime Minister but as a former Minister of Munitions.[1] Birmingham was built up into an arsenal, devoting the whole of its vast organization to war purposes, and adapting all its ancient energies to secure one massed concentration of effort. In the process, factories were extended, plants increased in scale, and new industrial buildings were erected. By 1918 the industrial structure of the city had been changed irrevocably from the pre-1914 model. There could be no return to normalcy.

There was no realization at first in 1914 that the war with Germany would develop into a total struggle, in which the manufacture of materials would count as much as the mobilization of men. The first effect of the outbreak of war in Birmingham was to send civilians to the colours, and to make business men look to their markets. Some of them were compelled in the first week of the war to put their workers on short time or to dismiss them altogether. The jewellery trade, for instance, employing 40,000 people, was placed on a half-time basis, some operatives working only from 9 a.m. until 1 o'clock. Tangyes reduced the working day from 6 a.m. to 5 p.m. to 9 a.m. to 5 p.m. and closed the works on Saturdays. Evereds closed on Monday as well as Saturday, and the Metropolitan Wagon Works went on to short-time working. There was so much local

[1] *B.P.*, 6 February 1921.

unemployment that from 2 August onwards the Central Labour Exchange was open from 6 a.m. until 6 p.m. and had to deal with about double the average number of pre-war applicants.

These were the immediate repercussions of the outbreak of war. Before very few days had elapsed, local industry had not only accepted the official slogan of economic endeavour, 'Business as Usual', but had come to believe that business could and would increase with the elimination of Germany as a trade rival. In early August 1914 business was practically at a standstill, and many hundreds of orders and running contracts were suspended, but by 14 August trades were rallying. It was believed that although practically no trade could be carried on with Europe, the markets of America, Africa, Asia, and Australia would be open as soon as shipping services were back to normal.

A fortnight later the chairman of the Chamber of Commerce emphasized the practical opportunities of capturing German markets. 'In the mind of every business man the thought is that as much trade as possible should be captured.'[1] It was the duty of local manufacturers to make a bold bid for the German trade. Austen Chamberlain, the Chancellor of the Exchequer, gave his blessing to these ambitions when he told the Chamber of Commerce, at a conference to discuss practical problems brought about by the war, that 'if we can only work through these critical weeks there will be a great deal of trade to be done, both new and old, in the near future'.[2]

In this atmosphere of confidence all sorts of bright ideas were put forward. Cornelius Chambers advocated a national mark to identify British-made goods. The Rotary Club and the Chamber of Commerce suggested a Birmingham Fair, on the lines of the Leipzig Fair, to welcome traders from all over the world. The Board of Trade gave a conditional approval to the idea in February 1915. 'Germany's misfortune is Britain's opportunity,' reported the *Birmingham Daily Post*, 'but it is imperative that this opportunity shall be immediately grasped. . . . Never before in commercial history are so many markets with such volumes of business at our disposal. For some time we shall be the only fully-equipped manufacturing nation in Europe.'[3]

These were the first dreams inspired by an international conflict which was to shatter irrevocably the pre-war conditions of

[1] *B.P.*, 27 August 1914.               [2] Ibid., 1 September 1914.
[3] Ibid., 4 February 1915.

multilateral world trade. By the spring of 1915 the conversion
of local industry to a war footing awakened business men, and
underlined new realities. There was too little time and too few
materials to expand foreign markets: the production of munitions of war was the major preoccupation. German leaders
realized the need for a full mobilization of their country's resources before British leaders did, but by the end of 1915 not
only were Birmingham manufacturers supplying to the Armed
Forces a greatly increased flow of pre-war products, like rifles,
cartridges, saddlery, and tin-plate goods, but many of them
were converting their plants from the manufacture of peace-
time to war-time products. The engineering firms were drawn
in 1915 into the heart of the war effort, being almost entirely
occupied with the production of munitions under government
control. Shells and fuses, previously regarded as outside the
range of local products, were being turned out in large quantities. Other firms followed the engineers' lead. New factories
and workshops were built, many of them of a permanent type,
and in design far superior to those existing before the war. With
both eyes on the poverty of the labour market, labour-saving
and automatic machinery were introduced. Where men could
not be employed, women were, in many repetition and other
processes, which had hitherto been performed only by men. In
1915 new products like armoured cars and aeroplanes flowed
out of the Birmingham workshops.

If it took time to build up this great arsenal and to grasp the
full implications of its organization, it also took time to realize
how far the war had interfered with the established laws of
supply and demand. 'At the beginning of the first World War,
when huge administrative structures such as the Ministry of
Munitions had not as yet even been dreamt of, the mainspring
of industrial mobilization was by necessity economic demand,
not sovereign command.'[1] The result was bottlenecks and price
and contract speculation. There was more than a suspicion in
Birmingham, as elsewhere, that contracts were being 'farmed'
by enterprising speculators, who did no manufacturing themselves, but acted as non-necessary and unpatriotic intermediaries
between the service departments and the munitions manufacturers. Even where bona fide direct contracts were made, a
private bidding-up process for labour and materials by muni-

[1] W. K. Hancock and M. M. Gowing, *British War Economy* (1949), p. 11.

tions makers was not calculated to make for the most efficient use of Birmingham's men and resources.

In April 1915, when it was realized that far more shells and fuses had to be produced if the campaign in France and Flanders was to be prosecuted successfully, inquiries relating to engineers and metal manufacturers in Birmingham showed that total output in the city alone could be increased by not less than 20 per cent. and probably by 50 per cent. 'if works were reorganized and contracts allocated by a body of men possessing practical knowledge of manufacturing conditions in Birmingham'.[1]

The War Office Armaments Output Committee asked Captain Hilton, secretary of the Birmingham Gas Department, to convene a meeting of the principal local manufacturers of armaments to set up a Local Munitions Committee, similar to that which had already been set up in the North of England. In consequence of this proposal a local Munitions Committee was organized, which included representatives of both capital and labour, and which was responsible, apart from general work of oversight and co-ordination, for the establishment of the National Shell Factory at Washwood Heath. By the time the Ministry of Munitions was set up in May 1915, their work was already well under way, and their local experience proved of great value to the Ministry's detailed regional organization.

The setting up of the Munitions Committee, although it recognized the new condition of 'siege warfare', by no means marked a complete abandonment of the 1914 attitude of seeking to capture new channels of trade. At the meeting which created the organization, Lord Elphinstone said that the great desire of the government in securing a greater output of munitions of war was 'not to upset legitimate and necessary trade more than is absolutely imperative. The general prosperity of the country must, as far as possible, be preserved in order that when the time comes to pay for the war, we shall be the better able to do it.'[2]

It was in the second half of 1915 that the enormous war-drive dominated the local scene to the exclusion of all else. Firms turned over to new products. The motor manufacturers diverted their attention from pleasure cars to army transport vehicles, aeroplane components, tanks, and, of course, shells, while

---

[1] *B.P.*, 17 April 1915.
[2] Quoted by R. H. Brazier and E. Sandford, op. cit., p. 116.

American manufacturers developed familiar Birmingham peace-time lines. The metal and bedstead trade turned down export orders and concentrated on hospital beds. The stove industry produced insulated canteens and field service lamps.

The last Birmingham trade to be converted to the manufacture of munitions was the jewellery trade, which had been badly hit by the war. Shortage of labour, shortage of precious metals, and decline in luxury demand crippled the industry. 'You may go into workshop after workshop', wrote a local newspaper in 1916, 'and see one side tenantless, idle, machinery still, tools lying on the bench. There is only one simile that leaps to the mind. It is that of a body paralysed down one side.'[1] In December 1916 the jewellers decided to offer their plant and services to the government with a view to the manufacture of munitions, particularly in the smaller shops, and an emergency committee of the trades decided on 28 December 1916 to arrange a census of available plant and labour. The census results, published in January 1917, showed that 300 firms were willing to engage in munitions making, some of them already having done so. The jewellers felt that the best contribution they could make was to approach large firms in the district who were already on government work with a view to getting sub-contracts for component parts. The measures taken were successful, and in addition to the increase in the flow of munitions, the jewellers themselves were enabled to tide over what otherwise would have been a very difficult economic period.

Munitions came first, far above all else, for all trades. Cycle manufacturers produced shell-fuses and 18-pounder shells. The B.S.A. produced Lewis guns on a programme far beyond anything which the Ministry conceived as possible during the early days of the war. The famous Mills hand grenade was invented in the city and produced in hundreds of thousands by the meter-makers. As for shells, between May 1915 and the end of the war, 15 million finished shells were produced in the district, enough to form end to end a line 3,000 miles long, or enough, when packed in 10-ton trucks, to fill a train which would stretch from Birmingham to Bournemouth.[2] All these statistics belong to the grim, record-breaking story of war production.

Some of the individual contracts placed by the government

[1] *B.P.*, 14 September 1916.
[2] R. H. Brazier and E. Sandford, op. cit., p. 127.

in the city were enormous by any standards. Kynoch's, for instance, which underwent very large extensions in 1915, contracted to produce each week 25 million rifle cartridges, 300,000 revolver cartridges, 110,000 18-pounder brass cases, and 300 tons of cordite. In 1918 in the final spurt to meet the demands caused by the successful German offensive the output of rifle cartridges was raised to nearly 30 million a week.

The B.S.A. speeded up all its processes of production. In the first six months of the war the rate of output of rifles increased more than six times: within seventeen months it was up twelve times: by the end of the war the average weekly output for the five years before 1914 of 135 rifles was up to 10,000. Lewis guns were produced at the rate of 2,000 a week as compared with 50 in 1914. They were supplied in considerable numbers not only to the British forces but also to the Russians and the Belgians. In all, 145,397 complete Lewis guns were produced, irrespective of spares.[1]

In the transport industry the Vickers subsidiary, Wolseley Motors, turned out over 4,000 cars for war purposes, 4,500 aero-engines, and 700 complete aeroplanes, while nearly 300 British warships were fitted with director firing gear and gunsights made at Adderley Park.[2]

The size and character of these contracts necessitated new scales of economic enterprise and new forms of economic organization. One of the best examples of a war-time expansion in scale was that of Austins'. At the outbreak of war, the Longbridge factory employed 2,800 men. By 1918, 20,000 people were working there. Quiet homesteads and green fields had given way to vast engineering shops with great chimneys and miles of railway sidings. A special railway station was constructed, where every morning 10,000 passengers thronged the platform. A large service of motor-buses was organized, and storage accommodation arranged for 6,000 bicycles. No fewer than 20,000 meals were served during 24 hours. The complete contrast between an enormous industrial unit of this kind—a world in itself—and the small factory-workshop of the middle of the nineteenth century reflects a revolution, just as important in its repercussions as the industrial revolution of the eighteenth century. Many factories expanded during the war to such an extent

---

[1] D. M. Ward, *The Other Battle* (1946), p. 28.
[2] R. H. Brazier and E. Sandford, op. cit., pp. 124–6.

that they were over-capitalized at the end of it and left with units completely unbalanced from the point of view of their peace-time needs. In other factories some departments had swollen disproportionately to the size of the factory as a whole, thus making necessary an expensive process of readjustment. But some factories stayed large, and transformed the economic structure of the neighbourhood.

Not only scale was changed: in addition new forms of organization emerged. On all sides there was an acceleration of production, a greater willingness to install new labour-saving machinery, to scrap old-fashioned processes and introduce modern ones. Individual firms were required to standardize, or at any rate to concentrate on fewer types and sizes. Government specifications often involved important reorganizations of this type, and the brassfounders, for instance, ruthlessly cut down the number of their patterns. Specialization increased along with the development of bulk outputs, and modified the attitudes of many local business men. Necessity was the mother of organization. In the hardware industry, for example,

it is beyond doubt that the exigencies of the war have done a good deal to demonstrate the value of organisation in quarters where it was very imperfectly appreciated before. The rationing of raw materials to different branches of the trade has brought manufacturers into a closer association, and they have had to learn that unity is strength and the individualism which their fathers practised may become a danger if opposed to the promptings of modern industrial development.[1]

The same story was true of engineering.

The attainment of the maximum output from available resources in plant and labour became a dire necessity in the war. It has opened the eyes of manufacturers to what is our indispensable condition of post-war success. The component parts of such a scheme do not sink their own identity but acting unitedly they are able to effect economies and command markets which would be beyond isolated efforts.[2]

This seemed to be the lesson taught by Birmingham's war-time industrial experience to the manufacturers of the city, great and small. The language of specialization and efficiency was the current jargon in 1918, just as talk of capturing trade provided the slogans of 1914. In both cases the war was conceived of as an opportunity as well as a burden.

[1] B.P., 27 December 1918.     [2] Ibid., 16 November 1918.

V

The real cost of the war lay in the sacrifice of men, who were taken away from their peace-time pursuits in large numbers to take part in the more active operations of war. It has been estimated that about 150,000 men and women of Birmingham served in the forces from August 1914 to November 1918. The men represented 54 per cent. of the local male population of military age. That such a high percentage existed in one of Britain's leading arsenals shows the high—indeed total—demands made by twentieth-century war. Thirty-five thousand men who went came back disabled, and thirteen thousand never returned. The names of the dead are enshrined in the Hall of Memory, which was opened in July 1925.

The first group of men from Birmingham to go to the war were the Reservists and the Territorials. Their numbers were soon augmented by the City Battalions and later on by other volunteers.

Some of the Territorials were in camp when war broke out. They had left Birmingham for Rhyl on the morning of Sunday, 2 August 1914. Among them was the Lord Mayor, Colonel E. Martineau, the Officer Commanding the 6th Battalion of The Royal Warwickshire Regiment. On the evening of the 3rd, a telegram arrived telling them that a movement order might be expected, and implying that war was near. The following day the Territorials were mobilized, and Martineau resigned from the Lord Mayoralty to take up military duties, handing over his civic responsibilities to the Deputy Mayor, Bowater. The Territorials went on to play an important part in the war-time exploits of the Royal Warwickshire Regiment.

The City Battalions were an interesting and later much-criticized war-time innovation. In the second half of August 1914 the idea had been conceived in Liverpool and Manchester of collecting battalions of 'pals' from the same neighbourhood to serve together. Birmingham quickly followed the example set by the North of England, and at the end of the first week of recruiting over 4,500 men had registered, instead of the 1,000 demanded. Money poured in from well-wishers in the city to provide for their equipment. Before 1 September 1914 over £10,000 had been raised. Because of a shortage of uniforms, the first distinguishing mark of the City Battalions was merely a

PLATE XXXII

Volunteer Helpers, 1915

PLATE XXXIII

2nd Battalion (Birmingham) Royal Warwickshire Regiment, leaving Sutton Coldfield for

buttonhole badge, and they were very proud when their first uniform and equipment arrived. The later history of a brave body of volunteers is once again bound up with the war-time exploits of the Royal Warwickshires.

Apart from the rush of volunteers, dispersed among all types of regiments, infantry, artillery, and technical, and the Navy, many men were drawn into the forces during the course of the war more slowly, as a result of the government's man-power policy. The man-power problem proved serious in a war on the scale of that of 1914–18. 'The search for the best methods of distributing it and using it to satisfy the requirements of war is not merely a technical problem of war economy; it is also a political problem of national consent.'[1] The first step taken in Birmingham was the setting up, early in November 1914, of a Local Branch of the Parliamentary Recruiting Committee. A vigorous campaign followed throughout the neighbourhood with appeals for volunteers being made at meetings, demonstrations, and local places of entertainment. Forms were sent round to all householders whose names appeared on the lists of voters, in each district. The response was disappointing, and recruiting was spasmodic, until the Lord Mayor made a special appeal in May 1915. There was an encouraging spurt in response to his exhortations, but numbers dropped off again by the autumn. It was against this unsatisfactory setting that the National Register was drawn up and Lord Derby was appointed to the position of Director of Recruiting in October 1915. He attempted to speed up the process of recruitment in an effort to bring $1\frac{1}{2}$ million recruits into the services. Locally in Birmingham his efforts were supported by the Birmingham and District Labour Recruiting Council, which drew attention to the seriousness of the military situation, and to the need for a regular supply of trained troops. It pointed out that 'this is our last chance to prevent conscription. The Premier and Lord Kitchener have agreed, for the time being, to depend on the trade union effort (1) to find all the men required for the front; (2) to supply all munitions required by our soldiers and sailors. Whatever other parts of the country may do, let the Midlands prove its capacity in both directions.'[2] The Lord Mayor supported this appeal and hoped that the voluntary system would prove adequate to secure

[1] W. K. Hancock and M. M. Gowing, op. cit., p. 24.
[2] Quoted by R. H. Brazier and E. Sandford, op. cit., p. 20.

all the men required. 'I trust', he said, 'that this final effort on
the part of organised labour will bring a full realisation of the
great sacrifices which it is now necessary for the people of this
country to make to carry through the war to a successful issue.'
The local Labour party underlined the meaning of the appeal
by pointing out that 'failing a satisfactory response from all
classes it will not be possible for trade unionism further to oppose
compulsory methods'.

There was a considerable boom in local recruiting as a result
of the introduction of the Derby Scheme, many of the volunteers
coming forward under the group system, whereby men were
lumped together in terms of their age, occupation, and whether
they were married or single. But the recruiting was not sustained
in the country as a whole. The scheme brought in only 800,000
volunteers, and although Birmingham was ahead of many other
cities of the country, the response was so small that it became
clear that greater compulsion was necessary if man-power was
to be drawn into the forces in large enough numbers. Neville
Chamberlain had already come to this conclusion in June 1915,
but he saw it in terms of a wider policy, related to the context
of an industrial city. He wrote to Mrs. Chamberlain:

The more I think over it, and the more I hear and see of the attitude
of the men in the factories, the more certain I feel that National Service
is the only solution of the present situation, which is rapidly becoming
intolerable. It must, however, be accompanied by either a surtax on,
or a limitation of profits for all, because workmen will never consent
to restriction which would have the effect of putting money into their
employers' pockets. Personally I hate the idea of making profits out of
the war, when so many are giving their lives and limbs, and I hope
and pray that the new Government will have the courage and the
imagination to deal with the situation promptly and properly.[1]

Promptness was not offered Chamberlain, for it was not until
May 1916 that the National Service Act was passed, but in
December 1916 he was afforded the opportunity of taking over
the national task of labour recruitment, when he became
Director-General of National Service.

Chamberlain found it impossible in his new task to secure
any satisfactory balance between the needs of military and
industrial man-power. This was a national problem, which
could be traced in miniature in a city like Birmingham. There

[1] K. Feiling, op. cit., pp. 56–7.

was a local as well as a national scramble between government departments, recruiting officers, and tribunals. The scramble was complicated in Birmingham by the complexity of local occupations, and the Local Tribunal, set up in January 1916, and holding its final meeting in July 1919, found itself faced with one of the most difficult tasks in the country. In 90,721 decisions 34,760 men were made available for the Army and 7,749 received exemption certificates. The complexity of the industrial background necessitated the formation of trade advisory committees for deciding who were the essential men. Although Chamberlain resigned from his official post in August 1917, mainly on the issue that recruiting should continue primarily to be based on age and not on occupation, his policy finally had to be put into practice in the last phase of the war, when in March 1918 the government at last decided to call out men under twenty-three from protected occupations, and munitions gave up 104,000 men in six months.

The withdrawal of large numbers of men created one other difficult problem in man-power policy: the substitution of women for men in many local jobs. Women had been employed on a large scale in Birmingham before the war, but between 1914 and 1918 the lines of demarcation between the economic province of women and that of men became so blurred as to be almost invisible. Their economic position was dealt with in a series of statutory rules and orders, consolidated in Order 546 of June 1918, and they had secured by the end of hostilities a recognized place in the economy and in society, which had done far more to encourage their emancipation than any of the political activities of the suffragettes before 1914. Although after 1918 serious problems were raised by their demobilization and replacement, women continued to play an essential part in Birmingham industry.

For all the workers who remained on the 'home front' during the war years, labour relations were controlled more tightly than they had been before 1914. An increasingly centralized framework was devised to regulate the labour market throughout the whole country, so that Lloyd George could proclaim 'a new chapter in the history of labour in its relations with the state'. The agreement of trade-union leaders to sign away the right to strike for the duration was followed by the development of arbitration tribunals and by official investigation of actual or

impending disputes. All these war-time developments were
accepted in Birmingham, where the labour market had been
considerably transformed by the influx of workers from other
parts of the country into the munitions factories. Despite all the
difficulties there was little loss of production on account of strikes
or lock-outs in the city.

The tradition of local industrial peace was maintained within
the new institutional framework. The Birmingham Trades
Council welcomed the Munitions Bill of July 1915, and listened
intently a year later to a proposal made by the president of the
Chamber of Commerce suggesting that a Standing Committee
composed of an equal number of workers and employers should
be set up to discuss trade-union matters. Kesterton, the secretary
of the Birmingham Trades Council, thought that the war had
taught employers that the future of the trade and commerce of
the nation depended upon the recognition of the mutual interests of both parties, and that they were prepared to consider
regular consultation more than ever before.

In 1915 a new local organization was set up—the Industrial
League, which aimed at uniting employers and employed in
friendly co-operation for the avoidance of misunderstandings
and industrial disputes. Its immediate roots were in the 90's,
although it could trace back its ancestry deep into the nineteenth century, to the days of Attwood and the early Chartist
movement. The League regarded itself not as an organization
with a single axe to grind, but as 'an instrument for widening
toleration and for effecting a more complete understanding of
recurring differences and vital interests'.[1] It remained active
after the end of the war, urging that mutual discussion was 'the
best protection against any possible spread of the revolutionary
spirit which exists among a minority of the workers in this
country'.[2] In the post-war world it enlisted the support of men
as far apart as George Isaacs and Neville Chamberlain, J. R.
Clynes and H. G. Williams.

The post-war world was to be full of problems, more indeed
than were posed during the course of the fighting. But Birmingham labour emerged at the end of the war conscious of the real
contribution it had made to the war effort. It had been exhorted
to action in the battle for increased output and had responded

1 *B.P.*, 5 July 1915.
2 Ibid., 10 October 1918.

willingly. 'It would be a kindness even to our enemies', said one Birmingham workers' representative in 1915, 'for the workers of this city to speed up munitions.' These efforts were recognized by those in authority. As Sir John French said, 'the issue is a struggle between Krupps and Birmingham',[1] and in the course of that struggle labour played a decisive part.

### VI

The end of the war came almost as suddenly as its beginning. On Monday, 11 November, work was begun in the factories and warehouses of the city in just the same way as usual. It continued normally until the prearranged signal was given, which announced a few minutes before eleven o'clock that a long struggle had at last ended. Birmingham had had few opportunities during the war to celebrate victories with popular demonstrations or any sort of colourful interruptions of the drab routine of war-time living, so that Monday, 11 November, and Tuesday, 12 November, were days of festival—festival mixed with sorrow and prayer. There were, indeed, so many people anxious to attend a service of prayer and thanksgiving in the Cathedral that three services had to be held in succession, many people patiently waiting outside for their opportunity to go in later.

The end of hostilities was followed by the demobilization of large numbers of the new labour force attracted to Birmingham during the war, and by the return of the servicemen. It soon became clear that the war had left a legacy of troubles and that peaceful readjustment was more difficult than had been anticipated. But that was not the mood of 11 November 1918. There was relief at the end of a wearing struggle, regret for the lost but hope for the future, and a belief that the city and the country should forge ahead in peace-time reconstruction. The Lord Mayor, Sir David Brooks, caught the mood when, in addressing a large crowd which had gathered in Victoria Square on 11 November, he declared that 'today is the greatest day in the history of our country, and it marks the beginning of a new era in human development. . . . We must take care to use this great opportunity aright so that the world may be better and not worse by reason of the overthrow of the old order.'[2]

[1] *B.P.*, 5 July 1915.          [2] Ibid., 12 November 1918.

B 1567.2                    Q

# VIII
## NEW CIVIC POLICIES

### I

THE First World War acted as a catalyst in English social history. The facts of war-time change, described in the last chapter, produced a new social environment: the hope of further changes in the future widened the horizons of civic policy. Neither the facts nor the hopes were new, but the process of change was quickened.

Developments in Birmingham can only be seen clearly in terms of a broader set of national changes. The war forced new social groups into positions of accepted importance both in politics and in economic life. Through its effects on wages, profits, prices, and taxation, it remoulded the relations between social groups. Through its enforced disruption of family life and its enforced emancipation of women, it radically altered the place of women and youth in society.

Most of these transformations were the result of long-run trends, which can be traced in the fifty years before 1914. Labour, particularly unskilled labour, had become increasingly assertive in the pre-war world; the system of direct and graduated taxation had begun to compress the scale of disposable incomes; and the extension of mass production for the home market along with a growing interest in the needs and tastes of the common people had made for a more unified material civilization which was beginning to be available for all.

The war, by emphasizing the key importance of labour, by increasing the pressure of taxation, and by stimulating and accumulating dreams of new material well-being, accelerated existing trends. But it did more than this. By delaying the provision of essential services like housing and education, it left a huge programme of arrears to be made up. It quickened social processes by making the problems behind them seem more urgent. In consequence both central government and local authorities were stirred into action.

The best illustration of this sequence of change was the new attitude to the housing problem. It was clear before 1914, as the Special Committee Inquiry showed, that housing would be one of the most important local issues of the future. The reduction of building during the war and the new demand for the provision of 'houses fit for heroes to live in' made the question an urgent one, which could be tackled only at a national level.

Before the war ended a national committee was appointed, under the chairmanship of Sir John Tudor-Walters, to consider the problem of the rehousing of the working classes. It made a series of important recommendations concerning minimum housing standards and the density of house-building. In July 1917 the government issued an appeal to local authorities, pointing out that private enterprise would be quite unable to deal successfully and speedily with the problem of the arrears of house-building; and later offered substantial financial assistance to local authorities to carry through, at the conclusion of the war, programmes of housing for the working classes.[1] In March 1918 a further government communication set out the terms of government assistance, and in 1919 the Housing and Town Planning Act was passed.

Birmingham did not act as the passive agent of a national scheme: it co-operated in national inquiries and it took its own independent line of action. In the spring of 1917 the increasing gravity of the housing situation in the city was discussed at a conference of the Public Health and the Housing and Town Planning Committees, and, as a result, a new Housing and Town Planning Committee was set up. In July 1918 its first extensive report was accepted by the Council. It calculated that the estimated normal requirements of the city amounted to 2,500 houses a year. On that basis the total deficiency in the provision of houses during the previous ten years was 12,000, not taking into account any clearance proposals for the central areas of the city, where there were still many insanitary back-to-back houses which had been condemned before the war, and many other houses which failed to reach accepted twentieth-century standards. The committee's proposals were passed on by the city to the government as the reply to the official circular of March 1918. They included the acceptance of the government's scheme concerning assistance to local authorities; the demand for additional powers for encouraging, promoting, and financing public utility services; and new measures to encourage private enterprise. The answers to some

[1] See Ministry of Reconstruction, *Reconstruction Problems*, No. 2 (1918).

of these problems involved dependence on national legislation: others were dealt with by clauses in the Birmingham Corporation Act of 1919.

All these steps to push housing into the centre of the picture were taken before the war ended in 1918. Plain facts and new hopes had conspired together to stimulate the community to social action. The foundations were laid for what was later to become, after many vicissitudes, an objective of general public policy—the promise to give the citizen 'a legitimate expectation of a home fit for a family to live in', with the promise no longer confined to heroes.[1]

Housing policy was important not only in itself or because it illustrated the general sequence of change, but because it touched many other frontiers of civic policy, particularly in a large city like Birmingham. The building of large numbers of new houses on the fringes of the city was the most important feature of Birmingham's civic history in the inter-war years. One new housing estate alone, Kingstanding, had a population slightly larger than that of Shrewsbury, while the population of all the new Birmingham municipal housing estates was as large as that of Leicester or Plymouth.[2] The new housing estates were the basic social products of the twentieth century. A historian must understand their structure and grasp their importance if he is to interpret the twentieth century, just as a nineteenth-century historian must understand the new industrial town or a historian of the eighteenth century the country house.

There were four ways in which housing problems posed complementary problems in other fields of policy. In the first place the fact that the new estates were far removed from the old civic centre raised new problems of transport policy—how and where to provide additional services, whether to offer buses or trams, and what was the wisest pricing policy to cover both long-distance and short-distance passengers.[3] Secondly, the distance between the estates and the factories accentuated the social and economic problems of the growing city of pre-war years. Thirdly, the fact that the estates were usually peopled by younger married people with children raised the question of the provision of new schools. Fourthly, the demand for electricity as the essential

[1] T. H. Marshall, *Citizenship and Social Class* (1950), p. 61.
[2] See M. P. Fogarty, *Town and Country Planning* (1948), ch. iii.
[3] See Ministry of Health, *The Management of Municipal Housing Estates* (1938).

means of lighting and a supplementary form of cooking and heating greatly expanded the work of the Electricity Department. Transport, education, and electricity thus met housing at the new frontiers of civic policy.

Finally, alongside these moving social frontiers, the ever-expanding geographical frontier was drawing Birmingham into closer touch with outside authorities. As a Birmingham newspaper put it in January 1931, 'Wider still and wider shall thy bounds be set'.[1] Birmingham found itself concerned increasingly with the problems of the government not of a city but of a region. The Birmingham of the 1920's and 1930's was very far removed from the Birmingham of Joseph Chamberlain.

II

Housing policy comes first in a study of new civic policies, since it provides the central theme, but the history of housing policy is complicated from the start by the interweaving of the pattern of local and national legislation. Neither local nor national policy was fixed. If the Birmingham policy vacillated and fluctuated, the policy of the government frequently changed, sometimes abruptly and drastically. In studying the changing fortunes of Birmingham housing programmes, it is difficult to say how far Birmingham determined its own policy and how far it anticipated or merely followed that of the government.

Between 1 January 1919 and 1 January 1939, according to the Building Surveyor's Department figures, a total of 50,268 municipal houses, housing about 200,000 people, were built in Birmingham. During the same period 54,536 houses were built by private enterprise. The closeness in the size of the two total figures over the twenty years obscures the marked variations in the building rates of the two types of houses. If the twenty years are broken down into shorter periods, significant differences emerge. Between 1924 and 1931, the annual production of municipal houses was always greater than the production of private-enterprise houses, and in all 32,829 houses of the former type were built as against 14,869 of the latter. Between 1932 and 1938 the trend was reversed. The number of council houses built in any single year was never as great as the number of

[1] *E.D.*, 23 January 1931.

private houses, and in all 38,070 private-enterprise houses were built as against 13,485 council houses.

The dividing line in this story as in many other inter-war stories was the economic depression of 1931, which was accompanied by serious national and local economy cuts. Birmingham led the way in advocating a policy of financial retrenchment to meet the economic crisis, even before the Ministry of Health issued a circular in 1931 stressing the need for concentration on the provision of cheap houses, which could be built at low cost and at a rent of not more than 10*s*. a week.

Before the dividing line had been reached, Birmingham had built up an impressive municipal housing scheme, often in face of initial misgivings and serious practical difficulties. Between 1921 and 1931 the net addition to the number of houses in Birmingham was 502 per 10,000 of the population as measured at the 1921 Census, as against figures varying from 267 to 359 per 10,000 in eleven other big cities. Birmingham's population increased relatively fast, and if the surplus of houses per 10,000 of the population over and above the number needed to contain the increase of population is taken as the test of progress, only Cardiff of the eleven other cities did better than Birmingham. In this first bout of building, by far the largest sector was municipal.

The administrative agencies responsible for the programme of municipal building were, from 1919 to 1922, the Housing and Estates Committee and, after 1922, a sub-committee of the Public Works and Town Planning Committee.

The Housing and Estates Committee worked within the framework of the national Housing and Town Planning Act of 1919, which made it an obligation for local authorities to consider the requirements of their areas for working-class houses, and to submit adequate housing schemes to the Ministry of Health. The government offered financial assistance sufficient to limit the loss, which the local authorities might sustain as a result of their action, to the product of a penny rate.

The Housing and Town Planning Act made Birmingham willing to consider large-scale municipal enterprise in a way it would not have done before 1914. Already in 1918 the Council had acquired 400 acres for post-war building. Now, as a result of the Act of 1919, a Housing and Estates Department was set up with a regular committee and a Housing Director as a full-time official, specially briefed to arrange the planning and supervision of houses built by contractors for the Corporation, the management and maintenance of new estates, and the collection of rents. The new committee had to begin its work in face of grave post-war difficulties, particularly a shortage of labour and materials, which caused delays and greatly increased costs. As soon as the Corporation issued contracts, prices soared and costs became alarmingly high. An attempt to float £1½ million of 6 per cent. Housing Bonds in the spring and summer of 1920 proved difficult, so that financial stringency was added to the earlier troubles. Between 1919 and 1923 only 3,234 houses were built under the 1919 Act out of 10,000 originally planned.

The problems raised during this difficult phase of house-building led to a Council inquiry in April 1921, and although the report of the committee, when it appeared in 1922, was critical without being antagonistic to the existing Housing Committee, an administrative rearrangement was made as a result of the investigations. The Housing and Estates Committee lost its powers to plan and build houses, and they were transferred to a Housing Sub-Committee of the Public Works Committee, which was already responsible for town-planning. Behind the transfer of authority there were political and personal differences, involving the extent and character of a municipal building programme. The changes of 1922 led to more permanent division of authority. The Housing Sub-Committee of the Public Works Committee, strongly in favour of private enterprise whenever possible, was concerned with the erection of houses. It was assisted by the City Engineer and Surveyor acting as Executive Officer. The Estates Committee retained control of the management of all municipal houses erected throughout the city, and had the responsibility of allocating houses to applicants.

The same battle which was going on behind the scenes in Birmingham between those who favoured direct, official, municipal responsibility for house-building and those who preferred to rely on private enterprise, was being fought out also at the centre. With the collapse of the post-war boom the government decided to limit the financial liability of the State. Chamberlain's retrospective Housing Act of 1923 reduced the maximum government subsidy to local authorities to an annual grant of £6

per house for twenty years. The next year Wheatley's Act increased the subsidy again to £9 per house for forty years, on
condition that an additional contribution not exceeding £4. 10s.
per house per annum should be made by the local authorities.
This Act was the basis of a vast expansion in municipal house-
building, although the amount of the subsidy continued to vary
between 1924 and 1933.

Against this background of shifting local and national action,
municipal house-building in Birmingham, despite all its initial
difficulties, had reached a high rate. By 1926 the city had built
13,008 municipal houses, more than any other local authority
in England. The increase in houses did not solve the problem,
and the social hardships hidden behind the high demands for
housing still remained acute. The percentage of housing
occupied by two or more families, for instance, had increased
from 19 per cent. in 1914 to 30 per cent. in 1922, and it was
estimated by the Public Works Committee in that year that
about 100,000 new houses would be required in the following
twenty years—25,000 on account of slum clearance, 3,000 a year
to meet the normal growth of the city, and 15,000 small houses
to meet the immediate needs of people without accommodation.
In July 1926 the City Council expressed its willingness to increase
the financial loss which it would bear as a result of its programme
to the product of a 4d. rate, and a year later this figure was
increased to 5d.

Although little was done before 1930 to embark upon a
general slum-clearance policy, by July of that year 30,000
municipal houses had been built. In 1930 alone, the peak year
of inter-war municipal building history, 6,715 Council houses
were erected. The 30,000th house was opened by the Minister
of Health, Mr. Greenwood, who in a national Act of that year
launched a great drive to clear away the slums. His 1930 Act,
which provided a special subsidy for houses or flats erected to re-
house persons displaced by slum-clearance, was welcomed by
the Birmingham authorities, who informed the Ministry that
they would build 30,000 houses in the next five years, 7,000 as
part of a plan of slum-clearance and 23,000 under the 1924 Act.
The year 1930 was a year when the Council was still prepared to
think in large terms. Not only did it authorize this impressive
building programme: it also sent out a special delegation of the
Estates and Public Works Committee to visit towns in Germany,

Czechoslovakia, and Austria to study the system of tenement and flat dwellings. The Committee recommended that up to 1,000 tenement dwellings should be included in the five-year programme for slum rehousing.

It was in the midst of this atmosphere of ambitious expectancy that the economic depression cut the ground from beneath the city's housing programme. The prevailing economic orthodoxy of the day, both local and national, conceived of retrenchment as the best method of dealing with the crisis. Housing schemes were cut, the register of applicants for municipal houses was slashed, and social improvements came to a halt. In 1932 only 1,757 Council houses were built, and the Public Works Committee decided to build only 3,500 houses in the next eighteen months under the 1924 Act instead of 6,900 planned as part of the 1930 programme.

Sometimes during these days of retrenchment there was a conflict of interest in the Council between an economy party, tending to look on municipal housing as a burden on rates and taxes, and a small minority group, including some members of all parties, attempting to maintain a more active city policy despite the economic situation. Orthodoxy prevailed. The chairman of the Public Works Committee asked for housing to be carried out in 'an economic manner',[1] while the chairman of the Finance Committee intervened in a housing discussion in September 1931 to say that it was the duty of any municipality to follow the lead of the government and effect wise economies, how and when it could.[2]

While the number of municipal houses fell off, the number of houses built by private enterprise increased. The building rate of private-enterprise houses trebled between 1930 and 1935, increasing from one-quarter to six times the Council's output. The high demand for private houses depended on the sharp fall in building costs, the low rate of interest, the relatively favourable unemployment record in the city, rising real wages for those at work, and the favourable terms offered by building societies, which made a special point of helping those areas which enjoyed a 'particularly favourable record of employment'.[3] As a result of this burst of private-enterprise housing, about one-

[1] B.G., 10 June 1931.                    [2] B.P., 23 September 1931.
[3] H. Bellman, The Thrifty Three Millions (1935), p. 233; 'The Building Trades' in Britain in Recovery (1937), pp. 395–437.

fifth of the housing in Birmingham's outer ring was developed on these lines.

Despite the high rate of private-enterprise building, there was still a long list of applicants on the waiting list for Corporation houses in February 1935, when a new wave of municipal house-building began. Private-enterprise building had catered for the needs of the middle and lower middle class and the better-paid artisans, but it had still left a gap in the supply of houses for the lower-income groups. It also left the slums untouched, and in many central areas of the city, apart from the installation of a separate water-supply in many houses previously without, little had been done since the Committee of Inquiry in 1913. In 1935 there were still 38,773 back-to-back houses; 51,794 houses without a separate W.C., and 13,650 houses without a separate water-supply.[1] The position was far more serious socially than in many other cities, such as Manchester.[2]

It was extremely unfortunate that the Council had not been able to build suitable houses to replace slum property of this type during the worst years of the depression, when building costs were low and there was some unemployment in the building trade. Such a policy would have been anti-cyclical, and would have been in accord with the best canons of Keynesian finance. As it was, when the Council returned to house-building in 1936, costs were rising again, although the rate of interest was low. In a new drive between the end of 1935 and the end of 1938, 7,931 municipal houses were built as against 3,851 in the previous three years. The rate of private-enterprise building remained high, the number of private-enterprise houses in each of the years 1936, 1937, and 1938 surpassing the peak municipal total of 1930.

Between 1935 and 1938 the City Council accepted the implications of a housing policy for the poorest families in the city in a more comprehensive way than it had ever done before. In the 1920's it had tended to choose its tenants on the same principles as the private landlords did. Under the scale used in 1926 a man with a wife and three children was accepted as a 'good tenant' of a three-bedroom, non-parlour-type house, only if he had an income of 70s. a week or more; and the minimum wage for a

[1] See Bournville Trust, *When We Build Again* (1941); J. C. Rushbrooke and others, *Birmingham's Black Spots* (1934).

[2] See E. D. Simon, *The Anti-slum Campaign* (1933).

PLATE XXXIV

CITY OF BIRMINGHAM

BIRCHES GREEN ESTATE

H. H. HUMPHRIES. M. Inst.C.E.
CITY ENGINEER & SURVEYOR
COUNCIL HOUSE. BIRMINGHAM.

SCALE OF FEET

The Plan of a Housing Estate

PLATE XXXV

'good tenant' of a three-bedroom parlour house was 80s. There was no organized policy of looking after poor families. In the 1930's, under the stimulus of the slum-clearance scheme, which reached its peak in the national Housing Act of 1936, the Council realized both the urgent need to provide good housing for poor families—a need which could not be met by private builders—and the wisdom of controlling clearance, re-housing, and development through a single agency. Municipal building was recognized as a permanent duty of the city. Vince's picture of a blurred sense of perspective in local housing policy had at last become out of date.

Between 1935 and 1938 the Council took an active and positive part in several controversies concerning national policy. It protested against the proposed enforcement of the house assessment provisions of the Rating and Valuation Act of 1925 so long as rents were at a high level, and it called for an extension of rent restriction in 1938. This last proposal was in marked contrast to the Council's vigorous opposition to rent restriction in 1922 and 1923.

During the years immediately before the war, the Council decided, too, to take a more direct interest in planning the welfare requirements of the new municipal housing estates. The estates had grown up with little in the way of communal facilities. They had good roads, plenty of open spaces, a low building density, and neat trim gardens, but they lacked the facilities associated with older communities. The example of Kingstanding is interesting. In 1932, when the population of Kingstanding was already about 30,000, a comparison was made locally between the communal services offered by Kingstanding and Shrewsbury, an old town with a slightly smaller population. Shrewsbury had 30 churches, 15 church halls and parish rooms, 5 other halls, and 2 public libraries; Kingstanding had 1 church and 1 hall.

To some extent voluntary agencies were beginning to interest themselves in this problem, as they always had done in the story of the emerging conurbation of the nineteenth century. The Birmingham Common Good Trust, a charity founded by George Cadbury, Junior, in 1917, provided an amenities fund, which offered trees and flowering shrubs to tenants on the estates, and an endowment fund which enabled land to be purchased for road widening, new roads, park extensions, allotments, and open spaces. The Birmingham Council for Community Associations, helping to fill the social gap caused by the retrenchment policy of the 1930's, was responsible first for organizing community centres itself, and later for encouraging and co-operating with the City Council. Finally, as far as private building was concerned, much useful voluntary work was carried out by Copec, the Conference on Politics, Economics, and Citizenship Home Improvement Society, set up in 1925, which set out with the clearcut objective of reconditioning slum houses in Birmingham and converting them into reasonably habitable dwellings. In line with the pre-war scheme of J. S. Nettlefold, Copec carried out invaluable work.

In the two years before 1938 the City Council itself began very tentatively to interest itself in a community policy on the estates, which only really blossomed out during the Second World War and after 1945. It had agreed as early as July 1930 to build an experimental community centre at Kingstanding, but the proposal was abandoned in consequence of the financial crisis of 1931. In 1934 the question was reopened, and eventually in November 1936 the first Council community centre was opened on the Billesley Farm Estate, where there was a great need for accommodation of this kind, and where there were already fifteen organizations in existence which could make use of it. In 1938 the Edgbaston Golf Club House was converted into a community centre for the Quinton and Harborne Estates, and a year later, to mark the meeting-point of the different branches of new civic policy, the powers under the Housing Acts concerning the provision and maintenance of community halls were transferred from the Public Works Committee to the Education Committee. There can be no better example of the adjacent frontiers of a new civic policy.

III

In the case of education, as in that of housing, the war years were important not only in leaving a backlog of arrears to be made up but in stimulating a new interest in education as part of a social programme. The Boer War had had a similar but less powerful effect in preparing the way for the 1902 Education Act: indeed, the Boer War ended on the day that the debate on the 1902 Act began. The First World War quickened trends 'which had been working silently and unsuspected beneath the surface to create a new desire for education'.[1]

As in the story of housing it was a national Act which symbolized the new social ideals of the post-war world. The Education Act of 1918, based on Fisher's investigations at the Board of Education, placed the onus of reconstruction on the local authorities. It called upon the Birmingham Education Committee, in common with the other local authorities, to submit to the Board of Education schemes showing 'the mode in which their duties and powers under the Education Acts were to be performed', in order to ensure progressive development and comprehensive organization. In 1920 the Education Committee submitted its scheme. It described the organization of education during the war, carried on in face of serious handicaps and dislocation, and made various proposals concerning the problems of post-war reconstruction. It laid stress not only on the curriculum and internal organization of schools but on the role of education in the process of the formation of citizenship, and on the interdependence of schools and other organizations, commercial and cultural, in the life of the community.

The Education Committee of 1920, which sent in this Report, was one of the most efficient organizations of its type in the country. It had gained much from the long record of public service of Sir George Kenrick, who, after twenty-three years on the old School Board, acted as chairman of the Education Committee from 1902 to 1921. Even after his retirement from the chairmanship he continued to serve on the Education Committee until 1933. Many tributes were paid to his fifty-three-year record of service, and the Minutes of the Education Committee for 27 October 1933 expressed the high regard in which Sir George's work was always held by the Council. As Alderman Byng Kenrick, his relative, who rendered sterling service as chairman of the committee from 1922 with a short break to 1943, put it, 'his work has helped to place firmly in the minds of the people of Birmingham the conviction that Birmingham must, at least, be in the first flight and that the members of this committee should be satisfied with nothing else'. There were others on the Education Committee, too, who represented ideals of long service and devoted interest. Miss Clara Martineau, in particular, was a member of the Education Committee for

[1] *Report of the Board of Education*, 1924.

fifteen years and was chairman of the Special Schools Sub-Committee. She left the sum of £1,000 in her will to the cost of securing the permanent establishment of the sea-side holiday school for Birmingham children at Towyn.

The Education Committee did most of its work at the sub-committee level. There were many sub-committees covering all branches of its work—elementary education; higher education; technical education and evening schools; the school of art; hygiene; special schools; appeals; continuation schools; juvenile employment and welfare; buildings; and finance. In 1919, after the retirement of J. A. Palmer, the Clerk and Secretary, it acquired the services of Dr. P. D. Innes, who was given the new title of Chief Education Officer.

One of the most important tasks facing the Education Committee in the 1920's and 30's was the provision of new schools, particularly on the large housing estates which were being erected as part of the building programme. The policy of the Corporation Estates Committee in letting houses was to give preference to young married applicants with children. This meant that a close relationship between housing policy and education policy was essential. In all, forty new schools were built between 1923 and 1935, all of them of very different type from the old Board Schools. At first economic necessity alone dictated a change: in the early 1920's the schools had to be different because of the high cost of building materials. The Board of Education sanctioned a departure from the former specifications, and permitted local authorities to experiment with cheaper types of construction—'light' construction, and 'semi-permanent'—such as the school at Nansen Road, Saltley, and the Pineapple Farm Estates School at King's Heath. Necessity encouraged experiment. The Billesley Council School, erected in 1925, was frankly experimental. It was designed with open-air classrooms, fitted with screens, opening on to verandas sufficiently wide to protect children from the direct glare of the sun. Heating was secured from a system of pipes laid underneath the floors. This was not the only experiment. Another change in style was expressed in the Ilmington Road elementary school, built in 1933–4 of timber on brick foundations because of the cuts in educational expenditure enforced by the Great Depression.

Because of their location some of these new schools were designed to cater for very large numbers of pupils. The Peckham

Road school with four departments catered for 1,568 children, and cost £66,350 to build. Nine other schools were designed to accommodate more than 1,000 children. It was agreed that the children were to be housed in smaller classes, and the condition was enforced that classrooms should be designed to hold not more than 40 children in the Senior Schools and 48 in the Junior Schools, as against 50 in both cases previously. Unfortunately both then and since it has been necessary to overcrowd them.

There was thus a relationship between the form and shape of school buildings and the methods of school internal organization. The 1920's were years when the purposes of education were being questioned and discussed on all sides. The Hadow Report on the Education of the Adolescent advocated the remodelling of school education for children aged between eleven and fourteen. For a rigorous central code, which ran to a document of 76 pages in 1902, it substituted the irreducible minimum of regulations demanded by statute, leaving local education authorities and teachers free to develop independently. At the same time it set out a view of education as a whole, treating elementary education not as a separate problem but as a stage in a longer development. It emphasized that the education of the child between five and eleven should be considered as a primary process, and that all children over the age of eleven should be given the benefit of a form of secondary education, suited to their capacity and their bent of mind. It aimed at making senior schools separate and distinct from earlier educational institutions, and separating children into different age-groups. The size of the top classes was to be reduced to achieve a maximum amount of educational specialization in terms of the needs of the adolescent, the specialization being fitted into a general framework of a comprehensive system. The curriculum was to be broadened so that 'the age of the three Rs' was to be finished for good.

In 1926 the Hadow Report was welcomed in Birmingham. Indeed, in some respects, it had been anticipated, for as early as March 1925 the Education Committee had decided that the statutory requirements for the new housing estates in the Stechford and Small Heath districts might best be realized by the provision of three schools in different parts of the area, one for infants and juniors from five to eleven years of age, and two schools for senior boys and girls respectively. After 1926 the process of school reorganization was speeded up. Not only did the new Council schools in the suburban areas follow the changed principles of planning and layout, but an attempt was made in addition to convert existing older schools in the central area of the city.

These schools, all of them dating from the pre-war period, faced two sets of serious problems—first, because a high proportion of them were non-provided schools, still run by voluntary bodies, and second, because the birth-rate was falling in the older parts of the town as the migration to the municipal housing estates increased. The problem of giving old schools new life was most serious in the case of the black list of schools—five of them Council schools and twenty-one non-provided—scheduled previously by the Board of Education as either wholly condemned or requiring substantial structural alterations before they could qualify for continued recognition. The economic crisis of 1931 interfered with the programme of conversion, for education was 'the first and easiest victim of the would-be economiser'.[1] No new buildings could be erected, except in cases of necessity, including the provision of school facilities for housing estates. Many progressive schemes had to be abandoned. Despite these setbacks, real improvements were made, although in 1938 five voluntary schools still remained on the black list, all of them in the older areas of the town. The result of the long-term programme of school reorganization was that the elementary schools were far brighter, cleaner, friendlier places than they had been under the old School Board system.

As the elementary schools were reorganized, secondary education, in the old sense of the word—higher education—underwent a parallel process of expansion, which has been compared to 'a social revolution of the first magnitude'.[2] There was a pressing need for improved secondary education in Birmingham, for in the provision of facilities for secondary education the city was badly off in 1918 compared with many other similar areas. A survey carried out at the end of the war showed that Birmingham offered only 6·6 secondary school places per 1,000 of its population, compared with 11·8 places in other large provincial cities. It was in the light of this deficiency that the

---

[1] *The Economist*, 3 December 1932.
[2] E. Halévy, *History of the English People, 1895–1905*, p. 205.

Education Committee proposed a more vigorous higher-education policy, which virtually transformed the pre-war system. In 1920–1 the Education Committee began to aid the King Edward VI Foundation Schools and the two Roman Catholic grammar schools. In addition, by 1930 a new school for 316 girls had been opened at Erdington; a school for 500 boys had been provided at Moseley; a mixed school for 500 pupils had been built at Saltley; and a new school for 500 girls had been erected at King's Norton, where the old school had been remodelled so as to provide for 500 boys. In the light of this advance and the extensions in the schools of the King Edward VI Foundation, it was anticipated that the number of secondary school places per 1,000 of the population in 1931 would be up to 9·6. The Committee considered this a minimum figure rather than an ideal percentage of secondary school places.

This expansion of secondary education—still inadequate in 1930—was accomplished quietly in response to both working-class aspirations and changes in the social outlook. There was a double emphasis on the frustration of rights of equal opportunity and on the magnitude of social waste. In the story of expansion 1931 and 1932 were years of disaster. The Ray Committee Report recommended the imposition of an income-test on the parents of scholarship holders, and a severe cut in expenditure. Even if a local authority had not accepted the necessity for such measures, it would have found it difficult to rebel, for in 1930, out of £2 million spent annually on education in Birmingham, rather more than half came from the national exchequer.

Although, after the economic crisis had ended, there was an attempt to restore the rate of progress, Birmingham was aiming at a 9·4 per 1,000 objective in 1935, a figure actually lower than the 1930 aspiration for 1931. 'Neither in Birmingham nor probably in any other part of the country, are there sufficient secondary school places for all the children who could occupy them with profit', said the *City of Birmingham Handbook* in 1935.

Despite the difficulties, great improvements were made in the inter-war years. The pre-war system of financial assistance on a small scale gave way to an elaborate system of free or special places and maintenance allowances. Pressure was great, and in 1934, for instance, 7,000 to 8,000 candidates presented themselves for 2,000 places. Unfortunately a substantial number of parents refused places at grammar schools even when their children qualified for maintenance allowances. Only a limited number of candidates was admitted to the King Edward VI High Schools on the results of these examinations, the main examination to these schools being conducted by the governing body of the schools themselves.

This system enabled bright children to climb the first rung of an educational ladder which might eventually lead to the university. It also enabled the city to secure a ready flow of soundly trained juveniles for selected local employment. While the first service was being carried out on the basis of an entrance scholarships scheme for the University of Birmingham, and a smaller scheme for entrance to other universities, the second service was being interpreted in a new spirit. There was a closer contact between the secondary schools and the industrial and commercial world; and the curriculum was broadened to cover subjects not taught in the older grammar schools. The Birmingham secondary schools played a big part in making possible the continued existence of Birmingham as an expanding twentieth-century industrial city.

So, too, did the technical schools, and during the inter-war years a serious attempt was made to develop technical education at all levels, from the junior school to the adult class. The First World War had made the task of maintaining technical education, even on its pre-war basis, extremely difficult. In February 1915 class-rooms and laboratories at the municipal technical college had been lent to the University, and later on were devoted almost entirely to the training of munitions workers. After 1918, while the demand for technical education increased, the supply position remained awkward, particularly because of the inadequate accommodation in the central technical college which was shared with the central grammar school. One of the most important inter-war developments—the large increase in the number of full-time day classes, and the increased number of apprentices sent by local firms for part-time classes—was held back because of lack of accommodation.

In the 1920's and early 30's hand-to-mouth expedients were adopted, and it was not until March 1935 that preliminary measures for the building of a new central combined technical college came under serious consideration. In November 1937 as the result of an open competition H. V. Ashley and Winton

Newman were appointed architects. Their scheme provided for a large and impressive building which would house the Technical College, the Commercial College, and the College of Art. The proposals were ambitious.

Though each college is independent one from another, joint accommodation, in the form of gymnasia, refectory, library, staff and students' common rooms, etc., is to be provided on an upper floor, in the hope that this accommodation will give students of each trade, profession, or calling ample opportunity, by social intercourse, to understand the outlooks, aspirations and ideals of all members of the colleges as a whole.[1]

A large joint assembly hall was to be provided where students' entertainments could be arranged with ample space for an audience of at least 1,500 people. Provision was made for further extensions to all parts of the building, and it was hoped that before the building expanded that portion of the site not immediately required would be laid out as an open space for quiet rest and study, 'much in the same way as the quadrangles of our older universities'.

The Central Technical College was still a dream in 1938, and technical education continued to be carried on in the existing central buildings, in the colleges at Aston and Handsworth, in the commercial schools and college, and in the College of Arts and Crafts. Although these premises were inadequate, a real effort was made to make technical education correspond to local needs. There was an increasing systematization and grouping of subjects and tests. The City of Birmingham Engineering Apprenticeship Certificate Scheme, formulated by the Education Committee acting in conjunction with the Birmingham District Engineering and Allied Employers' Association, provided a recognized qualification for young men in the engineering industry, who had completed training at work, together with suitable courses of technical instruction. 'A modern apprenticeship is essentially a combination of practical and theoretical training', said a former chairman of the Birmingham Employment Committee in 1938, 'and obviously such a combination requires the closest co-ordination and co-operation between education and industry.' Evening institutes attempted to assist young workers already employed by day to carry forward their knowledge and training. The driving force of individual ambition was still the

[1] See *City of Birmingham Official Handbook*, 1939.

most important force operating behind the demand for technical education.

Apart from these structural adjustments in the development of elementary, secondary, and technical education, the years between 1918 and 1938 saw a marked broadening of the range of special services offered to children in the city's schools. Some of the services went back to pre-1914 days, but they were all greatly expanded. In addition to the provision of special schools for blind and partially sighted children, the deaf, the physically defective, the mentally defective, and juvenile delinquents, the Schools Medical Service and the Schools Meals Service were greatly expanded. The Schools Medical Service, begun in 1908, was given a new impetus after the Education Act of 1921. The service made possible X-ray, ophthalmic, ultra-violet ray, and orthopaedic treatment for every child who attended an elementary or secondary school. The visits to the schools of medical and dental staff became an accepted part of school routine. The full-time school medical staff under the School Medical Officer greatly increased, and there were eleven clinics distributed throughout the city, including a special orthopaedic clinic and a child guidance clinic, set up experimentally in 1932 as a result of an initial grant from an anonymous donor and from the Commonwealth Fund of America. The Schools Medical Service, with its highly trained staff, was able, by 1938, to develop not only routine examination and supervision, but also experimental research. The care of the child by 1938 was far in advance of that even twenty years before. This in itself was one of the greatest social revolutions of the twentieth century.

The Free Schools Meals Service went back to pre-war years, the first meal to be provided in Birmingham being breakfast.[1] Under the terms of the Education Act of 1921 the Education Committee exercised its power to supply meals to those children in public elementary schools who 'by reason of lack of food are unable to derive full benefit from the education provided for them'. The criterion was that family income had not to be in excess of a certain figure of income *per head* per week, after house rent had been deducted. In 1929 the sum fixed varied from 2s. 9d. to 5s. 6d., and there were separate scales for summer and winter. In September 1931 as an economy measure the winter

---

[1] Before 1905 a charitable association called the Birmingham Schools Dinner Society had for twenty-three years provided meals for the poorest children in the schools.

scale was abolished, and the summer scale operated throughout the year. There were sharp annual fluctuations in the supply of free school meals. In 1921, for instance, £3,608 was spent by the committee on this service and 138,767 meals were provided, a daily average of 380. In 1922 £31,085 was spent and 1,454,914 meals were provided, a daily average of 3,986. This figure was not reached again until 1933, although the annual number of meals provided never fell below 200,000 between 1922 and 1932. It needed the Second World War, employment demands for mothers in factories, and a food shortage to stabilize the demand for school meals, and make a new comprehensive service a recognized part of the welfare state.[1]

In the inter-war years another service offered by the city to its children was that of assisting them to secure employment of a suitable character. After-care work was first made possible by the Education (Choice of Employment) Act of 1910, and in 1911 the Central Care Committee was set up in Birmingham, charged with the duty of seeing that, as far as possible, boys and girls leaving school should be directed into occupations offering them reasonable prospects in the future, and the opportunity of learning a skilled trade. Until 1924 the committee acted in an advisory capacity, but in April 1924 the Education Committee, with the authority of the City Council, took over the responsibility of administering the Unemployment Insurance Acts in so far as they applied to juveniles under eighteen. The number of children seeking guidance from the committee increased greatly, varying with the local employment position. In 1925 there were 90,187 visits to the committee's office of young persons seeking help and advice: in 1931, the peak year, there were 319,618. Application did not necessarily mean successful adjustment. Despite the disparity in annual applications between 1925 and 1931, the number of vacancies filled in the depression year chosen was only 9,356 as compared with 7,786 in 1925. Despite the fact that it could not find suitable openings for all the applicants, the committee played an important part in maintaining contact between schools, factories, and offices. Employment conferences were held at all schools each term, at which parents of children about to leave were invited to be present. A network of group care committees was constructed, drawing on the services of over a thousand voluntary helpers.

[1] R. M. Titmuss, *Problems of Social Policy* (1950), p. 149.

From 1924 onwards the committee realized the importance of expert child guidance, and began to investigate the possibilities and value of the study of industrial psychology. In 1925 two members of the staff of the Juvenile Employment and Welfare Department were sent to London to receive a course of training at the National Institute, and two years later two experiments were carried out to try to ascertain the practical value of selection tests relating to innate aptitude and ability for engineering work and to study the use of psychological tests in relation to vocational guidance as a whole.

In all these ways the Education Committee showed that it had the interest of the children of the city very closely at heart. It went on to extend its range of interests to cover leisure as well as workaday activities. The Juvenile Organisations Committee, for instance, which had been established on a voluntary basis to organize club and sports activities among adolescents, was taken over in 1928 by the Education Committee as a section of the Juvenile Employment and Welfare Sub-Committee. Voluntary action was supplemented rather than abandoned, for there was a continued partnership between the two, as there always had been in the earlier shaping of Birmingham's social policy. After 1928 a great army of voluntary workers continued to run the thousand affiliated clubs which existed throughout the city.

Quite naturally, with all this expansion of educational activities, the amount of money spent by the city on education increased, although the rate of increase was, as in the case of housing, dependent on general economic conditions, not only in Birmingham but in the country as a whole, and on the attitude of the national authorities.

Before 1918 the grants made by the Board of Education towards the expenditure of the local authority were based on the unit of average attendance, and bore no direct relationship to the total expenditure undertaken. By the Education Act of 1918 provision was made along the lines suggested by the Departmental Committee on Local Taxation in 1914 for the payment of such an amount by the central authorities as would bring the minimum Education Grant up to 50 per cent. of the net expenditure of the authorities. This was a most important, if overdue, reform.

The Committee on National Expenditure of 1922 led to a greater emphasis being placed by the central authorities on economy, and the Board of Education tried to ensure the success of this policy in its own field. In 1926 by the Economy (Miscellaneous Provisions) Act, it secured a stringent control over local estimates. Pleading that there were serious national difficulties caused by fluctuations in local education budgets, it asked local authorities to make a return of the programmes of work they hoped to carry out in the three-year period beginning 1 April 1927. By this means it hoped to ensure a greater stability in educational expenditure, and to enable the local authorities to plan ahead with a fair amount of certainty concerning the future. The Birmingham City Council approved its committee's first Three-Year Programme on 4 January 1927, and although some queries were raised by the Board of Education, which was endeavouring to standardize and limit its grants, there was no really serious educational dislocation until 1931, when the economic crisis brought the whole programme into question.

The May Report of 1931[1] was followed by a White Paper on Reductions in Expenditure and a Board of Education circular directed towards reductions of local educational costs and the 'contractionist' Report of the Ray Committee in 1932. By the National Economy Act of 1931 the government was given powers to alter by means of Orders in Council the proportion of educational expenditure which the local education authorities were entitled to receive in the form of Exchequer grants.

On 1 October 1931 the Board of Education issued a circular to local authorities indicating that grants would be calculated on the assumption of a reduction of 10 per cent. in teachers' salaries, which accounted for about two-thirds of the expenditure of the Board. The Birmingham authorities responded with an immediate 10 per cent. cut in teachers' salaries, and a 'voluntary abatement' in salaries of officers other than teachers. As a result of these steps a saving of nearly £100,000 was secured. The capital programme was cut down, too, and reduced to essential projects only. As a result, although teachers' salary cuts were made good in 1934 and 1936, the whole educational horizons of the city were inevitably narrowed.

Despite these cuts, it was only in 1932-3 that the total expenditure on educational services in the city fell, and in

---

[1] The May Report, while concerned with national expenditure, 'earnestly' recommended an economy campaign 'to the attention of every local authority in the country'.

1933-4 it was up again above the pre-slump figure, nearly £200,000 more than in 1929-30. Quite apart from the government grants, the amount taken from the rates to be spent on education had increased over 400 times since the first School Board had asked for £3,000 from the rates in 1871.

## IV

A study of civic expansion in the inter-war years easily becomes a study in superlatives. The development of municipal transport, in particular, was so rapid that it became a bigger undertaking than gas or water, and was beaten only by the still more rapidly developing Electricity Department. The scale of municipal enterprise in Birmingham could be compared with that of the largest public companies.[1] In 1938 the municipal transport undertaking was the second largest in the country.

In some branches of municipal transport, Birmingham was a pioneer. In 1922 it was the first undertaking to introduce a double-decker, top-covered trolley omnibus system. At that time there were no top-covered motor-buses in operation, and the Corporation's own engineers began to investigate the possibilities of a new invention. Eventually, after long tests, they designed a chassis having a track wider than the standard width. A body was then constructed by the Brush Electrical Engineering Company and a chassis by the Associated Equipment Company, and the new type of bus was put into service in the summer of 1924. With slight alterations it became after a time the standard pattern.

The most important problem facing local transport authorities in the post-war years was that of the balance between tram and motor-bus services. In an age of growing motor traffic, the chief difficulty about trams was that they served congested areas, that they were route-bound, and that they had to unload in the middle of the road, thereby adding to the congestion of the following traffic. The Birmingham tramway authorities tried to improve the existing system by developing new sleeper tramtracks, with two carriage-ways divided by a tram-track, and by introducing bigger trams with high-powered motors, which would permit greater speed and frequency. In 1931 the Birmingham

---

[1] See J. H. Warren, *Municipal Administration* (1948), esp. p. 11, where he compares Glasgow and Birmingham with Unilever and I.C.I.

PLATE XXXVI

A Nursery School

PLATE XXXVII

1872

190

CIRCA 1882

1911/12

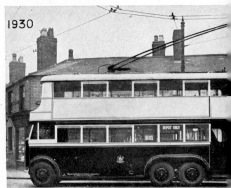
1930

Development in Tram and Omnibus Design, 1872–1930

Transport Manager, A. C. Baker, admitted the difficulties of making even the new system work. The increased volume of traffic hindered further progress, and the new system was merely leading to a great increase in the consumption of electric current.[1]

The trams had obvious advantages. They had a large seating capacity of from 60 to 64 passengers; they were operating at the rate of 1 every 2 or 3 minutes during rush periods. Their cost of upkeep was lower per passenger than those of trolleys and buses. Their owners were responsible under the Tramway Act of 1870 for maintaining the roads up to 18 inches on each side of the outer rails, thereby subsidizing other repairs. They paid in rates to the city £80,000 a year. All these considerations were important ones, and although the Royal Commission on Transport of 1931 believed that tramways were 'in a state of obsolescence, and cause much congestion and considerable unnecessary danger to the public' and recommended that 'it will be to the advantage of the inhabitants of the towns, where they exist, to get rid of them by degrees',[2] the policy adopted in Birmingham was to try to combine trams, trolleys, and motor-buses in one common transport scheme, where the merits of each particular form of transport would be brought out to the full. As Baker pointed out in 1931, if the tramways were scrapped the rates would have to be found from another source; the cost of 80 miles of road would begin to fall wholly on the general rate fund; it would be necessary to proceed to pay the outstanding capital; and there would be a loss to the city's Electricity Department of a large element in its income.

As a result of these and other considerations, Birmingham kept its trams—indeed it added to the length of its routes—and took over the running of the routes of neighbouring authorities. In 1924 it began to run the tram services of the Corporation of West Bromwich, taking over from a private company whose lease had not been renewed. Four years later it took over the tramway services in Smethwick, Oldbury, and Dudley, after an agreement had been signed with the Birmingham District Power and Traction Company. Both these extensions of the city transport system provided that the traffic receipts should be handed to the authority owning the lines, and that Birmingham Corporation

[1] A. C. Baker, in the *Journal of the Institute of Transport*, March 1931.
[2] Royal Commission on Transport (1931), *Final Report*, p. 163.

should be paid a sum in respect of their operating expenses, along with a contribution based on the capital cost of the rolling stock. A closer integration of routes and services was secured, the Corporation being enabled to work the whole of the tramway services running into the city, and the passengers securing the benefits of through routes, which took no account of artificial local government boundaries.

While the tramway system was being improved, the motor omnibus system was developing rapidly. In the year ending March 1927 the omnibus route-mileage was 63 miles, as against a tramway mileage of 77 miles; the trams were running 19 million miles as against the buses' 5 million; and over 238 million passengers were being carried by tram as against 43 million by bus. In the year ending March 1938, the omnibus route mileage had increased to 153 miles, while the tram mileage had gone down to 65 miles; the trams were running 15 million miles, and the buses 26 million miles; and over 225 million passengers were being carried by bus as against 174 million by tram. Buses had over trams the advantage of greater flexibility both as to route and as to adjustment to other traffic in the road, and they were playing an essential part in the life of the whole city area, particularly in carrying workers from the new housing estates to their places of work, often miles away. The Birmingham Corporation owned the largest fleet of municipal omnibuses in the world.

The transport system was operated as a whole. The underlying principle was to provide services on all the arterial roads leading from the city centre and then to link these together by means of circular and inter-communicating omnibus routes. There were three complete circular routes, the Inner, the City, and the Outer. The Outer Circle Route, 25 miles long with a running time for omnibuses of 2 hours and 20 minutes, was started in April 1926. It allowed for 30 connexions with other tramway and omnibus routes. The Inner Circle omnibus service, approximately 11 miles long and intersecting the radiating routes at a distance of rather more than a mile from the city centre, was opened in 1928. Four years later the City Circle Service, $6\frac{3}{4}$ miles in length and intersecting the radiating routes at a distance of approximately 1 mile from Victoria Square, was inaugurated.

The building of this network of local transport services involved three important sets of new civic problems—first, the

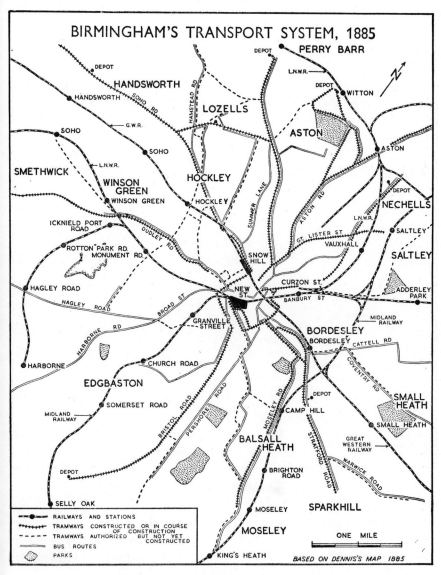

BIRMINGHAM'S TRANSPORT SYSTEM, 1885

BASED ON DENNIS'S MAP 1885

RAILWAYS AND STATIONS
TRAMWAYS CONSTRUCTED OR IN COURSE OF CONSTRUCTION
TRAMWAYS AUTHORIZED BUT NOT YET CONSTRUCTED
BUS ROUTES
PARKS

ONE MILE

FIG. 9

planning of an enormous business undertaking, on the routine efficiency of which the whole economic and social life of the community depended; second, the implementation of a pricing policy, which would be unfair neither to long-distance nor to

FIG. 10

short-distance passengers; and third, the design of an effective system of traffic control, whereby trams, trolleys, buses, private cars, and commercial vehicles could move round and through the city quickly—but not too quickly—and safely.

Birmingham had already had a wide experience of organizing large-scale municipal undertakings. The transport concern was no new departure. In March 1938 there were 701 tram-cars, 863 motor omnibuses, and 78 trolley-buses under the care of the Transport Manager. There was a pay-roll of nearly 8,000, a weekly wages bill of approximately £27,000, and a cash turn-over of over £50,000 a week. There were 11 tram depots and 9

motor omnibus garages, 3 of which were situated on the Outer
Circle omnibus route. The omnibus repair works at Tyburn,
completed in December 1929 and further extended in 1938,

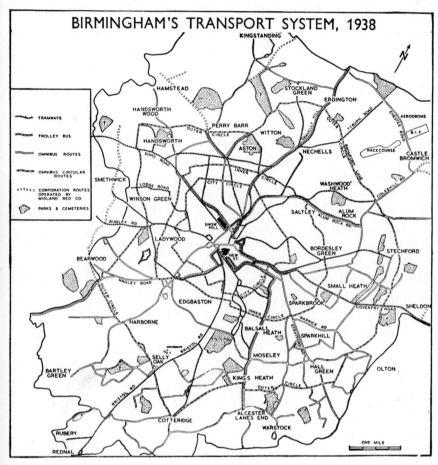

FIG. 11

covered an area of over 15,000 square yards and were designed
according to the most up-to-date principles. A staff of 350 was
employed in the works, and the vehicles which passed through
were completely overhauled and repaired. The same methods
were adopted at the tramway repair depot, where 301 men were
employed.

All the drivers and conductors employed by the Department
were trained in the Department's own school, and when they
were considered competent were tested by the Department's

Chief Examiner before they appeared before the Traffic Commissioners' Examiner to take their national test.

Most of this side of the transport undertaking was taken for granted by the citizens of Birmingham. What they could not and did not take for granted was the pricing policy put into effect by the Transport Committee. The rate of migration from the central area of the city to the outer districts had an important effect on the evolution of the transport system, and posed many pricing problems, for as the number of long-distance passengers travelling backwards and forwards from the housing estates increased, the number of short-distance passengers, hitherto an important asset to the Department, showed a substantial falling off. The committee decided to try to deal with this problem, first by discontinuing the use of trams on certain of the older routes, and secondly by raising the short-distance bus and tram fares and using the proceeds to subsidize passengers on longer routes.

Workmen's tickets on trams and omnibuses were issued, from August 1930, to passengers who completed the first portion of their journeys before 9 a.m.; and the maximum return fare was fixed at 5*d*. There was no restriction as to the time or period during which the return ticket was available. Passengers living in the most distant areas of the city were thus enabled to travel 14 miles on the two journeys for an outlay of 5*d*. This low rate meant a subsidy from other users, and Birmingham's figures compared well with those of a sample of 33 other municipalities, where the average tram distance allowed for 5*d*. was just over 12 miles, and the average bus distance was only 8½ miles.[1] The subsidy was increased by the low daily traffic outside the peak-load periods. Sixty-nine per cent. of the rolling stock lay idle between 9.30 a.m. and 4.30 p.m. Baker pointed out in 1932 that even during the peak-load periods buses operated almost empty in one direction, and had to travel 26 miles to earn 300 pence, about 11½*d*. a mile, which did not even cover operating expenses.[2]

So serious were these problems of maintaining an efficient transport service, which would at least meet its way, that there were some critics who were suggesting in the inter-war years that Housing Committees should consult Transport Committees

[1] *Report of the Annual Conference of the Municipal Tramways and Transport Association*, 24 June 1936.

[2] A. C. Baker, *The Effect of the Development of Housing Estates on Municipal Passenger Transport*, Paper read to the Annual Conference of the Municipal Tramways and Transport Association, 1932.

before selecting sites for the rehousing of slum-clearance areas. In Birmingham it was clear that housing estates, fully equipped with schools, cinemas, shops, and social centres, would change the balance of the transport services. Transport, like education, could not be divorced from the housing question, which from this angle too was the central issue of civic policy.

The third problem raised by the widening net of local transport services was that of traffic control. The rapid growth of motor traction after the war gave special importance to traffic problems, and in 1926 the congestion in the centre of the city had become so acute that the General Purposes Committee appointed a Joint Committee—consisting of representatives of the Public Works and Town Planning Committees, the Tramways Committee, and the Watch Committee—to make a thorough investigation of the traffic problem. The Report of this committee was approved by the City Council in March 1927. It suggested the provision of public parking places; a limitation on the amount of time vehicles could remain in certain central parts of the town; the widening of certain streets; the introduction, in some of the central areas, of the gyratory system which had been in operation at Six Ways, Erdington, since 1926; the creation of one-way traffic streets; and the re-arrangement of certain omnibus routes. Two amendments to these proposals were defeated: first, an instruction to the General Purposes Committee to consider and report upon the possibilities of establishing municipal garages in Birmingham, and second, the suggestion that a centralized garage department should be opened for all motor-cars belonging to the Corporation.

The programme of traffic control accepted in 1927 was merely a beginning, and in 1930, when the traffic problem still remained acute, the General Purposes Committee recommended the setting up of a consultative traffic control committee, without executive powers, as a standing committee of the Council. In January 1931 the committee evolved a one-way traffic system for the city centre, which was approved by the Council, and the scheme was put into operation on Whit Monday 1933.

All sorts of new forms of traffic control were developed. The first traffic islands had been erected temporarily in 1920. Ten years later they numbered 500, and in 1935 approximately 1,150. The first automatic traffic-control signals were introduced in 1929, before the Ministry of Transport announced that where signals were erected with its approval, contributions from the Road Fund towards the cost of installation and maintenance would be made to the rate of 60 per cent. of the expenditure incurred. In 1934–5, under the Road Traffic Act of 1934, pedestrian crossings were provided. Finally, in 1935, almost the whole of the city area was defined as a 'built-up' area. Motorists expressed their opposition to this step at a public inquiry conducted by an Inspector of the Ministry of Transport, and the Minister wrote to the Corporation expressing the view that a number of dual-carriage roads should be excluded from the thirty miles per hour speed limit. The Council reaffirmed its original decision, and finally secured its acceptance.

There was one other development in Birmingham's transport services which showed that the city was keeping pace with the times. In February 1928 the City Council requested the General Purposes Committee to make a survey of available sites in or near Birmingham suitable for the purpose of building an aerodrome. It was felt that the rapid development of the city and the reduction in available sites made the problem an urgent one, and it was hoped that 'much of the continental traffic by air might be diverted from London to Birmingham direct, thereby stimulating the present and future trade of the city'.[1] Valuable assistance and encouragement was given by the Air Ministry, and in 1930 it was hoped to acquire a site at Shirley, less than seven miles from the city centre, which might be secured not by agreement but by compulsory acquisition procedure under the Public Works Facilities Act of 1930, which aimed at providing public works schemes for the relief of unemployment. Progress on this scheme was held up partly because the sub-committee was attracted by other sites, but mainly because of the government's economy proposals of September 1931. The Council abandoned the Shirley scheme and shelved the whole question of an aerodrome until a letter from the Air Ministry in June 1933 drew attention to the importance of municipal airport development. By that time housing developments in Shirley had ruled out the possibility of choosing a site in that locality.

In December 1933 the Council approved the acquisition of a site at Elmdon, seven miles from Birmingham and ten miles from Coventry, and in November 1934 an Airport Committee was set up as a standing committee of the Council. Upon this body

[1] J. T. Jones, *History of the Corporation of Birmingham*, vol. v, pt. ii (1940), p. 563.

was placed the responsibility for the layout, responsibility, and management of the site. The committee sent a deputation to visit representative airports in Holland, Belgium, and Denmark.

The Birmingham Corporation Act of 1935 secured statutory approval for the building of the aerodrome. Lord Londonderry welcomed 'the establishment of an airport by Birmingham, and hoped the example would be followed by great municipal authorities all over the country'.[1] The Corporation withdrew a clause giving them power to run an air service of their own, after this ambitious proposal had been attacked by speakers in both Houses, who argued that commercial air services were entirely different from road and tramway services, which were local in character, and that air-transport services were not therefore a suitable subject for municipal provision and management.

Work proceeded on the airport in 1936, 1937, and 1938. Miles of hedges were taken up and hundreds of trees removed. The scheme was not completed by the end of 1938, although the City Handbook covering the events of that year pointed out that

it is significant that the period of greatest activity in the development of the airport should coincide with the centenary of the grant of Birmingham's Charter of Incorporation, and this newest form of municipal activity, the effect of which is that for the first time in its history Birmingham becomes a port, serves to illustrate the intention of the Corporation to ensure that Birmingham is provided with every possible means of extending its commercial and industrial activity in the future.

## V

These developments in the field of social and transport services were accompanied by parallel changes in the volume and scope of municipal trading. In particular the balance between the old departments of gas and electricity was changed, as a result of the greatly increased demand for electricity on the part of domestic consumers. So rapid was the expansion in the Electricity Department that by 1935 Birmingham's electricity undertaking had become the largest municipal electricity supply system in Great Britain.

The period began with the war-time dislocation. After many delays, the government gave the Council authority to build a temporary electricity station close to the Nechells site and the

---

[1] *The Municipal Review*, May 1935.

new plant began to operate in 1915, within nine months from the date of the beginning of its construction. It proved inadequate to meet the heavy load and its capacity was more than doubled, thus reaching the maximum that could be accommodated on the site. Emergency supplies had to be obtained before 1918 from the private generating station of the Dunlop Rubber Company at Fort Dunlop, which ran in parallel with the city supply, furnishing supplies in bulk to the Corporation. Before the end of the war negotiations were completed with the government, which permitted the active resumption of the work on the large permanent station at Nechells, but it was not until 1923 that the new works were opened by the Prince of Wales, and not until 1929 that they were completed.

Between 1918 and 1938 various national Acts of Parliament regulated the general conditions of local electricity supply. The Electricity Supply Act of 1919 provided for the appointment of Electricity Commissioners, who were granted powers to regulate the generating side of the supply, to determine the boundaries of electricity districts, and to set up in those districts Joint Electricity Authorities, consisting of representatives of the supplying agencies, large consumers, and other interests. In 1920 the Electricity Commissioners, under the authority of this Act, gave notice that they intended to recommend the setting up of a South-West Midlands Electricity District; and three years later, in June 1923, an Advisory Joint Committee came into being, consisting of representatives of the Corporation and the Shropshire, Worcestershire, and Staffordshire Electric Power Company. Its functions were to advise on a time-table for the interconnected generating stations in the district to provide the best load factor obtainable, to conserve fuel, and to standardize systems.

This first scheme was reorganized after the passing of the Electricity Supply Act of 1926, which set up a Central Electricity Board for Great Britain and a National Grid system. Birmingham became the central point of the Midlands area. The technique and management of its Electricity Department were reorganized on the basis of a standardized plan, which it was hoped would provide a better utilization of capital investment in all the generating stations. Since it was laid down that the standard of frequency of supply to be adopted by the country as a whole should be 50 cycles, a change-over had to be made in the 25-cycle system which was operating at the Birmingham works. The Central Electricity Board bore the cost of the change-over, and these costs, together with those incurred in other cities, became a charge on all electricity undertakings throughout the country.

Within the framework of this national structure the Birmingham Electricity Department embarked on substantial new investment. In 1926 the Council decided to build and equip a large new power station at Hams Hall. The first section, which cost about £1½ million, was opened by the Duke of York in 1929. It was further extended in 1930 and 1934 and was completed in 1939. In 1938 work was in progress on a second Hams Hall station known as 'Station B'. As a result of the development of the large-scale plant at Nechells and Hams Hall, the early power stations were converted into sub-stations. There was a consequent saving in production costs, which enabled the Electric Supply Committee to make large reductions in rates to all classes of consumers.

Demand kept pace with the enormous increases in supply, and one day's output from the Corporation's undertaking in the winter months of 1934 was equal to nearly a month's needs for the area supplied by the Corporation in 1914. The number of premises supplied with electricity had increased over eighteen times, while in the year ending 31 March 1938, 33,499 new customers were connected to the system, more than the total number connected during the first 34 years (1891–1925) of the private and municipal undertaking. Taking the 10 years from 1928 to 1938, the number of consumers increased from 57,161 to 251,864 and the gross annual revenue of the Department rose from £1,577,553 to £3,040,518.

Part of the advance can be explained as a result of the enterprising pricing and supply policy of the Committee. A favourable tariff was offered to local manufacturers, who were not slow to take advantage of the facilities offered. Motors were offered to manufacturers on hire and maintenance terms at fixed rentals, and large workshops were provided with high-pressure current at low prices. Shopkeepers were encouraged by specially low rates to light their windows after the normal closing hours, and to use illuminated signs.

Civic as well as industrial progress was made. A modern system of street lights was installed in part of Broad Street near the centre of the city in 1925, while from the start the new housing

estates were offered not only good electric lighting but also
many other electricity services. As early as March 1922 a comprehensive scheme for the development of electricity supply in
suburban and outlying areas in the eastern and southern districts
of the city was approved by the Council. Mains were extended,
and the whole distribution system enlarged. In 1926 the range of
electricity supply stretched far beyond the boundaries of the
city, and covered 192 square miles.

At first a differential rate was charged for the city and for the
surrounding areas in Warwickshire, but in 1937 a uniform scale
was introduced on the lines recommended in 1936 by the
McGowan Report on the Distribution of Electricity. It was hoped
that this would give an even greater stimulus to the high rate of
growth.

To interest private consumers, and to educate them in the
many different uses of electricity, extensive showrooms were
opened in Paradise Street in 1923, in Solihull in 1927, in Harborne in 1930, and later on in Acock's Green, Cotteridge, Handsworth, and King's Heath. The domestic use of electricity was
further encouraged by the introduction of the domestic contract
tariff whereby current was supplied to residential users for all
purposes at fixed quarterly charges plus low running rates. In
the case of tenants of municipal houses, arrangements were
made for the fixed charge to be paid in small weekly instalments,
collected at the same time as the rent. Customers were induced
to use more electricity not only by these special pricing agreements, which included special prices for electricity used for
domestic water heating and for cooking, but also by a comprehensive Council hire-purchase and rental scheme, for equipment like large-sized cookers, electric fires and fans, immersion
heaters, automatic storage water-heaters, and wash-boilers.

The impressive statistics of electrical progress naturally had
their repercussions on the Gas Department, but although
suggestions were made from time to time at meetings of the City
Council that there was unnecessary competition between the
Electricity and Gas Departments, the two Departments continued to prosper side by side. The view was taken that each
Department had a well-defined place in the public service, and
that in regard to management each should be kept separate and
distinct. A joint sub-committee, for advisory purposes only, dealt
with overlapping problems.

In the case of gas there was steady but substantial progress. Like the Electricity Department the Gas Department supplied gas beyond the city boundaries over a very large area, including, by 1938, Wednesbury, Coleshill, Darlaston, and Sutton Coldfield. Special Orders made by the Board of Trade under the Gas Regulation Act of 1920 extended the statutory area of supply from 125 to 195 square miles, and despite the competition of electricity a record daily output was secured on 21 December 1938, when 75,452,000 cubic feet of gas were distributed.

In 1938 there were 341,024 consumers, many of whom took advantage of the Council's hire-purchase and sales scheme for cooking and heating appliances. Some of the progress made in extending gas services to domestic consumers came surprisingly late in the history of the city. Between 1929 and 1931, for instance, the Gas Department undertook to run gas-supply pipes to about 21,000 court and terrace houses previously without it, and to fix in them repayment meters free of charge. The cost of the internal pipes was borne by the consumers, the amount due being paid back gradually through the slot-meters. This necessary social advance was long overdue.

For more experienced consumers, the gas show-rooms both in the centre of the city and in the outer districts were well equipped and advertised, and a travelling show-room was put into commission for use in districts outside the areas served by the permanent branches. A trained demonstration staff dealt with domestic consumers' requirements, and a Women's Gas Circle was formed which had a membership approaching 3,000 persons. A wider range of gas gadgets was offered to consumers. As early as 1923 some of these new devices were exhibited at the first National Gas Exhibition to be held in Birmingham. By 1938 automatic gas appliances, like heat-controlling devices and self-igniting boilers, had been invented, and were being developed and advertised on a large scale.

In 1938 about one-third of the enormous quantity of gas sold by the Corporation was used for manufacturing purposes, the great variety of trades carried on in the district affording plenty of opportunities for the use of gas. During the economic recovery of the 1930's the amount of gas used for industrial purposes greatly increased in many different trades. One firm alone annually consumed over 290 million cubic feet. To assist local industrialists and government departments in discovering the best uses of gas, the Gas Department maintained and extended its Industrial Research Laboratories, where investigations were made into manufacturing processes, and where facilities were provided for the testing of materials and the standardization of apparatus. A comprehensive range of gas-heated furnaces was in constant use for carrying out general heat-treatment work, for such necessary local industrial processes as the hardening of moulds and tools for plastic moulding, or the annealing of drop forgings.

In addition to these domestic and industrial uses of gas, the city continued to use gas for public lighting purposes on a large scale. Victoria Square was probably the best example of gas lighting in the country, the lighting being carried out by means of high-pressure gas-lamps each having a total candle-power of 4,500. In November 1934 a system of high-pressure gas-lamps was also installed in New Street and Corporation Street, the lamps being suspended from cables hung over the street. In the later 30's an improved system of low-pressure street lighting was installed in parts of Hagley Road, where staggered lighting, double-side lighting, and centrally hung lamps were used.

It was thus possible in 1938 for both the Gas and the Electricity Departments to flourish side by side, benefiting in fact from their competition with each other, and still anticipating a period of peace and prosperity in the future.

There was one important inter-war change in Birmingham which reflected new trends in all branches of municipal trading activities. The pre-war policy of using trading profits to subsidize rates was challenged and curtailed. Before 1914, and particularly in the Birmingham of Joseph Chamberlain, it had been believed that a progressive civic policy meant acquiring profits from the trading undertakings in order to improve the public services of the city. After the war exactly the reverse policy began to be conceived of as progressive, and in local trading Acts of new authorities, clauses were included to secure that charges should be so regulated that the undertakings should make neither profit nor loss. By the national Electricity Act of 1926, it was laid down that appropriations in aid of rates could not be paid at all until the accumulated Reserve Fund reached a certain minimum, and, even when that occurred, that no more than a sum of $1\frac{1}{2}$ per cent. of the outstanding debt might be so appropriated. This provision compelled the Electricity Department to make no contributions to the Rate Fund as such after 1929–30.

In the case of gas, Birmingham was compelled to conform with the new parliamentary policy. In 1925 the Gas Reserve Fund had had to be raided to balance the year's accounts, and although thereafter the profit of the enterprise would have made a return to the pre-1914 policy possible, the Birmingham Corporation (General Powers) Act of 1929 laid down that 'the charges to be made by the Corporation for gas supplied by them shall, after March 31st, 1933, be not more than sufficient, so far as can be estimated, to enable the Gas Undertaking of the Corporation to be carried on without loss'. This provision can be contrasted with Section 163 of the Birmingham Corporation (Consolidation) Act of 1883, which, discussing municipal trading, stated that 'the Corporation shall from time to time carry to the credit of the improvement rate leviable under this Act the net surplus remaining after the fulfilment of the several purposes aforesaid and the annual proceeds of the reserve fund when amounting to one hundred thousand pounds'.

Until 1933 the Gas Department continued to hand over considerable sums for direct rate relief: it even handed over £25,000 in the year of depression 1931–2, but times were changing and gas profits were no longer regarded as a means of enriching local government as a whole.

The acknowledgement, however involuntary, of this new approach to municipal finance marked the end of a period in the trading history of the city. It was true that the trading undertakings continued to pay large sums as rates and taxes— £134,918, for example, in the case of the Gas Department for the year ending 31 March 1938—but the stark simplicity of the trading outlook of the business-men Councillors of pre-war years had been undermined. The view was gaining ground, particularly among managing officials, that provision to 'plough back' and develop the undertakings should come first, and that thereafter pricing policy should be so regulated as to sell as near to cost as was reasonably 'safe', and 'to hasten the day when consumers and rate-payers were practically the same body'.[1] This was the mood of what was to prove the last chapter in the history of the local gas and electricity concerns.

[1] W. E. Foden, 'Some Aspects of Municipal Electricity Supply Finance', Manchester I.M.T.A. Report, *Proceedings*, 17 June 1937.

VI

There was one other welfare service in the city which was developed in the inter-war years, and which reached its historical climax in 1938—the creation of a Birmingham Hospitals Centre.

The provision of hospitals had been organized in Birmingham as elsewhere during the eighteenth and nineteenth centuries on a voluntary basis and as a result of voluntary action. The General Hospital had been founded in 1765, when the population of the town was under 30,000, and it was not until 1897 that a new building was opened by Princess Christian, designed according to the most up-to-date ideas of its time. A second Birmingham hospital, the Queen's Hospital, was founded in 1840 in connexion with the Birmingham School of Medicine and Surgery. After thirty-five years, when admission was by subscriber's ticket, entry was made free in 1875. There were other voluntary hospital services in Birmingham in 1914, including the Homoeopathic Hospital, opened in 1847; the General Dispensary, founded in 1793; the Orthopaedic Hospital, first established in 1817; the Eye Hospital, dating back to 1824; the Ear and Throat Hospital, set up twenty years later; the Dental Hospital, begun on a very small scale in 1859; the Birmingham and Midland Counties Sanatorium at Blackwell, launched out of money raised at the time of the Cotton Famine during the American Civil War; the Birmingham and Midland Hospital for Women, opened in 1871; the Birmingham and Midland Hospital for Skin and Urinary Diseases, founded in 1881; and the Moseley Hall Convalescent Hospital for Children, established in 1892.

This was a comprehensive list of voluntary hospitals for a great city. They raised their income from subscriptions, benefactions, and organized charities. Hospital Sunday, first sponsored in 1859, largely as a result of the initiative of the Rev. J. C. Miller, the Rector of Birmingham, was so successful in raising money—often small sums from large numbers of people—that the example was copied by London and many other large cities in England. Hospital Saturday, inaugurated in 1869, aimed at tapping the pockets of working men, and once a year weekly collections were made in the factories and large workshops of the district. In addition large sums of money were collected at special rallies and festivals, like the Triennial Music Festival, the first grant from 'the benefit of an oratorio' being received as early as 1768.

During the eighteenth and early nineteenth centuries it was not considered necessary or desirable that either the State or the city should organize hospital services, and it required the smallpox epidemic of 1871–2, as well as the new reforming Liberalism of the civic gospel, to turn the attention of the authorities to hospital questions. During the epidemic of 1871–2 the Board of Guardians of Birmingham Parish prepared small-pox wards in the grounds of the Workhouse, but the disability of pauperism attached to persons admitted to them made them unpopular with the population as a whole. In 1874, as a response to a newly recognized problem, the Corporation acquired the Borough Hospital, at first a very small building, for the treat-ment of smallpox and scarlet fever. It was extended and developed, and finally divided into two, one for each of the diseases, but there was still a serious shortage of accommodation during periods of epidemic like that of 1893–4, when many temporary expedients had to be adopted. In 1901, after long delays, a third hospital was opened for diphtheria and enteric fever, and ten years later five hospitals belonging to the old local authorities were added to the city as a result of the Greater Birmingham scheme. In the ten years before the outbreak of war, the Corporation also made a determined effort to hold in check the spread of pulmonary tuberculosis. Before national action had been taken to deal with this serious problem, two sana-toria had been opened in Birmingham, one in Birmingham itself and one on the hills beyond Cheltenham, in addition to a Tuberculosis Centre and Dispensary in the city. During the next ten years two more sanatoria were established in or near Birmingham—the anti-tuberculosis campaign being carried out largely through the inspiration of the Medical Officer of Health, Sir John Robertson. There was considerable progress but many disappointments, 'for the problem to be solved was soon found to be a social as well as a medical problem, offering difficulties with which the Corporation was not fully competent to deal'.[1]

While these hospital services were being developed by the Council out of the rates, the Birmingham Infirmary, opened in January 1889, was being maintained by the Board of Guardians out of the poor-rates. It was by far the largest hospital in 1914.

[1] C. A. Vince, *History of the Corporation of Birmingham*, vol. iv (1923), p. 136.

Two other hospitals were administered by the Guardians until 1930.

This patchwork of uncoordinated hospital services was inadequate for the needs of the war and the peace which followed it, and in December 1924 the City Council passed a resolution 'that it is desirable in the best interests of the City that there should be a properly co-ordinated scheme of development for the hospitals of the City, and that the General Purposes Committee be requested to get in touch with the Hospital Consultative Committee on the matter and to report to the Council thereon'. The Hospital Consultative Committee, a voluntary organization, later transformed into the Birmingham Hospitals Council, decided, after consultation with the Minister of Health, Neville Chamberlain, that the idea of co-ordination and expansion of the hospitals on existing or adjoining sites in the centre of the city would have to be abandoned. Instead a site sufficiently large for all further extension would have to be found either within or adjoining the city boundary. Opposition was encountered from those, both medical and lay, who considered that a new hospital centre on an unknown site, probably some miles from the city centre, would be a serious inconvenience to staff and visitors.

A generous gift to the city by Cadbury Brothers of a hundred and fifty acres of land adjoining the University materially altered the situation, and a Joint Committee of the General and the Queen's Hospitals, presided over by Sir Charles Grant Robertson, prepared a scheme for a new centre. Four main recommendations were made. The first was the final abandonment of any idea of extensions to the old hospitals, and the suggestion that new premises should be built on land presented to the city by Messrs. Cadbury for hospital purposes. The second was that the General and Queen's Hospitals should be amalgamated by Act of Parliament, so as to form a single administrative hospital unit. The third was to transfer the Medical School in Edmund Street, more than a mile away from each of the teaching hospitals, to the Edgbaston site, so as to be in direct and close contact with the new hospital. The fourth was that, when the amalgamation had been carried through, any other of the specialist hospitals in Birmingham should be free to transfer to this central site, so as to be linked ultimately in a single, unified organization with the General Hospital and the

Medical School. By this fourth recommendation the Grant Robertson plan clearly endorsed the principle of a Hospitals Centre for Birmingham.

The formulation of this well-contrived plan, like so much else in Birmingham's welfare policy in the inter-war years, seems to anticipate the national discussions and solutions of a later generation. The Hospitals Council sent out a deputation to Europe and America to study the layout and design of the most modern hospitals there, and in 1927 appointed an Executive Board, representative of the Hospitals, the City Council, the University, the Chamber of Commerce, and the subscribing bodies, to take charge of the first section of the proposed new hospital and to collect funds. With a view to obtaining the legal powers necessary to carry out the scheme, the Executive Board was reconstituted and registered as a private company in June 1930, under the Companies Act of 1929.

The first appeal for the necessary capital funds for the scheme was launched in 1930, and met with a magnificent response, but when everything seemed hopeful for the early start of the project, a strong current of criticism was raised as to the necessity of a Hospitals Centre in its scheduled form. The current was so powerful that a meeting of subscribers was called to ascertain their views, and even after a vote had been carried in its favour, a conference was called by the Lord Mayor to investigate the whole question. The first meeting of the conference was held in March 1932, and after many sittings a report was issued in November indicating the anticipated increase in hospital accommodation that would be required and recommending that the Executive Board should take the necessary steps to proceed with the erection of the first section of the scheme, consisting of a General Hospital of 500 beds and new buildings for the Medical School of the University.

The new hospital when completed provided 516 beds, but with all ancillary services for a total of 732 beds. A Nurses' Home was built from a gift of Lord Nuffield, and the Medical School was financed by the Public Appeal Fund and the University. Sir Harry Vincent as Treasurer, and other citizens, gave much time and personal care to the raising of the capital funds, and in checking detailed estimates of this great undertaking.

In June 1934 the Prince of Wales laid the foundation-stone of the Centre and cut the first sod on the site of the Medical School.

It was completed and opened by the Duke of Gloucester on 14 July 1938, during the Charter Centenary celebrations. Illness prevented the King and Queen from visiting Birmingham on this occasion, but in March 1939 they travelled to Birmingham, where the Queen named the new hospital 'The Queen Elizabeth Hospital'.

The General Hospital in Steelhouse Lane continued, and still continues, its invaluable services in the centre of the city, and is an integral part of the teaching hospital of the University. In April 1941 the Queen's Hospital in Bath Row, which also continued its work as part of the Birmingham United Hospitals, was transferred to a new authority set up for the purpose, and became the Birmingham Accident Hospital and Rehabilitation Centre, the first of its kind in the country.

These important developments in the making of the city's Hospital Centre should not obscure the local effects on health services of the national break-up of the Poor Law as a result of the Local Government Act of 1929. By that Act, from 1 April 1930, the functions of the Poor Law authorities, as carried out by the Boards of Guardians, were transferred to the Councils of counties and county boroughs. Already as a result of the Greater Birmingham Act of 1911 the three local Boards of Guardians had been merged into one Board to secure maximum local unification, and the Birmingham Poor Law Union became the largest Union in the country in respect of population and rateable value. In 1930 the Board of Guardians was abolished, some of its work being taken over by the new Public Assistance Committee of the Council, the rest by the Education Committee and, more important, the Public Health and Maternity and Child Welfare Committee. Those hospitals taken over by the Public Health Committee ceased to be poor law hospitals in most senses of the term and became general hospitals. Modernization and extension schemes were carried out. Birmingham Infirmary remained under the direction of the Public Assistance Committee, and in 1938 had nearly 2,000 beds and a staff of over 350.

In 1938, then, the responsibility for local hospitals was divided, and there was nothing like a uniform system. The Public Health Committee, however, had greatly expanded its services, and was employing a staff of nearly 3,000. Birmingham was a healthy city compared with most other English cities, and,

PLATE XXXVIII

Sir Charles Grant Robertson

PLATE XXXIX

Part of the Civic Centre

with the exception of 1929, from 1915 to 1938 the mortality rate
for the city was below that of the country as a whole. Infant
mortality of babies under one year of age had fallen from an
average of 101 per 1,000 for the years 1915–19 to 66 per 1,000
for the years 1930–4. The improvement was not accidental. As
early as 1899 women health visitors were appointed. In 1939
there were thirty-one welfare centres in the city, where clinics
were provided for expectant mothers, for infants under one year,
and for small children from one to five. A municipal midwifery
service was instituted, and two maternity homes and a convalescent home for mothers built. These services were in regular
demand. In 1934–5, for example, ante-natal advice was sought
by 54 per cent. of expectant mothers, and 71 per cent. of the
children born in the city attended clinics.[1] It has been said that
'infant mortality provides society with the first major index of
the reaction of a new human life to its surroundings. It is a
measure of man's ability and willingness to control his environment.'[2] There was still much to be done in Birmingham in
1938, particularly for poorer families, as the Reports of the
School Medical Officer, with their emphasis on malnutrition
caused by lack of food due to poverty, show,[3] yet another 'silent
revolution' was in progress. Birmingham was justifying a
comment made in the introduction to its official publication,
*Birmingham and its City Managers*, in 1928: 'The modern municipality's interest in her citizens extends from the cradle to the
grave; nay, even longer, from the ante-natal clinic to the City
Cemetery.'[4]

## VII

The many civic changes outlined in this chapter were pushed
ahead either by national delegation of powers or by local action.
Although the House of Commons was becoming increasingly
preoccupied with social policies for the country as a whole
and could not afford to tolerate wide local divergences, local
initiative, expressed in local Acts of Parliament, still had an
important part to play. The best example of its influence in

[1] J. T. Jones, op. cit., p. 207.
[2] R. M. Titmuss, *Birth, Poverty, and Wealth* (1943), p. 11.
[3] See City of Birmingham, *Report of the School Medical Officer* (1938); Birmingham
Social Survey Committee, *Nutrition and Size of Family* (1942); *Our Towns, a Close-up*
(1943).
[4] City of Birmingham, *Birmingham and its Civic Managers* (1928), p. 1.

Birmingham can be traced in the peace-time legislation concerning the Municipal Bank and in the successful attempt in the 1930's, already described, to acquire a municipal aerodrome. Another new venture was the sponsoring of a civic orchestra in 1919.

At the end of the war the Corporation determined to have a permanent Municipal Bank, and a clause was inserted in the General Powers Bill of 1919 to make the war-time institution permanent. It was freed of many of its former shackles. The coupon system which had been adopted in the old bank was abandoned, and the Bank became a normal savings bank with eventual power to advance money on the mortgage of houses. Its head office was sited in the Council House and seventeen branches were immediately opened. By a later Corporation Act of 1929 it was allowed to set up branches outside the city, with the consent of or at the request of adjoining local authorities. The regional influence of Birmingham was thus further extended.

To meet the increase of business in all departments, the Central Committee of Management decided in 1931 to build a new Central Bank and Head Offices. These were completed in 1933, and officially opened by Prince George. In his speech he claimed that the success of the Bank had been due to its own intrinsic merits—'to the fact that it meets a public need; that it is, in fact, part of the city's administration, backed by the security of the rates'.[1]

In 1938 the Bank, which had 450,000 depositors and had granted 8,000 mortgages which were still in force, was closely associated with other sides of municipal government. Rate-payers might pay their municipal accounts at the Bank: indeed 600,000 accounts amounting to well over £1 million were collected by it during the year 1938-9. The Water Department had been the first to sponsor this procedure in 1921. In addition, children, with the co-operation of the Education Committee, might save weekly through their schools. Deposits were taken as low as 1d. and might go up to £500 in one year. All these services made the Bank popular, but in addition, as Alderman Harrison Barrow, the chairman of the Bank Committee, put it in 1938, 'there is no doubt that the fact of the Bank being a possession of the citizens of Birmingham, contributes to its

[1] *B.P.*, 28 November 1933.

continued popularity'.[1] Neville Chamberlain, when Minister of Health, paid tribute to the Bank as compared with a parallel national institution. 'One has only to compare the methods of the Municipal Bank in Birmingham with those of the Savings Bank of the Post Office', he told a conference of administrators in 1929, 'to see an entirely different scheme of keeping in touch with the public.'[2]

Local acts were necessary not only to allow for the development and extension of special institutions like the Bank, but also for the purposes of extending the boundaries of the city. As the powers of the city grew, so, too, did its area.

By the Birmingham Extension Act of 1927, the central part of the Urban District of Perry Barr was added to the city. The first suggestions of incorporation had been made in January 1926 by the Perry Barr Urban District Council, which wrote to the Birmingham Corporation pointing out that its General Purposes Committee had under consideration the future development of Perry Barr. In subsequent discussion with the Perry Barr authorities the Birmingham representatives made it clear that while they wished to make sure that such development should not run counter to that of Birmingham, unless a general desire for incorporation was forthcoming from Perry Barr, no steps would be taken by Birmingham unilaterally to press for amalgamation. The Perry Barr Council agreed unanimously on 8 September 1926 'that this Council considers that the best interests of the Urban District of Perry Barr will be served by its incorporation as soon as possible with the City of Birmingham'. It gave five grounds for its desire to be incorporated—that there was a 'community of interest' between Perry Barr and Birmingham; that Perry Barr could not afford necessary sewage and sanitary services if it had to meet them entirely out of its own rates; that in view of the rapid development of Perry Barr the area should be developed on well-planned lines and that Perry Barr itself could not afford the expenditure which a town planning scheme would involve; that the rates of Perry Barr and the contributions from the Ministry of Transport did not enable the Council to put and keep its roads in a sufficient state of repair; and that Perry Barr, being an outgrowth of Birming-

---

[1] Harrison Barrow, 'The Municipal Bank, an Example to the Nation', in *B.G. Centenary Celebration Supplement* (1938).

[2] Neville Chamberlain in *Public Administration*, vol. vii (1929).

ham, 'could be more economically and efficiently administered as one unit with Birmingham'. There was a flicker of local opposition to the proposals, but a referendum among the ratepayers on the question of incorporation revealed that 1,232 ratepayers out of 1,539 wanted to join Birmingham. The Birmingham Extension Bill, although it went through the House of Commons without difficulty, did not include within the city the whole of Perry Barr; and West Bromwich Corporation, which promoted its own Bill, and Sutton Coldfield Corporation, which proceeded by Provisional Order, secured substantial slices of the old Urban District.

In 1931 Birmingham was still further extended. This time the city took the initiative and raised the problem of taking over very large parts of Castle Bromwich and Sheldon, which would bring up the city's total area to 51,147 acres. The Birmingham race-course at Bromford Bridge, the British Industries Fair buildings, and the aerodrome at Castle Bromwich were to be brought within the boundaries. The transfer aimed at anticipating the city's future needs for housing and industrial expansion, and was carried through by an Order of the Ministry of Health under Section 46 of the new Local Government Act of 1929. By this Act County Councils reviewed with the Councils of the districts within the county the desirability of effecting boundary changes. In 1930 Birmingham entered into negotiations with the Warwickshire County Council, the Council was willing to transfer land, and a local inquiry was held at Warwick by the Ministry of Health. After some initial opposition from the Earl of Bradford, the Castle Bromwich Parish Council, and the inhabitants of Tile Cross, minor adjustments were made and agreement was reached.

The Perry Barr transfer added one new ward to the city, but no further changes were made in 1931, the new land being attached to the five contiguous wards. The General Purposes Committee of the Council instructed the Town Clerk to inform the Home Office that a general readjustment of ward boundaries would take place within two years or, with the consent of the Home Office, longer. A new scheme was issued in July 1934, the number of wards being increased from 31 to 34 and the size of the Council by 5. The new wards were Hall Green, Stechford, and Bromford.

There was talk of further expansion in the later 30's, and the possibility of Shirley's being transferred from Solihull was widely discussed after the Shirley Residents' Association had brought the question into the open in 1937. The number of houses in Shirley had doubled in the previous five years, and the rapidity of development posed urgent problems of government. The Birmingham Council, on account of its size and character, was unwilling, however, to consider further expansion in 1937 and the issue did not become a practical one. It was clear in any case to everyone that, if Birmingham wished to expand its borders farther, it would be far more interested in areas which were not built up than in new urban centres.

In 1938 Birmingham City Council was already an example of very large-scale complex local government. It had 136 members —3 councillors from each of the 34 wards plus 34 aldermen. The secrets of its successful operations were shrewd apportionment of work between committees and departments and sensible co-ordination at many levels.

As far as apportionment of work was concerned, great power had always been allowed to committees, although the Council as a whole reserved powers to borrow money and to levy rates. With the exception of the Watch, Mental Hospitals, and Public Assistance, the committees were required to report not less than twice a year to the Council. In 1938 there were thirty-three committees in all. Not every committee had its own department; the officials were the officials of the Council, not of the committees.[1] One department—the Treasurer's—served many committees, while the Birmingham Markets and Fairs Committee employed the whole services of the Markets Department and the Weights and Measures Department, which were not amalgamated. The Birmingham Fire Brigade was administered as an entity distinct from the Birmingham Police, although both came under the supervision of the Watch Committee.

For the efficient management of its business, the Council had developed certain common services, particularly for staff and labour questions, for the purchase of goods and stores common to more than one department, and for information.

Before 1914 the Joint Committee on Labour, a body consisting of two representatives of each of the chief employing committees, had dealt with such problems as 'the fair wages clause',

[1] F. C. Minshull, 'The Departmental Organisation of the Work of Local Authorities', in *Public Administration*, vol. vii (1929).

which was accepted in principle in 1891, and 'decasualization'. It had begun quite informally in 1900 under the chairmanship of Alderman Beale, and had dealt with manual labour alone. It is significant that its administration was in the hands of the Water Department, a manual-labour employing body. In 1915, when the city was the largest employer of labour in the district, and there were serious general labour problems to be dealt with, the Joint Committee was transformed into a Standing Committee of the City Council. Two important changes followed. In January 1918 the Labour Committee was renamed the Salaries, Wages, and Labour Committee, and its responsibilities were extended from manual labour questions to cover salaries as well. In 1919 administration was taken over by the Town Clerk's Department, because of the character and growth of the work.

In the inter-war years far greater attention was paid to co-operation and joint consultation between officials and labour on the one side and the Council on the other. In 1919 the City Council began by accepting the principle of regulation by Joint Industrial Councils of wages and conditions of employment for its manual workers. Each of the four large trading departments —gas, electric supply, water, and tramways—was provided with a separate Joint Council, consisting of an equal number of representatives of employers and workers, and a composite Council was set up for the non-trading departments. In 1929 a Joint Consultative Committee of council members and staff was also created to consider matters of common interest in relation to service conditions of the non-manual staff, and to make recommendations to the Salaries, Wages, and Labour Committee. Consisting of seven members of the Council and of seven staff members, it aimed at developing and fostering 'the efficient administration of the public services by maintaining good relations between the Corporation and its officials'.

These examples of a recognized procedure of consultation reflect one of the big changes in local government. It was the growth of trade unionism and collective bargaining which first impressed on the departments the necessity for taking steps to deal with labour questions on a collective basis, but it was the growing size of the city's administrative machine and the need for conditions of uniform service which established the new system. Recognizing the new methods needed for a large-scale organization, the Joint Consultative Committee recommended a scheme, which was accepted by the Council, of choosing junior non-manual staff for the Corporation's service on a centralized basis by a Board of Selection, consisting of Council members, heads of departments, and representatives of the Juvenile Employment Branch of the Education Department. The whole scheme was administered by a section of the Town Clerk's Department.[1]

The second example of the development of effective centralized common services by the Council was in the field of buying. The General Purposes Committee was given instructions to act 'for the purpose of co-ordinating the purchase of all goods and stores required by the various departments of the Corporation, which are common to more than one department, and for the standardization of stores'. It was given the task of obtaining annually from the various committees a list of stocks and of goods required, and, although there were no central store-rooms, of making provision for the storage and distribution of goods and stores purchased by the Corporation, where possible departmentally. Two sub-committees carried out these tasks—the Stores and Contracts Sub-Committee of the General Purposes Committee and the Officials' Advisory Committee, which consisted of a chief official of each of the principal departments of the Corporation, appointed to watch price movements, to collect samples, and to give advice concerning tenders and the placing of contracts.

The Central Purchasing Department was an extension of the earlier Stationery Department. Of stationery alone in one year just before the Second World War the Department bought 30 million printed forms, 400,000 books, 16 million cash bags and wages bags, 30 million sheets of paper for school and office use, and $2\frac{1}{2}$ million exercise and drawing books.[2] In addition to stationery the Department dealt in food—some of it by weekly tender—drugs, household goods, and coffins. Coal for all departments of the Corporation, with the exception of the Gas and Electric Supply Departments, was purchased by the Coal Purchasing Sub-Committee of the Stores and Contracts Sub-Committee, while the purchase of non-domestic articles for all departments was arranged by that committee of the Council

---

[1] See Ministry of Health, *The Qualification, Recruitment, Training and Promotion of Local Government Officers* (1934).
[2] City of Birmingham, *Official Handbook* (1939).

which was the largest user of the articles in question—thus, for instance, the Transport Department purchased all the supplies of petrol.

The third example of a common service falls into a different category. By the General Powers Act of 1929—two years before the Local Authorities (Publicity) Act was passed as a national measure—the city secured powers to permit the establishment of an Information Bureau 'for the purpose of supplying information with regard to the City and neighbourhood'. In 1930 an Information Bureau was set up as a sub-department of the Town Clerk's Office. It was concerned not only with the municipal activities of Birmingham—described each year in the *Official Handbook*—but also with matters concerned with industrial development. It maintained a comprehensive register of factories and industrial sites, and provided all types of information at home and abroad for interested manufacturers. In addition, it assisted journalists and visitors, its free and centralized information being much in demand.

Alongside the development of these joint procedures, necessary in a large-scale organization, the task of co-ordination of different committee activities became increasingly important. Before 1914 the work of integration had been efficient, particularly as a result of the co-ordinating role of the Lord Mayor and of the General Purposes Committee. These two agencies continued their invaluable work after 1918. The retiring or Deputy Mayor was usually the Chairman of the General Purposes Committee and presented the General Purposes report at each Council meeting. The general policy of the Council in its choice of committee members was to arrange for inter-representation and liaison by at least one member.[1] Standing instructions issued to committees were designed to prevent overlapping and competition. Thus, for example, two or more committees were prevented from negotiating for the same piece of land, and steps were taken to avoid the indiscriminate breaking up of streets for the purpose of laying pipes, drains, and cables by different committees.

The effective work of the Council continued to be done at the committee level, some of it by co-opted members, whose co-operation was welcomed in a report of the General Purposes

[1] For details of the liaison system in practice, see H. R. Page, *Co-ordination and Planning in the Local Authority* (1936), pp. 195–7, 259.

Committee in 1933. The Council itself was the final forum. Meeting once a month, except in August and September, it retained its traditional forms of debate. No action was taken in 1927 when, as a result of the increasing volume of work, the General Purposes Committee was requested to consider the question of the desirability of regulating, by standing order, the length of speeches. Forty-six members constituted a quorum, and although at times the Council was talked out, the standard of service remained high in face of an increasing volume of paper and of pressure on time. In 1938 manufacturers were still the biggest single occupational group represented on the Council with 20 members, but there were 17 company directors, 16 solicitors and barristers, and 7 trade-union and Co-operative Society officials. There were 10 women, and 13 people who were described as 'retired'.[1]

The Council was the pivot of the civic life of the city, and the attempt was well under way to give the city a new administrative centre worthy of a great community. As a result of negotiations started as early as 1918, several acres of land were bought by the Corporation in the Broad Street area, and in 1926 the Corporation arranged an open competition to secure a layout for a new civic centre. The winning scheme, designed by Maximilian Romanoff of Paris, was considered beyond the resources of the city, and in 1934 a second project was approved by the Council and parliamentary powers were sought. The layout of the new centre made provision for the erection of two large blocks of administrative offices—urgently necessary as a result of the congestion in the Council House—a Natural History Museum, a City Hall, and a Public Library. The whole site was to be organized in relation to the Hall of Memory, which was opened in 1925.

In September 1937 the Council gave its consent to the first new building on the site, part of a block of administrative offices, and it was fitting that the foundation-stone of the new enterprise should be laid by the Lord Mayor in June 1938, in the middle of the Centenary year. The pageant of Birmingham, performed in July, gathered together the historic threads of Birmingham's past: the newly begun Civic Centre was a work for the future.

[1] Cf. the figures given on p. 128.

# IX

## THE FORTUNES OF INDUSTRY

### I

THE whole-hearted attention of Birmingham to the war effort, and the consequent large-scale conversion of the local industrial structure, naturally made it difficult for the city to find its feet again when the war ended. Although in 1918 there was an enormous pent-up demand for peace-time products, and it was plain that Birmingham would play an important part in the process of national rejuvenation and revival, there were serious problems of local readjustment. Some of the problems were short-term in character, particularly the speedy transfer of men and plant to new jobs; others were more difficult, part of the long-run task of adapting the city to a changed post-war economy.

The short period of transition proved longer than had been anticipated. It began with the abrupt termination of war orders. On 24 October 1918 contractors were informed of a decision by the Ministry of Munitions that 'contracts for such stores as will serve no useful purpose in peace should be terminated abruptly'. A week after the Armistice had been signed in November, the Treasury stressed that 'even if termination involves the sacrifice of expenditure already incurred, it may well be more in the public interest, on general economic as well as financial grounds, to avoid further expenditure of money and the use of labour and materials, which will ultimately be required elsewhere, than to complete munitions of war that are no longer required'.[1]

Birmingham was immediately affected by these decisions. Demobilization began with the women munition workers, and some firms tried to be logical by beginning with the dismissal of those women married to their male employees. Other firms tried to be kind by introducing a shorter working week until all their workers were gradually demobilized. By this method it was possible to retain the services of a large number of girls over the transition period, and to give them a living wage. Other firms were ruthless or thoughtless, discharging large numbers of workers with the shortest possible notice. There were complaints

[1] Quoted by A. C. Pigou, *Aspects of British Economic History* (1947), pp. 24–25.

that skilled men were being discharged from some factories before unskilled men, even before 'dilutees', and in some cases, it was alleged, before 'friendly aliens'.[1] The trade unions, growing in strength in the Birmingham area, contended that a specific undertaking should be given that 'dilutees' should be discharged before skilled artisans.

Between the Armistice and the end of April 1920, in the country as a whole the number of males employed in the armed forces and in civil work decreased by 600,000, and the number of females by about the same number. This contraction of employment was accentuated by the fact that, during this period, hours of work were reduced on the average by about 10 per cent. Birmingham, with its legacy of excess capacity and its serious difficulties of readjustment, suffered from considerable unemployment throughout the transition period. In order to deal with the unemployed, it was necessary to open new decentralized labour exchanges in various parts of the city. The government had given every member of the fighting forces below commissioned rank a free unemployment insurance policy, which entitled him to benefits while he was seeking work, and in 1920 the range of trades covered by the 1911 Unemployment Insurance Act was widened.

It was not unemployment, however, which symbolized the years 1918–20, but the price-boom, which pushed up prices to levels never reached during the war itself. The price-boom worked itself out in an atmosphere of uncontrolled business activity. After the end of hostilities, the demand by business men —and Birmingham men were in the vanguard—for the restoration of economic freedom became the categorical imperative of the day. 'The vital factor', said *The Economist* just after the Armistice, 'in procuring abundance of productive employment is not raw materials, but freedom.'[2] The government willingly divested itself of its war-time responsibilities, and Birmingham saw the war-time controls, which had conditioned its efforts, wither away. In November 1918, for instance, all restrictions on the purchase or manufacture of machine tools were removed, and control orders limiting the manufacture of wire rope, forgings and castings, motor and aero engines were withdrawn. Stocks of non-ferrous metals were released for non-priority purposes, without the need for special permits, and in May 1919

[1] *B.M.*, 13 February 1919.     [2] *The Economist*, 16 November 1918.

the Birmingham Iron Exchange, of great regional importance, opened on free and unrestricted lines for the first time for many years. 'For the past few years', wrote a local paper, 'the iron and steel trade has been in a state of bondage. It has been governed in all essential respects by the Government through the Ministry of Munitions. Now the trade has been set free.'[1]

The rise in prices, the reabsorption of labour, and the abolition of controls did not secure anything like a lasting boom. Labour disputes in the iron industry caused complications in the autumn of 1919. In July, August, and September 1920 there was a further and more serious slackening off, made worse by a coal strike. The trade-union figures for unemployment rose from 0·9 to 3·7 per cent. between April and November 1920. In March 1921 they were up to 10 per cent., and as a result of the serious coal strike of April 1921 they rose to 23·1 per cent. Taking the industries covered by the Unemployment Insurance Act, the percentage of unemployed rose from 6 in January 1921 to over 16 in December.[2]

Birmingham felt the impact of this collapse, and the memory of this post-war unemployment persisted even in the more prosperous years ahead. Although employment in the electrical engineering industry was moderate, most of the metal trades were badly hit. The tendency of local business opinion was to blame the delayed effects of the war for all the troubles. It was only in the last six or eight months, a speaker told the Chamber of Commerce in April 1920, that the business community had realized the depths of the depression and what it meant to the nation and to the world. Capital and labour blamed one another, he said, and both blamed the government. But the people really responsible were the Germans.

It was the Germans who brought the great earthquake that had come over the world. It was obvious that even if the relations between capital and labour and conditions of international trading were perfect, it would take a very long period before we could rebuild the world. We had got to step down from a high level of prices in industry to a low level. . . . It would take some time before we could adjust ourselves to the new conditions, and until then we could not look for any great improvement.

This attitude, contrasting already with the limitless optimism of 1918, led to a restatement of Birmingham's characteristic

[1] B.M., 1 May 1919.    [2] Ministry of Labour Gazette, January 1922.

traditional philosophy, which went right back to the eighteenth century, that in face of crisis the interests of labour and capital were not antagonistic but complementary. 'Industry stood upon three legs—labour, capital and management. If any one of those fell, the other two could not stand up.'[1] This inherited philosophy was reaffirmed in vigorous terms, while at the same time the need for constant attention to the export trade was emphasized. Many speakers stressed that the country was dependent for its very existence on the maintenance of its foreign trade and that Birmingham occupied a strategic position in the prospect of revival.

The revival was delayed. 'Business remains patchy,' wrote an economic weather forecaster in 1922; 'where there is any accession of buying, it is apt to have a spasmodic character, which betrays the hopes it encourages.'[2] The Annual Report of the Chamber of Commerce for 1922–3 complained that 'the progressive movement towards trade recovery is painful and slow, and the depression unprecedented in severity and duration'. Conditions improved in 1924 and 1925, although down to that date, as Professor Pigou has said, Britain was 'in the doldrums'. During these years, and in an exodus of 1926, Birmingham lost many of its workers to other areas.

II

The long-run process of readaptation to the needs of a postwar economy was tackled more successfully in Birmingham than in many other parts of the country. The presence of plentiful local capital equipment, skilled labour, and managerial experience attracted new industries, which more than counterbalanced the decline of older ones. In any case Birmingham was more adaptable in modifying its older industries than were most of the other parts of England, and succeeded in retaining its industrial supremacy even though all the initial advantages it had possessed in the early stages of its industrial development—close proximity to natural resources of coal, iron-ore, and limestone —were lost.

The crisis in the Black Country was intensified. The decline of the south Staffordshire and Worcestershire native iron industry continued after its short war-time revival. Many furnaces which were put out of action during the coal lock-out of 1926 were never relit. In 1927 the output of iron-ore was down to

[1] B.P., 4 April 1920.          [2] Ibid., 7 November 1922.

12,000 tons. The same story of decline applies to coal. By 1926 there were only 6,500 people working in the Staffordshire and Worcestershire coal-mines, compared with 25,000 in 1860. The Black Country area round Birmingham had to turn to the re-rolling of steel ingots, bars, and sheets, and the development of foundries, press and machine shops, instead of blast furnaces. While the iron trade declined the demand for iron and steel in Birmingham and other near-by centres was maintained, and one of the most important inter-war features of industrial organiza-tion was the greatly increased imports of continental, semi-manufactured steel for use by the local metal trades.

Metal still remained the preoccupation of Birmingham and its region. At the time of the 1931 census 37·1 per cent. of all those engaged in industry, trade, and commerce in Birmingham were concerned with metal in some capacity, as compared with a national proportion of 10·5 per cent. While there was a further decline in some of the old metal trades like nail-making, there was an increase in the new lighter metal industries in engineering, and in the non-ferrous metal trades.

Birmingham made metal products of all kinds for all parts of the world. In 1924 it manufactured a coining press for Tibet; in 1928 it sent out the rolling stock for the electrified suburban lines at Buenos Aires; in 1932 it manufactured the pipe-lines to carry oil through Iraq; and in 1934 it was supplying tribal umbrellas for African chiefs. Apart from special orders like these, its normal output of both consumers' and capital goods gave it a position of industrial pre-eminence. It was the natural centre of industrial exhibitions of all kinds, including the engineering section of the British Industries Fair.

There were two main forces brought to bear on Birmingham's industry during the inter-war years—on the supply side, the development of a new technology; on the demand side, the con-tinued influence of fashion on local economic activity. A high rate of technical change, particularly in the metal alloy in-dustries and the machine-tool trade, led to the discovery of new products and the exploitation of new methods. Special steels were invented and manufactured, particularly for the motor industry. Alloys like 'duralumin' or nickel-manganese were pro-ducts of a new scientific metallurgy, while the increased use of electrical ball-bearings and precision control gave a new character to old forms of production. On the demand side,

PLATE XL

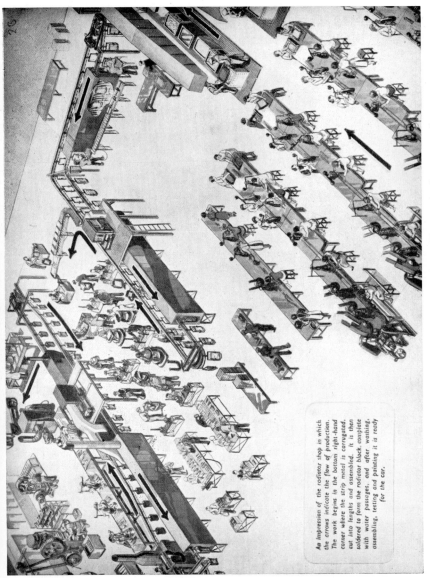

An impression of the radiator shop in which the arrows indicate the flow of production. The work begins in the bottom right-hand corner where the strip metal is corrugated, cut into lengths and assembled. It is then soldered to form the radiator block, complete with water passages, and after washing, assembling, testing and painting it is ready for the car.

Flow Production in a Birmingham Factory about 1938

changes of fashion were enforcing industrial switch-overs in smaller trades. While iron bedsteads disappeared from modern homes, and women abandoned hairpins, as they adopted the bobbed and shingled hair styles of the 1920's, Birmingham took over a new set of demands for light metal goods, like 'hearth furniture' in brass, bronze, and rustless steel, or for office and shop equipment. Through all the changes of technology and fashion, some out-of-the-way trades, like the manufacture of jews' harps, continued to exist, although like everything else they were subject to the depression.[1]

In addition to the pulls of fashion and the new technology, there were forces at work in Birmingham industry which went back before 1914—the tendency towards amalgamation or the unified control of companies; the increasing specialization of plants; the development of flow production; and the revolution in management. The war itself, while it diverted attention from the problem of costs, did much to encourage these tendencies. Firms which before 1914 had relied on hand labour came to use machine tools for the production of munitions, and after the war adapted them to the manufacture of their normal range of products. The influence of the productive methods pursued during the war was reflected in post-war factory administration. On all sides there was a speeding-up of production, and an increase in standardization. Manufacturers were apparently less conservative-minded and less individualistic in thought than they formerly were. There was a greater use of electricity for driving plants; there was a more general utilization of automatic machinery; a greater willingness to scrap old-fashioned processes and to install new ones; and a stronger disposition to take advantage of the aid of scientific research in relation to industrial processes. Pre-war methods of sub-contracting were further discouraged, and Birmingham's industrial structure was brought more into line with a general pattern. When members of the Birmingham Chamber of Commerce visited Fort Dunlop in 1927 they were told that Dunlops 'were in close relationship with American manufacturers, and were able to co-operate with Americans when a new size of tire was introduced, since it was necessary that they should produce a tire which, when it went overseas, could be interchanged with any of recognized size'.[2] This was a sign of the times.

[1] See E.D., 2 February 1934.    [2] B.P., 25 October 1927.

The transformation in Birmingham's economic pattern, with its profound social repercussions, was not unaccompanied by economic loss. As Professor Allen has written,

with a centralised system of management, responsibility is shifted from below, and the vast store of experience, inventiveness, and initiative among the rank and file remains largely untapped. The introduction of 'suggestion schemes' and of similar methods for interesting the worker in the problems of manufacture has thus become much more necessary in modern times than it was when a great deal of responsibility rested with the men in the shops.[1]

As firms grew in size, they often found it necessary to specialize on their managerial side in setting up labour departments to smooth over relations between employers and employed, or to encourage Joint Factory Councils where employers could meet employees round a common table. The more intimate and direct but sometimes more arbitrary relations between masters and men which had characterized the pre-war social pattern were disappearing in the larger firms, and there was sometimes tension and even strikes about the introduction of new methods of production and payment.[2] At the same time, the growth of firms made a new sort of relationship between producers and customers equally necessary. The specialization of sales departments—along with large-scale advertising, the building of branch showrooms, and the multiplication of travelling representatives and agents—was as necessary as the specialization of labour departments. Both became a recognized part of the business milieu of the twentieth century. In 1938 all the talk was of staggered hours and holidays for labour as a whole, and of the 'definitely increased production' brought about by 'music while you work'.[3]

The growth in the size of firms and in the number of trade associations was continued in the inter-war years. The war itself had reinforced the tendency. Manufacturers who had previously been competitors drew more closely together. In the case of the sporting-gun industry, for instance, in 1919 the Birmingham Registered Gunmakers Ltd. were registered as a Company,

---

[1] G. C. Allen, *Economic Development of Birmingham and the Black Country* (1929), p. 45.

[2] E.g. the strike at Austins' over a grading scheme in March 1929, or at Perry Barr over the introduction of the Bedeaux system in February 1932. In 1933 the Birmingham Trades Council attacked the Bedeaux scheme as 'an inhuman system' (*B.G.*, 13 November 1933).

[3] *E.D.*, 18 November 1938.

with the specific object of co-ordinating the resources of individual firms. The identity of each firm was preserved, but the principle was introduced that each firm should specialize in that department for which it was pre-eminently fitted. The guns could then be sold co-operatively on the market. In the case of metals, the Copper and Brass Extended Uses Council advertised co-operatively the new uses to which non-ferrous metals could be put, while, on the production side, brass-manufacturers were encouraged to abandon their lavish catalogues, advertising a large variety of articles in a wide range of patterns, and to concentrate on more specialized production.

Such associations were easier to construct than complete combinations, for there were strong forces working against complete fusion, particularly in the older trades. While relatively small undertakings were sometimes willing to join forces with others of their own type, and to pursue common policy in relation to output or price, they were loath to abandon their complete independence. The price and output arrangements arrived at often did not survive changes in markets and internal conflicts of interest. In jewellery, brush-making, and pens, to take a few examples, the immense variety in the design and quality of finished products made it difficult to enforce price agreements. Small men were interested in known low-price markets, and knew that they could often live in relative isolation from the expanding orbits of the larger firms.

Large firms themselves were being drawn increasingly into national combinations. The best early post-war example was the fusion of Cadburys' and Frys', which was announced in May 1919, after it had been virtually in operation for several months previously. A new holding company, the British Cocoa and Chocolate Company, took over the shares in the two older firms, and divided the profits between the shareholders of the two old companies. The firms continued to be separately managed by their own Boards of Directors, but it was arranged that meetings of the Joint Board should be held periodically at Cheltenham, a convenient half-way house between Birmingham and Bristol. An attempt was made to pool the organization and experiences of two businesses, through the medium of joint committees on factory management, finance, export buying, West African buying, agency sales, and advertising. The fusion was carried through with an eye to foreign markets. 'Whilst the combination may serve to strengthen and develop trade in the home market, one of the most important objects is to enable the British firms to meet the growth of competition which may be expected after the war from American, Swiss and Dutch houses.'[1]

The same story of combination can be traced in the metal industries, and it is interesting to trace the impact of large national combines like Vickers and I.C.I. on the structure of local industry. In 1919, for instance, Vickers acquired the whole of the share capital of the Metropolitan Carriage, Wagon and Finance Company Ltd., which had itself been built up on a basis of pre-war combinations. In 1928, after further amalgamations, it controlled 60–70 per cent. of railway rolling-stock output. I.C.I. controlled old-established firms like Elliott's Metal Company, which had itself acquired the older Muntz's Metal Company.

New industries, like electrical equipment and motor-vehicle manufacture, also had their combinations. Lucas, for instance, absorbed two large firms in 1925 and two more in 1926, while in the motor-vehicle industry Morris acquired Wolseley Motors in 1927, and although some spectacular attempts at combination later failed, there were important tie-ups in the 1930's, such as that between B.S.A. and Lanchesters'.

The growth of large combines helped to revolutionize local conditions of work more than anything else. In the 1930's there were many Birmingham factories employing thousands of people, some of them sited away from the old industrial parts of the town. The willingness of new firms to settle there was a recognition of the special advantages Birmingham seemed to offer. Old small firms continued to survive, and even to retain something of their *élan vital* as well as their economic importance, but conditions in the city as a whole had changed, and changed for ever.

### III

The new Birmingham industries changed more than the old ones. They were the pace-makers, encouraging a relatively rapid rate of technical advance. They were responsible also, by reason of their relative prosperity during the inter-war years, for the blessing that Birmingham escaped the worst impact of the Great Depression. The Birmingham area was more fortunate than any

[1] *B.P.*, 24 May 1919.

of the other old industrial districts of the country in escaping large-scale involuntary unemployment. Between 1923 and 1937 the total insured population of the city increased by 40 per cent. as against 22 per cent. in the country as a whole, and this expanded population found it far easier to secure work than the more stable population of South Wales or Tyneside. Birmingham led the national revival in employment after 1931, and recognized that its good fortunes depended not only on the variety of its trades and the adaptability of its business men, but also on the continued resilience of the new industries. Wensley and Florence have shown the key importance in the recent economic history of the Birmingham area of the fact that it happened to contain industries which were growing relatively fast, wherever they were established, and to exclude industries which were declining, wherever they were sited.[1]

The motor industry and electrical engineering stood out above the rest, the former especially important in Birmingham because of the indirect employment it attracted for the producers of components of all types. Birmingham produced many of the components and sub-assemblies of cars finally completed elsewhere. The pull of the motor-car industry gave an impetus to mechanization and mass production in many of these subsidiary trades;[2] it also encouraged the expansion of relatively new industries like rubber, steel alloys, and non-ferrous metals.

The successful motor-car magnates of the inter-war years realized from an early stage, although less clearly than their American opposite numbers, that they would increase their profits by concentrating their capacity on a few specialities, designed to meet the demand for well-modelled cars at popular prices, and cutting down their manufacturing costs to the minimum by standardizing component parts and producing them in bulk. They were hampered at first in the pursuit of this policy by the great increase in costs during the post-war boom, which made it very difficult for them to tap wider markets. Although they persevered in new methods of production—large-scale flow production, the reduction of internal transport costs, the standardization and interchangeability of parts, and so on—they were still dependent to some extent on external contracts for com-

[1] A. J. Wensley and P. Sargant Florence, 'Recent Industrial Concentrations especially in the Midlands', in the *Review of Economic Studies*, June 1940.
[2] G. C. Allen, *British Industries and their Organisation* (1933), p. 193.

ponent parts. Austins' were offered one item, for instance, at four times the pre-war price, and although, as a result of negotiations, the order was cut to a tenth of its original size and the price to a half, such bargaining could not always be used successfully.[1] There was a gradual reduction in dependence on outside producers during the inter-war years.

During the 1920's the price of cars fell and the markets widened. The industry flourished despite the large excess of productive capacity at the end of the post-war slump. The Baby Car was offered to the public in 1924. The Austin Seven, described in advertisements as 'the Mighty Miniature', cost £168, and it was followed later by the Morris Minor. Despite the competition of America, which could turn out more cars and chose to manufacture cars of a bigger and more powerful type, English cars sold well in the home market and the Empire. The Empire dominated all other foreign markets before and after protection had been developed. In 1925, the Empire took 87·6 per cent., by number, of British cars exported; in 1929 it took 86·4 per cent.; and in 1937, 84·6 per cent. Access to other markets was limited. There were many complaints that the British were trying to make too many varieties of cars, offering a far wider range of choice than the American manufacturers, who turned out far larger quantities,[2] but in 1938 Britain was second only to the United States both in total production and in exports.

Birmingham owed much of its prosperity in the inter-war years to the motor-car industry, even though it was freely said that old Birmingham trades, like jewellery, suffered as a result. 'The introduction of the cheap motor-car has obviously influenced the recession of the jewellery trade,' Alderman Roberts of Birmingham told the Royal Commission on the Distribution of Industrial Population in 1938, 'but it is fortunate for Birmingham that it has shared much of the fortune which this great new industry has produced.'[3] The motor-cycle industry too should be given part of the credit, as the annual reports of a company like B.S.A. show, while in the later 30's the aircraft industry was again important.

[1] B.P., 20 February 1918.
[2] e.g. The Economist, 26 July 1930. The seven largest English producers produced forty-two models. The seven largest American producers, whose complete output was twenty times that of their English rivals, produced only thirty-two models.
[3] Barlow Report.

The effects on local employment of the development of the motor-vehicle industry can be traced through the multiplier effects on other sectors of local business. Between 1927 and 1932, for instance, there were five building extensions at Austin's, costing £280,000. One extension alone in 1935, at the Morris factory at Adderley Park, cost £250,000 and was designed to employ 1,500 more men.[1] In 1938 there was some local controversy when a site which had been acquired by the Corporation for building purposes was turned over to an aircraft factory planning to employ 12,000 to 15,000 workers, but the opinion prevailed locally that many working-class people would be quite prepared to say, 'I'll be just as pleased with a job as with a house.'

The timing of the extension of the motor-vehicle industry was significant in relation to the local level of general business activity. The bottom of the slump in Birmingham and the Black Country was reached in 1931, but even in that year, after slackness in the motor-vehicle trades in January and February, there was a 'boomlet' in March and April, when the Birmingham unemployment figures fell for several weeks in succession, as a result of orders for component parts, from nuts and bolts to magnetos.[2] There was a decline again in the middle of the year, but while unemployment became more serious in England and Wales as a whole between 1931 and 1932, the position slightly improved in Birmingham from September 1931 onwards. Some foreign firms were attracted to the city, including a Swiss firm, manufacturing motor-tire valves, which had previously only been produced outside the country. In September 1932 about 53,000 people were unemployed in the city, about 14 per cent. of the insured population, as compared with a figure of about 20 per cent. for the conurbation and over 20 per cent. for Great Britain as a whole. Over 20,000 people were receiving poor relief, but this was only a fifth of the numbers in Glasgow. In the spring of 1933, when the Birmingham cycle firms were working to capacity, Birmingham touched its lowest unemployment figures since July 1930: 2·25 per cent. of the population was receiving poor relief as against 7·38 per cent. in Manchester, 8·72 per cent. in Liverpool, and 10·38 per cent. in Glasgow.[3] In November 1933 Geoffrey Lloyd, in the House of Commons,

---

[1] B.P., 22 November 1935.
[2] Ministry of Labour Gazette, March/April 1931.   [3] B.P., 15 June 1933.

referred to the extent of Birmingham's revival, and mentioned the existence of labour shortages in certain skilled trades.[1]

Birmingham was leading the country's trade revival, and there were complaints from one of the distressed areas that 'in the Midlands and South, you just don't know what we in the North have been through'.[2] A breakdown of the unemployment figures for December 1933 showed how Birmingham's unemployed were distributed. Forty-six per cent. had been unemployed for less than 3 months, 15 per cent. from 3 to 6 months, 15 per cent. from 6 to 12 months, and 24 per cent. for 12 months or more.[3] There were still many grim local tragedies of unemployment—one of them was recounted in May 1934 in a painful broadcast talk by John Evans, an unemployed mechanic—but Birmingham was relatively prosperous, and jealous eyes were cast on its prosperity by less favoured parts of the country.

During the years 1934 to 1937, the peak of the inter-war revival, when the unemployment figures were the lowest since the revision of the system in 1920, there was a marked movement of population into Birmingham and the surrounding area. At the same time the natural increase of population in Birmingham and the Black Country came to exceed that of any other commensurable population in the country.[4] Although there was a trade recession in Birmingham as in other parts of the country in 1938, and there were some local complaints concerning the influx of workers from outside,[5] there was a revival in 1939 in which the rearmament programme played a large part.

Other new industries besides the motor-vehicle industry must be fitted into this picture. The electrical trades were of special importance, because they never suffered any serious recession throughout the inter-war years, and the employment position was, at worst, 'fair'. In 1931, in the manufacture of heavy electrical equipment, such as power plant, Birmingham employed 33 per cent. of the workers in the industry, as against London's 16 per cent., Manchester's 24 per cent., and the rest of the country's 27 per cent. In the manufacture of light electrical equipment London was far ahead with 50 per cent., but Bir-

---

[1] *House of Commons Debates*, 5 s., 735–8.

[2] *E.D.*, 30 June 1934.                          [3] *B.M.*, 20 January 1933.

[4] G. Walker, 'The Growth of Population in Birmingham and the Black Country between the Wars', in the *University of Birmingham Historical Journal*, vol. i, no. 1 (1947).

[5] *B.P.*, 15 September 1938.

mingham employed 12 per cent.[1] Between 1911 and 1921 the
number of workers in the electrical engineering and apparatus
manufacturing trades in Birmingham and district rose from
6,000 to 17,000. By 1927 it was up to 20,000 and continued to
rise until 1938.[2] Employment in the new electrical trades and
radio followed the new lines of twentieth-century production.
A journalist described in 1930 how at the Midland Electric
Manufacturing Company 'all the workers' time is booked up to
specific jobs, all idle time is checked, and all causes of dislocation
are traced to their origins and remedied'.[3] Not only the technique of production but the costing system, 'the brain and nerve
department', followed 'the most modern methods'.

Alongside motor vehicles and electricity, plastics, like bake-
lite, also took their place. In 1933 it was estimated that thirty
Birmingham firms produced plastics, most of them having
started within the previous ten years.[4] In 1938 one firm, Elliott's,
employed over 700 employees: it had developed plastics as its
main interest from humble beginnings in the imitation stones
and cheap-jewellery business. In the same year, 1938, the golden
jubilee of the pneumatic tire was celebrated in Birmingham.

All these new industries, which revolutionized the social life
of the city and had an important effect on its economy, represented a new technology, which was seeking to emancipate
itself, skilfully and scientifically, from the old coal and iron technology on which the eighteenth-century prosperity of Birmingham had been based. All of them catered for the individual
material well-being of the consumer. The consumer—particularly the consumer in the upper and middle income groups, who
could afford a new house, a new car, and a houseful of electrical
gadgets—occupied a central position in the industrial revolution
of the twentieth century. But the firms who were meeting his
requirements were often joint concerns, employing thousands
of people and relying on elaborate conveyor systems of production and automatic connexions to produce their products, and
on mass advertising to reach their public.

The growth in material well-being was still compatible with
large pockets of unemployment and severe sectional distress,
and with the failure to rebuild the shattered structure of inter-

[1] A. Plummer, *New British Industries in the Twentieth Century* (1937), p. 58.
[2] *Conurbation* (1948), Table XXV, p. 120.
[3] *B.G.*, 28 October 1930.                    [4] *B.M.*, 6 September 1933.

national trade. Society was thus divided even in years of recovery, and different interests jostled together. Before 1929, while there were cries for welfare on the one hand, there were urgent requests for economy on the other. The height of social tension was reached during the General Strike of 1926, when the Joint Trade Unions Emergency Committee on the one side and the Volunteer Service Committee on the other organized their respective supporters. The President of the Trades Council claimed that 'the working class must let the government know that their hostility to the workers was at last coming up against a rock and was going to split'. After the collapse of the Strike the propaganda of a body like the National Industrial Alliance seemed to find new support in the Mond–Turner conversations and the formation of the National Industrial Council. 'People had come to see today that it was not by the earthquake that things happened that were good', the president of the Trades Union Congress claimed in Birmingham in 1930.[1] But the earthquakes did not subside. First the Great Depression and then the international disturbances of the 30's continued to provide an undercurrent of strain. Sectional pressures continued, even if they were sometimes apparently submerged. After 1929 the old demand of Birmingham business men for tariff reform acquired real driving force and influenced the new economic orthodoxy of the 1930's, while the memory of working-class unemployment was to stretch forward into the future to influence policy in years to come. It was Neville Chamberlain, who realized his father's gospel of tariff reform, who also said as early as 1923 that 'the fear of unemployment is by far the most serious and most justifiable indictment the workers have against the present industrial system'.[2]

### IV

The response of Birmingham business men to the economic ups and downs of the inter-war years was important in so far as it registered and in many cases anticipated changing national moods of thought and action. In some cases it reflected the prevailing canons of public policy, for during those years business men played both a background and a foreground role in policymaking. The Birmingham Chamber of Commerce, with its large number of members (1931, 3,000) and complex organization,

---

[1] *B.P.*, 19 February 1930.          [2] Ibid., 20 January 1923.

was a well-established body with recognized representative authority, but there were other local organizations as well, like the district branch of the National Union of Manufacturers set up in 1915, and the local branch of the Federation of British Industries, established in 1918. As a capital of industry, Birmingham provided leaders for many national bodies of this type.

Some of the special interests of Birmingham manufacturers were concerned with the immediate needs of the locality. Because of Birmingham's distance from the sea and its dependence on railway connexions, local business men had always been specially interested in questions of transport. In the nineteenth century there had been prolonged pressure politics concerning railway rates. In the inter-war years there was considerable discussion of canal ownership and policy, and of the possibility of linking Birmingham more closely with Bristol, Liverpool, or, after the Grand Union Canal Bill of 1929, with London. There was a persistent but unavailing attempt to secure a return to the penny post. All these local issues were eclipsed in importance, however, by the pressure of Birmingham to secure a set of national demands. Industrial needs turned attention to the framing of a national policy.

There were some complaints, for instance, against the return to gold in 1925. A militant amendment to the Annual Report of the Chamber of Commerce was carried, claiming that the return to the gold standard 'would make it still more difficult for the manufacturers of this country to meet competition in the export markets of the world'.[1] With faint echoes of post-Napoleonic Attwoodism, one speaker said that 'the question was so big that the livelihood of our workers was absolutely wrapped up in it'.[2] When the gold standard was abandoned in 1931, the Birmingham press spoke of a new 'fillip to trade'.

The needs of competition in the export markets of the world were never allowed to overshadow the greater need for protecting the home market and the growing desire to expand the empire market.

In the same year as the return to the gold standard, 1925, the idea of 'Buy British' was pressed by the Lord Mayor and the president of the Chamber of Commerce, who in a joint statement, strongly attacked by free traders, advocated more buying of British goods as a means of raising employment. 'Every pound

[1] B.P., 18 May 1925.          [2] Ibid., 12 May 1925.

spent in the purchase of a foreign made article', they claimed, 'contributes to the purchasing power of our foreign competitors, and involves a heavy consequential loss to Great Britain.'[1] In 1930 the campaign was pressed with great vigour, and a year later the first Empire Shop was opened in Birmingham under the aegis of the Empire Marketing Board. It was felt that, important though these measures were, they did not in themselves go far enough. A new tariff policy was necessary.

It was in the field of fiscal policy that the influence of Birmingham was strongest. In the post-war world Birmingham welcomed the Safeguarding of Industries Act, and objected to the proposed repeal of the war-time McKenna duties in 1924. When some members of the Chamber of Commerce protested against the discussion of a 'political question' like free trade, the president told them that 'such matters were business long before they were politics'.[2] In 1926 at the annual meeting the president told the members that he hoped the time would come when their Tariff Committee would be able to make suggestions to the government, which the government would be enabled to pass on to foreign countries 'with some threats of possible reprisals behind these suggestions'.[3]

In 1928 Sir Gilbert Vyle, who expressed the full gospel of twentieth-century protectionism in terms which allowed for no doubt or equivocation, said just after receiving his knighthood that 'in order to get full employment for every British worker, it was essential to have a logically controlled system of national trade, which ensured that our workpeople should not be exposed to the competition of other countries unless an adjustment was made that put them on an equality with ourselves'.[4] The same philosophy was propounded by Alexander Ramsay, chairman of the Engineering and Allied Employers' Federation, and author of *The Economics of Safeguarding*. 'Safeguarding' was one of the key-words of the late 20's, and there was little support in Birmingham for the idea of a 'tariff truce' propounded in 1930 by the government. The Association of British Chambers of Commerce meeting in the Midland Institute in Birmingham in 1930 preferred the idea of 'a self-supporting empire';[5] and after the Budget of 1931 had been announced, Ramsay attacked Snowden's 'Victorian free trade traditions' and added that there

[1] *B.P.*, 1 December 1925.    [2] *B.G.*, 29 April 1924.    [3] *B.P.*, 23 April 1926.
[4] *E.D.*, 2 July 1928.    [5] *B.P.*, 27 September 1930.

was no hope for the country until a different government was in power which would take a different point of view.[1]

Around this time there was some talk of a new government— preferably a coalition—or at least of joint action to secure a national policy. 'Undoubtedly the best remedy of all would be for everyone to work together to see how trade conditions could be improved',[2] said one prominent local figure. The National Government of 1931 seemed to many to represent the building of a common front to meet all emergencies, and Neville Chamberlain caught the mood when he wrote after the General Election of that year that he hoped 'we may presently develop into a National Party, and get rid of that odious title of Conservative, which has kept so many from joining us in the past'.[3]

Chamberlain joined the government convinced in his own mind like most of the Birmingham manufacturers that 'a tariff levied on imported foreign goods will be found to be indispensable'.[4] It was appropriate that he should be given the task of announcing the return to protection a year later in the House of Commons. He spoke with sincere filial piety of the aspirations of his father. 'His work was not in vain. . . . I believe he would have found consolation for the bitterness of his disappointment if he could have foreseen that these proposals which are the direct and legitimate descendants of his own conception would be laid before the House of Commons, which he loved, in the presence of one and by the lips of the other of the two immediate successors of his name and blood.'[5] Birmingham could admire the statement of tariff reform in these terms, but it could claim that its own interest in it went back even farther still, and that 'it was engraven in the industrial attitudes of many generations of business men'. There was a vested interest in protection in Birmingham. *The Economist* might head its leader on the speech 'Stark and Unashamed', but Birmingham did not fear the choice of such adjectives, nor the denunciation of 'all the antique paraphernalia for building a tariff of any height or absurdity that may result from the pressure of vested interests or the clamour of partisans'.[6]

The demand for fiscal reform was the lustiest call in Birmingham

[1] *B.P.*, 28 April 1931.　　　　　　　　[2] *B.G.*, 13 June 1931.
[3] Quoted by K. Feiling, *The Life of Neville Chamberlain* (1946), p. 58.
[4] Election Address at Edgbaston, October 1931.
[5] *House of Commons Debates*, 5 s., 296.
[6] *The Economist*, 6 February 1932.

in the 20's and early 30's, but there were many other sister songs—rationalization, economy, and even faint murmurs of 'Back to the land', the old Jesse Collings panacea.[1]

The demand for economy was historically the most significant, for it had widespread ramifications[2] and provoked a marked reaction. As early as 1925 the National Union of Manufacturers was attacking high taxation and the social services burden on industry. The gospel of thrift was pressed to its extremes first in good years—'save to create sunshine'[3]—then in bad—'nothing but the most rigid economy, national, municipal and industrial, drastic retrenchment by all . . . are all urgently required to arrest our national landslide'.[4] The financial crisis of 1931 seemed designed to drive the lesson home. 'At last the whole nation became alive to the simple fact that a nation, no less than an individual, must keep its expenditure within its income.'[5] After the up-turn in the 1930's there was some revulsion in Birmingham both to the idea of economy and to the dominance of 'sound finance'. While *The Economist* proclaimed that 'vicarious asceticism at the expense of the ignorant and the needy is not the royal road to trade revival',[6] the president of the Birmingham Chamber of Commerce in 1933 claimed that 'the man today who is in a position to spend and is not spending is an enemy to his country and not a benefactor'[7]—and another critic of official policy claimed that if any intelligent clerk in an accountant's office had been given the figures he could have prepared a Budget as good as the current one.[8] Such complaints died away in the later 30's, but while they lasted they were significant as intimations of ideas still to be thought out in the future.

V

Behind all the grumbles, the panaceas, and the philosophies of Birmingham business men, there was the steady routine practical organization of a 'capital of industry'. In 1938 small firms and big firms existed side by side in mutual dependence. There was considerable co-location, implying a linkage between related

---

[1] e.g. *B.G.*, 3 December 1930; 28 January 1931.
[2] See above, Chapter VIII.                          [3] *B.P.*, 11 December 1928.
[4] Sir Gilbert Vyle, reported in the *B.G.*, 31 December 1930.
[5] *Annual Report of the Birmingham Chamber of Commerce*, 1931–2.
[6] *The Economist*, 3 December 1932.                 [7] *B.P.*, 4 April 1933.
[8] Ibid., 27 June 1933.

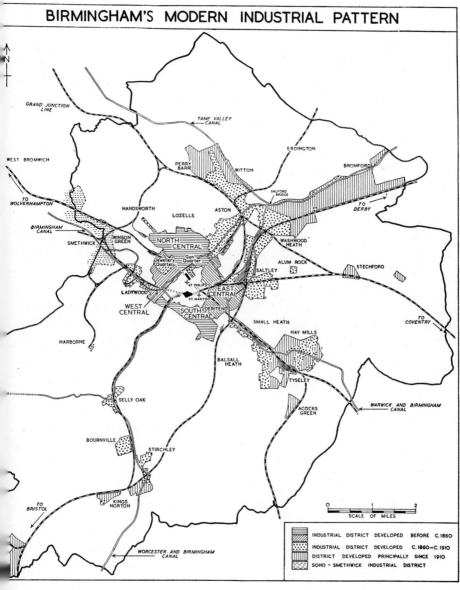

# BIRMINGHAM'S MODERN INDUSTRIAL PATTERN

N

GRAND JUNCTION LINE

TAME VALLEY CANAL

WEST BROMWICH

PERRY BARR

ERDINGTON

WITTON

BROMFORD

TO WOLVERHAMPTON

SALFORD BRIDGE

BIRMINGHAM CANAL

HANDSWORTH

LOZELLS

ASTON

TO DERBY

SMETHWICK

WINSON GREEN

NORTH CENTRAL

WASHWOOD HEATH

Jewellery Quarter

Gun Quarter

ALUM ROCK

STECHFORD

SALTLEY

ST PHILIPS

LADYWOOD

ST MARTINS

EAST CENTRAL

WEST CENTRAL

DERITEND

SOUTH CENTRAL

SMALL HEATH

TO COVENTRY

HARBORNE

HAY MILLS

BALSALL HEATH

TYSELEY

SELLY OAK

ACOCKS GREEN

WARWICK AND BIRMINGHAM CANAL

BOURNVILLE

STIRCHLEY

KINGS NORTON

TO BRISTOL

SCALE OF MILES
0        1        2

INDUSTRIAL DISTRICT DEVELOPED BEFORE C.1860
INDUSTRIAL DISTRICT DEVELOPED C.1860-C.1910
DISTRICT DEVELOPED PRINCIPALLY SINCE 1910
SOHO - SMETHWICK INDUSTRIAL DISTRICT

WORCESTER AND BIRMINGHAM CANAL

FIG. 12

groups of industries; and many main and auxiliary processes, which could all be performed within the walls of one factory, were organized independently by a great number of firms.[1] The number of firms was a legacy of the past: their interdependence was often a guarantee of their survival, for the city of Birmingham reproduced in itself 'without conscious effort' the main advantages of a large single plant—the physical juxtaposition of consecutive services and auxiliary services, which reduced costs of transport and frequency of contacts.[2]

The actual location of firms in Birmingham in 1938 showed that the old lines of district demarcation had not been completely obliterated, particularly in the old central core of the city. The jewellery quarter still remained concentrated within the triangular area bounded by Great Hampton Street, Vyse Street, and Warstone Lane. Three-quarters of the silversmiths, jewellers, needle- and lock-making firms were confined to two telephone exchange areas. The gun district, dwindling in size and importance, extended just beyond the limits of Steelhouse Lane in the south, Lawley Street in the south-east, Lancaster Street in the east, Tower Street in the north, and Livery Street and Caroline Street in the south-west. There were still traces of the old brass-foundry complex in Ladywood and Deritend, although new industries, like aluminium, and service trades, like baking, had found a place there.

The inner ring of Birmingham industry, with its small specialized workshops, was surrounded by the middle ring, much of which had been built up in the fifty years before the First World War, and some of which was older, based on local growth before the expansion of Birmingham. There were concentrated pockets of industry at Aston, Nechells, Saltley, Bordesley, Small Heath, Greet, and Balsall Heath, all conveniently placed in relation to road and rail and often to canal facilities. In some of these districts there was a more variegated industrial pattern than in the older parts of the city, and often the differences could be traced back to historical causes.

Aston, with its traditions of independence, had been blessed not only by abundant transport facilities but by good water-supplies. It had a series of wells which provided water ideal for brewing purposes, so that in consequence most of the brewers

---

[1] P. Sargant Florence, *Investment, Location and the Size of Plant* (1948), ch. iv.
[2] Ibid., p. 74.

both of beer and vinegar in the neighbourhood of Birmingham were located at Aston. Food industries had been developed as well. The industrial basis of the area was varied, most of the works being grouped together close to the banks of the Birmingham and Fazeley Canal, the Digbeth Branch of the Birmingham Canal Navigation system, and the Aston Goods Branch of the railway. While the Nechells area, lying close to Aston, enjoyed many similar advantages and shared the variegated industrial pattern, by contrast Saltley had a far narrower industrial base, its main activities being limited to the production of railway rolling stock and gas. Alongside these two major industrial activities, closely tied to the railway system, there was a restricted development of industries like non-ferrous stamping.

The Bordesley area manufactured a wide range of products, to a large extent interdependent in character. Paint works, for instance, were located in close proximity to a large motor-car factory. Biscuit and cake works were conveniently placed alongside a factory producing cardboard boxes for the final packing of the food products.

At Small Heath and Greet, the metal industries predominated. The B.S.A. and the Singer Motor Works were in the Small Heath neighbourhood, and alongside them complementary firms producing paint and varnishes, steel tubes, and non-ferrous castings. The Greet area, lying south of Small Heath, had as its central feature the manufacture of cycles, side-cars, and radiators, with tools, foundry products, and light engineering as subsidiaries.

The Balsall Heath industrial pocket, less well favoured from the point of view of transport than most of the other industrial neighbourhoods within the middle ring, had many light industries centred in small factories, dispersed among poor working-class houses. Nails, wire, and perambulator-wheels were made in Balsall Heath, as were furniture, paints, and food and drink products.

Within this old Birmingham, including the middle ring, factory conditions varied a great deal. In the jewellery quarter, many streets which had once been residential in character became the centres of small-scale production. Some other central buildings were less dignified, although there were some survivals of picturesque old workshops. In the middle ring there was often considerable industrial congestion, many of the factories consisting of extensions and stories built at different times to fill up all the available ground space. There were also in the middle ring many modern factories designed to provide efficient layout and high working efficiency.[1]

It was in the outer areas of Birmingham, where the inter-war industrial expansion was centred, that factories were newest and available space greatest. Some factories began to be located at a distance of three to five miles from the city centre. The demand for cheap land, for increased floor space, and room to expand encouraged the location of sites on the fringes of Birmingham. Often, because of the necessity for quick communications, there was industrial ribbon development on the main roads out of the city.

The most striking feature of the changing industrial pattern of the city in the inter-war years was the industrialization of the valley of the Tame from Perry Barr in the west to Bromford and Castle Bromwich in the east. The wide flood plain of the Tame, drained and canalized, seemed ideal for the erection of large factories. Fort Dunlop, lying between the main Birmingham–Derby railway and the Fazeley canal, was the best example of these, but the new aeroplane factory, situated to the east of Fort Dunlop and completed during the Second World War, was a further example. The main roads of this district were lined with smaller factories, producing electrical and motor accessories, with the Tyburn Road bounding the area to the north, an excellent example of ribbon factory development. The northern side of the Tyburn Road marked the residential fringe of the region, the outskirts of the Erdington housing estates, from which a large proportion of the labour-supply of the Tame valley region was secured.

At the far end of the city, in the south-west, there was a rapid growth of the built-up area beyond Selly Oak towards Bournville, Stirchley, and Northfield. The Selly Oak region itself was concerned with the production of non-ferrous metal products, and in the north of the area forging, engineering, machine tools, motor-cycles, guns, rifles, and cardboard boxes. Beyond Selly Oak, Bournville and Northfield had developed large-scale branches of modern industry. Modern Northfield grew up round the Austin works at Longbridge, Bournville round the Cadbury factory. Their dependence on one large factory was exceptional.

[1] For pictures of factories, see *Conurbation*, ch. ix.

Going round the outer ring from the north through Smethwick, Stirchley, Acock's Green, Stechford, and Bromford, the main feature of industrial development was still its variety, with the metal trades providing the base. In many cases twentieth-century factory building in these areas, like house building, was a natural over-spill from adjacent districts—thus rapidly changing districts like Tyseley and Hay Mills represented an extension of the earlier industrial neighbourhoods of Small Heath and Greet.

The development of new factory areas helped to reshape the topography of the city, to modify the balance of homes and workshops, and to provide a new framework for daily living. The effects of these and other changes can be fully appreciated only if one turns from industry to social life as a whole—to a fuller picture of what Birmingham was like in 1938 as a place in which to live and work.

# X

## BIRMINGHAM IN 1938

### I

IN 1938, the year of the centenary of the Incorporation, Birmingham had travelled far from the turbulent but compact town of the Chartist riots. With a population estimated by the Medical Officer of Health in 1938 at 1,048,000, it was an enormous, widely dispersed, but peaceful city, which still maintained the tradition of local pride grounded in its past.

The geography of the twentieth-century city can itself be contrasted with the topography of the nineteenth-century town. Birmingham in 1938 could best be considered from the point of view of housing as well as industry in terms of three rings, corresponding largely to its industrial layout. The inner-ring areas, covering the old central wards of the nineteenth-century town, were the core of the city, containing within them the Parish Church and the Bull Ring, the main railway stations, the City Centre, and the busiest thoroughfares, which with their shops, offices, and places of entertainment attracted visitors from miles around. Although they retained some of the features of the early nineteenth century, the seven central wards were now far less important as places of residence than they ever had been before. The fall in their population, which went back to the nineteenth century, continued at a faster rate. Between the censuses of 1921 and 1931 the population declined from 242,350 to 213,095.

Despite these falls in population, which were accompanied by rapid development of non-residential property, the central wards were still the most densely populated parts of the city, twice as densely populated as the Middle Ring and four times as densely populated as the Outer Ring. St. Martin's and Deritend had a population density of 96 persons to the acre, which, while it was a great deal less than the most densely populated wards in other cities, like St. George's in the East, Stepney, with 238, or Netherfield, Liverpool, with 227, contrasted markedly with the average population density of 20 persons per acre for the whole city area of Birmingham.

Into the densely packed core of Birmingham people flocked

by bus, train, and tram to secure the eagerly sought-after amenities of a large city, yet despite the influx of this floating population[1] the central wards still managed to retain something of their neighbourliness and cohesion. The busy thoroughfares like New Street or Corporation Street were to many of the regular inhabitants of the central areas great urban sheep-tracks: behind the tracks, as in Councillor White's day, there was often a vivid world which was less well known. There was still much overcrowding, and with it a mass of half-concealed poverty and malnutrition, but there was a vigour and a character there, sometimes lacking in the new municipal or private housing estates.

The older areas were often natural 'neighbourhood units' in themselves. Their inhabitants 'met on a common ground within their own area for primary social activities and for organized and spontaneous social contacts'.[2] The roots of the inhabitants were in the neighbourhood. There was a higher proportion of old people in the centre of Birmingham than in the outskirts— single and widowed older folk—for whom no provision had been made on the new housing estates. They maintained a thread of continuity with an older city, when neighbourliness was not a function of a restricted area, defined by sociologists after careful and prolonged research, but of the thriving activities of a relatively compact territorial society.

The central areas of Birmingham contained not only the civic centre, many of the biggest shops and places of entertainment, and facilities like the Library and the main line stations. They also included, and it was part of the legacy of old Birmingham, many of the small workshops and factories, where people from the outer areas were still employed. The invaluable publication of the Bournville Village Trust, *When We Build Again*, published in 1941 but based on research carried out from 1935 onwards, explained how 58·2 per cent. of the wage-earners who lived in the central area of the city were employed there, and that in addition 34·4 per cent. of the inhabitants of the municipal housing estates, mainly in the Outer Ring, were also employed within the central wards. It was these central workshops, some

[1] The Census return of 1921 showed that 33,525 people came into Birmingham each day from outside the boundaries to work in the city. *Census General Report*, p. 190.

[2] See R. V. Glass, *The Social Background of a Plan: a Study of Middlesbrough* (1948), ch. ii.

of which have already been described, which provided a link between new ways of home life in the modern houses of the suburbs and traditional ways of work, which, while they frequently depended on new techniques, were carried out in an old environment.

Between the central area of shops and the central factories there were slums; and before 1938 schemes of redevelopment were evolved, which it was hoped would extend both the relatively small shopping area and the cramped industrial sites. It was clear that any physical redevelopment would have to come about not by street widening, which was rendered prohibitive by high land values and enforcedly small and uneconomic building plots, but by slum clearance and 're-zoning'. In 1937 an area of 267 acres in Duddeston and Nechells, about 90 per cent. of the total area of the seven central wards, was declared to be a redevelopment area, and it was hoped that active redevelopment would begin in 1940, at a cost of about £6½ million. By revising the street plan and demolishing residential property it was anticipated that 22 acres of land could be released for the concentration of factories in zoned areas and the provision of flats and maisonettes for the inhabitants of the area, not very far away from their old homes. Flats were not very popular, and willingness to build them or live in them cut across social and political party lines. Of families living in the central wards who wished to move house in 1938, no more than 5·4 per cent. wished to exchange a house for a flat, but it was becoming increasingly clear that if they also wished to continue to live near the centre of the city, flats were the only possible means which would enable them to do so. The City Council realized this when in December 1938, after having frequently turned down the idea before, it finally decided to provide flats on a large scale. In 1939 the first block of flats was completed in Emily Street.

Flats appeared to many to be an agency which would undermine from within rather than from without the traditional ways of life of the older central wards. And 'flatted factories' would be even more revolutionary in their effects than 'flatted houses'. The resistances to them were great, but it was already clear in 1938 that many of the resistances would eventually be overcome, and would have to be overcome if the central areas of the city were to be worthy of an enlightened community. The lack of open space alone was an even more important problem than it had been in Nettlefold's day, for in 1938 there was less than three-quarters of an acre of open space per 1,000 inhabitants in the fourteen innermost wards of the city, containing two-fifths of the population of Birmingham, as against 4 or 5 acres per 1,000 in the outskirts, and 7 to 10 acres in the south and south-west. The National Playing Fields Association considered that 6 acres of open space per 1,000 inhabitants were desirable for playing fields alone.

The fourteen innermost wards of the city included not only the central core but also the so-called Middle Ring. In 1938 a little over one-seventh of Birmingham's houses were in the central wards, and nearly two-sevenths in the Middle Ring,[1] most of the latter built before 1914 but less old than the oldest houses in the centre. Building development had been as haphazard as in the centre of the city and far more dull, and with notable exceptions the Middle Ring districts lacked the colour of the older areas. Many of the houses, built in the nineteenth-century waves of suburban expansion, were of the 'tunnel back' type, constructed in long rows. Although structurally they were often soundly built, from an architectural point of view they lacked style and character, and they were designed to fill space rather than to fit into neighbourhoods, with provision for local social amenities and open space. The liveliest parts of the Middle Ring areas were the major roads leading into Birmingham, the main arteries along which both passengers and goods moved. Local shopping centres, churches and chapels, public houses and clubs tended to cluster round these roads, some of the shopping centres being sufficiently large to cater for all the daily wants of the people who lived round about.

These main roads led right out from the centre of the city through the Middle Ring to the Outer Ring, much of which had been built over since 1920. Four-sevenths of Birmingham's citizens lived in the Outer Ring in 1938. Most of the phases of Birmingham's growth can be studied in the bricks and mortar of main roads leading out of the city, like the Bristol Road or the Coventry Road. Out through the still attractive central districts, past the Edgbaston Estate with its charming Georgian houses, the Bristol Road forges its way through nineteenth-century Selly Oak and twentieth-century Northfield. The rows

---

[1] *When We Build Again* (1941), p. 51.

of shops, the distribution and age of churches, chapels, and public houses reflect the waves of migration, the forms of urban expansion, and the vicissitudes of taste.

The Outer Ring of the city cannot be clearly defined, and was still changing rapidly in 1938 as a result of the double influence of private and municipal building. A patchwork quilt of new houses of all types and styles and mixtures of styles could be traced in most parts of the new districts, although some of the new municipal estates, like Weoley Castle, set a very high standard both of building and unified layout. All the new areas, by comparison with the central wards and the Middle Ring, were characterized by their spaciousness. Modern housing estates, it has been said, have been 'designed not to draw people together, but rather to divide them from each other'.[1] In the sense of space, this was certainly true, and it had wider applications in other respects as well.

Social life in the Outer Ring, by its essential conditions, differed from that in the old crowded city centre. Neighbourliness was less obviously fostered by a congenial environment, and the first estates lacked new communal facilities to replace services provided naturally in the other parts of the city. Even climatic conditions seemed to differ. 'In winter the estates are colder than the concentrated living quarters in the older districts, and not uncommonly the tenants on the windswept roads and shopping centres compare their new homes to Siberia.'[2]

There was a time-lag on the municipal estates before local social life developed spontaneously, and although by 1938 much had been done to provide the areas with new facilities, there was still a great deal more to be accomplished. As late as 1938 the only parts of the Outer Ring of the city where the population served by each public library was higher than in the central wards and the Middle Ring were the north-west, where it was approximately the same, and the north-east. In the case of public baths, the north-west, south-west, and southern parts of the city were as well supplied as the centre, but the east side was far worse off. Perry Barr had no more than thirteen licensed premises, including clubs, for its 64,000 inhabitants—one licence to nearly 5,000 people—as compared with one for every 350–700 people in the central and Middle Ring districts. As far as church accommodation was concerned, there were obvious time-lags.

[1] R. V. Glass, op. cit., p. 12.    [2] *When We build Again*, p. 96.

PLATE XLI

A Nineteenth-century Inn

PLATE XLII

A Suburban Public House

Despite the fact that by the end of 1937 £100,000 had been raised and used for the provision of new Anglican churches in the outlying areas, there was still a deficiency in seating accommodation as compared with the central areas. The establishment of new Roman Catholic parishes kept pace with the migration of Catholics to the new districts, and various nonconformist bodies pushed ahead with 'forward' movements, but there was a far greater difficulty in offering effective church facilities than in the declining city areas, where some old churches and chapels faced serious problems of their own. The question was not a new one—it had been anticipated by Dale eighty years before—but it had become an urgent one, in an age when religious indifference appeared to be increasing.

With these important differences in social amenities between city centre and suburbs, the centre continued to act as a magnet for entertainment and recreation, and some of the new-comers to the estates at first sometimes wished themselves back in their old districts.[1] Two forces helped to counteract this magnetic attraction—the growth of local amenities like the enormous new public houses on the outskirts of the city, reflecting in their style and size the century which produced them, and the spread of community centres, also twentieth-century products.

The new suburban 'public houses', completely different in character from the small nineteenth-century inns in the centre of the town, were often enormous, well-built structures, towering over their neighbours. 'Over the years there has gradually evolved a new type of house', wrote a local commentator in 1930; 'it is neither ale-house, nor "pub", nor inn, nor tavern. It is a so far un-named place of public refreshment and public entertainment.'[2] The building of these new houses coincided with a decline in the total number of licences allowed in the city. Between 1911 and 1930 there was a reduction of 600 licences for 40 new ones granted. For every new suburban public house many old houses disappeared, although there were still far more licences in central Birmingham than in the suburbs. In 1938 there were only 12 licences and 3 clubs in Perry Barr— as against 154 licences and 41 clubs in Market Hall. Not only suburban public houses were being developed, but also sub-

---

[1] *Weoley Castle Review*, no. 2, November 1932.
[2] *B.G.*, 18 March 1930. For descriptions by a visitor, see E. Selley, *The English Public House as it is* (1927), esp. pp. 111–12.

urban cinemas and suburban sports facilities, although in this respect, too, the centre still exerted a magnetic attraction.

The growth of special community organizations is a fascinating story. In 1929 the National Council of Social Science organized the New Estates Community Committee, and a year later the Birmingham Council for Community Associations came into being as a result of a meeting presided over by the Lord Mayor. First called the Consultative Committee for Community Associations, it set out to foster and develop community life and to promote the provision of suitable halls for community centres. It was assisted by private enterprise, religious organizations, and later by the City Council. In 1938 there were ten community centres of all types in existence, some of the best equipped of them having been sponsored by the private First National Housing Trust. Tenants on the estates of the Trust paid 2d. a week with their rent to develop community facilities—one penny going to provide centres, the other penny going towards their running costs.

The City Council was slower in accepting the necessity for community centres, but it was taking pride at the end of 1938 in the attempts made to make the larger estates 'as far as possible self-contained communities';[1] and later on, in 1943, in a Report of the Public Works Committee it accepted the full implications of a social policy for the new estates.

A desirable social unit (it said) is a 'neighbourhood unit', with a population not exceeding 10,000, where everyone would be within about ten minutes' walk from its centre. Such a neighbourhood should be furnished with the communal facilities required for its full development. . . . The building of the Community centre should proceed simultaneously with the building of the houses, so that the centre should be available for the residents from the commencement of their residence in the 'neighbourhood'.[2]

By this time many of the local communities were very proud of their progress, as the pages of the magazine *Community Review* and its earlier predecessors, the first of them duplicated, show. They were aiming from the start at producing models of sound organization. 'We are grateful to places like Bournville and Edgbaston for providing us with many examples and some

---

[1] H. J. Manzoni, *The Production of 50,000 Council Houses*.
[2] *Report of the Public Works Committee*, accepted by the Council 9 March 1943.

warnings,' they wrote in 1934, 'but we intend to use their standards as stepping off places to far higher things.'[1]

The Outer Ring areas, with their emerging forms of local pride and social life, touched the usually forgotten agricultural fringe of Birmingham, where at harvest-time 'practically on all sides, outside what one might call the suburban belt, the clatter of the reaper and the binder may be heard'.[2] In 1922 the Birmingham authorities allowed a hundred dogs to be kept within the city boundaries, without licences being paid, to look after sheep on pasture. In 1938, when some of the agricultural areas of 1922 had been invaded by the builder, oat-threshing went on within five miles of the city centre and foxes were caught at Edgbaston. Within the Birmingham–Black Country conurbation, 37,000 acres were officially classified as agricultural land.

For a great industrial city, Birmingham men had always taken a somewhat surprising interest in the land. Joseph Chamberlain, who had reached the limits of his urban radical programme, made land reform the base of his Unauthorized Programme: Jesse Collings preached the gospel of Three Acres and a Cow. Even before that a Chartist land company had bought an estate at Dodford, and the Birmingham Agricultural Society had begun the long sequence of its yearly shows. It was in line with accepted tradition that in 1920, under the provisions of the Land Settlement (Facilities) Act of 1919, the City Council purchased the Canwell Estate of about 3,600 acres, eleven miles from the city, in an effort to satisfy the needs of a class of tenant somewhat different from the usual rural smallholder and with little experience of farming life. The development of this estate, with its 142 holdings in 1938, was carried forward in face of many difficulties; but out of it a new community emerged. The Highbury trustees paid the cost of building a village hall, named after Alderman Quinney, the chairman of the Agricultural and Small Holdings Committee of the Council.

Allotments were in themselves a sign of the city's interest in gardening. In 1938 the number of allotments under the control of the Corporation was over 12,000, covering an area of 1,300 acres. The largest freehold site was the Wyrley Birch Estate, accommodating nearly 1,000 tenants. While the tenants on the new housing estates were beginning to organize their own local life—gardening playing an important part—the local voluntary

---

[1] *Community News*, January 1934.          [2] *B.M.*, 16 September 1922.

allotments associations were promoting their joint interests in a manner that could not be achieved by individual action. Naturally developing and expanding social life was a more valuable plant than that which could be produced by any form of external pressure.

## II

The changed twentieth-century topography of the city provides the background for many features of its social pattern in 1938. The character of local social groupings in 1938 and the separation of homes and work both depended to some extent on the new urban geography.

Traditional local social structure had been characterized by friendly economic and social relations between small masters and skilled artisans living in close proximity to each other. Although the nineteenth-century suburbs had been carved out by migratory waves first of business men and then of working men, each group choosing to live in its own area rather than alongside the rest, the twentieth century has witnessed a more pronounced social segregation than ever before. At a time when there were many local and national forces leading to an increased equality of status between individuals, the quest for new housing space often worked in the opposite direction.

Municipal and private-enterprise housing estates tended to be one-class areas, although it is important not to exaggerate the divergence between the social standing of municipal- and private-house occupiers. In 1938 owner occupiers were few, and even in the Outer Ring, less than a quarter of the houses were owner-occupied. Even of the owner occupiers, 65 per cent. made weekly mortgage payments analogous to rent.[1] As far as rent statistics were concerned the median rental of houses built by private enterprise was not very different from those built by the city. More significant social divergences—and even these can be exaggerated—were the possession of a car, which made a great deal of difference to choice of sites and accessibility to the city, the style of houses and the size of gardens.

The growth of socially homogeneous estates was not accepted uncritically in the inter-war years. There were many critics who objected to the trend which was breaking up mixed populations and separating them out, and considered that an admixture of

[1] *When We Build Again*, pp. 54–55.

different social groups was essential within the boundaries of new neighbourhood units. There were other perhaps less scientific observers who contrasted the Birmingham of the nineteenth century with its juxtaposition of all classes living side by side and the vast new and increasingly socially stratified city.

Of Birmingham's 260,000 families in 1934, it was estimated that only 5 per cent. earned more than £10 a week, 16·5 per cent. between £4 and £10, and 78·5 per cent. less than £4.[1] The average wage paid to general workers was £2. 6s. a week. Many of the wealthiest families were choosing to live outside the city boundaries, travelling in by car from across the Severn, or the Stratford neighbourhood, or even Malvern. This dispersal beyond the city boundaries into the counties round about was the logical extension of a process noted in the eighteenth century.

In the old part of the city, too, the population was more homogeneous, many of the 78·5 per cent. living there, often in bad conditions. Rents were low: 41 per cent. of the working-class families living in the central wards in 1938 paid under 8s. a week in rent, and 71 per cent. under 10s. These figures compared with 20 and 44 per cent. respectively for the entire city.[2] Life in the central area of the city was cheaper than on the periphery, where there were higher rents, sometimes higher retail prices, and often significant transport costs.

The existence of considerable transport costs and of long journeys to work was the second important consequence of the expanded city. In money terms fares for journeys from homes to work acted as taxes on wages. In the west of Birmingham 15·9 per cent. of the working-class population spent over 3s. a week on chiefly routine travel.[3] The problem of the cost of transport was not as serious as it was in London, for only 3·3 per cent. of the population spent over 5s. a week, but it was a real problem, felt acutely by many people living on the municipal housing estates.

Apart from money costs, the time spent in travel was significant, even if not of the same serious social importance as in London. On the municipal housing estates considerably more than half the principal wage-earners travelled over 2 miles to work.[4] At the Austin Factory at Longbridge over 1,000 people travelled over 10 miles to work, and 300 workers lived as far

[1] G. Harrison and F. C. Mitchell, *The Home Market* (1936), p. 67.
[2] *When We Build Again*, p. 59.  [3] Ibid., p. 73.  [4] Ibid., p. 75.

away as Wolverhampton.[1] At a later date the average time taken by a sample of Birmingham's adolescents to get from home to work was 24 minutes for boys and 28 minutes for girls.[2] Distance and time taken to reach work were not always correlated, however, for some transport facilities were better for more distant travellers than they were for those nearer their places of work, and it was a great convenience to live on a main road or near a terminus.

Taking the Birmingham of 1938 sector by sector, it was clear that most of the districts could not provide work within their own boundaries. Although some twentieth-century factories had moved out from the highly-rated and congested central districts to the outskirts of the city, there were other areas which, like Perry Barr, were no more than large-scale dormitories. The area surrounding the central core of the city was still the heart of the city's workshops. It included nearly one-fifth of the total population of Birmingham, and provided work for over one-third.[3] There was relatively little travelling across the city centre, and not very much travelling between the centre and the outer industrial districts. For most travellers the city centre was the terminus.

This was probably true of the other forms of travel besides the journey to and from work. Housewives and children were compelled to travel into the centre of the city not only for certain forms of shopping, and entertainment, but also for communal facilities, including hospitals and clinics. No system of branches or sub-departments could completely obviate this difficulty. It was part of the price—considered by many to be an acceptable price—of living in a large city.

That the price was not too high was maintained by the Birmingham representatives in their evidence before the Royal Commission on the Geographical Distribution of Industrial Population in May 1938. They stressed their conviction that Birmingham was not too large, and that a great well-ordered city had real advantages over scattered communities or smaller towns in providing services for the health and welfare of its inhabitants. Some of the advantages of largeness lay in the

---

[1] J. N. Jackson, 'The Regional Functions and Sphere of Influence of Birmingham', in *Birmingham and its Regional Setting* (1950), p. 331.
[2] *Eighty Thousand Adolescents* (1950), pp. 35–36.
[3] *When We Build Again*, p. 65.

provision of amenities. The journey to leisure is usually more attractive than the journey to work, and Birmingham's leisure activities in 1938 had changed as much as anything else, when compared with fifty years before.

## III

The emphasis on mass entertainment and mass leisure activity was more marked in Birmingham in 1938 than it had been fifty years before, although small groups of people with highly distinctive tastes had probably increased in numbers and widened in social background as a result of the development of education and the increased amount of working-class leisure time available. Certainly women were taking a more active part in all forms of social activity, from mass entertainment, including sport, to group action. It was no longer true in 1938 that women kept to the home or to the shops, while men went to the football match. Women played a very important part in Birmingham industry, and they were determined to secure the social pleasures of Birmingham as well.

Sport, especially football, played a big part in the life of the local community. Watching games was more attractive than playing them. The membership of the tennis, golf, bowling, football, and cricket clubs of the city was estimated at less than 5 per cent. of its inhabitants,[1] but the number of spectators watching Aston Villa, Birmingham, and West Bromwich Albion alone ran into many thousands each week, and the number of words used in a week in conversation to describe the state of local sport would fill more space than several histories of Birmingham.

The local football clubs had grown from tiny amateur associations to enormous professional organizations, well established and renowned in English football. The Aston Villa Club was founded in 1874 in connexion with Aston Villa Wesleyan Chapel. In those days, before the foundation of the Football League, it was on one occasion content to play fifteen a side against a rugby club to keep a fixture, and for its first pitch in Wellington Road, Perry Barr, it paid only £5 rent in its first year.[2] After the switch to professionalism in 1885 and the move to Villa Park in 1896–7,

---

[1] N. Tiptaft, *So This is Birmingham* (1947), p. 97.
[2] F. Ward, *The Story of Aston Villa* (1948).

the club prospered—in 1896-7 it won both cup and league—
and by 1938 it had gained most of the honours the game had to
offer—six times winners of the F.A. Cup, six times winners of
the League Championship, six times runners-up to the League
Champions, and in 1938, after a lamented relegation, champions of the Second Division. Birmingham City, founded in 1875
by a few pioneers attached to Trinity Church, had a somewhat
similar, though less well known, story of progress. In 1890 its
wages bill amounted to £70 for a full season; in 1938 this figure
had risen to £9,000. Not so many honours had been won, but
the club had established itself in the hearts of its many supporters. A third club, West Bromwich Albion, had once been
League Champion and had won the F.A. Cup three times.

Association football was the mass sport of the Midlands. It
had driven out older and sometimes fiercer forms of sport, which
still lingered in the nineteenth century. Although it was challenged by the growth of greyhound racing, the first Birmingham
track having been opened in 1927, it had successfully overcome
the earlier challenge of horse-racing. Before 1900 there were
several horse-race courses within a twenty-mile radius of Birmingham, which by 1938 had become extinct. Football had
established itself as a game for large crowds, for perpetual conversation, and indirectly for the most widespread gambling of
the twentieth century. Football pools grew enormously in the
1930's. During the football season of 1934-5 they took a weekly
average of £700,000, and in 1936 this figure was doubled. In
1937 a special mail train ran from Liverpool to Birmingham
carrying 235,000 football coupons each week for the Birmingham area.[1]

The summer game—cricket—maintained its hold, although
its milieu and embellishments were entirely different from those
of football. County cricket at Edgbaston attracted far fewer
spectators than football at St. Andrew's or Villa Park, but it
excited almost as much discussion and local interest. In 1895
Warwickshire County Cricket Club entered first-class cricket,
stimulating interest in a game which in mid-Victorian Birmingham had occupied 'an unimportant position among local sports'.[2]
By 1938, when large numbers of local clubs and leagues had come
into existence, cricket was more of a 'people's summer pastime'

[1] *E.D.*, 20 September 1937.
[2] R. K. Dent, *The Making of Birmingham* (1894), p. 543.

PLATE XLIII

The Aston Villa Football Team, 1896–7

F.A. CUP-WINNERS 1896–7 AND CHAMPIONS, DIV. I (THE DOUBLE-EVENT TEAM)

(*Back row*) G. B. Ramsay (*Secretary*), J. Grierson (*Trainer*), H. Spencer, J. Whitehouse, Mr. Margoshis, A. Evans, J. Crabtree, Mr. J. Lees, Mr. C. Johnston

(*Front row*) Dr. V. Jones, J. Cowan, C. Athersmith, J. Campbell, J. Devey (*Capt.*), F. Wheldon, S. Smith, J. Reynolds, Mr. F. W. Rinder (*Vice-Chairman*)

*Div. 1 League Cup*

*F.A. Cup (original)*

PLATE XLIV

The Musical Festival, 1912

than it had been fifty years before. The County Cricket Club was probably one of the few local organizations which directed the loyalty of masses of people inside Birmingham to the county of which the city formed a part.

While sport of all kinds, in addition to football and cricket, was appealing increasingly to the people of Birmingham in the inter-war years, other forms of mass entertainment were developing rapidly as well. The wireless was revolutionizing home life, and Birmingham itself had become the wireless capital of the Midlands, from the time of the first broadcast under the 2WR sign from the General Electric Company's works at Witton in November 1922. Over 280,000 people in the Birmingham area had wireless licences in 1938. At the same time, the cinema was becoming the Mecca of the city crowds. 'I have often wondered what they used to do with their evenings before moving pictures were invented', wrote a local commentator in 1936.[1] In 1937–8 five new cinemas were opened, one of them holding 2,500 people, and four were in course of building. There were over eighty cinemas in all, and it was considered doubtful whether any provincial town in England had a larger number of cinemas in proportion to the population.[2] They provided accommodation for over 115,000 people.[3]

The cinema in Birmingham, like football, had a chequered history from humble and picturesque beginnings. The pioneer was Wally Jeffs, who for many years had conducted at Curzon Hall a Christmas entertainment which combined music-hall turns with a panorama and travelogue. He introduced short cinematograph films on a tiny screen, and made some local films on topics like the Birmingham University Degree Day celebrations.

It was not until 1909 that the first cinema building was built. The early halls were far from palaces, although they sometimes bore that name. They were usually long narrow rooms with the screen at one end and the projection machinery at the other. Many of them lost money, and it was not until the First World War and just after it that the cinema became a habit. By then Charlie Chaplin had been introduced to the cinema audiences

---

[1] P. Marshall, 'After Office Hours. No. 1, Going to the Pictures', in *B.W.P.*, 28 February 1935.

[2] *B.G.*, Special Number, *Birmingham Charter Centenary Celebrations* (1938).

[3] *B.G.*, 21 January 1939.

as 'the greatest laughter-maker of our time', and Birmingham had been offered the opportunity not only of seeing him but of admiring early classics like *The Birth of a Nation*, shown at the Scala during the First World War.

By 1938 there were many different types of cinemas in the city, ranging from the central super-cinemas, with their neon lights, thick carpets, and expensive foyers, to the old picture palaces, still surviving, as the older inns survived, as monuments to a not very distant past. There were many suburban cinemas too, some of them super-cinemas, but the centre had the pull. Its seats were more expensive, but it showed films 'earliest' and added the element of ritual to that of habit. There were also in the centre of the city news cinemas, Birmingham leading the way in 1932 over the rest of the provinces.

Although the cinema was most important as a form of mass entertainment, it is significant that a small group of people in Birmingham attempted to treat it as an art form. The first informal meeting of what later became the Birmingham Film Society was held in 1930,[1] one year after the introduction of talking pictures. Like the supporters of film societies in other parts of the country, its members struggled to seek the best in films, not only the best that had been made, but the best that could be made, if the cinema were to be treated as an opportunity and a challenge as well as a box office with a projector attached.

In the story of the Birmingham theatre in the inter-war years the same contrast between standard mass entertainment and the quest for quality can be traced, perhaps a more significant theme in the history of entertainment than the more familiar story of the impact of the cinema on the theatre. While Birmingham increased the volume of its mass entertainment, the Birmingham Repertory Theatre indulged in daring experiments like the production of Shakespeare's *Cymbeline* in modern dress, in which the ancient Britons wore evening dress at Court, lounge suits in the day-time, and khaki when they went to war.

There were several theatres in Birmingham in 1938, among them the Theatre Royal, going back to 1774; the Alexandra, first opened in 1901, as the Palace of Delights; the Hippodrome, Birmingham's leading music hall, formerly known as the Tower Circus of Varieties; the Empire, which recalled memories of Day's Concert Hall; the Prince of Wales, which went back

[1] See T. C. Kemp, 'Film Society History', in the *B.P.*, 30 September 1948.

to 1856,[1] and was to be one of the victims of the air attacks
of the Second World War; and the Birmingham Repertory
Theatre, opened with Barry Jackson's production of *Twelfth
Night* in 1913.

Each of these theatres contributed in its own way to the entertainment of Birmingham. The Theatre Royal, which had once
held a monopoly of theatrical productions, was renowned for its
pantomime, as was the Alexandra, which also offered seasons
of repertory. The Hippodrome was the first Birmingham hall to
give twice-nightly performances, and along with the Empire
and the Aston Hippodrome maintained the traditions of popular
music hall when they were challenged by the cinema. The Prince
of Wales Theatre, which was managed for a time by Philip Rod-
way, who had been manager of the Theatre Royal, passed into
the hands of Emile Littler. The towering personality of the
Birmingham Repertory Theatre was Sir Barry Jackson, who
built his theatre at his own expense, subsidized it for years, and
finally made it well known throughout the world as a nursery
for dramatists and actors. In face of severe difficulties Jackson
made Birmingham proud of its repertory theatre, and its history
has been aptly described as 'the story of Barry Jackson versus
Birmingham'.[2] From the start, the factor determining production
never was 'Is it likely to pay?' but always 'Is it worth doing?'

The Birmingham Repertory Theatre had its ups and downs—
there was a time at the end of the First World War when the
audience at the theatre did not equal in numbers the actors on
the stage—but after the serious crisis of 1924, when the Birmingham Civic Society stepped in to guarantee its future, and the
financial reorganization of 1934, the Theatre established itself
as a local institution. The same spirit which it had shown in
its pioneer amateur days before the First World War, when
it began its productions in St. Jude's Mission Hall, was being
maintained by new amateur groups like the Crescent Theatre
and the Highbury Little Theatre. At the same time, from the
opposite side of the curtain the First Nighter Club was collecting
a body of 'discriminating play-goers', who wished to establish
'the right relationship between audience and stage'.

The ranks of the discriminating could be marshalled together

---

[1] It began as a music hall in 1856, and in 1863 was called the Prince of Wales
Operetta House in honour of the marriage of the Prince of Wales.
[2] T. C. Kemp, *The Birmingham Repertory Theatre* (1948), p. 2.

throughout all the different sectors of Birmingham's cultural and artistic life, from the frontiers of culture and entertainment to the frontiers of education and art. Times had changed, old institutions had gone, but an attempt was made to maintain and develop taste. This was as true of music as it was of the theatre, and any picture of the twentieth century which ignores this feature of the age lapses into propaganda. There were in the city in 1938 thirteen Art Clubs and twenty-two Musical Societies.

Before the First World War one of the most important features of Birmingham's musical life had been the Triennial Musical Festival, beginning in 1768 and reaching its finale in 1912. Large sums of money were handed over by the Festival organizers to the General Hospital, and widespread interest was taken in the performance of great choral works, not only well-loved ones like the *Messiah*, but new ones like Elgar's *Dream of Geronius*, given its first performance in 1900. Even before 1900 the Festival was being threatened by apathy, and although it was killed by the First World War, new musical events of a more regular character began to take its place. In 1918 popular Sunday Orchestral Concerts, instituted by Matthews, were the precursors of the concerts of the City Orchestra, set up in 1919 and subsidized by the Council. An annual season of thirty weeks, from October to May, was arranged in the form of popular Saturday and Sunday evening concerts, mid-week Symphony Concerts, and evenings devoted to light music. By 1938 it had extended the range of its activities by educational work in the schools and by visits to neighbouring towns. A section of it was engaged as the orchestra of the B.B.C. Midland Regional Station. The Orchestra had been a favourite scheme of Neville Chamberlain: it was the first of its kind to be established in the country, and although many people felt that there was a place for the Musical Festivals as well, there was little doubt that the work of the Orchestra corresponded more closely with the needs of the times than the spectacular festivals of Victorian England.

Entertainment and culture were more widely spread out than a hundred years before, and the demand was no longer for gigantic special occasions but for services in constant supply. A large city demanded neon lights to blaze each night rather than fireworks to crackle two or three times each decade. And for those who cared little for the bright lights, the football crowds, the dance-halls, the skating-rinks, or the greyhound-tracks, the city had more to offer in the form of societies, meetings, and clubs than at any period in its history. One of them, the Civic Society, founded in 1918, aimed at uniting the citizens 'who desire to stimulate a deeper concern in the beauty of their city, and a regard for the study and preservation of the best things of the past'.

Women were now allowed to join in most societies on equal terms with men, and, what was an equally significant trend in the mass age of the twentieth century, a special place was being found for 'youth'. Much was made in the inter-war years of 'the coming generation' as the hope of the future: youth was picked out from the rest of the population and given its own pedestal.

The trend had begun before 1914, indeed before 1900, although when the new century began no more than 3,000 youths out of 86,000 resident in Greater Birmingham were attached to youth movements of any kind other than Sunday Schools. Two sorts of organizations developed: the uniformed, like the Boys' Brigade—the first branch of which was set up in 1889—or the Boy Scouts, whose Birmingham Association was set up in 1909, one year after the publication of Baden-Powell's *Scouting for Boys*, and the non-uniformed, like the boys' clubs. By 1914 about 19,000 youths were attached to youth bodies. Many of the movements aimed not only at widening the horizons of youth and tapping its energies, but at inculcating a deep and practical religious sense, which would safeguard spiritual values in the future.

After the end of the war the different organizations were more closely co-ordinated, particularly after the foundation of the Girls' Union in 1919 and the Birmingham Federation of Boys' Clubs in 1928. By 1938, although only 40 per cent. of the nation's youth were attached to youth organizations,[1] Birmingham had developed a mesh of activities which offered a complete contrast to the situation in the nineteenth century. The way was prepared for a more vigorous drive in the Second World War, with youth far more willingly accepted at the helm than ever before. Organizations were flourishing which saved youth from the streets or from commercial mass entertainment, and offered them new perspectives in their leisure.

[1] *Eighty Thousand Adolescents*, p. 1.

## IV

In the great city of work and pleasure, both religion and politics sometimes seemed to play a less important part than they had done before. It is difficult to generalize about religion in the inter-war world even against the background of a city. Birmingham retained and extended its old religious institutions, adapting many outward forms to meet new needs, developing new forms of services to attract non-worshippers, indulging in a variety of current controversies concerning life and faith, and widening the range of 'outside' activities, organized around the churches and chapels. The changed balance of population between the centre and the periphery produced a new range of problems, which were being dealt with in 1938. Although religion did not obtrude so obviously as it had done in the nineteenth century, when it acted as the great dynamic in city development, and although many of the tendencies of the times encouraged increasing secularization, the churches and chapels still acted as focal points of their districts, and the values they taught influenced the daily conduct of thousands of citizens. At the same time powerful new religious leaders emerged who preached Christianity to a new generation.

Politics were directly affected by the 'rise of the masses' and by the extension of the franchise to women. Parties had to become large-scale national bodies, organized locally, rather than federations of local associations organized nationally. To organize effectively they had to develop club facilities, special services for women and youth, field days and rallies, as well as traditional types of meetings and canvassing. Against the background of social change, the Labour party took the place of the Liberal party as the second party both in the country and in the city, but while there were marked political ups and downs in England as a whole, Birmingham remained a stronghold of Unionism down to 1938.

In general elections the total electorate increased from 427,085 in 1918, of whom 165,839 were women, to 662,967 in 1937, of whom 352,661 were women. At the Election of 1924 Labour won one of the twelve Birmingham seats, the first it had managed to capture, and pressed Neville Chamberlain to a very close fight in Ladywood, which he won, after several recounts, with a majority of 77. In 1929 it won four of the twelve seats, and polled over 40 per cent. of the votes cast, but this was the inter-war high-water mark. At the election of 1931, fought in an atmosphere of 'patriotic fever and national fear',[1] all twelve seats were won by Unionists, Labour's share of the poll dropping to less than 27 per cent.; and in 1935 there was again another complete Unionist triumph, although Labour's share of the votes cast rose to about 35 per cent. 'Labour in Birmingham has little reason to feel proud of the General Election', wrote the Labour party's *Annual Report*.[2]

In local elections, where national party issues and organizations were beginning to play a more important part, the story is less simple. At the end of the war there was a swing towards Labour, as elsewhere, particularly after the post-war slump. In 1921 Labour did exceptionally well in the municipal elections, securing ten seats, including six gains, and in 1926 there was another peak, after the General Strike, when twelve seats were won, including eight gains, on a low poll, and Labour as a result held 30 places out of 120 on the Council. The Unionists had several local strongholds, where contested elections were rare. They included Edgbaston, where there were only three contested elections between 1921 and 1938, Moseley and King's Heath, and Sparkhill. Even when the Labour party was increasing its activities, it could make little impression on these areas.

The economic depression produced a marked swing to the Unionists in 1930 and 1931, the Unionists winning heavily on high polls. There was a pronounced Labour reaction in 1932, when Labour polled 10,000 more votes than the Unionists, and secured 13 seats, but in the four years before 1938 the Unionists were in a very strong position, safe and secure in local life, with 83 councillors and 20 aldermen in 1938 as against Labour's 20 councillors and 7 aldermen. There were only 3 Liberals and 3 Independents on the Council, and the attempt by small political groups like the Communists to secure a place on the Council had always failed, usually ignominiously.

There was some local discussion concerning the effects of the redistribution of the city's population on local politics. The newly built-up wards on the outskirts of the city, with the exception of Bournville, polled well below the city average, which was itself extremely low in 1936 and 1937. There seemed to be some evidence that the new housing-estate areas lacked a natural

[1] *Birmingham Trades Council and Labour Party Report*, 1931–2.　　[2] Ibid., 1935–6.

interest in politics, and that party organization had not yet been developed on new lines to meet the difficult tasks of organizing highly dispersed urban wards. The excitement of a fiercely contested election like those in Market Hall or St. Mary's before 1914 seemed to be lacking, and local government itself no longer appealed to electors and would-be councillors in the same magnetic way that it had done in the nineteenth century. In 1938 itself, the year of the Charter Centenary celebrations, there was a marked increase in the total poll, but few could have pretended that the obstacles in the way of the continued vitality of local politics had been knocked down. At election times many candidates had to spend a large proportion of their time and energy in persuading and even luring their known supporters to the poll, rather than in influencing local opinion on local issues or in convincing doubtful electors of the rightness of their cause: even when local elections were exciting it was usually because they were considered as 'dress rehearsals' of national struggles or 'indications of the way in which the tide was moving'.

There was one force in local life which came perhaps to matter more as the interest in local elections tended to diminish —the force of the Birmingham press. The correspondence columns often provoked livelier discussions on local issues than did meetings at election times, and editorial comment provoked argument and counter-argument and kept interest keen.

In 1938 Birmingham was one of the few provincial cities to have two morning and two evening papers: it shared with Manchester, Plymouth, Newcastle, and Glasgow the rare honour of also having a Sunday newspaper of its own. The Birmingham newspapers fell into two distinct groups—the *Birmingham Post* and the *Birmingham Mail* on the one hand and the *Birmingham Gazette*, the *Evening Despatch*, and the *Sunday Mercury* on the other hand. The first pair of papers was the property of Sir Charles Hyde, who inherited them from his uncle, while the second group, of which the *Birmingham Gazette* at one time had belonged to Lord Northcliffe, had become part of the Westminster Press group, a big provincial chain.

The *Birmingham Gazette* could trace back its history to the first publication of the paper by Thomas Aris in 1741 on an old hand-press in a small room behind a shop in High Street. In 1862 it became a daily. From 1929 onwards it was being produced, along with the other papers in its group, along mass lines at

Newspaper House, and being read by well over one-tenth of the population of the city. The *Birmingham Post*, an outgrowth of the *Birmingham Journal*, maintained the high standards of provincial journalism, which it had built up since its establishment as a daily in 1858, while the *Birmingham Mail*, begun as a halfpenny paper in 1870, was one of the most important evening papers in the provinces.

The different papers had tussled in the past about big local and national issues like Home Rule; they did not find themselves drawn into the same violent conflicts in the 1930's, when the Labour party had to rely on its weekly, the *Town Crier*, and on the national *Daily Herald*, which according to one estimate was read by 16·8 per cent. of families in the Midlands.[1] On the whole, the local daily papers held firm against heavy penetration by the national dailies, although it was the evening papers, more strongly placed relatively to possible competitors, which provided most of the local news and views. If the vigorous editorials of the late nineteenth century had given way to milder twentieth-century comment, they had not lost the sense of excitement and controversy.

A mere scanning of the pages of the local press, including its notices and advertisement columns, qualifies the picture of apathy concerning both religion and politics which some prophets of gloom have portrayed in the darkest colours. They bring to life the picture of a thriving community, the members of which still had many of the characteristics which Hutton had noted when he wrote his *History*. 'I am surprised at the people. They were a species I had never seen; they possessed a vivacity I had never beheld; I had been among dreamers, but now I saw men awake.'

v

The influence of the Birmingham press, like many other local institutions, was felt outside the geographical boundaries of the city. Birmingham was the centre of a region in 1938 as well as a city in itself, and this had an important effect on the character of its life, particularly in the centre of the city. Central Birmingham provided a market and financial centre for a large area. It offered specialist services in education, medicine, law, and industry, as well as supporting the regional offices of government

[1] *P.E.P. Report on the British Press* (1938).

departments and national organizations. Above all it had shops, cinemas, theatres, and sports arenas, which drew in men and women from all over the Midlands.

As far as the provision of these regional amenities was concerned, there were some deficiencies in the 1930's. The Census returns of 1931 show that the number of people in Birmingham engaged in the professions, in entertainment and sport, and personal service was lower than the national average. In the case of private domestic service, laundries, hotels, inns, and restaurants—particularly the first two—Birmingham figures were significantly less than for the country as a whole. Only in the case of funeral undertaking was the local service staffed by more workers than in England as a whole. In both medicine and education Birmingham had fewer professional representatives as a proportion of the total working population than the country as a whole. It has been suggested that the lack of services and amenities indicated by these figures kept many managers and salaried staff from working in the area, and explained the drift to London.[1] Certainly the function of the city as a distributor of specific services can be over-emphasized. Its primary role was as a capital of industry.

As far as distribution was concerned Birmingham, too, had fewer workers engaged in it, relative to the total working population, than the whole of the country, although its shops were far more varied and attractive than in most parts of the surrounding district. It was also true that although the central shopping area remained small, many shops did very large business. They included old family businesses, some of which had become limited companies at a later stage of their development, or which had been converted from one-line concerns into department stores. Some of these shops retained the intimate atmosphere of the nineteenth century, and prided themselves on their known clientele. Alongside these old-established firms there were many great branches of national shopping enterprises, some of them going back to the last century when the advertising methods of vast emporia were only in their infancy. Finally, there were independent specialist shops with a well-known reputation. Anderton noted in 1901 how the character of Birmingham's shops was constantly changing.[2] Many of the most important

[1] *Conurbation* (1948), p. 111.
[2] T. Anderton, *A Tale of One City* (1900), pp. 163–84.

changes came after his day, with the growth of mail-order business and telephone communications. When the first telephone exchange was opened in 1879 there were twelve subscribers; by 1936 there were 100,000, including over 40,000 residential service telephones. The growth of special delivery services and telephone orders revolutionized shopping methods. So, too, did cheap excursion tickets, which made a day's shopping in the city attractive to people for miles around, and which gave a great advantage to those shops which provided shelter, colour, warmth, and refreshment in addition to the wares they normally displayed.

With the great increase in the number of shops and the changed character of their trading, the position of the old markets was altered. The granting of Birmingham's first market charter in 1166 had set the town on its progress as a distributive centre. It first became important as a market town. From the time that the Town Council bought the market rights in 1851 many improvements were made as a result of the provision of bigger premises. The Market Hall, situated in High Street, had first been built in 1835, but in 1869 the Fish Market was opened, and was further extended in 1878 and 1882. In 1883 the Smithfield Wholesale Fruit and Vegetable Market was erected, and further extended in 1892 and 1903. It had a wide range of customers, who found the market cheaper than Manchester and unencumbered by porterage charges as at Covent Garden. The City Meat Market and Abattoirs were developed on the Bradford Street site from 1891, and with an eye to further extension the Corporation acquired an adjoining property in the middle 30's. General extension orders were considered, as a result of the increased trade arising out of the growth of the city and the central traffic congestion, and the Markets and Fairs Committee of the Council drew up a scheme and acquired land for the building of a new fruit and vegetable market on a greatly extended scale. The markets continued to attract both customers and vendors, including hundreds of market gardeners from the surrounding Midlands area. The oldest market in the city, in the Bull Ring, was still the most crowded place in the city. Held every Tuesday, Thursday, and Saturday, for the sale of poultry, rabbits, eggs, flowers, and shrubs, and sheltering under the shadow of St. Martin's Church, it was the most colourful and exciting corner of Birmingham.

The extent to which Birmingham could offer services to the

surrounding region depended not only on their extent and character, but also on the accessibility of nearby districts to the city centre. The rapid growth of road transport had changed Birmingham's relationship to surrounding areas. As bus services grew in frequency and importance, accessibility to bus-routes became one of the most important factors in the daily lives of people who lived in the nearby areas. Nearness to a bus-route affected the growth and character of local shops and entertainments. The time of the last bus determined the ability of citizens of many areas to enjoy evening functions in the city, like theatres or cinemas and society meetings. Buses were especially important in the Birmingham city area itself and had supplanted earlier dependence on trains. In 1937, for instance, a census taken at the Austin works showed that 27 per cent. of the workers travelled by tram, 25 per cent. by either bus or coach, and only 8 per cent. by train.[1] As far as trains were concerned—and this is important in estimating Birmingham's regional influence—a relatively distant station with fast trains was often nearer in time to the city than a local station with only slow trains. This affected choice of sites for homes outside the city as well as proximity to services.

J. N. Jackson has recently written that places which were more than ninety minutes from the city centre by any form of public transport, and villages more than three miles from a Birmingham bus-route or railway station, were unlikely to make regular use of the facilities and amenities provided by the city.[2] This assessment would leave out of the city's direct sphere of influence areas to the north-east of Tamworth and Nuneaton, to the north of Lichfield and Cannock, to the west of Wolverhampton, Stourbridge, Kidderminster, and Worcester, to the south-west of Redditch, and to the south-east of Stratford, Leamington, and Coventry. It would leave in a region far wider than the city's administrative boundaries, stretching across the whole of the Birmingham Plateau out to the river valleys beyond.

In 1938, in his evidence before the Royal Commission on the Geographical Distribution of Industrial Population, Alderman Roberts disclaimed any desire to extend Birmingham's boundaries still farther into any of the parts of this broad region, which looked to it as a sort of capital, although he recognized the need

[1] Quoted by J. N. Jackson, loc. cit., p. 328.
[2] Ibid., p. 330.

for co-operation with adjacent authorities.[1] 'The City Council has already enough to do', he said. He disowned the word 'conurbation'—as applying to the 300-square-mile area of land round about—on the grounds that Birmingham's interests were different in character from those of the area that adjoined it, and that a depression in the Black Country need not necessarily lead to a depression in Birmingham. Despite the existence of the Midland Joint Town Planning Council, an advisory body, it was only after 1939 that a conjunction of new forces tended to change the approach to problems of regional adjustment, but the story of readjustment is still an unfinished one, which cannot yet be seen in historical perspective.[2]

## VI

Birmingham in 1938 was proud of itself and of its century-old record. It had good reasons for 'our own good conceit of ourselves'.[3] It could turn behind its record in local government to its development as a great community. So long as it faced its problems squarely, and brought accumulated experience and energy to bear on their solution, it could still vindicate the city's motto of 'Forward'.

The 'it' is misleading. A city is not an entity in itself which can be divorced from the citizens who make it up. The forces which create social change can be described in anonymous terms, but their speed of motion and sometimes their direction depend on groups and on personalities. With the spread of democracy and the extension of social rights, the future of Birmingham depended upon the representatives of all classes of its citizens. It also depended upon continued leadership and the recognition of new tasks ahead.

Above all else, the future of Birmingham depended upon the work carried out in its factories and warehouses. Dickens's famous description of Birmingham in *Pickwick Papers* had stressed the dominance of work in the noisy self-assertive Birmingham of stage-coach days. 'The streets were thronged with workpeople,' he wrote, 'the hum of labour resounded from every house, lights gleamed from the long casement windows in the

---

[1] Some of the difficulties—particularly financial ones—in regional co-operation were discussed by H. Humphries in the *Local Government Journal*, 22 June 1929.

[2] See W. A. Robson, The *Development of Local Government* (1948 edn.).

[3] *B.M.*, 20 May 1938.

attic stories, and the whirl of wheels and noise of machinery shook the trembling walls.' In the age of the motor-car Birmingham was a bigger, a tidier, and, despite the roll of traffic, a more quiet city. Where there had been the rushing of steam and the blazing of fires, there was electricity, and 'the harsh music which arose from every quarter' could certainly not be heard among the housing estates. But work went on, even though the hours were shortened and staggered, and it had to go on incessantly if Birmingham was to remain a capital of industry. One of the two main problems of the twentieth century was the integration of work into the complex life of a giant community. The other was how to secure the active interest in the affairs of the city of those who worked there. 'Men come together in cities', wrote Aristotle, 'in order to live: they remain together in order to live the good life.' If Birmingham was to continue to prosper, it needed to be a city where men wished to live, and where some of them at least could learn to live their lives to the full.

Each generation produces its own problems. In the early nineteenth century the industrial city provided a challenge to government and to society. It posed problems of public health, of law and order, of smooth administration; and, until these problems were solved, it remained a dark and mysterious place to those who lived in a different environment. The crudities of urban life have gone, but the city still offers a challenge in the mass world of the twentieth century. The response to the challenge will vary from place to place, for generalizations are dangerous concerning either the industrial town or the city of suburbs. The response of Birmingham will be conditioned by its past, by the nature of its inheritance, as much as by hope in its future. As Bunce, the greatest of Birmingham journalists, and no mean historian, said on receiving the Freedom of the City in 1899:

There are towns which possess a living personality peculiar to themselves; one which by some mysterious power they impress, generation after generation, upon their people, endowing them with characteristic qualities of independent judgement, of energy and courage, of straightforward frankness, and of that sense of public duty which creates and guides the highest form of citizenship. Birmingham is one of these.

# APPENDIX A
## MAYORS AND LORD MAYORS OF BIRMINGHAM (1838–1938)

| | | | |
|---|---|---|---|
| 1838 | William Scholefield. | 1876 | George Baker. |
| 1839–40 | Philip Henry Muntz. | 1877 | William Kenrick. |
| 1841 | Samuel Beale. | 1878 | Jesse Collings. |
| 1842 | James James. | 1879–80 | Richard Chamberlain. |
| 1843 | Thomas Weston. | 1881 | Thomas Avery. |
| 1844 | Thomas Phillips. | 1882 | William White. |
| 1845 | Henry Smith. | 1883 | William Cook. |
| 1846 | Robert Martineau. | 1884–85 | Thomas Martineau. |
| 1847 | Charles Geach. | 1886 | Sir Thos. Martineau, Kt. |
| 1848 | Samuel Thornton. | 1887 | Maurice Pollack. |
| 1849–50 | William Lucy. | 1888 | Richard Cadbury Barrow. |
| 1851 | Henry Smith. | | |
| 1852 | Henry Hawkes. | 1889–90 | Francis Corder Clayton. |
| 1853 | James Baldwin. | 1891–92 | Edward Lawley Parker. |
| 1854 | John Palmer. | 1893 | George James Johnson. |
| 1855 | T. R. T. Hodgson. | 1894 | Thos. Stratton Fallows. |
| 1856–57 | John Ratcliff. | 1895 | James Smith (*First Lord Mayor*). |
| 1858 | Sir John Ratcliff, Kt. | | |
| 1859 | Thomas Lloyd. | 1896 | Sir James Smith, Kt. |
| 1860 | Arthur Ryland. | 1897–98 | Charles Gabriel Beale. |
| 1861 | Henry Manton. | 1899 | Charles Gabriel Beale. |
| 1862 | Charles Sturge. | 1900 | Samuel Edwards. |
| 1863 | William Holliday. | 1901 | John Henry Lloyd. |
| 1864 | Henry Wiggin. | 1902 | Hallewell Rogers. |
| 1865 | Edwin Yates. | 1903 | Sir Hallewell Rogers, Kt. |
| 1866 | George Dixon.[1] | 1904 | Rowland Hill Berkeley.[3] |
| 1867 | Thomas Avery. | | Charles Gabriel Beale. |
| 1868 | Henry Holland. | 1905 | Alfred John Reynolds. |
| 1869 | Thomas Prime. | 1906–07 | Henry James Sayer. |
| 1870 | G. Braithwaite Lloyd. | 1908 | Sir George Hamilton Kenrick, Kt. |
| 1871 | John Sadler. | | |
| 1872 | Ambrose Biggs. | 1909–10 | William Henry Bowater. |
| 1873–74 | Joseph Chamberlain. | 1911 | William Henry Bowater. |
| 1875 | Joseph Chamberlain.[2] | 1912–13 | Ernest Martineau.[4] |

[1] Mr. Avery was elected on the resignation of Mr. Dixon, July 1867.
[2] Mr. Baker was elected on the resignation of Mr. Chamberlain, 16 June 1876.
[3] Died 13 April 1905.
[4] Mr. Bowater was elected on the resignation of Mr. Martineau, Sept. 1914.

| | | | |
|---|---|---|---|
| 1913 | William Henry Bowater. | 1924–25 | Percival Bower, M.B.E. |
| 1914 | William Henry Bowater. | 1926–27 | Alfred Henry James, C.B.E. |
| 1915–16 | Arthur Neville Chamberlain.[1] | 1928 | Wilfred Byng Kenrick. |
| 1916 | Arthur David Brooks. | 1929 | Martin Lewis Lancaster. |
| 1917 | Arthur David Brooks. | 1930 | Walter Willis Saunders. |
| 1918 | Sir David Brooks, Kt. | 1931 | John Bedford Burman. |
| 1919–20 | William Adlington Cadbury. | 1932–33 | Horace Edward Goodby. |
| | | 1934–35 | Samuel John Grey. |
| 1921 | David Davis. | 1936 | Harold Roberts. |
| 1922 | Sir David Davis, Kt. | 1937 | Ernest Robert Canning. |
| 1923 | Thomas Oswald Williams. | 1938 | James Crump. |

[1] Mr. Brooks was elected on the resignation of Mr. Chamberlain, Jan. 1917.

## APPENDIX B
## FREEMEN OF BIRMINGHAM

THE Honorary Freedom of Boroughs Act of 1885 provided that borough councils might admit to be honorary freemen of the borough persons of distinction or those who had rendered eminent service to the borough. The Councils were to choose their freemen at meetings called specially for the purpose, and not less than two-thirds of the members present and voting had to give their support to the proposals.

The following is the list of the Freemen honoured by Birmingham.

1. Joseph Chamberlain (1888).
2. Philip Henry Muntz (1888).
3. Thomas Avery (1892).
4. George Dixon (1898).
5. John Thackray Bunce (1899).
6. Field-Marshal Earl Roberts (1901).
7. Edward Lawley Parker (1904).
8. Jesse Collings (1911).
9. William Kenrick (1911).
10. Francis Corder Clayton (1912).
11. Charles Gabriel Beale (1912).
12. Sir William Henry Bowater (1916).
13. William Morris Hughes (1916).
14. David Lloyd George (1921).
15. Earl Balfour (1922).
16. Sir George Hamilton Kenrick (1923).
17. Sir David Brooks (1923).
18. Sir Austen Chamberlain (1926).
19. Barrow Cadbury (1932).
20. Neville Chamberlain (1932).
21. John Henry Lloyd (1932).
22. William Adlington Cadbury (1938).
23. Wilfred Byng Kenrick (1938).
24. Ernest Martineau (1938).
25. Henry James Sayer (1938).

This list of twenty-five Freemen is an interesting one. Most of the persons chosen to receive the highest honour the city could give had rendered eminent services to the local community. Nineteen of the twenty-five had been Mayors or Lord Mayors of the city. It was fitting that Joseph Chamberlain should be the first to receive the honour, although three other Freemen went back to the pre-Chamberlain era. Philip Henry Muntz had played a big part in promoting and obtaining the grant of the Charter of Incorporation in 1838, and was given his Freedom on the fiftieth anniversary of the day of the signing and sealing of the Charter. The Mayor saluted him as 'one of the founders of our municipal liberty'. Thomas Avery was first elected to the Council in 1862, and George Dixon two years later in 1864. Dixon's record of public service was as remarkable as that of any man who has ever worked for the city. He was Member of Parliament for Birmingham from 1867 to 1876 and for Edgbaston from 1885 until 1898. In addition to his Council work, he was for many years chairman of the Birmingham School Board, and the resolution admitting him to the Freedom declared that the honour was conferred upon him 'in grateful acknowledgement of his eminent public services and in recognition of his untiring energy and devotion in the interests of Elementary Education'.

Apart from these three veterans of the rising city, some of the other Freemen were representatives of the golden age of Chamberlain's Birmingham. John Thackray Bunce, for forty years Editor of the *Birmingham Daily Post*, and author of the first volumes of the *History of the Corporation*, had played an important part in the proclamation of the civic gospel and in the encouragement of local initiative. Jesse Collings, like both Chamberlain and Bunce, was not a Birmingham man by birth, but he had followed Chamberlain from local life to national public service. William Kenrick, Chamberlain's brother-in-law, served on the Council for forty-four years, as well as representing North Birmingham in Parliament from 1885 to 1899.

A new generation was represented by Edward Lawley Parker, who piloted through the enormous Welsh Water Scheme after the death of Sir Thomas Martineau; Francis Corder Clayton, who, apart from his two years as Lord Mayor, was chairman of the Finance Committee from 1886 to 1913; and Charles Gabriel Beale, who had been elected four times to the Mayoral Chair, and who had played a leader's part both in the Council and in many other walks of Birmingham life. Sir William Bowater had been Lord Mayor three times before 1914 and saw the Greater Birmingham Scheme realized during his mayoralty; he accepted office again after Ernest Martineau had taken up active service at the outbreak of the war. Sir George Kenrick, who had been chairman of the Education Committee from 1903 to 1921, was made a Freeman in 1923, along with Sir David Brooks, who had played an active part in bringing about the extensions of 1911.

Most of the other Freemen of the inter-war years were members of well-known Birmingham families, who had contributed many generations of service. This family basis of civic life distinguished Birmingham from many other large modern communities. Active co-operation in the work of the community began with the family, and was rooted in traditions of kinship. Both Sir Austen and Neville Chamberlain were made Freemen, Sir Austen remarking that although most of his public work had been national and international rather than local, 'Birmingham is in my blood and in my bones, and wherever I am, I shall remain a Birmingham man, and for better or for worse, you must be content to treat me as such'.

Three Chamberlains were made Freemen; so, too, were three Kenricks. There were two Cadburys to represent a third of the city's

PLATE XLV

Charles Gabriel Beale

PLATE XLVI

John Thackray Bunce

leading families. All these men were honoured and renowned for their 'tradition of generous public spirit'. Other Freemen too were representatives of families which had played a continuous part in civic history. John Henry Lloyd, who became a Freeman in 1932, was the 'Father' of the Council, but his father had been Mayor of Birmingham in 1870 and was still a member of the Council during the mayoralty of his son. Another kinsman had been Mayor in 1859. Ernest Martineau was a son of Sir Thomas Martineau, Mayor in 1884–6, and a grandson of Robert Martineau, Mayor in 1846.

These long records of individual and family service provided the social cement for the building of the community of Birmingham: they ensured a continuity, founded on kinship and closeness of association, which is rare in industrial cities. Taken together, they explain much in the local history both of voluntary action and of civic government.

# APPENDIX C
## CHIEF OFFICIALS OF THE CORPORATION OF BIRMINGHAM

### Town Clerks

1838 William Redfern.
1840 Solomon Bray.
1852 William Morgan.
1854 Thomas Standbridge.
1869 Edwin J. Hayes.

1881 Edward Orford Smith.
1908 Sir Ernest Varvill Hiley.
1916 Joseph Beaumont Jones.
1918 Sir Frank Henry Cufaude Wiltshire.

### Borough or City Treasurers

1839 H. Knight.
1852 W. Beaumont.
1858 N. Kimberley.
1867 W. R. Hughes.

1900 T. H. Clare.
1918 A. Collins.
1922 J. R. Johnson.

### Medical Officers of Health

Before 1872 there was no permanent Medical Officer, but Dr. Alfred Hill was Borough Analyst from 1859 to 1872.

1872 Dr. Alfred Hill.
1903 Sir John Robertson.

1927 Dr. H. P. Newsholme.

### Borough or City Engineers and Surveyors

1852 J. Pigott Smith, who from 1838 to 1851 was Surveyor to the Street Commissioners.

1857 William S. Till.
1896 John Price.
1906 H. E. Stilgoe.

1919 Sir Herbert H. Humphries.
1935 H. J. Manzoni.

PLATE XLVII

Sir Ernest Hiley
Town Clerk 1908–1916

PLATE XLVIII

Sir Frank Wiltshire
Town Clerk 1918–1946

## APPENDIX D

# SELECT LIST OF LOCAL ACTS OF PARLIAMENT

1. The Birmingham Improvement Act of 1851 consolidated the governing bodies of the town and transferred local administration entirely to the Town Council, as representing the Corporation of the Borough.
2. The Birmingham Improvement Act of 1861.
3. The Birmingham Corporation (Consolidation) Act of 1883, consolidated the measures of the period between 1851 and 1883, which had been originally embodied in 21 Acts and Orders.
4. The Birmingham Corporation Water Act of 1892.
5. The Birmingham Corporation Water Act of 1896.
6. The Birmingham Corporation Water Act of 1899.
7. The Birmingham Corporation (Stock) Act of 1900.
8. The Birmingham Corporation Water Act of 1902.
9. The Birmingham Corporation Act of 1903.
10. The Birmingham Corporation Act of 1905.
11. The Birmingham Corporation Act of 1907.
12. The Birmingham Corporation Water Act of 1907.
13. The Birmingham Corporation Act of 1912.
14. The Birmingham Corporation Act of 1914.
15. The Birmingham Corporation Act of 1919.
16. The Birmingham Corporation (Tramways) Act of 1919.
17. The Birmingham Corporation Act of 1922.
18. The Birmingham Corporation Act of 1924.
19. The Birmingham Extension Act of 1927.
20. The Birmingham Corporation (Rivers Improvement) Act of 1929.
21. The Birmingham Corporation (General Powers) Act of 1929.
22. The Birmingham Corporation Act of 1935.
23. The Birmingham Corporation Act of 1937.

# APPENDIX E
## ROYAL CIVIC VISITS

1843. Prince Albert came to Birmingham to examine local industries.

1849. Prince Albert visited the Industrial Exhibition in Bingley Hall, and King Edward's Grammar School.

1855. Prince Albert laid the foundation-stone of the Midland Institute.

1858. Queen Victoria, accompanied by Prince Albert, opened Aston Hall and Park.

1885. *27–28 November*. The Prince of Wales opened Jaffray Hospital and the Art Gallery.

1887. *23 March*. Queen Victoria laid the foundation-stone of the Law Courts. The Law Courts were named the Victoria Courts and Small Heath Park was renamed Victoria Park.

1891. *21 July*. The Prince and Princess of Wales opened the Victoria Courts.

1894. *8 September*. The Duke and Duchess of York (later King George V and Queen Mary) laid the foundation-stone of the new General Hospital in Steelhouse Lane.

1897. *7 July*. Princess Christian of Schleswig-Holstein, representing the Queen, opened the General Hospital.

1903. *23 June*. Princess Christian of Schleswig-Holstein laid the foundation-stone of Rowton House.

1909. *7 July*. King Edward VII and Queen Alexandra opened the new buildings of the University of Birmingham.

1913. *23 April*. Princess Louise, Duchess of Argyll, laid the foundation-stone of the Children's Hospital, and unveiled the statue of King Edward.

1917. *11 May*. Princess Marie Louise opened the Y.M.C.A. Hut, Worcester Street.

1919. *21 May*. King George V, accompanied by Queen Mary, opened the Children's Hospital, Ladywood Road, held an investiture, and visited Bournville Model Village.

1920. *14 January*. Prince Henry (later the Duke of Gloucester), on behalf of the King, held an investiture, and visited the Highbury and Uffculme Hospitals.

1921. *1 March*. The Duke of York (later King George VI) visited the British Industries Fair.

*6 June.* Princess Mary visited the Scenic Fair at Bingley Hall, the Instructional Factory for Disabled Men, and the Infant Welfare Centre.

1923. *22 February.* The Duke of York visited the British Industries Fair.

*11–14 June.* The Prince of Wales stayed in Birmingham at Bishop's Croft; and visited a number of industrial towns near Birmingham, including Wolverhampton and Coventry. He inaugurated the Nechells Electricity Works; laid the foundation-stone of the Hall of Memory; received an Address of Welcome in the Town Hall; attended the Scout Rally at Handsworth Park; inspected members of the British Legion; and visited the Industrial Centre, Garrison Lane, for disabled ex-Service men.

1924. *26–27 March.* Princess Marie Louise attended the Symphony Concert given by the City of Birmingham Orchestra; and visited the University and the General Hospital.

*17 May.* Prince Henry visited the British Industries Fair.

1925. *4 July.* Prince Arthur of Connaught opened the Hall of Memory.

1926. *19 February.* The Duke of York visited the British Industries Fair.

*23 February.* The Prince of Wales visited the British Industries Fair, Castle Bromwich, and the Industrial Centre, Garrison Lane.

*30 November.* The Prince of Wales attended the Cattle Show, Bingley Hall; and called at the Hall of Memory and examined the Roll of Honour.

1927. *22 February.* The Prince of Wales visited the British Industries Fair and the Highbury and Uffculme Hospitals.

*20 August.* Queen Mary visited the Birmingham Art Gallery and Aston Hall (staying privately with the Dowager Countess of Bradford).

*2 November.* The Prince of Wales opened the Birmingham–Wolverhampton Road and visited the Royal Cripples' Hospital, Northfield.

1928. *24 February.* King George V and Queen Mary visited the British Industries Fair at Castle Bromwich.

1929. *22 February.* The Duke of York visited the British Industries Fair.

*6 November.* The Duke of York, accompanied by the Duchess of York, opened Kingston Hill Recreation Grounds; visited the Royal Cripples' Hospital; and inaugurated the Electric Power Station, Hams Hall.

1930. *20 February.* Prince George (later the Duke of Kent) visited the British Industries Fair.

1931. *18 February.* Princess Mary and Lord Harewood visited the British Industries Fair.

1931. *11 May*. The Prince of Wales made an industrial tour of Birmingham and the Midland towns, and, in company with Prince George, attended a dinner of business men at the British Industries Fair.

1932. *25 February*. The Prince of Wales visited the British Industries Fair.

1933. *20 February*. The Duke of York visited the British Industries Fair.

*27 November*. Prince George opened the new Head Offices, Municipal Bank, Broad Street.

1934. *27 February*. The Prince of Wales visited the British Industries Fair.

*23 October*. The Prince of Wales laid the foundation-stone of the Hospital Centre, Edgbaston, inspected occupational centres, and visited slum areas.

*29 November*. The Duke and Duchess of Kent drove from Snow Hill Railway Station through central Birmingham (on their honeymoon journey to Himley Hall).

*6 December*. The Duke and Duchess of Kent paid a private visit to the Birmingham Art Gallery.

1935. *23 May*. The Prince of Wales attended the British Industries Fair.

*2 December*. The Duke of Kent visited Birmingham Cattle Show, and opened the new Central Fire Station, Corporation Street.

1938. *14 July*. The Duke and Duchess of Gloucester opened the Hospital Centre and attended a performance of the pageant of Birmingham.

# APPENDIX F
# A NOTE ON FINANCE

BETWEEN 1865 and 1938, in order to keep pace with expanding local needs and with rising national standards, there was an enormous increase in the expenses of local government. The size and character of the expenditure raised new technical and administrative problems in municipal finance, and eventually by slow stages produced a new form of partnership between local and central government.

*Current Income and Expenditure*

Birmingham had four main sources of current income: (*a*) rates, (*b*) trading profits, (*c*) grants-in-aid, and (*d*) payments for the use of specific services.

(*a*) *Rates* were charges levied compulsorily on local citizens to help to cover the expenses incurred in co-operative action for common purposes. At first there were different local rating authorities serving different areas and different purposes. Eventually there was one single city authority. Like all other local bodies, Birmingham had no general authority to raise rates to cover all types of projected expenditure in the same way that Parliament raised taxes for the whole of the country. It could only raise rates for purposes prescribed by statute, and on terms laid down by Parliament. All new burdens on rates were thus covered by local or national Acts of Parliament.

The system of levying rates was the most convenient method of local finance. All that the authorities had to know was (i) the annual value of the properties of the persons liable as ratepayers, normally the rateable value. This might increase either automatically as a result of city growth, or as a result of changes in assessment or methods of valuation; and (ii) the amount of money they wished to raise. If they divided the total requirements by the rateable value, making some allowances for losses in collection, then they arrived at the rate in the pound which had to be levied.

This simple process of arithmetical division was made more complex in practice by the coexistence of different valuation agencies and different categories of exemption. For instance, until the Birmingham Rating Order of 1913, a special Improvement Rate was levied, which afforded higher discount benefits to the owners of small houses compounding for rates than did the Poor and Borough Rates, and exceptional benefits to railway and canal concerns and the occupiers of agricultural land. The distinction between the Poor Rate and the Borough Rate caused additional complications, although from 1853 onwards the same official acted as valuer for the Poor Rate in the parish of Birmingham and for the Corporation, and the tradition was carried on by his son. In 1911, by the City Extension Order, the power of appointing Overseers responsible for the Poor Rate was transferred from the Boards of Guardians of the several parishes to the City Council, and the Council secured and delegated to its Finance Committee effective control over all rating business by electing members of the Finance Committee as Overseers and by appointing the Town Clerk and the City Treasurer to serve the Overseers in the same capacity in which they served the city. As a result of the virtual identity of the Finance Committee and the Overseers it was at last possible to recommend to the Council the levy of a stated rate in the pound instead of a precept for a stated sum of money. Two years later, by the Rating Order of 1913, the Improvement Rate was abolished, so that at last it was no longer necessary to have two distinct funds and two sets of books to cover borough expenditure.

There were further changes leading towards final unification in the 1920's. As a result of the Rating and Valuation Act of 1925, the first Rating and Valuation Committee was appointed by the City Council in March 1926, charged with the duty of levying, collecting, and recovering rates, and with the preparation of draft valuation lists every five years. In 1928/9 the separate Borough and Poor Rates were consolidated, and from 1930 onwards, after the abolition of the Boards of Guardians, the city took over Poor Law administration altogether. Since 1930 there has been one City Rate in Birmingham.

Apart from the consolidation of local rates there was one other important development in Birmingham's approach to rating questions in the inter-war years. The experiment was tried of stabilizing and rationing the amount of money collected from the rates. In March 1921 the Finance Committee recommended to the City Council that instead of levying a rate to meet the estimated amount of expenditure desired by the various spending committees, the Council should work out a precept for an amount, which, along with the Poor Law precept, would be equivalent to a fixed rate in the pound, and that the total precept should be rationed among the various committees. The policy of rate stabilization was accepted by the Council and applied by the Finance Committee from 1923/4 onwards. The main motive was the desire to secure economy and to prevent any further increase in rates. It was also believed that local commercial activity would be encouraged by rate stabilization, and unemployment relieved. From 1923/4 until 1927/8 the rate was fixed at 16s.—in 1865 it had been 7s. 1d.—but after the first revaluation in 1928 under the Rating and Valuation Act of 1925 the rate was reduced to 14s. 6d. in the pound, and this figure was maintained until 1931/2. The economy campaign led to a cutting of expenditure and a further fall of the rate to 14*s*. in the pound, but in 1937 there was an increase to 14*s*. 6*d*. and in 1937/8 to 15*s*.

(*b*) *Trading Profits* were especially important in Birmingham because of the lack of corporate property or revenue and the natural aptitude of business men to consider the implementation of the civic gospel in business terms. After the foundations had been laid by Joseph Chamberlain and built upon in the last twenty years of the nineteenth century, regular annual profits passed to the city from its markets and gas, tramways, and electric supply undertakings. Between 1900 and 1914 over £1,200,000 accrued to the Corporation from these sources. The First World War and the aftermath of the war somewhat changed the previous picture. It was not always possible for the trading undertakings to make contributions, and after 1920 there was a national tendency to limit or prohibit such transfers. From 1924/5 onwards the Finance Committee encouraged the payment of fixed annual contributions for limited periods rather than fluctuating sums of money. At the same time the undertakings themselves consolidated their own reserves rather than contributed to general rate relief, and in 1937/8, for example, when the net profits of the trading undertakings amounted to over £500,000, only £10,000 of this amount was appropriated directly for rate relief.

(*c*) *Grants-in-aid* have become one of the most important sources of local revenue in the twentieth century, but in their early years they were often modest in size and were sometimes opposed by local opinion. It was only with reluctance, for instance, that in 1856 the Birmingham Council accepted by thirty-one votes to nineteen the Police Act which introduced government inspection and offered one-quarter of the costs to boroughs where it was certified that the police had been maintained in a state of efficiency. By 1887 many grants had been given for different specific purposes, most of them on the basis of actual expenditure, some of them on a unit footing, and one, the Education Grant, showing signs of recognition of the needs of specially backward areas.

In 1887 total grants to local authorities had reached such large figures that it was considered necessary to reconsider the whole question of financial relations between central and local government. The Chancellor of the Exchequer, Goschen, in an effort to separate national and local finance, changed the system of allocation. Direct payment from government funds of the principal grants-in-aid except education was discontinued, and in its place the local authorities received the proceeds of certain Assigned Revenues, mainly local taxation licences and probate duties. At first the new revenue provided from the Assigned Revenues was more than sufficient to compensate for the loss of the old grants, but in time the increase in the grant was insufficient when related to the increase in general expenditure. The sum received by the Birmingham Corporation increased from less than £40,000 in 1889 to over £70,000 ten years later, but after the turn of the century local expenditure rose more sharply still. The Exchequer was consequently compelled to absorb more and more sources of revenue or to make distinct new grants as the expenses of government increased. The whole position was reviewed by a Royal Commission on Taxation set up in 1896 and by a Departmental Committee appointed in 1911, which published its report in 1914.

In the 1900's two main blows were struck at the Assigned Revenues system in practice. The Finance Act of 1907 provided that the Assigned Revenues, instead of being paid direct into the Local Taxation Account, should be paid into the Exchequer, and the Finance Act of 1910 stabilized at the 1908/9 level the amount paid to local authorities from the licences for the sale of intoxicating liquor and motor-cars. Birmingham was one of the many cities which protested against the loss of the most resilient element in the Assigned Revenues system. It even claimed £100 from the Treasury to cover the cost of the administrative changeover, a claim which was rejected.

The pre-war paralysis of the Assigned Revenues system led not to an immediate and complete overhaul of the machinery, but to a prolonged period of disintegration. During the First World War itself, when it proved impossible to fashion a new local taxation policy, social policy was expanding and various special grants had to be made by the government to local authorities, for instance, the grants for maternity and child welfare. At the end of the war some of the grants, like the Education Grant, were constituted to ensure for each authority a minimum of 50 per cent. of its expenditure. Others, like the grants for the training of midwives, were provided on a unit basis.

The complicated system of payment of grants was finally changed by the Local Government Act of 1929. The main purposes of this intricate measure were to discontinue certain grants-in-aid, substituting for them a new block grant, and to relieve agriculture and industry of certain rate charges by comprehensive de-rating proposals. The remnants of the system of Assigned Revenues were finally discarded. Instead a pool was formed into which there was paid annually the equivalent of all the losses suffered by local authorities through the withdrawal of the previous grants and the loss of rates, in terms of the 1928/9 position. A limited amount of 'new money' was added, amounting to £5 million for the first grant period. The size of the pool was to be redetermined first after three years, then after four, and ultimately every five years. The pool was to be divided among the different local authorities, at first partly in relation to the losses actually incurred and partly on the basis of an empirical formula, which took into account the size of the population, the proportion of children under five years of age, low rateable value, the high proportion of unemployment, and (for counties only) the sparseness of population as compared with mileage of roads. Ultimately the formula was to be the only basis of the block grant. The formula took no account of local expenditure or local rates in the pound.

The block grant enabled the local authorities to know how much they would get from the government for several years ahead, and the Treasury to know how much it would be called upon to pay. Under the first grant, covering the years 1930/1 to 1932/3, Birmingham secured £946,774 and in the second period, from 1933/4 to 1936/7, £999,342. The losses incurred through de-rating were estimated at £563,730 and the discontinued grants at £292,519, a total of £856,249. The new grant was therefore in excess of the actual losses.

The block grant had advantages and disadvantages for a large and progressive city like Birmingham. Percentage grants had had to be earned. They were not paid until the expenditure had been incurred. The block grant, calculated on factors beyond the control of the local authority, was paid whether the authority made any corresponding payment itself or not, provided that health services were kept up to a reasonable standard. Under the block grant system Birmingham secured a large government grant irrespective of its expenditure. On the other hand, the government refused to compensate the city for further losses of rateable value due to de-rating after 1929; and new factories, set up in Birmingham in the 1930's, would have been paying a large sum in rates had they not been de-rated by the 1929 Act. This might-have-been sum of money represented a loss to which the city still has not become reconciled. Furthermore, the increase in Birmingham's population in the 1930's involved a time-lag between population growth and the adjustment of the grant, and in any case the formula contained no recognition that change of population itself is a disproportionately expensive factor in all branches of local government.

Quite apart from the block grant, other specific grants were made by the central government to Birmingham for police, education, and housing. These specific grants amounted to as much as two-thirds of all the grants made by the central government to local authorities. In 1934/5, for instance, in Birmingham over £1 million was received from the Board of Education, over £450,000 from the Ministry of Health under the various Housing Schemes, and nearly £300,000 from the Home Office for the police. All these grants implied a close working partnership between central and local government.

(d) *Income from Specific Services* accounted for a sizeable share of the total receipts of the Birmingham Corporation. It included such items as rents, licence fees, baths receipts, and so on.

*Capital Expenditure*

Alongside the increase of rateable value and the rise in the total of government assistance, the public debt of the city also increased extremely rapidly. In 1851 the Corporation inherited a debt of nearly £200,000 from the Street Commissioners. By the Improvement Act of that year it acquired the right to raise further loans repayable in fifty years, and not amounting to more than £150,000. By the second Improvement Act of 1861 the Corporation was empowered to raise further loans up to £100,000, repayable in thirty years. To cover interest on loans and to help to repay capital, a Sinking Fund was instituted. The Council had free discretion either to keep this fund invested in government securities or to employ it periodically for the liquidation of loans.

Many new loans were necessary after the 1851 and 1861 sums had been exhausted. In addition to new powers to borrow, conferred in various local Acts and summed up in the Birmingham Consolidation Act of 1883, additional powers were granted by national pieces of legislation, particularly the Public Health Act of 1875, which consolidated and simplified borrowing powers conferred in earlier sanitary enactments. It laid down certain important general principles—that borrowing should be for permanent works only, the cost of which should be spread over a period of years; that the sum borrowed was not to exceed the assessable value for two years, and that when the loan exceeded one year's assessable value, the consent of the Local Government Board should not be given until after a local inquiry had been held by a Board inspector; and finally, that the money was to be repaid either by annual instalments or through a sinking fund. Similar canons of public finance were reaffirmed in many other national Acts, relating to electric lighting, allotments, museums, and education.

Birmingham adopted various methods of raising money by borrowing. Before 1880 Corporation loans were obtained through the Public Works Loans Commissioners, from banks, insurance companies, and private individuals. In 1872 Avery, the chairman of the Finance Committee, urged that Debenture Stock ought to be issued at a low rate of interest on the same lines as that approved of in the case of London, which in 1863 had issued its first Metropolitan Consolidated Stock. Although by a private Act of 1872 Manchester obtained powers to issue such stock, it was not until 1880 that Birmingham succeeded. The first £2 million of Birmingham stock was issued in that year through the Bank of England, and was taken up within a month 'notwithstanding the unfavourable state of the money market'. A further issue was made in 1882 when the Corporation was authorized to advance money to other local bodies, the School Board, the Board of Guardians, and the District Drainage Board. In 1883 Powell Williams, anticipating the policy followed by Neville Chamberlain in the setting up of the Municipal Bank, arranged for the issue of Corporation Mortgages of sums of £10 at 3½ per cent., which he hoped would be taken up by artisans in the city.

There were many different issues of stock between 1884 and the turn of the century. Throughout the whole of this period the rate of interest was falling, from 3·5 per cent. in 1881 to 2·4 per cent. in 1896. The upward turn came in 1898 and was accentuated by the South African War and the financial stringency of the 1900's. By that time the local debt had increased to over £10 million, and many people were as alarmed at its rise as Englishmen had been in Macaulay's time, and since, at the great increase in the national debt. The timorous and the critical did not take into account the advantage to posterity of the capital outlay covered by loans which would be repaid before the value of the realized local improvement was exhausted. They did not note how much of the debt related to undertakings which were entirely self-supporting. Finally, they forgot that other things grew as well as the debt, and that the most important question raised by large-scale borrowing was not the total commitment but the effect of it on the ratepayers, who had to find annual payments and sinking fund.

One important economic problem concerning the debt emerged in the last quarter of the nineteenth century, that of the length of time of repayment. The Consolidation Act of 1883 laid down that terms of years for the liquidation of loans should be fixed in conformity with the purposes for which the loans were required, varying from short periods in the case of exhaustible investment up to periods of 100 years in the case of freehold purchases and the erection of permanent buildings. There was considerable local irritation, therefore, when in 1885 the Treasury refused to sanction a small building loan unless the Council would give an undertaking to repay it within thirty years. The Finance Committee not only protested, but called into question the competence of the Treasury to fix any limit at all. Powell Williams asked the Council 'to fortify the Finance Committee . . . in resisting the arbitrary principle which the Treasury wants to lay down. . . . The Treasury speaks of the increase of local indebtedness, but says nothing about the assets. The decision strikes a blow at local government and at social progress.' This was a widely held view-point at the time, although a few years later Clayton, Powell Williams's successor, supported a tight restriction of the period of repayment, and claimed that if the government had been more rigid earlier, much wasteful expenditure would have been avoided.

Questions concerning the period of repayment were discussed more frequently than questions concerning the consolidation of all the city's loans in one common fund. The Corporation Water Act of 1892 secured the right to use stock redemption funds for new capital schemes, and by the Corporation Act of 1903 all loans secured by mortgage of the various funds of the Corporation were consolidated into a general form of mortgage secured indifferently upon the revenues of the City. Liverpool, Manchester, and Edinburgh had all obtained similar powers by 1894. Many local authorities in the 1920's established Consolidated Loans Funds by means of which all loans, whether raised by mortgage or otherwise, were combined in a 'pooled' account from which advances were made to borrowing accounts at the average rate of interest. Birmingham secured the necessary powers to establish such a Fund in 1929, but on account of special difficulties they had not been put into effect by 1938.

During the twentieth century various experiments were made in new methods of raising funds. Stock continued to be issued, and for the first time in 1920 the joint-stock banks were employed rather than the Bank of England. The Birmingham Corporation Act of 1903 enabled the city to raise money by bills, issued and paid on maturity through the Bank of England. This power, which had already been conferred on the Metropolitan Board of Works in 1877 and on other cities at the turn of the century, was employed several times down to April 1920. In the inter-war years, further funds were raised on short-term mortgages and on housing bonds, authorized by the Housing Act of 1919. No money was raised by Corporation fixed interest-bearing bonds, although the Birmingham Corporation Act of 1929 authorized the issue of this form of security on lines already adopted by Coventry two years before.

As far as the national framework of borrowing was concerned, the Local Government Act of 1933 gave to all local authorities a general power to borrow for authorized purposes and provided a uniform code of procedure. While this Act made an attempt to crystallize methods, policy was far from static. Just as, in the case of current income and expenditure, a new partnership between local and central government was evolving, so too there were tendencies at work in the capital sector, which were extending the interest of central departments in local borrowing. In the 1930's, after the economy campaign had spent itself, the Ministry of Health began to encourage consistency and co-ordination in local finance by asking local authorities to draw up forward budgets of their likely capital expenditure over five-year periods, and to submit the information to all the departments concerned. This request was symptomatic of a new trend in central–local relations, although it was not until after the Second World War that economists stressed that, since the investment of local authorities had become a major constituent of total national investment, in any plan for controlling annual investment close co-operation between local and central authorities was essential. There had been no such plan during the post-war troubles of 1921–3, when the central government had followed the contradictory policy of trying to encourage relief works and to cut local investment.

*Administration*

Apart from having to deal with the increase in work caused by the growth of current and capital expenditure, the City Treasurer's Department also had to introduce routine methods and precision into its many tasks. The City Treasurer himself was a key official. He was not only Chief Financial Officer to the City Council, but also Chief Rating Officer, Registrar of Stock and Local Bonds, Treasurer to the Municipal Bank, and Treasurer to the Drainage Board. He was required to submit an annual return of income and expenditure to the Ministry of Health, and the evolution of the city's *Annual Abstract of Accounts* and its shorter *Epitome* reflects the increasing complexity and routinization of local finance.

The method of drawing up estimates of expenditure changed considerably throughout the period. Before 1890 the precept for the amount required by the Council in any one year was voted at the March meeting of the Council, when two months of the year had already run. In 1890, when the Council belatedly accepted the change from the calendar year to the national April–March year, the system was reviewed. The Finance Committee presented at the April meeting an approximate estimate of the requirements of the Council and the Council went on to approve a precept on account to cover one-half of the estimated requirements. It was not until the June meeting that the detailed estimates were considered and the remaining half of the rates fixed.

This was obviously a clumsy system, and in 1913, after the extension of the city, it was completely overhauled. The full estimates were now presented and the rate determined at the March meeting, that is to say, before the end of the financial year. The different committees thus knew from the start of the financial year exactly how much they had to spend instead of having to spend on account for two or three months. The Council was at last in a position to make a complete survey of its forthcoming expenditure at one meeting, and the Treasurer's office could finish its work on the estimates before starting on the preparation of the annual financial statement.

The system of audit was gradually refashioned to fit the needs of a complex city machine. According to the Municipal Corporations Act of 1835 the Corporation accounts were to be audited by three auditors, of whom two were annually elected by the burgesses and one nominated by the Mayor. Before the Local Government Act of 1933 consolidated and amended the law of audit, and enabled borough and county borough councils to appoint professional auditors, Birmingham had found it necessary to employ professional auditors, although not so early as other cities. By 1933 a carefully contrived system of internal audit, covering costing, had also been devised, and was carried out continuously by the City Treasurer. Certain accounts, such as Education, Public Assistance, and Rating and Valuation, were also subject to audit by the District Auditor, appointed by the Minister of Health.

### The Finance Committee

While the work of the City Treasurer ensured smooth day-to-day efficiency, the Finance Committee secured greater control over the timing and size of expenditure. In the age of Joseph Chamberlain, the Finance Committee had no authority to urge restraint, and it was quite exceptional when in 1886 the chairman of the committee opposed, and succeeded in having defeated, a spending recommendation of the Baths and Parks Committee on the grounds that the outlay was inexpedient in view of the depressed state of trade. The normal procedure was for capital expenditure to be recommended by the various committees of the Council and to be approved or rejected by the Council as a whole. If the Council approved, it instructed the Finance Committee to borrow the money after obtaining the consent of the Local Government Board.

From 1886 onwards a measure of control was exercised over the actual capital expenditure of the committees taken in relation to their own estimates. In August 1886 the Council authorized the City Treasurer to report to the Finance Committee any cases of capital expenditure exceeding authorized figures. Any excess of less than £100 was to be charged to the Revenue Account of the spending committee. No payment once made on Revenue Account could be transferred to the Capital Account except on authority of the Finance Committee, which would then become responsible to the Council.

In a Special Report on the Estimates in 1895 the Finance Committee suggested that tighter control was necessary. It stressed that enlarged capital accounts led to swollen administrative expenses, and asked for and received instructions to confer with the General Purposes Committee on the question 'whether it was desirable to adopt any system which might give to the Council a more effective control over expenditure on Capital Account'. The subsequent conference agreed, in face of the opposition of the Gas and Water Departments, that all committees should send to the Finance Committee, before the end of January each year, a statement of the amount and objects of their proposed capital expenditure in the financial year beginning on the following 1 April. The Finance Committee was instructed to incorporate its observations on these statements in its general report. The scheme broke down, largely because the committees found it impossible to draw up accurate forecasts of their anticipated expenditure, and the regulation was rescinded in 1899. Two years later the Finance Committee declined to recommend a new system of financial control, and the question was relegated into the background until after the extension of the city.

In March 1912 the enlarged Finance Committee was instructed by the Council to consider future control, and in June it reported that it should in future act as the adviser of the Council in reviewing the finances of the Corporation as a whole and in directing attention to the economic effects of committee recommendations, viewed not in isolation but in conjunction with the schemes proposed by other committees. It pointed out that every other large city, with one exception, had been entrusted with a larger responsibility for regulating expenditure than it possessed, and that Birmingham should adopt new procedures. It recommended first that before the presentation of the detailed estimates and the recommendation of a rate in the pound, the draft estimates should be reviewed by a consultative committee, consisting of the Finance Committee along with the chairmen of the nine spending committees. This proposal was accepted without a division. Second, it recommended that if any proposal not included in the estimates but imposing a charge on the rates was made after the approval of the estimates, it should be considered, in its financial bearings only, by the Finance Committee. Although this proposal did not apply to the trading committees, it was strongly opposed, particularly by Neville Chamberlain, and was carried by only forty-three votes to thirty-seven. Third, it recommended that in March of each year and from time to time when necessary the chairmen of the trading committees should confer with the Finance Committee on any revision of the scale of charges, in order that the effects of such a revision on the rates should be considered before reporting to the Council. This proposal was also carried without a division.

In November 1919 the General Purposes Committee recommended that the Finance Committee should examine all proposals involving capital expenditure before they were submitted to the Council. The instructions to committees were amended to provide for this, the committee making a proposal involving expenditure having the right of appeal to the Council if it was not satisfied with the decision of the Finance Committee.

The climax came in February 1920, when the Finance Committee itself reported that the proposals for new capital schemes had assumed such large proportions that it was possible that the city might be unable to raise sufficient money, particularly if it had to depend on short-term mortgages. After discussions the Finance Committee took upon itself the task of reporting to the Council the order of priority in which capital schemes approved by the Council should be carried out. This regulation of capital policy, coupled with the policy of rate stabilization, gave the ten members of the Finance Committee, presided over by the Lord Mayor, a far greater measure of control over city spending than had ever been exercised in pre-war years. Along with the General

Purposes Committee, the Finance Committee had become an indispensable agency of civic co-ordination. As Sir David Brooks told the
Royal Commission on Local Government, the one committee looked
to policy and the other to resources. Taken together—and they covered
overlapping rather than distinct fields—they acted as the most effective
'cabinets' in local administration.

## APPENDIX G

## OUTLINE OF A CHRONOLOGY

| | THE NATIONAL FRAMEWORK | LOCAL GOVERNMENT | THE LIFE OF THE LOCAL COMMUNITY |
|---|---|---|---|
| 1865 | .. .. | .. .. | The Birmingham Liberal Association founded. Newman's *Dream of Gerontius*. |
| 1866 | .. .. | Annual Balance Sheet and Stock Account first published. | Birmingham Trades Council founded. Reference Library opened. Dr. Miller left Birmingham. |
| 1867 | Second Reform Bill. | Land purchased for Sewage Farm. | First Art Gallery opened. |
| 1868 | .. .. | .. .. | Industrial School opened. |
| 1869 | National Education League founded. Royal Sanitary Commission. | .. .. | Trades Union Congress met in Birmingham. Hospital Saturday started. |
| 1870 | Education Act. First Tramways Act. | Report on Tramways. | Central Nonconformist Committee set up. |
| 1871 | Report of the Royal Sanitary Commission. Local Government Board set up. | Council Blue Book first published. Sewage Inquiry Committee set up. Birmingham School Board set up. | .. .. |
| 1872 | Public Health Act. | First Medical Officer of Health appointed. | .. .. |
| 1873 | .. .. | New Ward Boundaries. Joseph Chamberlain became Mayor. First Tramway constructed. | .. .. |

| | THE NATIONAL FRAMEWORK | LOCAL GOVERNMENT | THE LIFE OF THE LOCAL COMMUNITY |
|---|---|---|---|
| 1874 | .. .. | Council House begun. First Municipal Hospital. Watch Committee authorized to establish a Fire Brigade. | Aston Villa Football Club founded. |
| 1875 | Public Health Act. Artisans' Dwellings Act. Local Loans Act. | Gas Undertaking acquired. Water Undertaking acquired. Municipal Fire Brigade started. Birmingham Corporation Street and Improvement Scheme accepted. | Birmingham Football Club founded. |
| 1876 | Joseph Chamberlain became a Member of Parliament. Elementary Education Act. | Formation of Improvement Trust. | Small Heath Park presented by Miss Ryland. |
| 1877 | National Liberal Federation founded. Local Taxation Returns Act. | Birmingham, Tame, and Rea District Drainage Board set up. | Remodelled Conservative organization. |
| 1878 | .. .. | Council Governors of the Grammar School first elected. | First volume of *Corporation History* published. |
| 1879 | .. .. | Council House opened. | First telephone exchange started. Small Heath Park opened. Bournville begun. Fire at Central Library. Newman created a Cardinal. |
| 1880 | Joseph Chamberlain entered the Government. | .. .. | Mason College opened. |
| 1881 | Fair Trade League started. Royal Commission on Technical Education. | Reservoir at Shustoke authorized. First issue of Corporation Stock. | .. .. |

| | THE NATIONAL FRAMEWORK | LOCAL GOVERNMENT | THE LIFE OF THE LOCAL COMMUNITY |
|---|---|---|---|
| 1882 | Electricity Act. | Gas Committee Report on Electric Lighting. | Warwickshire County Cricket Club founded. |
| 1883 | .. .. | Birmingham Consolidation Act. | First Municipal School of Art set up. |
| 1884 | .. .. | First Birmingham Assizes. | Aston Riots. Visit of the Archbishop of Canterbury. |
| 1885 | Redistribution of Seats Act. | .. .. .. | Art Gallery opened. |
| 1886 | The Liberal Split on Home Rule. National Radical Union set up. | .. .. .. | .. .. .. |
| 1887 | The Royal Jubilee. Local Government Boundaries Act. | New Police Station in Bristol Road. Queen Victoria laid foundation-stone of the Law Courts. | Small Heath Park renamed Victoria Park. |
| 1888 | Electricity Act. Local Government Act. Assigned Revenues policy. | Greater Birmingham scheme proposed. | Liberal Unionist Association set up. First pneumatic tire produced. |
| 1889 | Technical Instruction Act. | Birmingham became a City. Lawrence Street housing scheme authorized. | John Bright died. Birmingham Electric Supply Company set up. Foundation of Boys' Brigade. Birmingham Infirmary opened. Birmingham's first Electric Tram. |
| 1890 | Final Report of the Royal Commission on the Housing of the Poor. Housing of the Working Classes Act. Police Act. | First municipal dwelling-houses built in Ryder Street. First Technical School Committee. | Joint Committee of Liberal and Conservative Unionists set up. |

| | THE NATIONAL FRAMEWORK | LOCAL GOVERNMENT | THE LIFE OF THE LOCAL COMMUNITY |
|---|---|---|---|
| 1891 | Free Elementary Education. Public Libraries Act. Select Committee on Unemployment. | First City extension. Welsh Water Scheme adopted. Fair wages clause accepted in principle. | First Municipal Technical School started. |
| 1892 | .. .. | Birmingham Water Act. | .. .. .. |
| 1893 | .. .. | .. .. .. | First Industrial Alliance. |
| 1894 | Local Government Act. | .. .. .. | .. .. |
| 1895 | Royal Commissions on Tuberculosis, Secondary Education, and the Aged Poor. | .. .. | Wolseley Motors started. Rear-wheel chain-driven safety-bicycle first made. Dr. Dale died. |
| 1896 | Report of the Royal Commission on Imperial and Local Taxation. | First Lord Mayor. | .. .. |
| 1897 | Royal Jubilee. Working Men's Compensation Act. | Gift of Mace. | .. .. |
| 1898 | .. .. .. | .. .. .. | Burne-Jones died. |
| 1899 | Foundation of the Garden City Association. | Electric Supply Undertaking acquired by Corporation. | .. .. |
| 1900 | Labour Representation Committee founded. | Milk Street Tenements built. | Edward VI School Act. Royal Charter granted founding University. |
| 1901 | Report of the Royal Commission on Imperial and Local Taxation. | Housing Committee set up. | .. .. |
| 1902 | Education Act. Report of Joint Select Parliamentary Committee on Housing. | .. .. | Birmingham and District Labour Representation Council set up. |

| | THE NATIONAL FRAMEWORK | LOCAL GOVERNMENT | THE LIFE OF THE LOCAL COMMUNITY |
|---|---|---|---|
| 1903 | Joseph Chamberlain began his Protectionist campaign. | First Education Committee set up. Tramways municipalized. Aston incorporated in city. | .. .. |
| 1904 | Tariff Reform Commission had its first meeting. | Elan water supply opened by King Edward VII. | .. .. |
| 1905 | Royal Commissions on Poor Laws, Relief of Distress. | .. .. | Austin's factory at Longbridge started. First Bishop of Birmingham. |
| 1906 | .. .. | Resolution carried in favour of town-planning legislation. | .. .. |
| 1907 | .. .. | .. .. | .. .. |
| 1908 | Old Age Pensions Act. | .. .. | .. .. |
| 1909 | Housing and Town-planning Act. Report of the Royal Commission on the Poor Laws. | Quinton incorporated in city. | First sanatorium opened. First Boy Scouts in Birmingham. |
| 1910 | Education Act. | Town-planning Act adopted. | |
| 1911 | National Health Insurance Act. | Large-scale extension of the city—Greater Birmingham. | Juvenile Employment and Welfare Department set up. |
| 1912 | .. .. | First Town-planning Scheme adopted. | .. .. |
| 1913 | .. .. | Quinton, Harborne, and Edgbaston Town-planning Scheme. Special Housing inquiry. | Birmingham Repertory Theatre started. |
| 1914 | Departmental Committee on Local Taxation. War declared. | Birmingham Citizens' Committee set up. | Joseph Chamberlain died. |

| | THE NATIONAL FRAMEWORK | LOCAL GOVERNMENT | THE LIFE OF THE LOCAL COMMUNITY |
|---|---|---|---|
| 1915 | .. .. .. | .. .. | .. .. |
| 1916 | .. .. .. | Municipal Bank started. | First attempt made to bomb Birmingham. |
| 1917 | .. .. .. | .. .. | .. .. |
| 1918 | The Armistice declared. Maternity and Child Welfare Act. Ministry of Health Act. | Salaries, Wages, and Labour Committee appointed. | Provisional Management Committee of Liberal and Conservative Unionists set up. Local Branch of Federation of British Industries set up. |
| 1919 | Electricity Supply Act. Land Settlement (Facilities) Act. Housing and Town-planning Act. | Municipal Bank made permanent. | United Unionist Association set up. Girls' Union founded. City Orchestra founded. |
| 1920 | Gas Regulation Act. Unemployment Insurance Act. | Canwell Estate purchased. | First traffic islands erected. |
| 1921 | Education Act. | .. .. | .. .. |
| 1922 | Committee on National Expenditure set up. Allotments Act. | .. .. | .. .. |
| 1923 | Chamberlain's Housing Act. Royal Commission on Local Government set up. | .. .. | .. .. |
| 1924 | Wheatley's Housing Act. Road Traffic Act. | .. .. | First double-decker bus used. |
| 1925 | Town-planning Act. Rating and Valuation Act. Weir Report on Electricity. | .. .. | British Industries Fair. |

| | THE NATIONAL FRAMEWORK | LOCAL GOVERNMENT | THE LIFE OF THE LOCAL COMMUNITY |
|---|---|---|---|
| 1926 | Economy (Miscellaneous Provisions) Act. Electricity Supply Act. General Strike. | .. | .. |
| 1927 | Hadow Report. | Birmingham Extension Act. | First greyhound track started. Hospitals Council Executive Board set up. |
| 1928 | .. | .. | Birmingham Federation of Boys' Clubs founded. |
| 1929 | Local Government Act. Block Grant Finance. | .. | Hams Hall Power Station opened. |
| 1930 | Greenwood's Housing Act. Public Works Facilities Act. Poor Law Act. Chelmsford Committee on Local Government. | Birmingham Board of Guardians abolished. Information Bureau set up. | First Empire Shop. Consultative Committee for Community Associations set up. Birmingham Film Society started. |
| 1931 | Formation of National Government. The May Report. National Economy Act. Local Authorities' Publicity Act. | New Municipal Bank head offices opened by Prince George. Extension of city. | .. |
| 1932 | The Return to Protection. Town and Country Planning Act. Rating and Valuation Act. The Ray Report. | .. | .. |
| 1933 | Local Government Act. | .. | One-way traffic system put into operation. |
| 1934 | Unemployment Act. | Airport Committee set up. | .. |

| THE NATIONAL FRAMEWORK | LOCAL GOVERNMENT | THE LIFE OF THE LOCAL COMMUNITY |
|---|---|---|
| 1935 General Election. | Birmingham Corporation Bill. Fire Brigade Headquarters opened by the Duke of Kent. | ..    ..    .. |
| 1936 Housing Act. | First Council Community Centre opened. | ..    .. |
| 1937 Air Raid Precautions Act. | Duddeston and Nechells Redevelopment Scheme. | ..    .. |
| 1938 Royal Commission on the Geographical Distribution of the Industrial Population. | Centenary of the Incorporation of the City. Foundation-stone of the new Civic Centre laid. | Pageant of the City. Queen Elizabeth Hospital opened. |

# INDEX

Compiled by H. M. Cashmore

Roman figures i and ii refer to Volumes I and II respectively. Arabic figures give page numbers and if *in italics* indicate the pages faced by plate illustrations.